To
Carlow Sisters. may Wisdom attend you always.

Alice m Dennott RSm

Gratitude for your warm
& generous hospitality.

THE PERSONIFICATION OF WISDOM

This book examines the personification of Wisdom as a female figure – a central motif in Proverbs, Job, Sirach, Wisdom and Baruch. Alice M. Sinnott identifies how and why the complex character of Wisdom was introduced into the Israelite tradition, and created and developed by Israelite/Jewish wisdom teachers and writers. Arguing that by personifying Wisdom the authors of Proverbs responded to Israel's defeat by Babylon and the loss of Davidic monarchy, and by retrieving and transforming the Wisdom figure the authors of Sirach, Baruch and Wisdom responded to the spread of Hellenism and the potential loss of identity for Jews. Sinnott concludes that Personified Wisdom functioned to reinterpret and transform the Israelite/Jewish tradition.

SOCIETY FOR OLD TESTAMENT STUDY MONOGRAPHS

Ashgate is pleased to publish the revived Society for Old Testament Study (SOTS) monograph series. The Society for Old Testament Study is a learned society based in the British Isles, with an international membership, committed to the study of the Old Testament. This series promotes Old Testament studies with the support and guidance of the Society. The series includes research monographs by members of the Society, both from established international scholars and from exciting new authors.

The Personification of Wisdom

ALICE M. SINNOTT
University of Auckland, New Zealand

ASHGATE

Published by
Ashgate Publishing Limited
Gower House
Croft Road
Aldershot
Hants GU11 3HR
England

Ashgate Publishing Company
Suite 420
101 Cherry Street
Burlington, VT 05401-4405
USA

Ashgate website: http://www.ashgate.com

British Library Cataloguing in Publication Data
Sinnott, Alice Mary
  The personification of Wisdom. – (The Society for Old Testament Study monographs)
  1.Wisdom (Biblical personification) 2.Wisdom literature – Criticism, interpretation, etc.
  I.Title II.Society for Old Testament Study
  223'.06

Library of Congress Cataloging-in-Publication Data
Sinnott, Alice M.
  The personification of Wisdom / Alice M. Sinnott.
    p. cm. – (Society for Old Testament Study monograph series)
  Includes bibliographical references and index.
  ISBN 0-7546-5124-X (hardcover : alk. paper)
  1. Wisdom (Biblical personification) 2. Wisdom literature – Criticism, interpretation, etc. I. Title. II. Series: Society for Old Testament Study monographs.

  BS580.W58S56 2005
  223'.064–dc22

                                                            2005002545

ISBN 0 7546 5124 X

Printed and bound in Great Britain by MPG Books Ltd, Bodmin, Cornwall

Contents

Acknowledgements

The first human never finished comprehending Wisdom,
nor will the last succeed in fathoming her. (Sir 24:28)

Biblical Wisdom has captivated me ever since I encountered these intriguing texts many years ago. An enduring abiding curiosity about the Wisdom figure and the literature where she appears has inspired me to continue my search. I am deeply grateful to all who helped sustain my interest by teaching, encouraging and supporting me, to all who accompanied me in my pursuit of Wisdom, and to all who assisted me in my struggle to write about wisdom. This monograph is a revised version of a doctoral thesis by the same title that I submitted to the University of Oxford in 1997. I extend my deep gratitude to the many people whose inspiration, interest, insights, and support enabled me to persevere and bring this work to completion. I particularly wish to thank:

John Barton, for his belief in my research and his unstinting willingness to share his wisdom and scholarship, inspiration and wise counsel throughout my time in Oxford, Dianne Bergant for inspiring my decision to engage seriously in the study of wisdom literature, John Day for providing extensive bibliographic resources and advice. Stephanie Dalley for sharing with me her astute insights and invaluable resources on Mesopotamia, Sue Gillingham for active support and insight in the beginning stages of my research, Mary Keen for guiding me through many Latin texts, Ernest and Hazel Nicholson, for their unfailing encouragement and warm hospitality, Oriel College for gracious accommodation and conference funding,

This work would not have been possible without the blessing and support of my Congregation, the Auckland Sisters of Mercy. Special thanks to Judith Leydon for her sustained confidence in me that enabled me to embark on this venture, my family for their love, concern, care and hospitality, as well as my many friends, particularly Clare and Alexander Eaglestone, Prue Wilson, Clare Hutton for reading the first draft of this work, the Sisters of Mercy at Abingdon, Oxford women of Ireland group, colleagues and students at the School of Theology, University of Auckland and the many others who have enhanced my work by their with friendship, interest, and support.

To Sarah Lloyd, Ann Newell and Ashgate Publishing I express my thanks for accepting the manuscript for publication and for the meticulous care with which the editing process has been undertaken.

Abbreviations

AA	Åbo Åkademie
ABD	D.N. Freedman, ed., *Anchor Bible Dictionary*. 6 Volumes. New York: Doubleday, 1992
AEL	M. Lichtheim, *Ancient Egyptian Literature*. 3 Volumes. Berkeley: University of California, 1971-80
AIO	*Acten Internationalen Orientalisten kongresses*
AIR	P.D. Miller, ed., *Ancient Israelite Religion*. Philadelphia: Fortress, 1987
ATR	*Anglican Theological Review*
ANEP	J.B. Pritchard, ed., *Ancient Near East in Pictures Relating to the Old Testament: Second Edition with Supplement*. Princeton: Princeton University, 1969
ANET	J.B. Pritchard, ed., *Ancient Near Eastern Texts Relating to the Old Testament*. 3rd ed., Princeton: Princeton University, 1969
ARW	*Archiv für Religionswissenschaft*
BHS	*Biblica Hebraica Stuttgartensia*
Bib	*Biblica*
BJRL	*Bulletin of the John Rylands University Library Manchester*
BN	*Biblische Notizen*
BO	*Bibliotheca Orientalis*
BRev	*Bible Review*
BSOAS	*Bulletin of the School of Oriental and African Studies*
BTB	*Biblical Theology Bulletin*
BVc	*Bible et Vie chrétienne*
BWL	W.G. Lambert, ed., *Babylonian Wisdom Literature*. Oxford: Clarendon, 1960
BZ	*Biblische Zeitschrift*
CBQ	*Catholic Biblical Quarterly*
DBS	*Dictionnaire de la Bible Supplément*.
DDD	K. van der Toorn, ed., *Dictionary of Deities and Demons in the Old Testament*. Leiden: Brill, 1995
DJDJ	*Discoveries in the Judaean Desert of Jordan*
Ebib	*Études bibliques*
EgT	*Église et Théologie*
ET	English translation
ETL	*Ephemerides Theologicae Lovanienses*
GKC	E. Kautzsch, ed., *Gesenius' Hebrew Grammar*. Translated by A.E. Cowley. 2nd ed., Oxford: Clarendon, 1980
HAR	*Hebrew Annual Review*
HBC	J.L. Mays, *Harper's Bible Commentary*. San Francisco: Harper & Row, 1988

HBT	*Horizons in Biblical Theology*
HR	*History of Religions*
HTR	*Harvard Theological Review*
HUCA	*Hebrew Union College Annual*
Int	*Interpretation*
ISW	L. Perdue, ed., *In Search of Wisdom*. Louisville: Westminster John Knox, 1993
JA	*Journal asiastique*
JAAR	*Journal of the American Academy of Religion*
JANES	*Journal of Ancient Near Eastern Society of Colombia University*
JAOS	*Journal of the American Oriental Society*
JBL	*Journal of Biblical Literature*
JCS	*Journal of Cuneiform Studies*
JEA	*Journal of Egyptian Archaeology*
JNES	*Journal of Near Eastern Studies*
JQR	*Jewish Quarterly Review*
JSJ	*Journal for the Study of Judaism*
JSOT	*Journal for the Study of the Old Testament*
JTS	*Journal of Theological Studies*
JWCI	*Journal of the Warburg and Courtauld Institute*
LEW	M. Lichtheim. *Late Egyptian Wisdom Literature in the International Context*. Freiburg: Freiburg University, 1983
MT	Masoretic Text
NJBC	R.E. Brown, ed., *New Jerome Biblical Commentary*. Englewood Cliffs: Prentice Hall, 1989
LXX	Septuagint
NAB	New American Bible
NEB	New English Bible
NJB	New Jerusalem Bible
NRSV	New Revised Standard Version
NRT	*La Nouvelle Revue Théologique*
OED	*Oxford English Dictionary*
OLZ	*Orientalistische Literaturzeitung*
OTP	J.M. Charlesworth, ed., *Old Testament Pseudepigrapha*. Garden City: Doubleday, 1983-85
PL	*Patrologia Latina* J. Migne
PMLA	*Publications of the Modern Language Association of America*
PNSP	M. Dahood. *Proverbs and Northwest Semitic Philology*. Rome: Pontifical Biblical Institute 1968
PSBA	*Proceedings of the Society of Biblical Archaeology*
RAC	*Reallexikon für Antike und Christentum*
RB	*Revue Biblique*
RES	*Revue des Études Sémitique*
RevQ	*Revue de Qumran*
RSB	*Ricerche Storico Bibliche*

RSR	*Recherches de Science Religieuse*
RTL	*Revue Théologique de Louvain*
SAIW	J.L. Crenshaw, ed., Studies *in Ancient Israelite Wisdom.* New York: KTAV, 1976
SAINE	J.G. Gammie, ed., *The Sage in Israel and the Ancient Near East.* Winona Lake: Eisenbrauns, 1990
SPAW	*Sitzungsberichte der Preussischen Akademie der Wissenschaften*
SPOA	*Sagesse du Proche-orient ancient*, 1963
TDNT	G. Kittel and G. Friedrich, eds. *Theological Dictionary of the New Testament.* 10 volumes 1964-76
TDOT	G.W. Botterweck and H. Ringgren, eds., *Theological Dictionary of the Old Testament.* 14 volumes. Grand Rapids: Eerdmans, 1974ff.
ThWAT	G.W. Botterweck and H. Ringgren, eds., *Theologische Wörterbuch zum Alten Testament.* 14 volumes. Stuttgart: Kohlhammer, 1970ff.
TOT	J.M. Crenshaw, *Theodicy in the Old Testament.* Philadelphia: Fortress, 1983
TLZ	*Theologische Literaturzeitung*
TRu	*Theologische Rundschau*
VT	*Vetus Testamentum*
VTSup	*Vetus Testamentum Supplements*
WAI	J. Day, ed., *Wisdom in Ancient Israel.* Cambridge: Cambridge University, 1995
ZA	*Zeitschrift für Assyriologie*
ZÄS	*Zeitschrift für Ägyptische Sprache und Altertumskunde*
ZAW	*Zeitschrift für die Alttestamentliche Wissenschaft*
ZDMG	*Zeitschrift der deutschen morgenländischen Gesellschaft*
ZKT	*Zeitschrift für katholische Theologie*
ZTK	*Zeitschrift für Theologie und Kirche*

Introduction

Wisdom, as a personified figure, appears in many guises in the Wisdom literature.[1] Wisdom speaks and is spoken about, "I will pour out my thoughts to you, I will make my words known to you" (Prov 1:23); "The Lord created me at the beginning" (Prov 8:22); "Whoever finds me finds life" (Prov 8:35); "Come eat of my bread" (Prov 9:5); "Truly the fear of the Lord, that is Wisdom" (Job 28:28); "Before the ages, in the beginning God created me" (Sir 24:9); "The first human did not know Wisdom fully, nor will the last one fathom her." (Sir 24:28); "She is the book of the commandments of God" (Bar 4:1); "She is an initiate in the knowledge of God and an associate in God's works" (Wis 9:4); "People were taught what pleases you, and were saved by Wisdom" (Wis 9:18). These varied and diverse Wisdom utterances suggest something of the complexity and charm of this enigmatic figure.

Personified Wisdom's first appearance in public is in Proverbs 1-9 where she calls out in the streets, and squares to all who will listen. Wisdom is a multifaceted, elusive, immanent, substantial, corporeal, tangible figure who takes up residence in the biblical tradition and to this day inspires and puzzles theological, religious and scholarly research. Wisdom in Proverbs calls out to the simple, urging them to pay attention to her teaching (1:22-33; 8:6-10a). She stretches out her hand and no one heeds so she threatens to laugh and mock those who do not listen (1:24-26). She holds long life in her right hand, riches and honour in her left hand (3:16). On those who embrace her she bestows a beautiful crown (4:9). She speaks truth and righteousness (8:7-8). She walks in the way of righteousness and in paths of justice (8:20). Finally, in 9:1-6 she provides and presides at a lavish wisdom feast.

In the Hebrew canon, we next meet her in the elegant Wisdom poem which asks, "But where shall wisdom be found? Where is the source of understanding?" (Job 28:12-13), and announces, "God understands the way to it, God knows its source" (Job 28:23). "Mortals do not know the way to it, and it is not found in the land of the living" (Job 28:19). Accepting that Wisdom is beyond the reach of humanity, the poem concludes with the traditional affirmation that "Fear of the Lord is wisdom; to shun evil is understanding" (Job 28:28). Images of Wisdom's inaccessibility contrast sharply with images portrayed in Proverbs, and the contrast emphasises Wisdom's incomprehensibility. However, for the author of

---

[1] I use the term 'Wisdom Literature' in this work as a term of convenience. Derived from ecclesiastical usage it designates the books of Proverbs, Job, Qoheleth and the deuterocanonical books of Baruch, Wisdom of Ben Sira, and Wisdom of Solomon. Egyptologists and cuneiform specialists adopted this label to denote a variety of extra-biblical literature sharing characteristics with the biblical works. I use the term to denote literature that speaks chiefly about 'wisdom'.

the poem in Job as for the author(s) of Proverbs "Fear of the Lord" is the sine qua non for attaining wisdom.

Successive descriptions of Wisdom enhance her growth and development as in Wisdom's hymn of self-praise (24:1-22) where Ben Sira identifies her with the Torah (24:23-34). Baruch describes how Wisdom, given by God to Jacob/Israel, lives among human beings as Torah (3:9-4:4), and the Wisdom of Solomon (7:7-10:18), describes Wisdom as a breath of the power of God, and a pure emanation of the glory of the Almighty; a reflection of eternal light, a spotless mirror of the working of God, and an image of God's goodness (7:25-26). 1 Enoch 42:2 says, "Wisdom went forth to make her dwelling among the children of men, and found no dwelling place" so she returns to live eternally with the angels. Wisdom also appears in Qumran 4Q185 11, and she may also underpin key Christological proclamations such as, Luke 7:35; 11:49; John 1:1-18; 17:5; Col 1:15-20; 1 Cor 1:18-31; 8:6; Heb 1:2-3. Clearly, Wisdom provides strikingly colourful, attractive and mysterious threads to the tapestry that is the bible.

With such a vibrant textual history, it is not surprising that personified Wisdom continues to generate substantial scholarly interest. However, while many scholars have investigated various aspects of wisdom, I am not aware of the existence of any study devoted exclusively to the particular subject of personified Wisdom in the Old Testament and Deuterocanonical books.[2] Consisting of a series of linked studies of personified Wisdom, this book offers an analysis of how specific texts portray the Wisdom figure, her relationships with God, with the created world and its inhabitants. Included in this investigation is a discussion of Wisdom's origins and/or antecedents, the contexts in which Wisdom appears, and her significance and function within the texts, which describe her. Each study aims to identify how and why biblical authors introduced and developed the complex character of Wisdom as portrayed in Prov 1:20-33; 8:1-36; 9:1-6; Job 28; Bar 3:9-4:4; Sir 1:1-10; 24:1-34; Wis 6:12-10:18.

A Note on Approaches

This book examines the personification of Wisdom as a female figure, a central motif in Proverbs, Job, Wisdom of Ben Sira, Wisdom of Solomon, and Baruch, with particular emphasis on the role and function of this phenomenon. Employing a combination of literary, historical-critical, form-critical and canonical approaches, I seek to discover personified Wisdom by asking: What or where are Wisdom's origins? What are the characteristics of her relationship with God and with human beings? What issues and situations does she address? What roles and functions does Wisdom fulfil in Prov 1:20-33; 8:1-36; 9:1-6; Sir 24:1-36; Job 28;

---

[2]   'Old Testament' in this work denotes both Canonical and Deuterocanonical texts. While the Wisdom of Ben Sira, the book of Baruch, and Wisdom of Solomon are not part of the Hebrew Bible, the Roman Catholic and Greek Orthodox traditions following the Greek canon consider the Apocrypha to be Deuterocanonical books and so retain them in their bibles.

Bar 3:9-4:4; Wis 6:12-10:21. Underpinning my approach to the texts are certain assumptions and understandings some which I can identify. The biblical texts in which Wisdom is personified are poetic compositions, which are expressions of the history and theology of the communities in which they were composed and from which they emerged. These texts incorporate perspectives and traditions from the Torah, historical, and prophetic traditions, and unique perspectives now considered characteristic of the wisdom tradition. Authors designed these texts to teach, to persuade, to inspire, and to influence their audiences towards behaviour in concrete social and historical situations, which may not now be recoverable.

As the texts selected for study are very varied, I employ a variety of approaches. Many of the passages that come in for scrutiny call for textual and literary criticism, form criticism, and redaction criticism. Regardless of the various methodologies brought into play, this enquiry is concerned primarily to examine and provide some possible explanations of how and why the biblical authors created and developed the figure of personified Wisdom from her earliest appearances in the Old Testament to her later manifestations and development in the Deuterocanonical texts.

Dating Proverbs 1-9

Inferences about Wisdom's origins inform conclusions about the dating of Proverbs 1-9, and findings about dating these texts affect judgements about her origins. Pre 1920's scholars were unaware that Proverbs was but one sample of a vast collection of ancient Near Eastern wisdom texts but they considered several questions that continue to vex contemporary scholars. From the 1920s, discoveries in the ancient Near East alerted scholars to something of the variety and extent of this ancient Near Eastern literature. The hope that these finds might eliminate uncertainty surrounding the dating of Proverbs was in vain. Proverbs 1-9 have been dated from the reign of Solomon, (twelfth century BCE), to third century BCE. However, because of a lack of any firm evidence, such as, specific historical context, references to the *Heilsgeschichte* narratives, references to Israel, its history, or its institutions to support these claims no definite date can be ascertained. While the traditional ascription of authorship to Solomon was understood to suggest a date in the tenth century BCE, attribution to Solomon appears in Qoheleth, Canticle, and Wisdom, where it is clearly a literary device, so such an ascription does not help to decide a likely date for Proverbs 1-9. Delitzsch, who took the Solomon heading literally, dated Proverbs 1-9 to that era citing stylistic and thematic evidence for his decision.[3]

Kayatz rejected claims of "lineal development" which would make these chapters post-exilic. Finding Israelite theology with a strong Egyptian influence in Proverbs 1-9, she proposed a date as early as the time of Solomon.[4] Brunner, Gese

---

[3]   F. Delitzsch, *Das Salomonisches Sprüchbuch* (Leipzig, 1873).
[4]   C. Kayatz, *Studien zu Proverbien 1-9: Eine form-und motivgeschichtliche Untersuchung unter Einbeziehung Ägyptischen Vergleichsmaterials* (Neukirchen-Vluyn, 1966);

and later Lang noted close links between Egyptian Instruction and Israelite teaching in Proverbs 1-9, and so argue for a Solomonic date.[5] Finally among those who favour an early date is Kitchen who claimed that "advanced" theological concepts could have been current among Israelites earlier than the sixth century BCE. Many such ideas, he noted, were known from documents common in the ancient Near East in the second millennium BCE. Gainsaying theories based on notions of unilinear development, he argued that the personification of Wisdom in Proverbs 1-9 is precisely the same as the personification of Truth, Justice, Intelligence, and Understanding, in third and second millennia BCE, Egyptian and Mesopotamian documents and in second millennium BCE, materials from Hittites, Hurrians, and Canaanites.[6] Characteristics of Egyptian influences on Israelite wisdom literature do appear in Proverbs 1-9.[7] As such influences could have been prevalent either during the time of the monarchy when international exchange may have been frequent, or after the exile when Egypt was no longer a major concern for the Israelites, they cannot be invoked to support arguments for particular dates for Proverbs 1-9.[8]

Robert, who was the first to investigate Proverbs 1-9 separately, concluded that these chapters exhibited unmistakable literary correlations with Deuteronomy, Isaiah, and Jeremiah. He found that Proverbs had enough in common with these writings to exclude a Hellenistic date and on identifying contacts with Malachi, dated Proverbs 1-9 to the fifth century BCE.[9] Oesterley noted Egyptian and Mesopotamian influences on biblical texts, but concluded that Proverbs 1-9 with its "developed" concept of wisdom was late third century BCE, as did Baumgartner, who examined the close correspondence of *Papyrus Insinger* and the *Instruction of 'Onchsheshonqy,* late Egyptian texts with Proverbs 1-9.[10]

Einführung in die alttestamentliche Weisheit BS 55 (Neukirchen-Vluyn, 1969).

[5] H. Brunner, *Altägyptische Erziehung* (Wiesbaden, 1957): 117; H. Gese, *Lehre und Wirklichkeit in der alten Weisheit* (Tübingen, 1958): 30; B. Lang, *Die weisheitliche Lehrrede* (Stuttgart, 1972); *Wisdom and the Book of Proverbs: A Hebrew Goddess Redefined* (New York, 1986): 4-12.

[6] See K.A. Kitchen, *The Ancient Orient and the Old Testament* (Leicester, 1966); see A.H. Gardiner, *Some Personifications.* Proceedings of the Society of Biblical Archaeology, 1915-17. 37/38/39 [*PSBA*] (1915-17): 253-262, 43-54, 83-95, 134-140, for the personification of Magic (*Hiké*), Understanding (*Sia*) etc. in Egypt; H. Bonnet, *Reallexikon der ägyptischen Religionsgeschichte* (Berlin, 1952): 586-588; H. Ringgren, *Word and Wisdom: Studies in the Hypostatization of Divine Qualities and Functions in the Ancient Near East* (Lund, 1947): 9-40, 124-5.

[7] R.J. Williams, "The Sages of Ancient Egypt in the Light of Recent Scholarship," *JAOS* 101/1 (1981): 7.

[8] P. Humbert, *Recherches sur les sources Égyptiennes de la littérature sapientale d'Israël* (Neuchâtel, 1929): 63, 107, 180.

[9] A. Robert, "Les attaches litteraires bibliques des Prov 1-9", *RB* 44 (1935): 502-525; see also B. Gemser, *Sprüche Salomos* HAT 16 (Tübingen, 1963): 5-6 who strongly rejected a post-Ezra dating.

[10] W.O.E. Oesterley, *The Book of Proverbs* (London, 1929); "Papyrus Insinger", in M. Lichtheim, ed., *AEL* vol. 3 (Berkeley, 1980): 184-217; "Instruction of Onchsheshonqy", in M. Lichtheim, ed., *LEW* (1983): 6-12.

McKane in arguing that Proverbs 1-9 is the latest part of the Book of Proverbs commented, "There is such unanimity on this as to make this an article of form critical orthodoxy."[11] Weeks detected evidence of Greek influence in Proverbs 1-9 and consequently opted for a fourth or third century BCE, date. The above discussion does not purport to an exhaustive account of the debate about the dating of Proverbs 1-9 and many studies that are more significant could be added.[12] However, of the many other scholars who have debated this topic most would belong in one of the above categories and therefore would not clarify this complex matter.[13]

Arguments concerning the dating of Proverbs 1-9 are inseparable from questions about the origin of the figure of Wisdom. Scholars who see her as a surviving remnant of a Hebrew goddess, or as based on Egyptian or Mesopotamian models, are likely to date Proverbs 1-9 as early as ninth century BCE, whereas those who view her more as a literary or theological creation posit an exilic or post-exilic date. When she is seen as a mediating figure based on women in the Israelite community, a post-exilic date is usually proposed.[14] Scholars, who place the collection in the fifth century BCE, or later, base this dating on a variety of

---

[11] W. McKane *Proverbs* (London, 1970): 1-22; R.N. Whybray, *The Composition of the Book of Proverbs* JSOT 168 (Sheffield, 1994): 163-164; *Wisdom in Proverbs 1-9* SBT 45 (London, 1965): 76-98; J. Schmidt, *Studien zur Stilistik der alttestamentlichen Spruchliteratur.* AA 13.1 (Münster, 1936).

[12] S. Weeks, *Early Israelite Wisdom* (Oxford, 1994): 57-73; see also R.B.Y Scott, "Wise and Foolish, Righteous and Wicked", *VTSup* 23 (1972): 146-165; *Proverbs, Ecclesiastes* AB 18 (New York, 1965): 15; F.M. Wilson, "Sacred or Profane? The Yahwistic Redaction of Proverbs Reconsidered" in K.G. Hoglund, E.F. Huwiler, J.T. Glass, and R.W. Lee, eds., *The Listening Heart:Essays in Wisdom and the Psalms in Honor of Roland E. Murphy* [*Listening Heart*] (Sheffield, 1987): 313-334; Humbert, *Recherches sur les sources Egyptienne de la Litterature Salientale d'Israel* (Neuchatel, 1929): 53; J. Hempel, *Die althebräische Literatur und ihr hellenistich-jüdisches Nachleben* (Wildpark-Potsdam, 1930): 49-55; R.H. Pfeiffer, *Introduction to the Old Testament* (New York, 1941): 656; Ringgren, *Word and Wisdom* (1947): 9; A. Bentzen, *Introduction to the Old Testament* (Copenhagen, 1952): 172; G.W. Anderson, *A Critical Introduction to the Old Testament* (London, 1959): 188; A. Weiser, *The Old Testament: Its Formation and Development* (New York, 1960): 296; Gemser, *Sprüche Salomos* (1963): 5; W. Zimmerli, "Ort und Grenze der Weisheit im Rahmen der alttestamentlichen Theologie" SPOA (1963): 121-37 (ET in *SAIW* 314-326); O. Eissfeldt, *The Old Testament* (New York, 1965): 472-82.

[13] C.H. Toy, *A Critical and Exegetical Commentary of the Book of Proverbs* (Edinburgh, 1899): xix-xxxi, dated chapters 1-9 to later than 300 BCE, citing evidence for monotheism and new international contacts; R.E. Murphy, "The Kerygma of the Book of Proverbs," *Int* 20 (1966): 4; *The Tree of Life: An Exploration of Biblical* ABRL (New York, 1990): 19, 160-162, opts for the post-exilic period, and suggests that Egyptian influence may be later than either Kayatz or Lang suggest.

[14] See C. Camp, *Wisdom and the Feminine in the Book of Proverbs* (Sheffield, 1985): 233-282, for a reconstruction of this period as the primary impetus for the development of Wisdom personified; L.G. Perdue, "Liminality as a Social Setting for Wisdom Instruction" *ZAW* 93 (1981): 114-126.

factors such as, the strange or foreign woman theme; Wisdom's apparently mythological background and her claim to have preceded creation (Prov 8:22-31); the word אֵטוּן "linen, thread , yearn" (Prov 7:16), which may be a Greek loan word; and the linking of Wisdom with "fear of the Lord" (Prov 1:7, 29; 2:5; 3:7; 8:13; 9:10).[15]

Whatever may have inspired or provoked the response that is the Wisdom figure she was, I believe, the product of a long process of reflection on Israel's relationship with YHWH by wisdom writers who expressed aspects of this relationship as Wisdom personified. The portrayal of this speaking female figure in Proverbs 1-9 suggests critical events and dramatic changes in the Israelite tradition. While no definite scientific facts can be established for Wisdom's emergence, I suggest that the theological point of departure for personified Wisdom may have been the Priestly tradition in the sixth and fifth centuries BCE. This tradition emphasises that God created human beings "in our image after our likeness" בְּצַלְמֵנוּ כִּדְמוּתֵנוּ (Gen 1:26); "in the likeness of God" בִּדְמוּת אֱלֹהִים (Gen 5:1); "in the image of God" בְּצֶלֶם אֱלֹהִים (Gen 9:6). A comparative reading of Gen 1:1-2:3 and Gen 2:5-25 reveals the theocentric view of the Gen 1:1-2:3 and the anthropomorphic view of 2:5-25. As many scholars consider Gen 1:1-2:3 and similar texts often called Priestly texts in the Pentateuch to be exilic or early post-exilic, it is reasonable to infer that the wisdom writers created the Wisdom figure around the same time. Links with Gen 1:1-2:3 suggest an exilic or early post-exilic date for Proverbs 1-9. Wisdom's association with the "tree of life" (3:18) also evokes imagery central to Gen 2:9, 16-17; 3:22, 24. She claims creation by YHWH, both in the sense of her origins, (Prov 8:22-31; Sir 24:3; Wis 7:22; 8:6), and in the creation of the world, (Job 28:27; Prov 3:19-20; Sir 1:9-10; 24:8-9; Bar 3:32-34). The God of the Wisdom texts is clearly Creator of Wisdom and Creator of the heavens, the earth and its inhabitants (Gen 1:1-2:3; Prov 8:22-30).

Conditions prevailing in the fifth century BCE provide some grounds for believing that the figure of Wisdom emerged during that period. By this time, the prophetic voice no longer had an impact and the monarchy had ceased to be effective. Assuming that the Wisdom literature of the Old Testament began to be formulated about this time I argue that Proverbs 1-9 is for the most part exilic or early post-exilic. The personal form of address common in chapters 1-9 as evidenced in, "Hear, my child, listen to your father's instruction, and do not reject your mother's teaching" (1:8); "How long, O simple ones, will you love being simple?" (1:22a); "Give heed to my reproof; I will pour out my thoughts to you; I will make my words known to you" (1:23); "To you, O people, I call . . . O simple

---

[15] Toy, *Proverbs* (1899): xxviii; Gemser, *Sprüche Salomos* (1963): 5; Ringgren, *Word and Wisdom* (1947): 8-13; Scott, *Proverbs, Ecclesiastes* (1964): 15; A. Barucq, *Le Livre des Proverbes* SB (Paris, 1964): 17; E. Sellin, *Introduction to the Old Testament* (London, 1923): 208; W. Baumgartner "Die Israelitische Weisheitsliteratur," *Theologische Rundschau* 5 (1933): 259-288; Eissfeldt, *Old Testament* (1965): 472-77; A. Weiser, *The Old Testament: Its Formation and Development* (New York, 1960): 296-298; Bentzen, *Introduction* (1952): 172; Pfeiffer, *Introduction to the Old Testament* (New York, 1941): 656; Anderson, *A Critical Introduction* (1959): 188.

ones, acquire intelligence, you who lack it. Hear, for I will speak noble things" (8:4-60), mark these texts as distinct from much of the rest of Proverbs, with its practical general advice and teaching. Forms of address heard in Proverbs 1-9 suggest an absence of highly ritualized modes of worship and teaching, and indicate that wisdom teachers at this time became more directly personal in their communications.

Outline of Study

Chapter 1 concentrates on possible antecedents for personified Wisdom focussing particularly on arguments positing Egyptian and Mesopotamian prototypes. Many scholars have sought to show that the figure of Wisdom was shaped either entirely or to a degree as an Israelite version of female deities in other ancient Near Eastern cultures. Hypotheses include the Babylonian goddess Ishtar; Sumerian Inanna; Egyptian Ma'at; Egyptian Isis; Sumero-Babylonian Gula; Asherah; Astarte; or an unnamed Canaanite wisdom goddess, but the identity of a likely predecessor continues to elude even the most persistent scholars. This is not particularly surprising since, for example, Ma'at's outlook on humanity and nature is in sharp contrast to Old Testament thought, which proclaims faith in a living and personal God. While it appears reasonable to suggest that Egyptian and Mesopotamian texts, which are usually considered more ancient than the comparable biblical material, could have contributed to the development of the Wisdom figure, the identity of an equivalent, a predecessor, or a prototype on which Wisdom may have been modelled continues to remain a matter of conjecture. Wisdom's own claims concerning her origins (Prov 8:22-31) present semantic problems for exegetes, as two crucial words resist definitive interpretations. The biblical figure has all the appearances of a biblical creation, but exegetical difficulties impede definitive interpretations of the decisive text (Prov 8:22-31). Wisdom is never portrayed as an independent personality, but as YHWH's "first" creation, speaking always within the tradition while also transforming it. This figure reflects essential differences between biblical texts and other ancient Near Eastern texts.

Chapter argues that personified Wisdom in Proverbs is an exilic creation as evidenced in her appearances in public places, without ritual or sacred space; the echoing of exilic prophetic motifs and styles; reinterpretation of prophetic teaching demanding a choice between life and death; claims that her words bring salvation or destruction, and 'justification' of the ways of God. The author(s) of Proverbs 1-9, I suggest, created the figure of personified Wisdom in an attempt to address the crisis following the events of 587 BCE, as the Israelites' understanding of how YHWH acted for them, before the fall of Jerusalem (587 BCE), could not effectively address the crisis resulting from the loss of Jerusalem, the Temple, the Davidic kingship, control over the land, and the exile. Taking into account earlier proposals regarding the dating of Proverbs 1-9 and given the historical context proposed, I argue that the portraits of Wisdom in Proverbs 1-9 were created in the period following 587 BCE. This is evidenced in the portrayal of Wisdom in public places, without ritual or sacred space; her echoing of exilic prophetic motifs and styles; her reinterpretation of prophetic teaching demanding a choice between life and death; her claims that her words bring salvation or destruction; her 'justification' of the ways of God in her teaching, which appears to echo, but in fact reinterprets, prophetic teaching.

Chapter 3 examines the depiction of elusive Wisdom in Job 28 and Wisdom as Torah in Baruch 3:9-4:4. As both these portraits allude to Wisdom's elusiveness, I have chosen to pair them in this study. Two popular Jewish motifs, woven through Old Testament wisdom are the search for Wisdom and Wisdom's elusiveness, Wisdom's accessibility and Wisdom's hiddenness. While the classic perception of Wisdom's elusiveness and inaccessibility appears in Job 28, the Wisdom poem in Baruch 3:9-4:4 also explores the apparent difficulty of finding Wisdom by posing the question which also appears in Job "who has found the place of Wisdom?" (Job 28:12, 28; Bar 3:15). Both poems emphasise the paradox of Wisdom's hiddenness and inaccessibility. I argue that Job 28 functions in the book to indicate that Job's questions cannot be resolved by his friends because the place of understanding is elsewhere, thus pointing to chapters 38-41. The author of Baruch 3:9-4:4 underscores issues threatening Jews in exile from their heritage and identity. They have forsaken "the fountain of Wisdom" and not walked "in the way of God" (3:12-13). This poem treats exile as a metaphor for the loss of identity brought about by unfaithfulness to Torah and claims that the Law was given exclusively to Israel thus implying that Israelite wisdom is the most ancient.

Wisdom's poem of self-praise in the Wisdom of Ben Sira 24 is the focus for chapter 4, where I argue that in this text Ben Sira attempts to address the difficulties faced by Jews who are struggling to retain and develop their distinct identity and heritage in a hostile environment. He calls on his audience to live within the Jewish tradition, which was under threat of being eroded or assimilated by the prevailing Hellenist culture. Ben Sira, by evoking traditional themes, metaphors, and symbols, such as the Garden of Eden, the rivers of Eden, the land of Israel including its trees, produce, and borders, Jerusalem, the Temple and its rituals, highlights and gives new expression to the unique history and development of the Jewish heritage. He transforms the Wisdom figure by identifying her as the Torah. Therefore, engages Wisdom in the reformulation of the Mosaic tradition through a theodicy that envisages personified Wisdom pervading the world. The centre of this world and the central point of humanity is Israel with its unique history guided by YHWH. In the Mosaic Law Israel was entrusted with the divine Wisdom, the orderer of creation who now calls Jews attracted by Hellenism to recognise the richness of their own heritage. Both Ben Sira and Baruch identify Wisdom with the Torah and claim that Wisdom was given to Jacob/Israel. However, Ben Sira places Wisdom/Torah in the Jerusalem sanctuary, while Baruch insists on a gift exclusively to the Jewish people.

The elaborate depiction of Wisdom in Wis 6:22-10:21 recalls and refashions the figure encountered in earlier biblical portrayals. In chapter 5, I argue that the author, through the figure of personified Wisdom, demands that the audience face onerous decisions concerning how to live in accord with their beliefs and traditions and how to nurture their Jewish faith in a culture that is threatening the survival of their Jewish tradition. By transforming Wisdom into a figure that reflects a Hellenistic background, but is deeply rooted in the Hebrew/Jewish tradition and sacred history, the author integrates earlier traditions with Hellenistic ideas and so fashions a Wisdom figure, who is the presence of God in the universe, a much more powerful figure than the popular Isis is. In describing Wisdom in the role of Saviour in the past, the author builds his case to present her as saviour for the Jews in the crisis they now face living in a Hellenistic culture. He credits this Jewish Hellenistic Wisdom figure with deeds elsewhere ascribed to God. Wisdom as the presence of God is vividly illustrated by the use of twenty-one images and a fivefold metaphor, which illustrate a uniquely intimate relationship between God and Wisdom.

Postscript

While many argue that the poem in Prov 31:10-31 about the אֵשֶׁת־חַיִל "woman of worth" is a concluding portrayal of personified Wisdom and is closely related to the depictions of Wisdom in Proverbs 1-9. I argue that this poem is a portrayal of an earthly woman/wife who is humanly real but idealised. The אֵשֶׁת־חַיִל who "fears the Lord" is, in all respects, the opposite of the "wicked women" depicted in chapters 1-9. She embodies the idea of the "good woman" who is the essential spouse for any man seeking wisdom. She is a wife and mother (v.28) who spins, weaves, produces handcrafts, buys and sells, chooses and purchases land, plants a vineyard, trades in the market, ensures adequate food supplies and warm clothing for her household and works tirelessly. References to the woman's household, maids, spinning, weaving, buying and selling, her husband and her children all contribute to make her a real, albeit exceptionally gifted woman and sought after wife to be treasured above all other possessions. Woman Wisdom (1-9) and the Woman of Worth (31:10-31) respectively open and close the book of Proverbs, but do not merge or even converge as one figure. I reject the popular equation that this figure is another portrait personified Wisdom, and argue that her specifically human characteristics clearly identify her as a human being, albeit a near perfect version. Consequently, I do not include a discussion of אֵשֶׁת־חַיִל in this work. I opted to engage with this fascinating figure in a different context.

Chapter 1

Origins of Personified Wisdom

Introduction

Approaches to understanding the personification of Wisdom are nearly as numerous as are commentators. Recent years have witnessed a rapid increase in interest in the personification of Wisdom. In 1979, J.A. Emerton noted, "a controversial problem of Proverbs 1-9 is that of the origin and meaning of the personified figure of Wisdom".[1] While scholars have addressed several aspects of personified Wisdom, her origin and function remain mysterious. R.E. Murphy, who over the past four decades has written frequently about the personification of Wisdom, notes, "From a literary-theological point of view, personified Wisdom is simply unequalled in the entire Old Testament."[2] Camp, and more recently Whybray, reviewed, in considerable detail, research concerning the personification of Wisdom, so I shall confine my comments in this chapter to works that specifically address issues pertaining to Proverbs 1-9.[3] Classifying previous work on this subject inevitably leads to some generalizations and loss of distinct voices. Yet some outline of the landscape is an essential instrument for charting a route through the rich and diverse material available. With this qualification, I shall survey a small sample of critical approaches to the personification of Wisdom in Proverbs 1-9. Some of the works examined in this section, while not so well know, are included for what I consider unique insights. Rather than attempting to produce an exhaustive review of literature pertaining to the personification of Wisdom, the aim of this study is to strive for a representative sample that outlines a wide and varied range of interpretations of the Wisdom figure, rather than in-depth appraisals of each scholar's work. I acknowledge that such a brief overview cannot do justice to how individual scholars nuance their interpretations, and the categorising of these brief outlines into general groupings is of its nature arbitrary. I shall be referring to pertinent studies throughout the book in the relevant chapters.

---

[1] J.A. Emerton, "Wisdom," in G.W. Anderson, ed., *Tradition and Interpretation* (Oxford, 1979): 214-237, particularly 231-2.

[2] R.E. Murphy, "The Personification of Wisdom" in J. Day, R.P. Gordon, H.G.M. Williamson, eds. *Wisdom in Ancient Israel: Essays in Honour of J.A. Emerton* [forthwith *WAI* (Cambridge, 1995): 232.

[3] C. Camp, *Wisdom and the Feminine* (1985): 23-68; R.N. Whybray, *The Book of Proverbs: A Survey of Modern Study* (Leiden, 1995).

During the past decades, scholars of personified Wisdom have taken many different approaches, so any strict categorisation tends to distort or misrepresent the work of many scholars. One large group uses approaches usually grouped as historical. Second are those concerned primarily with the origin of personified Wisdom. They use sociological approaches seeing the Wisdom figure as abstracted from the lives of Israelite women and reflecting particular social developments. Those who adopt literary approaches by which they regard the Wisdom figure as a hypostasis or a literary device to portray wisdom as an attribute of God can often be placed in one or both of the above categories. Such studies consider the Wisdom figure to be modelled on one or more ancient Near Eastern deities. Regardless of the approach favoured, scholars have persistently searched for the origins of personified Wisdom. In the first half of the twentieth century Schencke, Reitzenstein, Bultmann, Knox, Boström, Ringgren, and many others, examined biblical and other ancient Near Eastern texts for clues to the development of this biblical figure.[4] Discussions of the origins of the biblical Wisdom figure are often complicated unnecessarily when texts in which Wisdom is personified are treated together as if all of these books can be understood as of one mind on the matter of personified Wisdom. This study is concerned with the unfolding meanings and functions of the Wisdom figure in the Old Testament. To avoid conflating or confusing developments particular to the Wisdom figure in specific wisdom books I shall focus in this chapter on portrayals of Wisdom in the Book of Proverbs. I shall examine likely sources for evidence of personified Wisdom's origins. This involves a brief survey of studies of Proverbs 1-9 especially those concerned with the personification of Wisdom. Secondly is a study of biblical texts which portray the emerging and developing phenomenon that is the figure of Wisdom in the Old Testament and lastly there is an exploration of Egyptian and Mesopotamian influences, prototypes, and antecedents that may have contributed to the biblical Wisdom figure.

Historical Approaches

History of religion scholars regard the figure of Wisdom as something strange and enigmatic within the Israelite tradition. They seek to explain the language used to describe this figure by seeing Wisdom solely as an Israelite borrowing of a foreign deity or goddess. Some who have concentrated on perceived historical influences on the emergence and description of personified Wisdom, have proposed various origins, such as that this figure was modelled on a goddess borrowed from neighbouring peoples and demoted to serve as a subordinate to YHWH. Various foreign deities and mythological figures have been proposed as the prototypes of

---

[4] W. Schencke, *Die Chokma (Sophia) in der jüdischen Hypostasenspekulation: Ein Beitrag zur Geschichte der religiösen Ideen im Zeitalter des Hellenismus* (Kristiana, 1913); R. Reitzenstein, *Das iranische Erlösungsmysterion* (Bonn, 1921); W.L. Knox, "The Divine Wisdom" *JTS* 38 (1937): 230-237; G. Boström, *Proverbiastudien: Die Weisheit und das fremde Weib in Spr 1-9* (Lund, 1935): H. Ringgren, *Word and Wisdom* (1947): 89-171.

Wisdom. Reitzenstein claimed that the origins of the Wisdom figure lay in the Jewish-Hellenistic Isis-Sophia speculation ultimately based on the Egyptian goddess Isis, but with an admixture of an Iranian element.[5] Bousset and others, who held the view that Iranian beliefs influenced post-exilic Judaism, suggested that its origins lay in one or other of the Iranian angelic figures known as the *Amesha Spentas.*[6] Some other suggested models for Wisdom are Canaanite Asherah, Egyptian Ma'at and Isis, Astarte, or Inanna.[7] Theories that suggest Wisdom's dependence on Semitic sources can be traced back in this century to Albright who invoked a vast array of material evidence to support his claim for a "goddess of life and wisdom."[8] Schencke, proposed the Egyptian goddess Ma'at, a personification of truth and righteousness, as a partial model for the figure of Wisdom. However, after an examination of all the hypotheses proposed up to his time, he stressed the polytheistic character of pre-exilic Israelite religion and concluded that Wisdom was probably originally a distinct indigenous female deity worshipped side by side with YHWH as one of his consorts. Such worship, he believed, continued to be practised after the exile, but Wisdom was eventually absorbed into official Judaism and became simply a personification of YHWH's wisdom. He believed that the figure was influenced by various non-Israelite mythological figures, which could not be identified.[9] Coogan also proposes ancient Near Eastern goddess connections and suggests that the divine attributes given to the Wisdom figure in Proverbs 1-9, Job 28, and in the Deuterocanonical books are a legitimatisation of the worship of more "established" goddesses in Israel and Judah, such as Asherah.[10] Hadley challenges Coogan's claim for legitimating the

---

[5]   R. Reitzenstein, *Zwei religionsgeschichtliche Fragen nach ungedruckten griechischen Texten der Strassburger Bibliothek* (Strassburg, 1901); *Poimandres: Studien zur griechisch-ägyptischen und frühchristlichen Literatur* (Leipzig, 1904).

[6]   W. Bousset, *Die Religion des Judentums im späthellenistischen Zeitalter* (Tübingen, 1926).

[7]   H. Conzelmann, "The Mother of Wisdom," in J.M. Robinson, ed. *The Future of Our Religious Past: Essays in Honor of Rudolf Bultmann* (New York, 1971): 230-231; J.M. Hadley, "Wisdom and the Goddess" in *WAI* (1995): 234-243; B. Lang, *Wisdom and the Book of Proverbs* (New York, 1986); "Wisdom" in K van der Toorn, B. Becking, P.W. Van Der Horst, eds. *Dictionary of Deities and Demons in the Bible* [forthwith *DDD*] (Leiden, 1995): 1692-1702; C. Kayatz, *Studien zu Proverbien 1-9* (Neukirchen-Vluyn, 1966); J.M. Reese, *Hellenistic Influence on the Book of Wisdom and Its Consequences* (Rome, 1970); D. Winston, *Wisdom of Solomon AB* 43 (1979); J.S. Kloppenborg, "Isis and Sophia in the Book of Wisdom" *HTR* 75 (1982): 57-84; G. Boström, *Proverbiastudien* (Lund, 1935) proposes that the character of Folly is inspired by a goddess; cf., P.D. Miller, "The Absence of the Goddess in Israelite Religion" *HAR* 10 (1986): 239-248.

[8]   W.F. Albright argued for the identification of Wisdom with a hypothetical Canaanite goddess, the daughter of El in, "Some Canaanite-Phoenician Sources of Hebrew Wisdom" *VTSup* 3 (1955): 1-15, see also "The Goddess of Life and Wisdom" *American Journal of Semitic Languages and Literature* (1919/20): 258-294.

[9]   Schencke, *Die Chokma* (1913).

[10] M. Coogan, "The Goddess Wisdom—'Where Can She Be Found?': Literary Reflexes of

worship of "established" goddesses. She proposes that the apparent apotheosis of Wisdom is a literary compensation for an earlier eradication of the worship of these goddesses.[11]

Sociological Approaches

Sociological interpretations perceive personified Wisdom as a product of social impulses within Israel that drew upon the lives of Israelite women for their imagery. Foremost among those looking towards an internal origin for the feminine personification of Wisdom is Camp. She addresses the fundamental question of Wisdom's exalted position as a female figure in Proverbs in association with the notion that the Hebrew Bible generally exhibits a patriarchal perspective. Arguing that Wisdom is based on Israelite women rather than on any ancient Near Eastern goddess, she sees the implied role of Israelite women in Proverbs as reflecting the "kingless sociological configuration of the post-exilic era", when the family in some respects replaced the monarchy as the "defining element" in society. In her examination of the literary roles of women in the Bible and the relationship of these roles to the social roles of women of the time, Camp questions the potentially misogynist argument for a divine precursor of Wisdom, which ignores the real human role models that might have given rise to personified Wisdom in Israel.[12] Camp pinpoints features present in the Wisdom figure and the "strange or foreign woman" that she claims result from literary traditions about women in society. She concludes that social crises of the post-exilic period provided the impetus for drawing on family-centred imagery to authenticate the wisdom tradition embodied in Proverbs. Arguing that personified Wisdom is an abstraction from female sages and counsellors, she claims that social forces such as renewed emphasis on the home in the post-exilic period, the consequent elevated status of women and the need for a mediator between God and the people, propelled the development of the Wisdom figure.[13]

Popular Religion," in B.A. Levine, R. Chazan, W.W. Hallo, eds., *Ki Baruch Hu: Ancient Near Eastern, Biblical, and Judaic Studies in Honor of Baruch A. Levine* [*Ki Baruch Hu*] (Winona Lake, 1999): 203-209.

[11] J.M. Hadley, "Yahweh and 'his asherah': Archaeological and Textual Evidence for the Cult of the Goddess" in W. Dietrich and M.A. Klopfenstein, eds., *Ein Gott allein? JHWH-Verehrung und biblischer Monotheismus im Kontext der israelitischen und altorientalischen Religionsgeschichte* [*Ein Gott allein*] (Freiburg, 1994): 235-268; J. Day, "Asherah in the Hebrew Bible and Northwest Semitic Literature," *JBL* 105/3 (1986): 385-408.

[12] C.V. Camp, *Wisdom and the Feminine* (1985): 262-265, 290.

[13] C.V. Camp, "Woman Wisdom as Root Metaphor: A Theological Consideration," in *The Listening Heart* (1987): 45-76; *Wisdom and the Feminine* (1985); "The Female Sage in Ancient Israel and in the Biblical Wisdom Literature" in J.G Gammie; L. G Perdue *The Sage in Israel and the Ancient Near East* (forthwith *SIANE*) (Winona Lake, 1990): 185-203.

A similar way of thinking about personified Wisdom is evident in the work of Schroer, who suggests that women in the Old Testament who served as counsellors provided the literary and historical background for the Wisdom figure. She sees Wisdom as a counsellor as positive for contemporary women and for feminist spirituality.[14] By analysing the texts of Proverbs 1-9, 31 she seeks to reconstruct the post-exilic history of Wisdom's personification within the theological history of Israel and concludes that as the Wisdom figure is woman and Wisdom is God so the virtuous woman has attributes usually reserved for YHWH. The key to Proverbs is the unifying metaphor of Wisdom. Theologically the metaphor portrays the God of Israel in the image of a woman speaking the language of the goddess. Wisdom, she concludes, was part of a new post-exilic theology that was more inclusive and home-centred. She ascribes the erosion of that post-exilic position and image of woman to the later restoration of hierarchical structures.[15]

Klopfenstein in his examination of Proverbs 1-9 concludes that the feminine imagery of Wisdom amplified the post-exilic divine image, and this imagery gave women a means of participation in Yahwistic religion.[16] Even if we accept a human model for Wisdom, that is no more or less than what we claim for literary depictions of male and female gods that were presumably also based on data from the human realm. Clifford, Crenshaw, Blenkinsopp and others who have adopted a sociological perspective for the study of the Wisdom figure see her as a response by the wisdom writers to a major crisis besetting the people of Israel. Clifford in his study of Proverbs 1-9 argues that personified Wisdom appeared in Israel around the seventh century BCE as part of an Israelite polemic against Canaanite religion.[17] Proverbs 1-9 borrows from the "epic type-scene", such as, Gilgamesh and Ishtar, Aqhat and Anat, to exhort young men to yoke themselves to Wisdom and not to Folly.[18] Those who seek to account for what they call personified Wisdom's mythological character, propose the notion that Wisdom is the product of creative theological thinking within the Israelite tradition.

Conzelmann may have been the first to suggest that the appearance of personified Wisdom in Hebrew writing was a result of a process he called "reflective mythology".[19] Mack explores this notion further and proposes that the

[14] S. Schroer, "Weise Frauen und Ratgeberinnen in Israel" *Biblische Notizen* 51 (1990): 45.

[15] S. Schroer, "Die personifizierte Sophia im Buch der Weisheit" in *Ein Gott Allein?* (1994): 534-558; "Die göttliche Weisheit und der nachexilische Monotheismus," in M.T. Wacker, ed., *Der eine Gott und die Göttin: Gottesvorstellungen des biblischen Israel im Horizont feministischer Theologie.* QD 135 [*Der eine Gott und die Göttin*] (Freiburg, 1991): 151-182.

[16] M.A. Klopfenstein, "Auferstehung der Göttin in der spätisraelitischen Weisheit von Prov 1-9?" in *Ein Gott allein?* (1994): 531-542.

[17] R.J. Clifford, "Proverbs IX: A Suggested Ugaritic Parallel," *VT* (1975): 298-306.

[18] R.J. Clifford, "Woman Wisdom in the Book of Proverbs," in G. Braulik, W. Groß and S. McEvenue, eds., *Biblische Theologie und gesellschaftlicher Wandel* (Freiburg, 1993): 61-72.

[19] H. Conzelmann, "The Mother of Wisdom" in R.K. Bultmann and J. Robinson, eds., in

post-exilic question of theodicy is the context for the theological employment of myth to express faith in the continuing wisdom of YHWH as Lord of creation and redemption.[20] His study, which deals with the movement from *Sophia* mythology to *Logos* mythology, is a comparison of Jewish *Hokmah/Sophia* and Philonic *Logos*. In contrast to earlier attempts to explain personified Wisdom through the *Urmensch* myth and *anthropos* speculation, Mack finds that the relationship between Egyptian and Old Testament wisdom sources is a more fruitful approach to the question. His purpose is to pursue Conzelmann's opinion that there is a distinction between myth and myth-ology, (the employment of myth for theological reflection).[21]

Personified Wisdom is not a myth, but the result of a reworking of mythic materials as theological categories of thought. Earlier wisdom was experiential, but now Wisdom confronts human beings, and to accept it means salvation. In working out the objectification of wisdom, the myth-ology, Mack establishes a typology of wisdom: hidden Wisdom (Job 28; Bar 3:16-21; Wis 9:13-18; Sir 1:1-8); near Wisdom (Prov 8:22-31; Sir 24:6); disappeared Wisdom (1 Enoch 42; 2 Esdras 5:9-10; 1 Bar 48:36). He shows the relationship of these types of wisdom to early Egyptian (*Ma'at*) wisdom and to the Isis literature, and situates the development of the wisdom typology against the background of the trauma of exile. He sees Wisdom's promises as a reply to post-exilic faith questions. The mythical Wisdom figure becomes a category of thought by which one could understand the order of creation.[22] According to this myth, wisdom is that which orders or even creates the world. In the process of mythologization new linguistic formations were produced".[23] Mack claims that Proverbs 1-9 exhibits mythopoeic thinking, and it is through this process that Israel reappropriates wisdom. That Wisdom is ever portrayed as creating order or is even ever shown as actively involved in the work of creation in Proverbs 1-9 is very doubtful.

E. Schüssler-Fiorenza investigating the influence of Wisdom on early Christology, similarly claims that the personification of Wisdom was the result of "reflective mythology," a theological process by which a community appropriates living myth, and adapts and develops it for its own purposes to create a new myth.[24] O'Connor also considers the notion of "reflective mythology", and suggests that given the international character of Israelite wisdom literature, this process may have begun in Israel in the Persian period or even earlier, as a theological response to threats created by competition from neighbouring Wisdom

The Future of Our Religious Past (New York, 1964): 230-243.

[20] B.L. Mack, "Wisdom Myth and Mytho-logy," *Interpretation* 24 (1970): 46-60.

[21] B.L. Mack, *Logos und Sophia: Untersuchungen zur Weisheitstheologie im Hellenistischen Judentum* (Gottingen, 1973): 20.

[22] Mack, *Logos* (1973): 47-48.

[23] B.L. Mack, *Wisdom and the Hebrew Epic* (Chicago, 1985): 147-148.

[24] E. Schüssler-Fiorenza, "Wisdom Mythology and the Christological Hymns of the New Testament" in R. Wilken, ed., *Aspects of Wisdom in Judaism and Early Christianity* (Notre Dame, 1975): 17-41. Conzelmann may have introduced the term 'reflective mythology'.

goddesses.[25] According to this proposal, "personified Wisdom is the product of a long process of mythopoeic thinking in which Israel draws upon a pool of goddess myths from the ancient Near East" and transformed them into a new myth which gained prominence in Israel. She suggests that this transformed myth served to address the challenge presented to Israel's faith by the international Wisdom goddesses in the Hellenistic period. To hypothesise that personified Wisdom arose because of the Israelite authors' theological reflections on neighbouring myths is to assume that creative theological thinking within Israel was invariably based on "foreign" myths. O'Connor claims that such a hypothesis helps explain why earlier texts about personified Wisdom, such as Proverbs 1-9, are more subtle in identifying Wisdom with God, while later texts (Sir 1:1-10; 24:1-33; Wis 6:12-21; Bar 3:9-4:4) do so more directly.[26] She proposes that Wisdom is a symbol of God in her own right. The Wisdom figure is Wise-God, or the personification of wisdom, a mytho-poetic expression of divinity that both complements, and challenges depictions of God found elsewhere in the Old Testament.[27]

Wisdom's Biblical Origins

Within biblical wisdom texts, there is not much interest in the historical origins of the personification of Wisdom. The passages that clearly bear on this subject are Prov 8:22-31 and Job 28. Whether the figure of Wisdom in the Bible is an original creation of the biblical writers, or the result of the inculturation of borrowed ideas into the Israelite tradition, she now appears to be indigenous to her biblical settings because she has been enshrined in the biblical tradition and included in the biblical canon. Only in the late nineteenth century did the critical study of Proverbs begin to engage some scholars in spite of the reservations entertained by many concerning the appropriateness of the wisdom books as biblical texts. Some scholars have held that the wisdom literature cannot be considered a valid expression of Israel's beliefs. Koch, who proposed a deed-consequence theory as basic to wisdom teaching, excepted Israel's election and covenant from this.[28] His

---

[25] K.M. O'Connor, "Wisdom Literature and Experience of the Divine," in S.J. Kraftchick, B.C. Ollenburger, S.J. Kraftchick, C.D. Myers, eds., *Biblical Theology: Problems and Perspectives* (Nashville, 1995): 195; see also C.V. Camp, "The Female Sage in the Biblical Wisdom Literature," in *SIANE* (1990): 185-203.

[26] O'Connor, "Wisdom Literature" (1995): 195-6; Camp, "The Female Sage" (1990): 185-203; C. Larcher, *Études sur le Livre de la Sagesse* (Paris, 1969): 329-414.

[27] O'Connor, "Wisdom Literature" (1995): 187-188; see also, É. Bonnard, "De la Sagesse personificée dans l'Ancien Testament à la Sagesse en personne dans le Nouveau," in M. Gilbert, ed., *La Sagesse de l'Ancien Testament* (Louvain, 1979): 117-149; P. Ricoeur, "Towards a Hermeneutic of the Idea of Revelation", in P. Ricoeur, L.M. Mudge, eds., *Essays in Biblical Interpretation* (Philadelphia, 1980): 88.

[28] K. Koch, "Gibt es ein Vergeltungsdogma im Alten Testament?", *ZTK* 52 (1955): 1-42, expresses his conviction concerning order as basic to wisdom teaching. J. Barton responds to Koch's view in "Natural Theology and Poetic Justice", *JTS* 30 (1979): 1-14.

theory has had considerable influence among some biblical wisdom scholars. It is the underlying reason why Preuss, who has written extensively about the wisdom books, holds the view that wisdom literature presents an invalid theology.[29] Delitzsch in his analysis of the structure of chapters 1-9 found it to be a unified composition consisting of fifteen *Meschallieder* or *Lehrdichtungen, mᵃšᵃl,* songs or didactic poems.[30] Other scholars who commented on Proverbs 1-9 as part of larger studies in this period were Ewald, Wildeboer, Nowack, Frankenberg, Strack, and Toy, while Meinhold produced the first study devoted entirely to biblical wisdom.[31] Not surprisingly, scholars in this period, because of their history of religion approach, found Old Testament wisdom books difficult to place, as they knew of no similar literature. Although most biblical scholars of the time did not know the literatures of other ancient Near Eastern peoples sufficiently well for easy comparison, Gunkel attempted a comparison with Egyptian material.[32] Studies of the era located Proverbs in the development of Israel's religious ideas in comparison with other Old Testament and Deuterocanonical books especially the Wisdom of Ben Sira. Toy described Proverbs as "a manual of conduct" that addressed individuals and presupposed knowledge of the prophets and the Torah. Studies of Proverbs 1-9 suggested that monotheism was the norm since the text of Proverbs refers to no deities other than YHWH who is presented as universal Creator and orderer of nature; that religious consensus prevailed; that education was important; and that monogamy was customary.[33] Such ideas point to a late date for Proverbs 1-9.

The remarkable figure of personified Wisdom, who speaks, does seem to be uniquely Israelite. Such a character has not been identified in other ancient Near Eastern writings where wisdom remains, at most, a human quality, and is never portrayed as speaking. In the biblical texts where she is personified she appears in a variety of settings and in various roles: a mysterious and elusive figure; close associate of YHWH; present at the creation; a figure who speaks, calling out in public places like a prophet; a teacher who invites all present to "listen/pay attention" to her message, and threatens doom for all who ignore her; a hostess who prepares a banquet and issues invitations; a figure identified with the Torah, and located in the Temple. In view of the power, that personification provides some discussion of this literary convention seems in order.

[29] H.D. Preuss, *Einführung in die alttestamentliche Weisheitsliteratur* (Stuttgart, 1987).
[30] F. Delitzsch, *Das Salomonisches Spruchbuch* (Leipzig, 1873): 29-36.
[31] H. Ewald, *Sprüche Salomos. Kohélet Zusätze zu den frühern Theilen und Schluss.* DDB 4 (Göttingen, 1837); W. Nowack, *Die Sprüche Salomos* KEH 2nd. ed. (Leipzig, 1883); G. Wildeboer, *Die Sprüche* (Freiburg, 1897); C.H. Toy, *Proverbs* (1899); J. Meinhold, *Die Weisheit Israels* (Leipzig, 1908): 120-139.
[32] H. Gunkel, "Ägyptische Parallel zum Alten Testament" *ZDMG* 63 (1909): 531-539.
[33] A. Klostermann, "Schulwesen im alten Israel" in *Theologische Studien. Theodor Zahn zum Oktober 1908 dargebracht* (Leipzig, 1908): 193-232.

Personification: A Literary Convention

Some scholars have opted for purely literary interpretations of the Wisdom figure. Anderson, in an analysis of Prov 8:22-36, sees personified Wisdom as metaphorical, not as a goddess or as God.[34] The poem, he notes, invites exploration of other feminine images for relationship to humanity and the world. Habel, following Ricoeur's definition of 'symbol', argues that Wisdom is a symbol.[35] While his perception of personified Wisdom highlights Wisdom's many-sided character, the study underestimates the figure of Wisdom in favour of the "way of Wisdom." In explaining the importance of this motif, he overlooks to some extent the central position of personified Wisdom in Proverbs 1-9. Many scholars explain the close association of personified Wisdom with the divinity as a form of literary device. Among them are those who regard Wisdom as representing an actual person, or as a hypostasis of wisdom.[36] Sheppard offers a fresh approach maintaining that at a certain period in the development of Old Testament literature, wisdom became a theological category associated with an understanding of the canon that formed a perspective from which to interpret Torah, and the prophetic traditions. In this sense, Wisdom became a "hermeneutical construct" for interpreting Sacred Scripture.[37]

Personified Wisdom is, I believe, a literary creation rather than a person, or hypostasis. The term personification, with its variety of connotations in the English language, denotes the literary convention of attributing human

---

[34] B.W. Anderson, "Prov 8:22-36. Moving Beyond Masculine Metaphors," *BRev* 10/5 (1994): 22, 57-58.

[35] N. Habel, "The Symbolism of Wisdom in Proverbs 1-9" *Int* 26/2 (1972): 131-157; P. Ricoeur, *Freud and Philosophy: An Essay on Interpretation*, trans., D. Savage (New Haven, 1970): 9, "a double meaning linguistic expression that requires an interpretation".

[36] R. Marcus, "On Biblical Hypostases of Wisdom," *HUCA* 23 (1950-51): 57-171; H. Ringgren, *Word and Wisdom* (1947): 89-171; R.N. Whybray, *The Book of Proverbs* (Cambridge, 1972); H. Cazelles, "La Sagesse de Proverbes 8:22: Peut-elle être considérée comme une hypostase?" in A. Triacca, A. Pistoia, eds., *Trinité et liturgie* (Rome, 1984): 53; R.E. Murphy, "Wisdom Theses" in J. Armenti, ed., *Wisdom and Knowledge: Papin Festschrift* (Philadelphia, 1976): 187-200; "Wisdom—Theses and Hypotheses," in J.G. Gammie, W.A Brueggemann, W.L. Humphreys, J.M. Ward, eds., *Israelite Wisdom: Theological and Literary Essays in Honor of Samuel Terrien* [forthwith *IW*] (Missoula, 1978): 35-42; "Hebrew Wisdom," *JAOS* 101 (1981): 21-34; "Proverbs and Theological Exegesis," in D.G. Miller, ed., *The Hermeneutical Quest* (Allison Park, 1986): 87-95; *Tree of Life* (1990): 133-149; Conzelmann, "Mother of Wisdom" in *Future of our Religious Past* (1971): 232.

[37] G.T. Sheppard, *Wisdom as a Hermeneutical Construct* (Berlin, 1981); Although scholars have observed this phenomenon in the Wisdom of Ben Sira, it appears that no one had sketched the contours of this interpretation or explored the possibility of a similar perspective at points in the later redaction history of the Old Testament. For a discussion of Wisdom as a "theological idiom" in early Jewish literature see H.H. Guthrie, *Wisdom and Canon: Meaning of the Law and the Prophets* (Chicago, 1966); S.Z. Leiman, *The Canonization of Hebrew Scripture* (Hamden, 1976): 70 n. 305.

characteristics and personality to an element or abstract quality.[38] It is a way of speaking that endows things or abstractions with life. This convention has featured in poetry and song since ancient times.[39] Rhetorically it may be described as "a means of taking hold of things that appear startlingly uncontrollable and independent".[40] As a stylistic device, personification emphasises and vivifies Wisdom by its use of poetic diction, and simultaneously avoids the problems of abstraction. The personification of human characteristics is not confined to biblical literature. Plato's "ideas" and the scholastics' "universals" are parallels. Because the biblical authors used metaphorical language to portray Personified Wisdom, the figure operates on a symbolic level, so is dependent on the reader's ability to perceive its meaning.[41] Biblical writers did not confine personification as a literary device to portrayals of Wisdom. It appears in many other texts, for example,

Wine is a mocker, strong drink a brawler;
and whoever is led astray by it is not wise. (Prov 20:1)

Then your light shall break forth like the dawn,
and your healing shall spring up quickly;
your vindicator shall go before you,
the glory of the Lord shall be your rear guard. (Isa 58:8)

Surely his salvation is at hand for those who fear him,
.... Steadfast love and faithfulness will meet;
righteousness and peace will kiss each other.
Faithfulness will spring up from the ground,
and righteousness will look down from the sky. (Ps 85:9-11)

Righteousness and justice are the foundation of your throne;
steadfast love and faithfulness go before you. (Ps 89:14)

His lightnings light up the world:
The earth sees and trembles. (Ps 97:4)

---

[38] *Oxford English Dictionary* 2nd. ed. Prepared by J.A. Simpson and E.S.C. Weiner (Oxford, 1989): Vol. 11, col. 3: 605-11:1, defines personification as "the attribution of personal form, nature, or characteristics; the representation of a thing or abstraction as a person: esp. as a rhetorical figure or species of metaphor".

[39] I am indebted to John Arthos, "Personification" in *The Princeton Encyclopaedia of Poetry and Poetics* (London, 1975): 612, for several of the ideas presented here.

[40] T.B.L. Webster, "'Personification' as a mode of Greek Thought," *JWCI* 17 (1954): 12-21.

[41] Over the past half century, linguistic analysts, language philosophers, anthropologists, historians of religion, and biblical theologians have studied symbols and their functions. See M. Eliade, *Images and Symbols* (New York, 1969); C.G. Jung, *Symbols of Transformation* (Princeton, 1956); V.W. Turner, *The Ritual Process: Structure and Anti-Structure* (Chicago, 1969). E. Cassirer, *The Philosophy of Symbolic Forms* vol. 2 (New Haven, 1955). Several recent studies of wisdom literature discuss the nature and character of metaphor. See bibliographies in L. Perdue, *Wisdom in Revolt: Metaphorical Theology in the Book of Job* (Sheffield, 1991); *Wisdom and Creation* (Nashville, 1994).

In the texts above, the instances of personification exhibit common characteristics. Human actions are attributed to abstract qualities and inanimate objects by the use of active or complementary verbs, for example, "wine is a mocker strong drink a brawler" (Prov 20:1); your light shall "break forth"; your healing "shall spring up"; your righteousness "shall go before you", the glory of the Lord "shall be your rearguard" (Isa 58:8); salvation "is at hand"; glory "may dwell"; steadfast love and faithfulness "will meet"; righteousness and peace "will embrace" (Ps 85:9-11); steadfast love and faithfulness "go before" (Ps 89:14); "lightnings light up" the world; the earth "sees and trembles" (Ps 97:4).[42] However, these personified qualities and elements are not developed beyond the actions attributed to them. Interesting to note is the brevity of the personification, with most instances sustained for one or two verses only. A second point of interest is the predominance of words of masculine gender in Hebrew, in these texts, for example, הַיַּיִן "wine"; שֵׁכָר "strong drink"; אוֹרֶךָ "your light"; אֲרֻכָתְךָ "your healing"; צֶדֶק, "righteousness"; כָּבוֹד "glory"; אֱמֶת "faithfulness"; שָׁלוֹם "peace".

In contrast to the examples above the personification of Wisdom in Prov 1:20-33; 4:6-9; 8:1-36; 9:1-6; Job 28:12-28; Bar 3:9-4:4; Sir 1:1-10, 24:1-34; Wis 6:12-10:21 takes on a profound and dynamic character. It continues throughout several verses, sometimes forming complete pericopes. This allows for detailed portrayals of Wisdom and the development of a multifaceted literary character. The Wisdom figure is portrayed in particular settings, such as the marketplace, in her house of seven pillars, at the creation of the world, sitting by the throne of God. In addition, we hear that she performs actions, such as, calling out and threatening punishment (Prov 1:20-24); narrating her history (Prov 8:1-36); preparing a feast and offering an invitation to her banquet (Prov 9:1-6).

Invariably, the wisdom writers depicted personified Wisdom as a female character. Her intimate association with God is manifest in her divine origins, as in: יְהוָֹה קָנָנִי רֵאשִׁית דַּרְכּוֹ קֶדֶם מִפְעָלָיו מֵאָז "YHWH created me at the beginning of his work the first of his acts of old" (Prov 8:22). She is "throne-companion, the one who sits beside God" (Wis 9:4), and her activity ranges from involvement with human beings in the created world (Prov 8:31) to her position as YHWH's אָמוֹן (Prov 8:30), to τεχνῖτις "fashioner, architect" (Wis 8:6). Wisdom in Prov 9:1-6 issues invitations to all to partake of her banquet. In Sir 1:9-10 we hear, "God poured her out upon all his works, upon all the living". Job 28:12 and Bar 3:15 ask, "Where is Wisdom to be found?" Bar 4:1 proclaims, "She is the book of the commandments of God, the law that endures forever." In Wis 7:24 Wisdom

---

[42] According to a theory supported, among others, by E. Cassirer, *The Philosophy of Symbolic Forms* vol. 1 (New Haven, 1955), personifications replace mythical figures when rational attitudes supersede the primitive imagination. This theory had an ancient presentation in the Stoic doctrine, which taught that abstractions in the form of personifications express demonic forces; see also J. Arthos, "Personification" (1975): 612.

permeates the world, while remaining with God, "a pure effusion of the glory of the almighty".

Personification demands the use of poetic language as is particularly striking where the language intensifies and vivifies the depictions of Wisdom. Poetic language demands an imaginative approach. It gives a sense of mysterious, unexplored possibilities, an emotional resonance that delights and instructs, and thus captures a wider audience than would narrative or argument. Texts describing the Wisdom figure exhibit the highly concentrated character of poetry with the rich use of such rhetorical devices as symbolism, metaphor, simile, rhyme, parallelism and repetition.[43] Each text is a unity in which every detail is related, and within this unity, different orders of existence appear.[44] The power of personification as a form of rhetoric is evident in the authors' freedom to range from the human to the sublime, in the simplicity of vivid detail used to portray the figure of Wisdom, and in the engagement of the visual imagination without objective details. Wasserman expressed precisely the uniqueness of this device when he wrote, "Personification is a means of clothing the universal in imagery effective to the senses, of transferring the abstract from the intellect to the imagination. The creative imagination works only with the material of the senses."[45] Beattie, writing towards the end of the eighteenth century, aptly captured the effect when he said that personification conveys "many ideas in few words," and "descriptions . . . that are most vivid and picturesque will generally be found to have the most influence over our affections."[46]

Wisdom as a personified figure gives bodily form to an abstraction, with its attendant physical imagery, and links the senses with the understanding. The wisdom authors use this convention to convey to their audiences abstract knowledge in an attractive form. They utilise the universal image of woman, and the sympathetic desire of human beings to humanise everything, to create a character by analogy that is, therefore, not merely an artistic embellishment but the most accurate linguistic means of expressing an abstraction as it appears to the human mind. Far from being a mere abstraction, it is a means of vivid and detailed particularisation and materialisation. Personification cannot be separated from

---

[43] Poetry may involve sound as an extra sense thus providing the element of resonance. As we cannot be sure of the prevailing sound patterns of Hebrew and Greek when these texts were composed, the likely presence of this characteristic must remain undecided. A further consideration with regard to resonance is that sounds available in one language may not be available in another, so for example, Sir 24:1-33, which may have been composed in Hebrew but is known to us only in the Greek, may not have retained the full force of its personification in translation.

[44] In this brief analysis of poetic language, I am much indebted to Northrop Frye's, *Words with Power* (New York, 1990): 63-96; Lyn M. Poland, *Literary Criticism and Biblical Hermeneutics: A Critique of Formalist Approaches* (Chico, California, 1985).

[45] E.R. Wasserman, "The Inherent Values of Eighteenth Century Personification" *PMLA* 65 (1950): 456-457.

[46] See J. Beattie, *Essays on Poetry and Music* (London, 1779): 256-257, and *Elements of Moral Science* vol. 2 (Edinburgh, 1793): 474.

symbolism in its methods. Warren, in his analysis of Coleridge's theory of
symbolism, noted that the poetic symbol involves an idea (or ideas) as part of its
potential, but it also involves the specific complex of feelings associated with that
idea, the attitude towards that idea. The symbol is a device for making a welter of
experience graspable for the mind. It is not a mere sign but represents a focus and
acts like "picture language".[47] A symbol does not "stand for" a single idea, nor
does a system of symbols represent a simple rendering of a discursive sequence,
but implies the fusing of a body of ideas. An outstanding characteristic of a symbol
is that of its nature it points beyond itself. Characterisations of Wisdom illustrate
this in that they portray not a static being, but one who communicates and evokes a
reality of another order.[48]

Because of the extent and intensity of the personification of Wisdom in
Prov 8:22-33, some see this text as an example of hypostasis. Hypostasis—
endowed with a variety of meanings—is a precise term in Christian theology used
to describe the doctrine of three persons in one God, the Trinity, or the Hypostatic
Union.[49] The introduction of an expression from Christian theology to describe the
personification of Wisdom in the Israelite/Jewish tradition adds little of
significance to the discussion but may signal problems of a theological nature.[50]
While both חָכְמָה and Σοφια "Wisdom" are feminine gender, it seems most
improbable that the monotheistic Israelite tradition would ever have included the
notion of a female consort for YHWH. Biblical authors adopted and transformed
the fertility metaphor to speak of YHWH's relationship to Israel. The notion of
YHWH as the "husband" of Israel was a specially favoured metaphor of Hosea 2:2,

---

[47] S.T. Coleridge in *The Statesman's Manual* (London, 1816):192-93 observed that the
      symbol proceeds from, and gives the reader access to, a God's-eye view of experience.

[48] A traditional notion of a symbol was that of capturing an experience or insight in a form
      that went beyond everyday concrete information.

[49] W.O.E. Oesterley & G.H. Box, *The Religion and Worship of the Synagogue* (London,
      1911): 195, speak of 'a quasi-personification of certain attributes of God, an intermediate
      position between personalities and abstract beings'. However, they do not use the term
      hypostasis. See also, W. Schencke, *Die Chokma* (1913); S. Mowinckel, "Hypostasen" in
      Die Religion in Geschichte und Gegenwart II (1928): 2065-2068, defined "hypostasis" as
      'a personification of qualities, functions, limbs, of a higher god'; Ringgren, *Word and
      Wisdom* (Lund, 1947): 89-171; R. Marcus, "On Biblical Hypostases of Wisdom," *HUCA*
      23 (1950-51): 157-171, follows Ringgren; R.N. Whybray, *The Book of Proverbs CBC*
      (Cambridge, 1972): 50; H. Cazelles, "La Sagesse de Proverbes 8:22: Peut-elle être
      considérée comme une hypostase?" in *Trinité et liturgie* (1984): 53; *OED* 7, 579 columns
      2-3, defines hypostasis as "the making into or regarding as a self-existent substance or
      person; embodying or impersonating; endowing with personal existence, as in three
      hypostases in the Trinity".

[50] See D. Winston, *Wisdom of Solomon* (New York, 1979): 35; R.B.Y. Scott, *Proverbs,
      Ecclesiastes* (1965): 69-71; M. Hengel, *Judaism and Hellenism: Studies in their
      Encounter in Palestine during the Early Hellenistic Period* (Philadelphia, 1974): 154;
      156; 158; 163; D.G. Miller, "Female Language for God: Should the Church Adopt It?" in
      D.J. Miller, ed. *The Hermeneutical Quest: Essays in honor of James Luther Mays on his
      sixty-fifth birthday* (Allison Park, 1986): 97-114; Murphy, *Tree of Life* (1990): 133-149.

7, 16), and is found in Jer 3:20; 6:11; 31:32; Ezek 16:32, 45; and Isa 54:5-8. These examples, especially Hosea's forthright portrayal, demonstrate the significant transformation of this seemingly simple metaphor. Just as the prophets appropriated, and transformed this image to speak of the relationship between YHWH and Israel, the wisdom writers used and developed the metaphor to portray Wisdom as enjoying a relationship with God both as Creator and Saviour, unique in all the created universe (Prov 8:22-31; Wis 7:21-8:8). Characteristic of an extraordinary bond were imaged in the notion of a marriage. The typifying of Wisdom's relationship with God as the ideal for the relationship of human beings with God seems not to appear elsewhere in the Old Testament.

Although the Torah forbade the representation of YHWH by images, biblical anthropomorphisms are numerous. This is hardly surprising, as anthropomorphism appears to be integral to human language. The inevitable anthropomorphisms of human language accrued and the biblical authors who used many nevertheless maintained the notion of transcendence.[51] Since A. Marmorstein collected much of the relevant data in a seminal monograph devoted to the Rabbinic idea of God, scholars have recognised the extent to which anthropomorphic conceptions of God pervade Rabbinic and Biblical literature, although considerable debate over their meaning and historical significance continues.[52] Anthropomorphism may be viewed from the perspective either of corporeality, therefore as a problem of metaphysics; or as an issue in the semantics of religious language, an extreme instance of the dilemma concerning whether any human expression can truthfully be applied to the description of God.[53] Dogging any discussion of anthropomorphism is the fundamental question, did the authors believe in the anthropomorphic and anthropopathic features they attributed to the Creator?

An alternative approach to the question of anthropomorphism is to ask how expressions in which God is likened to a human being are used to personalise God and to affirm presence. To consider anthropomorphism from this perspective is to view it as a trope and figure, a turning of creative language to express truth.[54] In this approach, the biblical writers used the Wisdom figure to portray the

---

[51] Anthropomorphisms for YHWH appear in attributions of human characteristics to God: "I will put you in a cleft of a rock, and will cover you with my hand until I have passed by. Then I will take away my hand and you shall see my back but my face shall not be seen" (Exod 33:22-23); "The Lord laughs at the wicked" (Pss 37:13; 59:8).

[52] A. Marmorstein, *The Old Rabbinic Doctrine of God, II. Essays in Anthropomorphism* (New York, 1937); E.E. Urbach, *The Sages: Their Concepts and Beliefs* (Jerusalem, 1975), trans. I. Abraham (London 1987): 37-38; M.J. Klein, *Anthropomorphisms and Anthropopathisms in the Targumim of the Pentateuch* (Jerusalem, 1983).

[53] See D. Stern, *Parables in Midrash* (Cambridge, Mass., 1991): 96-98; D. Stern, "Language" in A.A. Cohen & P. Mendes-Flohr, eds., *Contemporary Jewish Religious Thought* (New York, 1986): 543-551.

[54] D. Stern, *Parables* (1991): 98 notes "Anthropomorphism is less a matter of metaphysics or semantics than of the construction of divinity: the intentional conscious use of language to represent character"; P. de Man, "Anthropomorphism and Trope in the Lyric," in P. de Man, ed., *The Rhetoric of Romanticism* (New York, 1984): 239-262.

Wisdom of God symbolically rather than anthropomorphically or metaphysically, by intimating, not a static divinity, but a God who communicates with all creation and in particular with human beings. As noted by Murphy, the obvious anthropomorphisms of the Bible do not sit well with notions of God based on the traditional Christian doctrines of divine impassability, transcendence, and omnipotence.[55] Portrayals of God in the Bible range over a vast array of images, such as creator and artist (Gen 1:1-2:3), potter (Gen 2:7-24), shepherd (Pss 23:1; 28:9; 80:1; Isa 40:11; Ezek 34:2, 15); one who repents of the evil he planned (Jer 18:8-10; Jon 3:9-10). Each characterisation of God points to a particular aspect of being. Only human images provide sufficiently complex models that can do justice to God, and this is the case for the personification of Wisdom. Just as the biblical description of change of heart concerning Nineveh, and the inhabitants of Jerusalem, pointed to a notion of God that encompasses change, so also personified Wisdom reflects some unique aspects of the deity. One of the most striking of these aspects is Wisdom's intimate association, if not identification with God, the intensity of which increases in the later wisdom texts, as in the term πάρεδρον "throne-partner, one who sits beside" (Wis 9:4).

Wisdom Speaks of Her Origins

I shall now investigate claims made by the Wisdom figure when she speaks of her origins. As a literary device, personification is particularly suited to this purpose, as the author can portray the figure of Wisdom giving a first person account of her origins, thereby emphasizing the authenticity of the account. This paradoxical figure who exhibits sharply contrasting, and even contradictory features, associates her own origins with God and the beginning of time, (Prov 8:22; Sir 24:3, 9), while third person accounts emphasise the mystery that surrounds her origins, and the consequent difficulty associated with searching for her. In Prov 8:22-31 Wisdom describes her status with God as having been present with him before creation as אָמוֹן. This word, which has generated much discussion leaves Wisdom's role in creation unresolved textually. In some later literature she is understood to be an "artisan" τεχνῖτις (Wis 7:21; 8:6; 14:2).

Wisdom's characterisations point to her association with the Hebrew tradition. This is evident in her prophet like location and speech (Prov 1:20-33; 8:1-36); her banquet preparations and invitations (Prov 9:1-6); her location in Israel and in the Temple (Sir 24:8-12); her status as a gift from God (Sir 1:9-10; Wis 7:7; 9:4); and in her identification with the Torah (Sir 24:23; cf. also Sir 1:25-27; 6:37; 15:1; 19:20; 33:2-3; Bar 4:1). Prov 8:22-31 has been much discussed in recent literature. Some argue that it is an elaboration of 3:19-20 where YHWH founded the earth and established the heavens by wisdom, so it is argues that YHWH used wisdom as an instrument in the creation of the world. I do not understand 8:22-31 as speaking of how Wisdom acts but of the nature and status of Wisdom's relationship to YHWH. This text highlights Wisdom's creaturely

---

[55] R.E. Murphy, "Wisdom Literature and Biblical Theology" *BTB* 24/1 (1994): 4-7.

position, while also stressing her authority in relation to human beings by invoking a variety of motifs from traditional sources.

Personified Wisdom recounts that she was the first of all creation, and was present at the creation (Prov 8:22-31), thus claiming a unique relationship with YHWH. However, these intimations do not provide a complete account of her beginnings. Rather, they generate much debate because of the confusion that surrounds the meaning of the very words spoken by Wisdom about her relationship to and her presence with God at the creation. These very words may give some clues to and illuminate Wisdom's role at the creation. It is not surprising that the debate about Wisdom's relationship to YHWH has generated much scholarly research into the possible meanings of the Hebrew words describing it.

Disputed Words

This section of the chapter discusses disputed words in their order of appearance. קָנָנִי is one of the most significant of these words that presents a problem of fundamental importance for the interpretation of Prov 8:22-33. The verb קָנָה with its cognates occur frequently in the Old Testament.[56] In most cases it means "to acquire or "to purchase" or "to possess", but this interpretation is disputed, and many contemporary scholars render it as "created".[57] The ancient translators did not agree concerning how קָנָנִי was to be understood. Two main schools of thought emerged. One group, which translated קָנָנִי as ἐκτήσατο "acquired" or "possessed", was represented by Aquila, Symmachus, Theodotion, and the Vulgate *possedit*, while another group, represented by the Septuagint ἔκτισέν, the Targum בראני. The Peshitta opted for "created". Humbert in his analysis of the use of קָנָנִי in the Old Testament argues that only in a small number of passages (Gen 4:1; 14:19, 22; Exod 15:16; Deut 32:6; Pss 74:2; 78:54; 139:13; Prov 8:22) is the meaning "create" possible.[58] Interestingly for most of these texts "create" is not the only possible interpretation and except for Gen 4:1 God is the subject of the verb in each. Humbert could find no way in which one of its supposed senses could have developed into the other, and suggested that קָנָנִי denoted two unrelated verbs in Hebrew. In the majority of cases, he claimed that קָנָנִי was the ordinary word "to buy", but in others, it denoted the acquisition or possession of an object, or slave, by means other than by the payment of money. He arrived at this view partly from context and partly by reference to the Ugaritic verb *qny*, which, he maintained, meant "to create", a function of Athirat as the creator *qnyt* (f.) of the gods. Several scholars accepted Humbert's interpretation of this verb though not always with his

---

[56] Apart from Prov 8:22, there are at least 12 references to the desirability of acquiring or getting wisdom, knowledge, skill (Prov 1:5; 4:1, 5, 7; 8:5; 9:9; 10:16; 11:16; 15:32; 16:16; 19:20; 23:4).

[57] In several texts this verb is interpreted as "to create" or "to make", as in "maker of heaven and earth" (Gen 14:19, 22), and in "you formed or created" (Ps 139:13).

[58] P. Humbert, "Qânâ en Hébreu biblique," in W. Baumgartner, ed. *Festschrift für Alfred Bertholet* (Tübingen, 1950): 259-267.

theory of two different verbs. One of those was Albright who posited a Canaanite goddess *Hokmôt*, daughter of *El*, as the origin of the Wisdom figure; others were von Rad; Schmidt; L. Boström, Irwin, Toy, and A. Meinhold who opted for "formed"; while de Savignac and Plöger proposed "produced".[59]

Several scholars propose that קָנָנִי be understood as "procreate" or "beget".[60] This interpretation is supported by a specific understanding Gen 4:1 and Deut 32:6; the interpretation of Prov 8:23-25 as referring to Wisdom's "birth"; analogies from extra-biblical material, such as the birth of Ma'at; or the claim that *qny* in Ugaritic can mean, "procreate".[61] Irwin and Gilbert interpret the Ugaritic evidence differently by introducing the idea of "to beget", or "to father (a child)", though they insist that the word is used here, not in the literal sense as for male deities in the surrounding Near Eastern societies, but figuratively.[62] Perdue notes, "One of the important theological metaphors in this first-person hymn of self-praise presents Yahweh as the divine parent. In this case, Yahweh's offspring is Woman Wisdom, at first a newborn infant and then a small child. Yahweh fathers and gives birth to Wisdom. As the father and mother of Wisdom, Yahweh 'procreated' her as the first-born of creation."[63] Both Lang and Gilbert distinguish a procreative meaning in this passage, and interpret נִסַּכְתִּי in verse 23 as "I was fashioned or woven [in the womb]."[64] Lang argues, "What later came to be considered a mere figure of speech started its career as a 'real' deity." He claims

---

[59] W.F. Albright, "Some Canaanite-Phoenician Sources of Hebrew Wisdom" *VTSup* 3 (1955): 1-15; W.A. Irwin, "Where Shall Wisdom be Found?" *JBL* 80 (1961):133-142; G. von Rad, *Wisdom* (1972): 198; W.H. Schmidt, "ηνθ θνη ερωερβεν", *THAT* II (1976): cols. 650-659; L. Boström, *The God of the Sages* (Stockholm, 1990); Toy, *Proverbs* (1899); A. Meinhold, *Die Sprüche* (Zürich, 1991); J. de Savignac, "Note sur le sens du verset 8:22 des Proverbes", *VT 4* (1954): 429-432; "Interprétation de Proverbes 8:22-32" *VTSup* 17 (1969): 196-203; O. Plöger, *Sprüche Salomos (Proverbia)* (Neukirchen-Vluyn 1984).

[60] W.O.E. Oesterley, *The Book of Proverbs* (London, 1929); H. Cazelles, "Review of Canaanite Myths and Legends" *VT 7* (1957): 422, 429; Irwin, "Where Shall Wisdom be Found?" *JBL* 80 (1961): 133-142; M. Gilbert, "Le discours de la Sagesse en Proverbes, 8. Structure et cohérence" *BETL* 51 (1979): 209-10; Plöger, *Sprüche Salomos* (1984): 91-92, sees Proverbs 1-9 as an enchiridion or handbook and dates them from 900-200 BCE. B. Lang, *Wisdom and the Book of Proverbs: A Hebrew Goddess Redefined* (New York, 1986): 77.

[61] C. Kayatz, *Studien zu Proverbien 1-9* (1966): 93-98.

[62] Irwin, "Where Shall Wisdom be Found?" (1961): 133-142; M. Gilbert, "Le discours" (1979): 202-218; For a discussion of the births of gods and goddesses (theogonies) in Egyptian mythology, see V. Notter, *Biblischer Schöpfungsbericht und Ägyptische Schöpfungsmythen SBS* (Stuttgart, 1974): 21-26.

[63] L.G. Perdue, *Wisdom and Creation: The Theology of Wisdom Literature* (Nashville, 1994): 90.

[64] Lang, *Wisdom* (1986): 63-65; 149-152; M. Gilbert, "Le discours" (1979): 202, 210; "La Sagesse personnifiée dans les texts de l'Ancien Testament" *Cahiers Evangelie* 32 (1980): 5-36; "Le discours menaçant de Sagesse en Proverbes 1:20-33" in D. Garrone & F. Israel, eds., *Storia e tradizioni di Israele scritti in onore di J. Alberto Soggin* (Brescia, 1991): 99-119.

that in an original version of the poem Wisdom was a goddess, literally begotten by the male deity El, "fashioned" as in the womb and eventually born. While acknowledging that he cannot provide much evidence for the existence of a goddess called Wisdom in the ancient Near East, who was the "divine patroness of scribal education and training", then reduced to a poetic personification, representing "wisdom teaching with its moral injunctions".[65] Camp, who opts for "conceive", bases her choice on Irwin's translation of this verb in Gen 4:1 "to parent", and notes "conceive" expresses the connotation of the whole pericope very well.[66] The interpretation of קָנָנִי as "begot" or "procreated me" if understood literally clearly has mythological and polytheistic connotations.

Vawter disagrees with the use of "create". He favours "acquire" or "get" claiming that Job 28 and Proverbs 8 speak of a "wisdom" which is neither creation nor his natural attribute, but rather a possession, which he has acquired. For Vawter's argument to stand one must accept the notion that "wisdom" was in existence and that YHWH had to "acquire" it, a notion seeming to run counter to the Israelite perception of God as Creator. His explanation that the figure of Wisdom had not been completely "digested by and homogenized in Old Testament thought" appears to beg the question.[67] It seems unlikely that the author of Proverbs 8 would have focused so clearly on personified Wisdom if the wisdom tradition had not fully integrated this figure and that the use of קָנָנִי was integral to its context. The presence of חוֹלָלְתִּי "brought forth" (8:24-25) suggests the notion of new life. In such a discussion concerning the meanings and possible interpretation of rare usages and debated words, the use by the author(s) of metaphorical language in the portrayal of personified Wisdom means that any attempt to arrive at a literal interpretation is to misunderstand the text.

Proposed interpretations such as, acquire, possess, make, create, beget, and procreate, all overlap to some extent, so that any judgement as to the exact meaning cannot be absolute. Claims by Nyberg and Ringgren that the two meanings "possess" and "create" need not be kept apart may be most apt.[68] In Gen 4:1 Eve's words קָנִיתִי could be interpreted as "I have acquired", "I have made", "I have given birth to".[69] In Gen 14:19, 22 קנה appears to refer to the Creator of heaven and earth.[70] Deut 32:18 images the nation of Israel as forgetting the God

---

[65] Lang, *Wisdom* (1986): 76-79, 135, "Wisdom" *DDD* (1995): 1693, notes similar contexts in Pss 2:6; 139:13; Job 10:11.

[66] See, Camp, *Wisdom* (1985): 306 n.7; Irwin, "Where Shall Wisdom be Found?" (1961): 136; J.N. Aletti, "Proverbes 8:22-31: Étude de structure" *Biblica 57* (1976): 25-37, opts for "begot" or "conceived".

[67] B. Vawter, "Prov 8:22: Wisdom and Creation," *JBL* 99 (1980): 206-216.

[68] H.S. Nyberg, "Studien zum Religionskampf im Alten Testament." *ARW 35* (1938): 352; Ringgren, *Word and Wisdom* (1947): 101, notes that the sense of 'acquire' is confirmed by the meaning of the root in other Semitic languages.

[69] Ringgren, *Word and Wisdom* (1947): 99-105.

[70] Whybray, *Proverbs* NCBC (Grand Rapids, 1994): 130, notes that this could also mean "possessor or master of heaven and earth".

who "gave you birth" מְחֹלְלֶךָ. It seems here the notion is used metaphorically, as is Deut 32:6 קָנֶךָ "is he not your father who created or begot you?" A literal interpretation of these texts would suggest the absurd notion that YHWH's "begetting" of Wisdom or Israel was the result of a sexual act. The Old Testament does not appear to have any texts depicting YHWH as a "father" in the sense in which the Canaanite *El* becomes a father in the Ugaritic poem of *Šaḥar* and *Šalim*.[71]

Any conclusions about this word are subject to the interpretation of its context (8:22-31). Although various interpretations have been proposed for דַּרְכּוֹ רֵאשִׁית its context suggests "at or in or as the beginning", since several other references to time occur throughout the passage perhaps emphasising that Wisdom's beginning precedes that of the rest of creation. "I was set up/installed" נִסַּכְתִּי fits the sense of this poem. In addition, its appearance in Ps 2:6 in reference to the enthronement of a king, may suggest that in 8:23 Wisdom is royal and has power over all the earth.[72] Since her authority or dignity is bestowed from the beginning, she possesses it intrinsically, by nature, as God does. The pre-existence of Wisdom in relation to the existence of the world is affirmed in 8:24-26 where the author may have had Ps 90:2 in mind, "before the mountains were brought forth or you had formed, (writhed in travail) with, the earth".[73]

Of primary concern is the generation of Wisdom as an act of the Creator. This precedes the creation of the world and at the same time is associated with it. While verses 27-28 are reminiscent of Egyptian and Babylonian creation texts, the notion of election and consecration before creation is attributed only to personified Wisdom.[74] Echoes of Isa 49:1: "The Lord called me before I was born. While I was in my mother's womb he named me"; and Jer 1:4-10: "Before I formed you in the womb I knew you, and before you were born I consecrated you," may also be intended here. The author has Wisdom claim to have come into being before YHWH created the world, and to declare her status as witness שָׁם אָנִי "I was there" (8:27) at the drama of creation. In this creation account Wisdom uses a series of "before" and "no" (vv.24-26) followed by first person reporting speech

---

[71] C. Gordon, *Ugaritic Manual* (Rome, 1955).

[72] According to 2 Sam 7:14 the relationship between God and the Davidic ruler was that of father to son, consequently the day of the king's accession to power was the day on which he was "begotten" as the son of God. Some commentators read Isa 9:5, "a son is born to us", as speaking of a coronation rather than of a birth. See A. Alt, "Die Weisheit Salomos" *TLZ* 76 (1951): 139-144; A. Robert, "Les attaches littéraires Bibliques des Prov. I-IX." Parts 1 and 2, *RB* 43 (1934): 42-69, 172-204, 374-384; 44 (1935): 344-365, 502-525; Ringgren, *Word and Wisdom* (1947): 102.

[73] The verb חוּל (8:24) usually suggests "writhing in birth pains" (Deut 32:18; Job 39:1; Pss 29:9; 51:7; 90:2; Isa 51:2). As the verb in 8:24-25 is in passive voice it can be rendered, "I was brought forth or I was given birth", so the subject is not identified, but as YHWH is the subject throughout this section YHWH is probably understood here also.

[74] Book of the Apophis, *ANET* 5; *JEA* 23 (1937): 172; Enùma Eliš, *ANET* 60-61; A. Heidel, *Babylonian Genesis* (Chicago, 1951): 7, 62.

"when he" (vv. 27-30) about the creation of the world.[75] Certainty about the meaning of קָנָנִי eludes us. Having considered three plausible interpretations, I deem "created" to be most in keeping with the poem as we now have it. While "acquired or possessed" seems a good choice in view of the number of biblical texts in which this verb is understood to have that meaning, it is unlikely from the context as discussed above that the text implies that God "acquired" personified Wisdom, as if Wisdom had been elsewhere prior to this episode. The use of "created" coheres with what is surely the logic of the text. Since God is named as the author of Wisdom throughout the biblical wisdom literature, the sense of "brought into existence" or "created," is the more likely understanding.

> YHWH created me at the beginning of his work,
> the first of his acts of long ago.
> Ages ago I was set up at the first,
> before the beginning of the earth. (Prov 8:22-23)

The second most significant of the disputed words is אָמוֹן in Prov 8:30. Biblical scholars have debated interpretations and understandings of this word since earliest times. Its importance for the understanding of the nature and function of personified Wisdom as depicted in Prov 8:22-31 continues to inspire research. Translations appearing in the Versions indicate confusion and disagreements about this term. Murphy respects the mystery surrounding אמון by refraining from attempting a translation.[76] The only other appearance of this rare Hebrew word is in Jer 52:15, and maybe in Song 7:2MT, which has אָמָן, a term usually interpreted as "craftsman" or "artist", or "master hand". Scholars are not agreed that אָמוֹן in Prov 8:30 is the same word as that in Jer 52:15 where הָאָמוֹן seems to denote artisans as workers. Exegetes have provided interpretations such as "artisan" "artist" "master craftsman", for אָמוֹן (Prov 8:30).

Rüger offers an exhaustive history of its interpretation.[77] If is understood as a participle, it would take a feminine ending as this is Wisdom חֹכְמֹה speaking— participles agree in gender with the noun to which they belong—so a case could be made that the most appropriate sense in this context is "artisan" or "architect". Some, including NRSV, suggest that this is a loan word from Accadian *ummânu*, "sage or craftsman".[78] Cazelles, who examines the meaning of אָמוֹן in the light of the description of Ahiqar as an *ummân* in a Seleucid tablet, concludes that Wisdom is understood as a steward, not a child.[79] Interestingly, Greenfield suggests that

---

[75] רֵאשִׁית "beginning" in Prov 8:22 (cf. Job 40:19; Pss 78:51; 105:36), may suggest that Wisdom is unsurpassed or paramount, see Jer 49:35; Amos 6:1.

[76] Murphy, *Tree of Life* (1990): 136.

[77] H.-P. Rüger, "Amôn—Pflegekind: Zur Auslegungsgeschichte von Prv. 8:30a" in *Übersetzung und Deutung: A.R. Hulst gewidmet* (Nijkerk, 1977): 154-163.

[78] S. Smith, "An Inscription from the Temple of Sin at Huraidha in the Hadhramawt" *BSOAS* 11/3 (1945): 451-464; Ringgren, *Word and Wisdom* (1947): 103.

[79] H. Cazelles, "Ahiqar, Ummân and Amun, and Biblical Wisdom Texts" in Z. Zevit, et al.,

this Accadian word assists in understanding Prov 9:1.[80] Such an interpretation has ancient roots as can be seen in the use of the Greek ἁρμόζουσα = אָמֹן, which may mean "one who organizes". Delitzsch, Duesberg, de Savignac, Ringgren, and several other scholars accept this meaning.[81] "Artisan or master craftsman" suggests a position of some responsibility and in this context could suggest that Wisdom collaborated with the Creator in the creation. However, the text of Proverbs 8 does not appear to support this notion, nor does it provide grounds for believing that such a sense was intended.

    Hurvitz summarizes attempts to interpret 8:30 as opting for one or other of two basic meanings, that of "skilled worker", which matches the references to the creation of the cosmos in Prov 8:27-29; or that of "foster-parent", (cf. הָאֹמֵן "nurse" Num 11:12), which fits if one accepts an allusion to childlike playing in verses 30b-31.[82] The Massoretic pointing invites comparison with similar forms such as בָּחֹון "assayer" (Jer 6:27), עָשׁוֹק "oppressor" (Jer 22:3) and יָקוֹשׁ "trapper" (Hos 9:8), suggesting that some kind of artisan is meant. He concludes, "'*amon* is a cognate of the Mishnaic form '*umman*, meaning skilled worker."[83] The alternative interpretation produced by adjusting the pointing to vocalise the word as אָמוּן, a passive participle, does achieve the notion of "nursling", "beloved child", or "faithful disciple" of the Creator. This form appeared at least as early as Aquila τιθηνουμένη who seems to have read אָמוּן in the sense of "nourisher".[84] Acceptance of this form implies that Wisdom is perceived as a little child at the creation of the world. It includes equally the sense of nurturing and of darling child. Von Rad, Rüger, Plöger, Lang, Meinhold, and several other translators favour this interpretation. It excludes any notion of Wisdom's active participation in the work of creation.[85] Some find support for this view in the reference to מְשַׂחֶקֶת

---

    ed. *Solving Riddles and Untying Knots. Biblical, Epigraphic, and Semitic Studies in Honor of J. C. Greenfield* (Winona Lake, 1995): 45-55.

[80] See J.C. Greenfield, "The Seven Pillars of Wisdom (Prov 9:1)—a Mistranslation", *JQR* 76 (1985): 13-20.

[81] Delitzsch, *Salmonisches Sprüchbuch* (1873); H. Duesberg, *Les Scribes inspirés* (Paris, 1938); J. de Savignac, "Note sur le sens", *VT* 4 (1954): 429-432; H. Ringgren, *Sprüche/Predigers* (Göttingen, 1967).

[82] Avi Hurvitz, "Towards a Precise Definition of the Term *noma* in Prov 8:30 [Hebrew]" in S. Japhet, ed., *The Bible in the Light of Its Interpreters* (Jerusalem, 1994): 647-650.

[83] Hurvitz, "Precise Definition" (1994): 647-650.

[84] Kayatz, *Studien* (1966); see also A. Gelin, *Le chant de l'infante, in Bible et Vie chrétienne*, 7 (1954): 89-95; Von Rad, *Wisdom* (1972): 178-180; While a similar idea may be expressed in Lam 4:5 "those who were brought up", the meaning is not certain; A. Robert, "Les Attaches Littéraires Bibliques de Prov. I-IX." *RB* 43 (1934): 42-68, 172-204, 374-84, especially 201.

[85] G. von Rad, *Wisdom* (1972): 180; H.-P. Rüger, "'Amôn—Pflegekind" (1977): 154-163; Plöger, *Sprüche* (1984); Lang, *Wisdom* (1986); A. Meinhold, *Die Sprüche* (1991); S. Terrien, "The Play of Wisdom: Turning Point in Wisdom Theology" *HBT* 3 (1981): 125-153.

"playing or dancing" before YHWH.[86] While this understanding of the word may work in Prov 8:30, it does not seem to fit the context for Jer 52:15.

Williams, who regards Prov 8:22-31 as an ode to Wisdom, notes that the issues surrounding it have triggered a wide array of Christological and pneumatological interpretations which attempt to explain the ontology of Wisdom and its relation to YHWH.[87] Christian theologians have applied these approaches so consistently to this passage that its exposition is impossible without at least an acknowledgement of its colourful hermeneutical history. Accordingly, he examines the history of its interpretation from Theophilus of Antioch through to modern readings. Recently, Fox surveyed what he believes are the three main interpretations of אָמוֹן offered by scholars, "artisan", "constant(ly)", and "ward or nursling", and argues for a fourth, which is a variant of "ward or nursling", by drawing upon the insights of two medieval scholars, Yonah Abu al-Walid Marwan ibn Janah and Moshe Qimhi. He concludes: "Lady Wisdom is declaring that while God was busy creating the world, she was nearby, growing up like a child in his care (v.30a) and giving him delight (v.30ba) by playing before him (v.30b) in a world that would be inhabited (v.31a)."[88] The notion that Wisdom was created as a child, who then grows up in YHWH's care, does not seem to fit well into the context of this poem.

Claims that the birth imagery of 8:24-25 support the choice of "little child" or "nursling" for אָמוֹן assumes that קָנָנִי has been interpreted as "brought forth or brought into being", in 8:22. It is difficult to imagine how the term "little child" or "nursling" would function in the context of this passage. Throughout Proverbs 1-9, personified Wisdom is portrayed as a character who speaks with authority. Her origins are highlighted to show that she is the first of creation.[89] It seems likely that such nuanced words as discussed above, and the elaborative verses surrounding them were intended to establish that Wisdom was with YHWH from before the creation of the world. The author intensifies the notion of Wisdom's incomprehensible antiquity by using words and phrases denoting time, (יְהוָה, קָנָנִי רֵאשִׁית דַּרְכּוֹ קֶדֶם מִפְעָלָיו מֵאָז<). "YHWH created me at the beginning of his work, the first of his acts of long ago", (cf. Isa 40:21; 41:4, 26; Deut 32:18).[90] Greater significance is given to the antiquity of Wisdom's origins than to the manner of her origins. In depicting Wisdom as the first creation of the Creator, the author perhaps highlights her knowledge of creation from the beginning. A certain irony surrounds the verbs הוֹלָלְתִּי נִסַּכְתִּי קָנָנִי, which appear to tell us

---

[86] To associate playing or dancing with childhood in this ancient Near Eastern context may be anachronistic. Playing or dancing before the Creator, or before any important figure, would almost certainly have been an activity performed by adults in the ancient world.

[87] D.H. Williams, "Proverbs 8:22-31," *Int* 48 (1994): 275-279.

[88] M.V. Fox, "'Amon Again" *JBL* 115/4 (1996): 699-702.

[89] "Little child" which implies "young human being", suggests that Wisdom is created in human form, an image that is not consistent with the figure of Wisdom in Proverbs.

[90] See R.N. Whybray, *Proverbs* NCBC (1994): 130-132.

something about personified Wisdom's origins and yet constitute such problems for scholars.

Keel, Scott, and von Rad, despite differences in their respective analyses of Proverbs 8, maintain that the real significance of 8:22-31 lies, not in Wisdom's claims about her ancestry and possible participation in creation, but in her relationship with and function in the world of human beings.[91] All three agree that the figure of Wisdom in this pericope is not a hypostasis.[92] Chapter 8, they claim, is pervaded by the theme of Wisdom's relationship to בְּתֵבֵל אַרְצוֹ "his inhabited world" as emphasised in verses 30-31, where Wisdom מְשַׂחֶקֶת "rejoiced" in YHWH's created world and delighted in the human race. Scott proposes a new interpretation of verse 30, which he claims should be the active participle *ōmēn*, meaning "foster-father or guardian". The verb *āman* can also mean to support or guide, so he opts for the sense of sociable or allied to.[93] Since YHWH "made the world by wisdom" (3:19), he argues that Wisdom in this passage personifies the principle of harmony or coherence in the world that God has created. Wisdom is thus the "living link" between God and human beings.

Keel, who holds that קָנָנִי in verse 22 means "made or created me", emphasises the presence of Egyptian imagery in Prov 8:22-31 and supports his claim by drawing extensively on Egyptian iconographical evidence. In his analysis of 8:30-31 he argues that אָמוֹן means "workman", but that it has been misread grammatically. It is YHWH, not Wisdom, who is the "master workman" or architect of creation. Wisdom's מְשַׂחֶקֶת "playing" denotes the way in which she "entertained" the Creator. He notes that this imagery suggests the Egyptian practice in which a woman or goddess entertained the king or a high god by dancing, acrobatics, and making jokes to put him in good humour.[94] While he cites iconographical evidence showing the goddess Hathor engaging in similar activities, he suggests that Ma'at may have been the model for the Wisdom figure. Interestingly, Wisdom not only "entertains" YHWH but also "rejoices in" creation.

Gilbert reads the Massoretic text of Prov 8:30 אָמוֹן as "master craftsman", and questions whether the word refers to Wisdom, as is often said, or to God?[95] He notes that the first interpretation is an ancient one and Wis 7:21; 8:6 seem to confirm that interpretation, but asks if this is in keeping with the context. The

---

[91] O. Keel, *Die Weisheit spielt vor Gott: Ein ikonographischer Beitrag zur Deutung des mesahäqät in Sprüche 8, 30f.* (Göttingen, 1974): 222; R.B.Y. Scott, "Wisdom in Creation: The 'amôn of Proverbs 8:30" *VT 10* (1960): 213-223; Von Rad, *Wisdom* (1972): 200-205.

[92] Both Von Rad and Keel see Wisdom as a personification, a quality, not of God but of the world.

[93] Scott, "Wisdom in Creation: The 'amôn of Proverbs 8:22-31", *VT* 10 (1960): 219.

[94] In Shakespeare's Anthony and Cleopatra Act II Scene 2, Cleopatra entertains Anthony in similar fashion. This scene may be based on the account given in *Plutarch's Lives* XXXV: "But Cleopatra . . . ever contributing some fresh delight and charm".

[95] M. Gilbert, "L'Éloge de la Sagesse (Siracide 24)" *RTL* 5 (1974): 326-348; Bonnard, *La Sagesse en personne annoncée et venue Jésus* (Paris, 1966) 21; M. Dahood, "Proverbs 8:22-31", *CBQ* 30 (1968): 518-519.

ancient Hebrew text did not vocalise the reading of consonants, so this rare word has given rise to several extremely different interpretations. Stecher sees the Greek word ἁρμόζουσα as a faulty reading.[96] The Targum reads אָמוֹן in the sense of "faithful"; thus understanding it in the same way as the Greek versions of Theodotion and Symmachus, ἐστηριγμένη.[97] Whatever the case may be, one cannot claim that any vocalisation of אָמוֹן can be determined beyond all possible doubt, to support the notion that Wisdom played an active role in creation.

Whether one opts for "little child", "nursling", "artisan", "master-craftsman", or finds another term that captures the intent of the passage more precisely some significant features inform the interpretation of the pericope. The repetition of the terms שַׁעֲשֻׁעִים; "delight", מְשַׂחֶקֶת "playing/rejoicing" (8:30-31) seems to create a sense of play.[98] In verse 31 "rejoicing", "delighting" are the same words as those used in verse 30 except that "my delight" is used here. The reversal of order gives a chiasmus and completes this pericope. "Delight" is further qualified by the reference to "playing" before YHWH on the surface of the earth.[99] It is possible that the verb מְשַׂחֶקֶת which is used twice in Prov 8:30 attributes to Wisdom a cultic dance. In this instance Prov 8:30-31 may be suggesting a relationship between cosmic Wisdom and the cult (cf. Sir 24:8). Wisdom here declares her purpose in speaking of her primeval origins. She dances for YHWH in the created world and she delights in human beings. The word "delight", like Wisdom, dances through these lines taking on different connotations with each appearance. Wisdom declares that she comes from God and delights in human beings. Wisdom's narrative in Prov 8:22-31 is pivotal in any discussion of her origins in the Old Testament. Underpinning such texts is Israel's sense of herself as called into being by God the Creator to be YHWH's people. The wisdom authors wrote from this worldview and their experience of the created world. The Wisdom figure they depict is inseparable from their experience of God manifested in their world when Wisdom speaks:

> YHWH created me at the beginning of his work,
> the first of his acts of long ago.
> Ages ago I was set up at the first,
> before the beginning of the earth. (Prov 8:22-23)

Wisdom describes the creation of the cosmos above and below—deep, fountains, sea, earth's foundations—from her viewpoint as witness beside the Creator, "rejoicing in his inhabited world and delighting in human beings" (8:24-31). Although Wisdom's role in YHWH's creative activity is much debated, I believe

---

[96] R. Stecher, "Die persönliche Weisheit in den Proverbien Kap. 8: 22-31" *Zeitschrift für Katholische Theologie 75* (1953): 411-451, especially 435.

[97] Gilbert, "L'Éloge de la Sagesse" (1974): 345, notes the translator may have confused 'amôn with hamôn and have read this word as "playing a stringed instrument".

[98] MT "delight", but Septuagint has "his delight" while NRSV (I was daily his delight), and note e indicates that the Hebrew lacks "his"; see also Jer 31:20; Isa 66:10.

[99] The psalmist "rejoices" over the Torah in Ps 119:24, 77, 92, 143, and 174.

that the emphasis is on her presence at and witness to creation rather than that of "helper", as exemplified in the repetition of delight in YHWH and human beings. In Prov 8:22-31, which is not primarily an account of the creation of the world, YHWH, not Wisdom is the central figure.[100] A change of tone is clear with the switch of subject at the beginning. The name YHWH opens the poem and precedes the verb.[101] This emphasis continues in the following verbs of which YHWH is subject (vv. 26-29). Wisdom's relationship to YHWH is defined by her witnessing to YHWH's creative acts (vv. 25, 27, 30-31).

Wisdom is not engaged in any autonomous activity, nor does she have an independent existence before, during, or after the acts of creation. Her role is to delight in YHWH's created world (v.31). Neither Wisdom's relationship to YHWH nor her appeal to human beings appear to have any parallels in other ancient Near Eastern literature. In attributing personified Wisdom's origin completely to YHWH, the biblical author insists that this figure is not a borrowed idea or quality from another culture or tradition. The use of metaphorical language throughout the narrative demands of the audience a mastery of the imaginative and poetic use of language. Any attempt to arrive at a literal interpretation of this pericope must flounder when confronted with such sustained use of symbolic language. The literary device of personification inhibits attempts to seek a literal interpretation, while the narrative sustains imaginative and creative engagement with the text.

Personification, as a rhetorical device, relies on the ability of the audience to engage imaginatively with the narrative and thus make the connections evoked by the description. In the later wisdom books, we will see that Wisdom is even more completely embedded within Israelite tradition. She is given her abode by God, in Israel Jacob, in the sanctuary (Sir 24:8); and is bestowed specifically on the people of Israel (Bar 4:1). Undeniably, she is integral to the Israelite tradition. However, many scholars claim to find within texts describing the wisdom figure clues that point to Wisdom's roots within other ancient Near Eastern cultures and mythological elements that have contributed to Prov 8:22-31 and other Wisdom texts. Some of these claims are discussed in the following section.

Wisdom's Egyptian Connections

Ever since the publication in 1923 of the Egyptian text called the *Teaching of Amenemope*, and the identification of apparent parallel material in Prov 22:17-23:11, the links between Israel's wisdom and that of the ancient Near East has been accepted.[102] Texts in which Wisdom is personified are but one component of a large and complex body of biblical wisdom literature, which itself is part of an

---

[100] The focus on YHWH in 8:1-21 distinguishes it from the rest of Proverbs 8, where Wisdom is central.
[101] *Gesenius Kautzsch* 142.
[102] *Papyrus 10474* in the British Museum. E.W. Budge, *Second Series of Facsimiles of Egyptian Hieratic Papyri in the British Museum* (London, 1923): Plates I-XIV.

extensive and more diverse corpus of ancient Near Eastern wisdom literature. Scholars have found that biblical wisdom texts share some striking similarities in vocabulary, literary forms, and interests with Egyptian and Mesopotamian texts. A cursory look at a type of Egyptian literature called *Sebayit* reveals characteristics in common with Proverbs.[103] An introduction or prologue announces the purpose of the work, as in Amenemope: "The beginning of the teaching of life, the testimony for prosperity, all precepts for intercourse with elders". The body of the instruction consists of admonitions or imperatives, which develop a theme, as in the wisdom poems in Proverbs.[104]

In this century, scholars investigating probable relationships between Egyptian, Babylonian, and Biblical wisdom writing, identified some common elements. Relating most directly to this study are occurrences of personification, and possible ancient Near Eastern prototypes for the Old Testament figure of personified Wisdom.[105] Similarities in content,[106] vocabulary, and literary forms were frequently identified.[107] References to the sages of other nations can be found within the biblical text itself, usually in passages that portray an Israelite surpassing a non-Israelite in wisdom, for example, Joseph in Pharaoh's court, "So Pharaoh said to Joseph, 'Since God has shown you all this, there is none so discreet and wise as you are'" (Gen 41:39); and Solomon's proverbial wisdom, "Solomon's

---

[103] *Sebayit* is an Egyptian word that occurs as a heading for various types of literature, for example, didactic treatise and tomb autobiography. Usually titles identify authors by name. The purpose of the writing is to instruct. It is characterised by word plays, parallelism and admonitions enjoining a way of life after the manner of Proverbs; *AEL* 1 (1973): 6-7. R.J. Williams, "The Sages of Ancient Egypt in the Light of Recent Scholarship," *JAOS* 101/1 (1981): 7.

[104] Examples of this occur in Prov 1:1-6; 22:21; see also *ANET* 421; *AEL II*, 148; *LEWL*, 242.

[105] Kayatz, *Studien* (1966); K.A. Kitchen, *Ancient Orient and Old Testament* (Downers Grove, 1966); Lang, *Wisdom* (1986); M. Lindenberger, *The Aramaic Proverbs of Ahiqar* (Baltimore, 1983): 68, 102-3, 114-5; J. Assman, *Ma'at: Gerechtigkeit und Unsterblichkeit im Alten Ägypten* (Munich, 1990); I. Kottsieper, *Die Sprache der Ahiqarsprüche* BZAW 194 (New York, 1990); H. Donner, *Geschichte des Volkes Israel und seiner Nachbarn in Grundzügen.* GAT 4 (Göttingen, 1984).

[106] Much of the literature of Egypt was didactic e.g. Instruction of Ptah-hotep; Instruction of Merikare; Instruction of Ani; Instruction of Amenemope; Instructions of Onchsheshonqy. Speculative literature: The Dispute over Suicide and the Song of the Harper on the impermanence of happiness. Speculative literature also emerged in Mesopotamia, The Dialogue about Human Misery; The Dialogue of Pessimism, a treatise on the injustice of life.

[107] R. Gordis in "The Social Background of Wisdom Literature," *HUCA* 18 (1943-44): 92, notes that in Proverbs commonly precious stones are used as objects of comparison and value; R. N. Whybray, *The Intellectual Tradition in the Old Testament* (Berlin, 1974): 70, identified a small group of terms he associates with an intellectual elite in Israel: "understanding", "stupid", "scoffer", "intelligent", "senseless", "prudent", "wisdom"; R.B.Y. Scott, *The Way of Wisdom in the Old Testament* (New York, 1971):121-122, suggests a list with a more general semantic range: sayings, proverbs, acrostics, and personification associated with wisdom literature.

wisdom surpassed the wisdom of all the people of the east, and all the wisdom of Egypt" (1 Kgs 5:10 *BHS* 1 Kgs 4:30 *NRSV*). Such biblical allusions to the existence of an international wisdom movement were substantiated, when at the beginning of the twentieth century, the discovery and translation of ancient Near Eastern wisdom texts alerted scholars to the international character of wisdom, and initiated some re-examination of assumptions and approaches.[108]   Erman's discovery and publication of the relationship between Prov 22:17-24:22 and the Egyptian *Instruction of Amenemope* marked the beginning of a series of studies investigating relationships between Biblical wisdom and foreign wisdom literature.[109]

Oesterley recognised the affinities of Proverbs with Egyptian wisdom literature and to a lesser extent with other foreign wisdom literature.[110]   Fichtner carried out a detailed comparison of Israelite wisdom with that of the ancient Near East and concluded that early Israelite wisdom, Proverbs, Job, and Qoheleth, was dependent on other ancient Near Eastern models.[111]   However, he noted some significant differences. From the time of Ben Sira, Israelite wisdom was completely integrated into Israelite belief and tradition, particularly with the Torah, and thus it lost its universal flavour. Humbert's groundbreaking studies dispelled doubts, at least temporarily, concerning the influence of Egyptian wisdom on Israelite wisdom.[112]   In the most complete study of the relation between Israelite and Egyptian wisdom up to his own time, he asserted that Hebrew dependence upon the Egyptian sources was primitive, original, and permanent, and extended throughout the wisdom literature. With the work of Humbert, the point was reached where the dependence of Israelite wisdom upon its Egyptian prototype was considered almost total. The Strasbourg colloquium contributed to the ongoing research into foreign influences and many studies have been carried out in recent decades.[113]

---

[108] Such as the commonly held view that the book of Proverbs was the only extant example of ancient Near Eastern aphoristic literature.

[109] A. Erman, "Eine ägyptische Quelle der Sprüche Salmos," *SPAW* 15 (1924): 86-93; H. Gressmann, *Israel's Spruchweisheit im Zusammenhang der Weltliteratur* (Berlin, 1925); F.L. Griffith, "The Instruction of Amenemope" *JEA* 12 (1926): 191-231; W.O.E. Oesterley, *The Wisdom of Egypt* (1927); *The Book of Proverbs* (1929); Humbert, *Recherches* (1929); H. Duesberg, *Les Scribes Inspirée* (1938); Albright, "Canaanite-Phoenician Sources," *VTSup* 3 (1955): 1-15; E.I. Gordon, "A New Look at the Wisdom of Sumer and Akkad" *BO* 17 (1960): 122-152.

[110] W.O.E. Oesterley, *The Wisdom of Egypt and the Old Testament* (London, 1927).

[111] J. Fichtner, *Die altorientalische Weisheit in ihrer israelitisch-jüdischen Ausprägung*. BZAW 62 (Giessen, 1933); see also L. Dürr, *Das Erziehungswesen im Alten Testament und im Antiken Orient* (Leipzig, 1932); W. Baumgartner, "Israelitische und altorientalische Weisheit" *TRu* 5 (1933): 259-288.

[112] Humbert, *Recherches* (1929); "La femme étrangère du livre des Proverbes" *RÉS* 6/2 (1937): 49-64; "Les adjectifs "Zar" et "Nokri" et la femme étrangère" in *Melanges Syriens offerts á M.R. Dussaud* (Paris, 1939): 259-266.

[113] J. Leclant, *Les Sagesses du Proche-Orient Ancien* (Paris, 1963); S. Morenz, *Egyptian Religion* (London, 1973); J. Nougayrol, *La Mésopotamie* (Paris, 1965); B. Gemser, "The

Although much of a general character has been done to establish the connections of Proverbs with foreign and especially Egyptian wisdom, Whybray was the first to base his treatment of Proverbs 1-9 on a direct comparison of these chapters with the Egyptian "Instruction" literature.[114] Kayatz points out the parallels between wisdom and the Egyptian Ma'at,[115] and by means of a careful comparison of datable Egyptian parallels with Proverbs 1-9, successfully destroys the critical distinction made by some scholars concerning early and late wisdom. Moreover, the lack of evidence for a comparable development in the wisdom literature of Egyptian and Mesopotamian materials eliminates the possibility of specific extra-biblical control in this matter.[116] She investigates the influence of Egyptian religion on the formulation of the figure of personified Wisdom systematically, and claims a wider and earlier stream of Egyptian influence than does Donner who postulates a connection between a wisdom figure in the Ahiqar text and the figure of personified Wisdom in Proverbs.[117] He sees the Ahiqar figure as the "connecting link" in a literary-historical chain that runs from Egyptian, as embodied in Ma'at, to what he regarded as a fully developed figure of Wisdom in Proverbs 8.

Against Donner's hypothesis can be set Lindenberger's work, which claims that the Aramaic Ahiqar text is of Assyrian origin.[118] Kayatz undertook an analysis of the formal structure of Proverbs 1-9 in relation to the Egyptian "Instruction". She claimed that Prov 8:1-36 was so heavily imprinted with attributes characteristic of Ma'at that Wisdom, a "poetic personification" in Prov 3:13-20 becomes a hypostasis of divine Wisdom in 8:22-31, an entity with an independent existence such as Ma'at has. As in the Egyptian texts, which proclaim that Ma'at existed before the creation, Proverbs also, announces Wisdom's authority by claiming her origin in antiquity, her existence before the creation of the world, her presence at and role in the event, and a claim to special intimacy with the Creator. Kayatz translates Prov 8:30 as "YHWH's darling child playing before him", and parallels this with "as a child Ma'at played before Re-Atum".[119] Wisdom is also like Ma'at in that she is depicted as the effective agent by whom the king is empowered to rule (Prov 8:15-16).

Instructions of 'Onchsheshonqy and Biblical Wisdom Literature" *VTSup* 7 (1960): 102-28; R.J. Williams, "The Alleged Semitic Original of the Wisdom of Amenemope" *JEA* 47 (1961): 100-106; D.E. Smith, "Wisdom Genres in RS22.439"; J. Khanjian, "Wisdom" in L. Fisher, ed., *Ras Shamra Parallels* II. AO 50 (Rome, 1975): 215-247, 371-400; *AEL* 2: 146-163; J. Greenfield, "Ahiqar in the Book of Tobit" in J. Doré, P. Grelot & M. Carrez, eds., *De la Tôrah au Messie* (Paris, 1981); F-J. Steiert, *Weisheit Israels: Ein Fremdkörper im Alten Testament?* (Freiburg, 1990).

[114] Whybray, *Wisdom in Proverbs: The Concept of Wisdom in Proverbs 1-9* (1965).

[115] Kayatz, *Studien* (1966): 76-134.

[116] W. McKane, *Proverbs* (London, 1970), discriminates between what he calls "old wisdom" and a later development of wisdom, but Kayatz questioned such hypotheses; S. Weeks, *Early Israelite Wisdom* (Oxford, 1994) argues against such distinctions.

[117] H. Donner, "Die religionsgeschichtliche Ursprünge von Prov. Sal 8" *ZÄS 82* (1957): 8-18.

[118] J.M. Lindenberger, *The Aramaic Proverbs of Ahiqar* (Baltimore, 1983): 68.

[119] Kayatz, *Einführung* (1969): 70; 74, 78-90.

However, Kayatz does not propose an immediate literary dependence of Proverbs 1-9 on Egyptian texts. She avoids Boström's Mesopotamian cultic theory, in which he claims that Ma'at replaced Ishtar.[120] She focuses on the role of Ma'at and that of personified Wisdom within the wisdom traditions of their respective cultures. Each functions as a central idea within the tradition, embracing the complex relationships of God, the world, and human life. Each is the product of wisdom's theological reflection, bringing cosmological and pedagogical thought into unity. Unlike Ma'at, however, personified Wisdom is not the "divine, eternally-valid order itself", but represents "the effort to learn from the secret orders by observation, and respect them in the execution of life". God is always independent of these orders in Israelite wisdom thought. Personified Wisdom is never elevated to the highest level, unlike Ma'at, to whom the gods themselves are obligated, as they must "live by Ma'at".[121] Wisdom is always in YHWH's control.[122]

Kayatz's view is unlikely for the following reasons. Ma'at is never personified in Egyptian wisdom books, and when she is personified in other Egyptian literature, she is never portrayed as speaking in the first person, nor is she given credit for any speech at all, whereas personified Wisdom is portrayed as delivering her teaching in the first person in Proverbs (1:20-33; 8:1-36; 9:4-6). In addition, some proposed parallels do not hold up under closer investigation. Kayatz notes that the Egyptian judge, the guardian of moral life, who called himself the priest of Ma'at, wore a symbol of Ma'at on a chain round his neck, and she draws a parallel between this instance of neck-wear and references to: (1) "parents' teaching" which is to be as "pendants for your neck" וַעֲנָקִים לְגַרְגְּרֹתֶיךָ (Prov 1:9); (2) sound wisdom and discretion which is to be "adornment for your neck" חֵן לְגַרְגְּרֹתֶיךָ (3:22); (3) "loyalty and faithfulness" that are to be bound "about your neck"; (4) teaching of father and mother which are to be "tied about your neck" (Prov 6:21).[123] However, in these verses the wearing of a symbol about the neck is to ensure that the wearer does not forget or lose the particular gifts mentioned. There is no indication that this is an allusion to the practice in Egypt, which may have been associated with particular ranks and the accompanying authority. There may not be any grounds for regarding these references as indications that

---

[120] Boström, *Proverbiastudien* (1935): 155-7 sees Prov 3:16-19 as a corrective to the "strange woman" character, and suggests that the harlot is a sacred prostitute to Astarte. This notion is unlikely since the description of her in the text sounds more like a public adulterer, "my husband is not at home" (Prov 7:19), and the fact that the wisdom writers do not seem to have been much concerned about foreign cults; see also J. Day, "Foreign Semitic influence on the wisdom of Israel," in *WAI* (1995): 55-70.

[121] Kayatz, *Studien* (1966): 102-4, 136, 138-42.

[122] Both Camp, *Wisdom* (1985): 31, and Lang, *Wisdom* (1986): 70, 76, support this notion.

[123] Kayatz, *Studien* (1966): 107-110; J. Day, "Wisdom" in *WAI* (1995): 21, suggests that a stronger claim could be made for the imagery being a free adaptation of Deut 11:18 "lay up these words of mine in your heart and in your soul; and you shall bind them as a sign upon your hand" (cf. Deut 6:8) He notes the close parallelism between Deut 11:18-19 and Prov 6:21-22, "bind them upon your heart always; tie them about your neck".

personified Wisdom is being equated with Ma'at, so that the "ornament", used here as a simile, can be interpreted as relating to or representing Wisdom.

Images of "wearing about the neck" appear to be common in many cultures as the use of neck ornaments is a well-attested practice, and so was unlikely to be peculiar to Egypt. Kayatz suggests that a prototype of personified Wisdom may be found in the speeches of the gods that constitute a literary genre in Egypt, and that the passages in Proverbs 1-9 where personified Wisdom gives "life" to her adherents (Prov 3:16, 18, 8:35a), are evidence of the borrowing of a Ma'at motif from Egyptian literature.[124] She acknowledges, however, that this piece of motif research does not throw any further light on what is meant by "life" in these verses. Even if it could be shown to be a direct borrowing of the motif or image this would not mean that the Egyptian beliefs underlying the motif were appropriated by the Old Testament wisdom writers along with the image itself. Allusions to "life" in Egyptian literature itself are usually found in writing concerned with death. These references were to be found particularly in rituals and cults connected with death, and with eternal life that was to be achieved after death. Death in the Old Testament is seen as the end of all living creatures (Qoh 2:15; Sir 44:9; Wis 2:2-4). Until perhaps the first century BCE it seems that everything had to be worked out within the limits of earthly life. In Proverbs, as in much of the Old Testament, life after death, if alluded to at all, is envisaged only as retirement to the rather obscure place called Sheol, for example, 2 Sam 22:6; Prov 5:5; 7:27; Pss 6:5; 18:6; 49:14; 55:15; 89:48; 116:3; Isa 28:15-18; 38:18; Hos 13:14; Hab 2:5. Concerns about life after death emerge in the Wisdom of Solomon where there may be a mention of an afterlife or immortality (Wis 1:1-6:21).

Descriptions of Ma'at that occur in Egyptian literature, for example, 'Ma'at loves' 'Ma'at as lover', 'Ma'at as companion' or 'beloved friend', may have provided some impetus for the Israelite conception of the female figure of Wisdom. Such individual expressions and phrases that have exact equivalents in Egyptian writing do suggest a general body of wisdom language in use throughout the ancient Near East.[125] Several scholars have investigated the connection between Egyptian and Old Testament love.[126] However, this does not necessarily

---

[124] Kayatz, *Studien* (1966): 76-79; 55, 102, does not accept Boström's theory that Wisdom is an opposite but sees her as based on Ma'at.

[125] Boström, *Proverbiastudien* (1935) believes the personification of Wisdom originated as a positive opponent of Astarte, goddess of Love, as she is of the foreign woman. However apt there are some complicating factors. Other Egyptian documents, in which the love motif is clearly in evidence, also exist. Boström's claim rests on the notion that the wisdom writers were merely constructing an opponent to Astarte.

[126] Ancient Egyptian love lyrics first became available to the general reader in 1874 and there followed several investigations of possible parallels with Old Testament texts. See C.W. Goodwin, "On Four Songs Contained in an Egyptian Papyrus in the British Museum", *Transactions of the Society of Biblical Archaeology 3* (1874): 380-388; G. Maspero, "Les Chants d'amour du Papyrus de Turin et du Papyrus Harris", *JA 8/1* (1883): 47; M. Müller, *Die Liebespoesie der Ägypter* (Leipzig, 1899): 8-9, claimed that "Hebrew and Egyptian poetry are just as different as Hebrew and Egyptian thought"; G. Gerleman, *Das Hohelied*

mean that the images used to describe personified Wisdom in Proverbs are of
Egyptian origin: they and the Egyptian songwriters may have shared a common
body of poetic language. A definitive motif in Wisdom's speeches is her love for
human beings which is evidenced in her promises (Prov 8:17, 20-22, 34) to which
may be added Prov 7:4 where she is called 'sister' 'intimate friend' 'confidante'.
Balancing this image of Wisdom as lover is the admonition to the seeker of
Wisdom: "Get wisdom, get insight, do not forsake her, Love her and she will guard
you" (Prov 4:5).

Kayatz, who sees this cycle of metaphors as originating in Egypt, claims
that there was an Egyptian stimulus for the conception of the figure of Wisdom
because so many individual expressions and phrases had equivalents in the
Egyptian Ma'at texts. Awareness of and familiarity with the Egyptian material and
the manner of Ma'at portrayals in Egyptian literature may be advantageous in
leading to some understanding of the figure of personified Wisdom, but one
wonders if sufficient grounds exist to warrant the conclusion that personified
Wisdom in the Old Testament is based on the Egyptian Ma'at. Without some
evidence of direct borrowing or adaptation by one group from another one can only
surmise as to the origins of the motifs used in traditional literature. As noted by
Kayatz, there seems to have been a considerable body of literary material that was
common over a wide area of the ancient Near East. This being so, it seems likely
that Israel both contributed to, borrowed from, adapted, and creatively
reinterpreted this material. The miniature portrait appearing in Prov 3:13-20 is
composed of a litany of praise of Wisdom plus an array of images depicting her
value in relation to material benefits.

> Happy is the one who finds wisdom
> She is more precious than jewels . . .
> Long life is in her right hand; in her left hand are riches and honour . . .
> She is a tree of life to those who lay hold of her. (Prov 3:13-18)

In a vivid turn of metaphor in Proverbs, Wisdom becomes a "tree of life", an
association (Prov 3:18; cf. Gen 3:22) that affirms her claim of power to give life.[127]
This life-death situation is also expressed in the portrayal of personified Wisdom as
"Long life in her right hand, in her left, riches and honour" (Prov 3:16), "she is
your life" (4:13). The former opens with a tribute to Woman Wisdom and her
benefits framed by an inclusio of the root meaning "happy" Prov 3:13-18. Wisdom

---

(Neukirchen-Vluyn, 1965): 3-4 and M.V. Fox, *The Song of Songs and the Ancient Egyptian Love Songs* (Madison, 1985) read the poems of the Song of Songs as love lyrics, formulations of the moods and experiences of lovers expressed in the language of poetic fiction. They argue from the perspective of the Egyptian parallels and note connections between Egyptian and Old Testament love lyrics; O. Keel, *The Song of Songs*, trans., F.J. Gaister (Minneapolis, 1994): 13-24, compares Egyptian and Old Testament poetry in detail.
[127] In addition to its appearance in Prov 3:18, "the tree of life" appears in Prov 11:30; 13:12; 15:4 and in Ezek 47:12 which uses the imagery of health-giving trees.

is described as the bearer of riches, long life, and honour (3:14-16); her ways are those of prosperity and peace (3:17). Moreover, for those who embrace her, she is a "tree of life." Kayatz sees this pericope as modelled on a representation of Ma'at holding an *ankh* symbol of life, in one hand and a sceptre, symbol of wealth and status, in the other.[128] Lang takes this connection further. He understands this text to portray Wisdom as a life-giving deity who, like her divine prototypes, Ma'at, Isis, Ishtar, holds long life in her right hand and wealth and honour in her left, and the Queen of Heaven who dispenses kingship, prosperity and esteem to those who love her (Prov 8:14-21). Those who answer her invitation find life, while those who spurn her favours experience death (8:32-36).[129] Camp argues against this reading, and observes that the garland and crown were typical elements in a variety of celebrations in the ancient Near East and consequently do not necessarily indicate an Egyptian source for this motif.[130]

In an extended investigation of Ma'at, Assman has produced a complex study of the importance of Ma'at in the Egyptian intellectual experience.[131] In dealing with the centrality of Ma'at in Egyptian thought he defines it as "primary religion" that Ma'at was not a simple concept of good and evil, but rather a principle of justification, inseparable from the unification of Upper and Lower Egypt. He stresses the importance of Ma'at for personal immortality, its role in the cosmic process, and in the Egyptian state. She was, according to Assmann, the fundamental state myth (*grundlegender Staatsmythus*) of the two kingdoms. Ma'at was not only the entire basis for the Egyptian understanding of the universe, but the myth extended beyond Egypt, and was part of the ancient Near Eastern intellectual milieu out of which grew the complex system of biblical theology. He sees Ma'at as one of the roots of Old Testament thinking, or at least an essential element of the soil from which Hebrew thought grew.

Recently Fox has challenged the view of many scholars that Ma'at, the central concept in Egyptian ethics, primarily means *order* or *world order*. Rather it provides a key to understanding both Israelite and Egyptian Wisdom.[132] To look to Ma'at, as the key to understanding the worldview of Israelite Wisdom is a mistake, says Fox. Nor is the figure of Wisdom in Proverbs 8 to be linked to the goddess Ma'at. "The Israelites, or their Canaanite predecessors, could draw on Egyptian wisdom, while not necessarily aware of its origins, without importing the entirety of the genre or even its most basic axioms".[133] Schmid also undertook an investigation of the nature and history of wisdom thought, discussing first Egyptian, then Mesopotamian and finally Israelite wisdom.[134] He was particularly concerned to stress that these wisdom literatures are not "timeless", as often suggested, but they had their own histories and underwent changes as part of

---

[128] Kayatz, *Studien* (1966): 105.

[129] Lang, *Wisdom* (1986): 71-81

[130] Camp, *Wisdom* (1985): 31.

[131] J. Assmann, *Ma'at: Gerechtigkeit und Unsterblichkeit im Alten Ägypten* (Munich, 1990).

[132] M.V. Fox, "World Order and Ma'at: A Crooked Parallel" *JANES* 23 (1995): 37-48.

[133] Fox, "World Order" *JANES* 23 (1995): 48.

[134] H.H. Schmid, *Wesen und Geschichte der Weisheit* (Berlin, 1966).

historical developments. In the case of Israelite wisdom, Schmid was specifically interested in the late developments in which teaching, originally indistinguishable from its Egyptian prototype, became systematised and eventually was turned into a rigid theology dominated by the concept of the Law. He did concede that the understanding of human beings in Proverbs differed from that of Egyptian wisdom, in that the emphasis was on human character rather than actions dividing human beings into good and evil. This he sees as an influence of Yahwism, which personalised the anthropology of Proverbs as a retribution dogma. He characterised the eventual rational-intellectual systematisation of wisdom thought, including Proverbs 1-9 in this, as having lost touch with reality.

Murphy is among those who reject Schmid's thesis, maintaining that he has failed to demonstrate wisdom's relationship to history.[135] His work was "a premature and hence an ineffective presentation of the history of the wisdom movement". Steiert rejects the assumption, made by several scholars, that Israel's wisdom is an alien body in the Old Testament. He contends that scholars have overemphasised the affinities of Proverbs with Egyptian sapiential literature, because they have failed to give due weight to the pronounced underlying differences of content between the two bodies of material. Some of these matters are: the conception of God, the centrality of the "horizontal" aspect, or what may be called the element of personal piety, and the role allotted to magic.[136] He believes the links with Egyptian wisdom may not to be regarded as mere borrowing, although undoubted similarities appear, but each set of texts should be looked at in their own contexts.

G. von Rad sees in Prov 8:22-29 the borrowing of a "style of a specific Egyptian divine proclamation", and in verses 30-33 the Egyptian idea of a deity caressing personified truth (Ma'at) which has, with internal modifications, found its way into the poem. Perhaps his reflections on this insight are of more import. "But what does all this prove? Only that ideas that had their roots elsewhere came to Israel's help when she needed them, in order [for her] to be able to progress in her thinking within her own domain".[137] L. Boström points to the distinctiveness of the monotheistic presuppositions of Proverbs as showing its independence of Egyptian wisdom, while Steiert emphasises that the affinities of Proverbs with Israelite traditions and beliefs are far greater than with those of Egypt. Many recent studies of Proverbs, while not denying Egyptian influence completely, are moving to a view that this book is much more closely related to Israelite traditions, than to other ancient Near Eastern influences. Preuss is a notable exception to this view.[138]

---

[135] R.E. Murphy, "Assumptions and Problems in Old Testament Wisdom Research" *CBQ* (1967): 102-112; "Wisdom Theses", in *Wisdom and Knowledge* (1976): 187-200.

[136] F.-J. Steiert, *Weisheit Israels* (Freiburg, 1990), mentions in particular H.H. Schmid and H.D. Preuss as failing to recognise how intimately Proverbs chapters 1-9 and 10-31 are related to the teaching of the Law and the Prophets, thereby coming to distorted notions of the place of wisdom in the canon. Steiert stresses links of expression and thought in Proverbs with the prophetic and Deuteronomic traditions.

[137] Von Rad, *Wisdom* (1972): 153.

[138] H.D. Preuss, "Das Gottesbild der älteren Weisheit Israels", *VTSup* 23 (1972): 116-145;

Wisdom's Mesopotamian Connections

Research into Mesopotamian influences on the figure of Wisdom is meagre if viewed against that which exists on Egyptian influence. Connections between Israelite wisdom and Egyptian wisdom have generally taken pride of place in discussions about foreign influences.[139] However, affinities with Mesopotamian literatures are increasingly but sporadically considered.[140] These separate but related languages and cultures flourished in the area covered by the Tigris-Euphrates basin. Sumerian domination can be dated from about 3000 BCE until the rise of Babylonian culture primarily in the eighteenth and seventeenth centuries, particularly under Hammurabi (c.1848-1806). Babylonian culture was greatly influenced by the Sumerian. Gradually the Accadian, rather than the Sumerian language became dominant. Two main dialects of Accadian were Babylonian and Assyrian. Sumerian texts were translated and understood more recently than Egypt texts. Gordon's studies of this literature greatly enriched and extended our knowledge of the field.[141] More recently, Alster has made the *Instructions of Shuruppak* available.[142] This composition in Sumerian is usually dated to the mid-third millennium BCE. It was translated into Accadian before the neo-Assyrian period. Like Sumerian, Accadian was also written in cuneiform signs. In the first millennium BCE, Aramaic began to replace Accadian and eventually became the official language. Aramaic was the spoken language and was used for official documents in the late Assyrian empire.

Accadian wisdom texts became available to a wide readership through the work of Lambert.[143] W. Baumgartner, van Dijk, Schmid, Crenshaw, L. Boström, and Murphy among others have documented stylistic affinities between the book of Proverbs and Mesopotamian literatures.[144] McKane assumes such affinities in his work on Proverbs in which he includes a lengthy section entitled "International

---

Einführung in die alttestamentliche Literatur (Stuttgart, 1987).

[139] C.I.K. Story, "The Book of Proverbs and Northwest Semitic Literature" *JBL* 64 (1945): 319-337; M.J. Dahood, *Proverbs and Northwest Semitic Philology* [forthwith *PNSP*](Rome, 1963); W.A. van der Weiden, *Le Livre des Proverbes* (Rome, 1970).

[140] Mesopotamian as used here includes Sumerian (non-Semitic), Accadian (east-Semitic, Babylonian and Assyrian), and Amorite, Canaanite, Ugaritic (west-Semitic) strands. I am indebted to Dr. Stephanie Dalley for her clarification of these terms.

[141] E. Gordon, *Sumerian Proverbs* (Philadelphia, 1959); "A New Look at the Wisdom of Sumer and Akkad," *BO* 17 (1960): 122-152.

[142] See B. Alster, *The Instructions of Shuruppak* (Copenhagen, 1974). This work resembles the royal instructions genre common in ancient Egyptian literature. Ziusudra, the receiver of instruction, is Utnapishtim's Sumerian counterpart, the hero of the flood story in the Atra-hasis and Gilgamesh epics. See Lambert, *BWL* 92-94; *ANET* 594-96.

[143] *BWL*: 213-282.

[144] Baumgartner, "Die Israelitische Weisheitsliteratur" *TRu* 5 (1933): 259-263; J.J.A. van Dijk, *La Sagesse suméro-accadienne* (Leiden, 1953): 42-47, 100-118; Schmid, *Wesen und Geschichte* (1966); J.L. Crenshaw, *Old Testament Wisdom: An Introduction* (Louisville, 1998): 20-30; Boström, *God of the Sages* (1990): 24-27; Murphy, *Tree of Life* (1990): 153-159.

Wisdom", where he discusses the literary forms of Egyptian, Babylonian and Assyrian wisdom literature and devotes a large section of his material to Babylonian and Assyrian Instructions and Proverbs.[145] Interestingly an Accadian text, *The Counsels of Wisdom* (about 140 lines in length, and dated probably between 1500 and 1200 BCE), exhibits literary forms that are similar to the Egyptian "Instructions" and to the Book of Proverbs, such as using the address "my son", and the giving of advice and instruction concerning daily life.[146] The *Epic of Gilgamesh,* dated from about 1600 BCE, while not regarded as wisdom literature, has the quest for immortality as its dominant motif.[147] Wisdom's preoccupation with the choice between life and death (Prov 2:19; 3:2, 16, 22; 4:10, 13, 22, 23; 5:6; 6:23, 26; 7:23; 8:35) echoes Gilgamesh's quest for immortality. Another such text, the *Poem of the Righteous Sufferer,* often denoted by its first line, *I Will Praise the Lord of Wisdom,* is dated to about 1290 BCE. It is frequently compared with the Book of Job, since in tablet two the sufferings of a person claiming to be righteous are detailed.[148] However, the poem is mainly praise of Marduk, "lord of wisdom", for having delivered his servant from suffering. Lambert uses stylistic considerations to date *The Babylonian Theodicy,* also known as *The Dialogue about Human Misery,* to about 1000 BCE.[149] It is an acrostic poem with twenty-seven stanzas of eleven lines each. Like Psalm 119, each line in the stanza begins with the same letter, or sign.[150]

Personification in Mesopotamian Texts

S. Dalley observes, "It has sometimes been claimed that the Babylonians did not personify abstract concepts in the way that Wisdom is personified in the Bible. This is not so, for deities such as Mīšarum 'Justice', Kittum 'Righteousness', Hasīsu /Hasīsatu 'Wisdom', are abstract nouns in origin".[151] Some links may exist between texts showing Mesopotamian personifications of abstract divine qualities and Biblical texts describing personified Wisdom, since several images appearing in the Mesopotamian texts are similar to those associated with the Wisdom figure. If one interprets the much-debated Prov 8:30 to say that personified Wisdom was beside YHWH and was actively involved in creation, this verse would be reminiscent of the *Epic of Atrahasis,* composed about 1700 BCE, which portrays

---

[145] McKane, *Proverbs* (1970): International Wisdom is discussed on pages 51-210.

[146] *BWL,* 101-105; *ANET,* 595-596; Egyptian *Sebyait,* occurs as a heading for many types of literature designated Instructions.

[147] *ANET,* 95-96.

[148] The "Poem of the Righteous Sufferer," exists in both Sumerian and Babylonian. See *BWL* 21-62, 343-345; *ANET,* 596-600.

[149] *BWL* 27; 63-91; *ANET,* 601-604.

[150] Prov 31:10-31 is also an acrostic poem of 22 verses; see W.M. Soll, "Babylonian and Biblical Acrostics" *Biblica* 69/3 (1988): 305-323.

[151] S. Dalley, ed., *The Legacy of Mesopotamia.* I wish to thank Dr Stephanie Dalley for giving me access to her unpublished research and for her suggestions and help regarding this material on Mesopotamian influences.

the goddess Mami working alongside Enki/Ea to fashion human beings.[152] Interestingly, this epic uses the epithet "wise" *eristum* several times to describe Mami. In *The Babylonian Theodicy*, Mami, called *pātiqtu* "the female who creates/fashions" is present at creation.[153] Loretz, in his book on Qoheleth, notes a close parallel between Qoh 9:7-9 (about enjoying life) and the speech of the alewife/barmaid Šiduri (whose name has the divine determinative).[154] Šiduri exhorts Gilgamesh on the same issue in the Babylonian *Epic of Gilgamesh*.[155] H. Grimme first noted the interesting parallel between Qoheleth's advice and that of Šiduri.[156] S. Dalley remarks, "It seems to me that Šiduri, also known as Šabitu, resembles Old Testament Wisdom in being a woman who lives alone, without a father or brothers, in her own house, and dispenses food and drink. Her speeches are clearly wisdom speeches."[157]

Another claim for Mesopotamian influence on personified Wisdom appears in an article by Greenfield in which he argues that various interpretations proposed for Proverbs 9:1 are mistaken.[158] He notes, "Babylonian literature and tradition preserved, although in a fragmentary form, the myth of the seven Apkallus or "sages".[159] The Apkallus "ensure the correct functioning of heaven and earth".[160] Like *Ea*, the god of the depths, who was also the god of wisdom, was credited in various myths with bestowing useful information upon humanity. They were credited with teaching humanity, wisdom, and social forms.[161] They were also known as *ummânu*, a broad term appearing to denote "scribe/scholar/master/craftsman/officer".[162] The seven Apkallus were credited with writings about omens, magic and other "wisdom" texts.[163] Greenfield claims

---

[152] W.G. Lambert, and A.R. Millard, eds. *Atra-Hasis: The Babylonian Story of the Flood, with the Sumerian Flood Story by M. Civil.* (Oxford 1969)

[153] *BWL*, stanza xxvi; The Babylonian Theodicy is dated to the twelfth century BCE.

[154] O. Loretz, *Qoheleth* (Freiburg, 1964): 167-180.

[155] *BWL*, X.iii.6-14; *ANET*, 594-596.

[156] H. Grimme, "Babel und Koheleth-Jojakhin", *OLZ* 8 (1905): 432-438.

[157] S. Dalley made this comment in a conversation with the author on Mesopotamian influences.

[158] J.C. Greenfield, "The Seven Pillars of Wisdom (Prov 9:1)—a Mistranslation", *JQR* 76 (1985): 13-20.

[159] Greenfield noted a growing literature on the apkallus; see van Dijk, *La Sagesse* (1953): 20, n. 56; E. Reiner, "The Etiological Myth of the 'Seven Sages'" *Orientalia 30* (1961): 1-11; J.H. Tigay, *The Evolution of the Gilgamesh Epic* (Philadelphia, 1982): 205-6; R. Borger, "Die Beschwörungsserie Bīt Mēseri und die Himmelfahrt Henochs", *JNES* 33 (1974): 183-189.

[160] E. Reiner, "The Etiological Myth" *Orientalia* 30 (1961): 10-11.

[161] H. Galter, *Der Gott Ea/Enki in der akkadischen Überlieferung* (Graz, 1982).

[162] S. Parpola, *Letters from Assyrian Scholars* (Neukirchen-Vluyn, 1983): 270 notes that an ummânu was a "master" or highly trained expert in specific arts.

[163] See W.W. Hallo, "On the Antiquity of Sumerian Literature", *JAOS* 83 (1963): 167-176; van Dijk, *La Sagesse* (1953): 42-47; W.G. Lambert "Ancestors, Authors and Canonicity" *JCS* XI (1957): n.8.

that "the word *ummânu*, appears in Hebrew in the form '*āmōn* in Prov 8:30".[164] He
suggests a return to Albright's claim that behind the Greek ἀμμουναίον we have
some reminiscence of *ummânu*, "compositions in the enigmatic script of the
ammunīm which have been obtained from the inner rooms of temples".[165]
Albright's intricate argumentation appears in his review of Clemen's *Die
phönikische Religion*.[166] Greenfield concludes that the Hebrew text of Prov 9:1 was
misunderstood during transmission, so the tradition of the seven wise ones was
forgotten, thus changing the meaning. He proposes that the translation of Prov 9:1
should read, "Wisdom has built her house; the Seven have set its foundations". The
"Seven" are the Apkallus or primeval sages in Mesopotamian mythology, who
were endowed with wisdom by Ea, and became the ancestors of civilisation. This
interpretation could function in isolation from the remainder of the text, but is
problematic within the whole poem.   One wonders about the introduction of the
"Seven" at this point in the text when personified Wisdom in Prov 1:20-33; 8:1-36
claims a unique relationship with YHWH, and speaks with the authority of one
dependent only on YHWH.

Wisdom's speeches in Prov 8:4-36 highlight her character. Clearly, the
purpose is to persuade the audience to devote themselves to Wisdom. The means
employed to that end is a lengthy recommendation in which Wisdom speaks of her
power, her authority and the gifts that are hers to bestow.[167] This speech of self-
praise is reminiscent of a literary genre attested in Egyptian, Mesopotamian and
other Near Eastern texts, in which a character, usually a goddess–Ma'at, Isis,
Astarte/Ishtar, Gula–praises herself.[168]   Von Soden suggests possible cultic
significance for first person texts of this type, and claims that this genre may be
restricted to goddesses.[169]   An example is a prayer by Bullusta–Rabi where his
spouse Gula, the goddess of healing, speaks her own praise, a well-attested mode
in Accadian. Whatever the literary background, Gula's self-predication gives her
praises authority. She discourses upon her many attributes, such as her astral
character, her position of authority, her interest in agriculture, unalterable word,

---

[164] A claim by J. Ewald, *Sprüche Salomo/Kohélet* (Göttingen, 1837) cited by W.F. Albright,
in *JBL* 60 (1941): 210; Albright, "Canaanite-Phoenician" *VTSup* 3 (1955): 8; S. Smith,
"An Inscription from the Temple of Sin at Huraidha in the Hadhramawt" *BSOAS* 11/3
(1945): 451-464 suggested the derivation of '*āmōn*; see McKane, *Proverbs* (1970): 357-
58.

[165] See Greenfield, "Seven Pillars of Wisdom" (1985): n.31; L. Dürr, *Mitteilungen der
Vorderasiatisch-aegyptische Gesellschaft* (Leipzig, 1938); C. Clemen, *Die phönikische
Religion nach Philo von Byblos* (Leipzig, 1939); J. Stamm, *Die akkadische
Namengebung*, (Leipzig, 1939).

[166] See W.F. Albright, "Islam and the Religions of the Orient" *JAOS* 60 (1940): 298 n.53;
Eissfeldt, *Ras Shamra und Sachunjaton* (Halle, 1939): 9.

[167] YHWH also speaks in self-praise in Isa 42:8-9; 44:24-8; 45:5-7, but the contents of these
speeches are very different from those of Wisdom in Proverbs.

[168] Boström, *Proverbiastudien* (1935): 172-3; Kayatz, *Studien* (1966): 77-98; Lang, *Wisdom*
(1986): 56-59; Ishtar II. 4, IV. 53.

[169] W. von Soden, "Die Unterweltsvision eines assyrischen Kronprinzen" *ZA* 43 (1936): 1-
31.

healing ability, control of destinies, sexual attraction, upbringing and education, marriage and scholarship. Gula is portrayed as a complex character and has several names.[170] In the Old Testament, it seems likely that some imagery of self-praise in Proverbs 8 may have been shaped by literary conventions derived from polytheism. However, whatever polytheistic connections this text may have had in an earlier form, the speech in its present form is monotheistic. Wisdom is intended to be understood as the creation of YHWH with whom she has a unique relationship. This she expresses by her presence in the created world and especially by her delight in humanity.[171]

Traces of Mythological Figures

Gemser, in his study of personified Wisdom in Proverbs, especially Prov 8:22-31, notes that one might be tempted to find traits of mythological figures and the beginning of later hypostasis speculation in this chapter. Conceding that the personification passages in Proverbs show a progression and deepening reflection by the wisdom writers, he notes that what is striking in any comparison with ancient Near Eastern mythology and Hellenistic speculation is the sober and prudent way in which such ideas are handled without prejudice to ethical-religious Yahwism. These mythological-speculative forms of expression are "nationalised" or better "Israelitised" in the earlier wisdom literature. Gemser denies that the figure of Wisdom can be explained as derived from any mythological figure whether Iranian, Babylonian, Egyptian or other.[172]

Ringgren, in a comprehensive study of the hypostatization of divine qualities and functions in the ancient Near East, develops some of Gemser's ideas. In his discussion of Israelite Jewish concepts of Wisdom, he investigates those appearing in Job, Proverbs, Wisdom of Ben Sira, Wisdom of Solomon, Baruch, and later Jewish literature. However, he concedes that problems arise from the reading back of later developments into earlier portrayals of Wisdom in Proverbs 1-9. Wisdom's personification as a teacher (Prov 1:20-33) might, he thinks, be no more than a literary device. Nevertheless, he sees the Wisdom figure in 8:22-31 as neither an abstraction nor a purely literary personification but "a concrete being, self-existent beside God. He claims that Wisdom was originally simply a divine quality, a "hypostasis", but as occurred frequently in some Near Eastern religious systems, she became in time objectified as a distinct being worthy of devotion. Despite the Near Eastern analogy, he emphasises that the Israelite-Jewish figure of Wisdom cannot have been derived in the first place from external mythological sources. Theories that deities such as Ishtar or Isis are her prototypes tell us nothing: they are unable to explain, "how a great goddess has become a relatively unimportant divine being with an abstract name".[173] Gemser and Ringgren argue

---

[170] See B. Foster, *Before the Muses* (Leiden, 1973): 491-95.
[171] R.N. Whybray, *The Heavenly Counsellor in Isaiah xi 13-14* (Cambridge, 1971) discusses this topic in detail.
[172] B. Gemser, *Sprüche Salomos* (Tübingen, 1963).
[173] Ringgren, *Word and Wisdom* (1947): 104; 131-135.

that the form of Prov 8:24-26, in which the various acts of creation are referred to in a series of negative clauses each beginning with "before", points to a common ancient Near Eastern tradition and has prototypes in Egyptian and Babylonian accounts of creation.[174] However, several differences exist between these texts and Proverbs 8. Existence of comparable texts from other parts of the world suggests that the theory of a common Near Eastern tradition must remain in doubt.[175]

Over the past few decades, discoveries of drawings and inscriptions at Kuntillet Ajrud and Khirbet el-Qom have provoked much discussion, especially the interpretation of what may be a reference to YHWH's Asherah. Keel and Uehlinger in a recent study have used iconographic sources to illustrate the biblical text and the cultures that influenced it. They survey the evidence from about 1800 to 450 BCE, shedding light on ancient Near Eastern gods and goddesses and their symbols. Their work is particularly pertinent because of the recent discussions of monotheism in Israel and the feminist-oriented investigation about a divine partner such as Asherah for YHWH in the pre-exilic period. Their verdict on Kuntilleth 'Ajrud is clear. "The discoveries at Kuntilleth 'Ajrud and Khirbet et Qom, provide no compelling argument against the thesis of a broad monolatric worship of YHWH in the Israel of Iron IIB, approximately eighth century BCE, but rather arguments against the recognition of a female πάρεδρον of YHWH in this period".[176] Hadley has reviewed various identifications of Wisdom with a goddess, and investigated Proverbs 8 and Job 28 to "examine whether or not this personification of Wisdom refers to an actual person, divinity or hypostasis, or is merely a literary device".[177] She concludes, "The apparent apotheosis of Lady Wisdom in the biblical literature is not a legitimating of the worship of 'established' goddesses, but is rather a literary compensation for the eradication of these goddesses".[178]

M. Smith, in a recent study, also suggests that the Old Testament personification of Wisdom derives from the goddess Asherah.[179] Both, he claims, are feminine divine figures and appear to have some shared characteristics. For example, Wisdom's association with the "tree of life" (Prov 3:18; 9:30; 15:4), evokes the Asherah stylized tree, and the use of the word אַשְׁרֵי "blessed" which occurs in Prov 3:18. This hypothesis, while appearing plausible, lacks some coherence. The goddess Asherah is not associated with wisdom in Ugaritic texts.

---

[174] Book of the Apophis, *ANET*, 5; Enuma Elish, *ANET*: 60-61; The Creation of the World by Marduk, in A. Heidel, *The Babylonian Genesis* (Chicago, 1951): 62.

[175] R.N. Whybray, "Proverbs 8:22-31 and its Supposed Prototypes" *VT* 15 (1965): 504-514 for a discussion and translation of some of the texts.

[176] O. Keel & C. Uehlinger, *Göttinen, Götter und Gottessymbole* (Freiburg, 1992): 237-282.

[177] J.M. Hadley, "Wisdom and the Goddess" in *WAI* (1995): 234-243; see also J.M. Hadley, "The Khirbet el-Qom Inscription" *VT* 37 (1987): 50-62; "Some Drawings and Inscriptions on two Pithoi from Kuntillet 'Ajrud" *VT* 37 (1987): 180-213; "Yahweh and 'his asherah': Archaeological and Textual Evidence for the Cult of the Goddess" in *Ein Gott allein?* (1994): 234-268.

[178] Hadley, "Wisdom" in *WAI* (1995): 236.

[179] M.S. Smith, *The Early History of God* (San Francisco, 1990): 94-96.

Old Testament writers portray Wisdom as having a unique relationship with YHWH. She is the first creation, and delights in humanity, but they never that she is wife or consort. The macarism אַשְׁרֵי "blessed" is a sapiential keyword occurring throughout the Old Testament. It appears often in Proverbs and Psalms exhibiting wisdom style and concerns (Prov 8:34; 14:21; 16:20; 20:7; 28:14; 29:18; Job 5:17; 31:7; Pss 89:15; 94:12; 106:3; 112:1). Other occurrences are in contexts reflecting wisdom nuances (Deut 33:29; 1 Kgs 10:8; 2 Chr 9:7; Isa 30:15; 32:20; 56:2; Dan 12:12). It takes several forms, and mixes a surprising number of themes. Terrien warns that the interjection must not be confused with "blessing" בָּרוּךְ, which is a passive participle implying a ritual transfer of power to a static recipient.[180]

An Aramaic text, *The Proverbs of Ahiqar*, features Ahiqar, a figure whose earliest appearance in literature is now deemed to be as the wise scribe who was chief counsellor to Sennacherib and Esarhaddon, seventh century BCE. He appears in a number of texts, the earliest being the Aramaic text from Elephantine.[181] This ancient Near Eastern Semitic, Aramean/Assyrian, wise man appears several times in the Book of Tobit (Tob 1:21-22; 2:10; 11:17-18; 14:10-12).[182] Here he has been transformed into a northern Israelite from the tribe of Naphtali. He is Tobit's nephew, the son of his brother Anael, and a benefactor of Tobit (Tob 1:21-22; 2:10; cf. 1:1). It seems likely, as Cazelles maintains, that behind Achior the Ammonite in Judith 5:1-21 (*Vulg.* 5:1-25), stands the "profile figure of the celebrated Ahiqar" a wise man, reputed to be the author of a wisdom book containing many proverbs and fables. Moore notes "that the author of Judith was familiar with the Ahiqar figure becomes more probable when one realises that Tobit, a book whose composition many scholars date to the same general period as Judith, alludes to what was obviously a well-known story" (Tob 14:10).[183]

Since the *Ahiqar* text presents similarities to the sayings typical of biblical wisdom, scholars have searched this work for likely influences on Old Testament wisdom.[184] Although the text reflects an Assyrian background, it was probably

---

[180] S. Terrien, "Wisdom in the Psalter", in L.G Perdue, ed., *In Search of Wisdom: Essays in Memory of John G. Gammie* [forthwith *ISW*] (Louisville, 1993): 54-55; J. Crenshaw, "Method in Determining Wisdom Influence upon 'Historical' Literature" *JBL* 88 (1969): 132; R.N. Whybray, *The Intellectual Tradition in the Old Testament* (Berlin, 1974): 125-126; A. Hurvitz, "Wisdom Vocabulary in the Hebrew Psalter" *VT* 30 (1981): 43.

[181] The leaves of the Aramaic version of Ahiqar discovered at Elephantine (1906-8) are dated fifth century BCE. A. Cowley, *Aramaic Papyri of the Fifth Century B.C.* (Oxford, 1923): 204-208; Recent editions of Ahiqar are J.M. Lindenberger, *The Aramaic Proverbs of Ahiqar* (Baltimore, 1983); I. Kottsieper, *Die Sprache der Ahiqarsprüche* (Berlin, 1990); B. Porten & A. Yardeni, *Textbook of Aramaic Documents* (Jerusalem, 1993): 24-57; J.C. Greenfield, "The Wisdom of Ahiqar" in *WAI* (1995): 43-52 gives a comprehensive account of the textual history of Ahiqar.

[182] On Ahiqar and Tobit, see Greenfield, "The Wisdom of Ahiqar" *WAI* (1995): 45-48; "Ahiqar in the Book of Tobit" in *De la Tôrah au Messie* (1981): 329-336.

[183] H.A. Cazelles, "Le Personnage d'Achior dans le Livre de Judith" *Recherches de Science Religieuse* 39 (1951): 125-137; C.A. Moore, *Judith* AB 40 (New York, 1985): 161-169.

[184] Cowley, *Aramaic Papyri* (1923): 204-206.

written in Aramaic in the sixth or seventh century BCE. Its history suggests that it was reproduced in many ancient languages, such as Syrian, Armenian, Arabic, and was added to in the process. Grimme, who examined the parallels between Proverbs and Ahiqar, noted that the sayings section of the *Ahiqar* text came into the biblical text through the Aramaic version of the sayings. While the relationship between the story and the sayings is not clear, some hold that the proverb collection probably existed separately once. The Aramaic text containing fables, numerical sayings, admonitions, a prayer, and popular sayings exhibits a form similar to that of ancient Near Eastern wisdom.[185] Parallelism is frequent. Its contents are reminiscent of Proverbs with sayings about, the king, control of speech, discipline of the young, diligence, retribution, riches, and honesty.

Lindenberger notes, "Genuinely close parallels between the Aramaic proverbs and the Bible are few." The most commonly cited parallels are Prov 23:13-14 and lines 81-82 about the disciplining of children, Jer 9:22 [23] and line 207 concerning the rich man glorying in his riches. Parental discipline is also treated in other sayings of Ahiqar and in Proverbs.[186] Of the several other similarities between these two works the most noteworthy in this context is the statement about personified Wisdom (lines 94b-95) but the text is uncertain: "To gods also she is dear. F[or all time] the kingdom is [hers]. In he[av]en is she established, for the lord of holy ones has exalted [her]".[187] While this seems to resemble personified Wisdom in Proverbs, the term "wisdom", which does appear in lines 92 and 94a, has been partially restored.

Lang, who deems Wisdom to be a personification of school wisdom, argues that she speaks as a teacher, queen and goddess in Proverbs. He believes Israel to have had a polytheistic past in which a Canaanite goddess called "Wisdom" was honoured. He writes, "Wisdom is the goddess of school and instruction, or more precisely, the divine patroness of scribal education and training", and claims that the Ahiqar story "refers to a goddess who bears the same name as Israel's divine patroness of wisdom". Like the Ahiqar story as a whole, he suggests that the home of this goddess called Wisdom must be seventh-century Mesopotamia or perhaps Syria, but concedes that the passage on Wisdom in Ahiqar is too brief and fragmentary to allow for further conclusions. Portrayals of personified Wisdom in the Old Testament do not exhibit traits of an Assyrian goddess, nor is there any instance of speech by a wisdom goddess. While Lang cites other instances in the ancient Near East of female patron deities, no evidence is forthcoming to support the notion of a Canaanite goddess called Wisdom.[188]

Emerton notes that in the fragmentary text of Ahiqar it is never explicitly stated that Wisdom is a goddess, and it must be borne in mind that the word

---

[185] See B. Porten, *Elephantine Papyri*, ABD 2: 445-455.

[186] Lindenberger, *Proverbs of Ahiqar* (Baltimore, 1983): 20, 25; Prov 13:24; 19:18; 22:15; 29:15, 17; Sir 30:1-13; humility is mentioned in Ahiqar as it is in Sir 3:17; 4:8; Jam 1:9-10.

[187] The power of the soft tongue appears in lines 105-6; Prov 25:15; Sir 28:17; Hunger makes the bittersweet appears in lines 188; Prov 27:7; see *ANET*: 428.

[188] See Lang, *Wisdom* (1986): 129, 131-3, 172.

"wisdom" is restored in a lacuna.[189] While the themes are common in wisdom texts, dependence of one source on another has not been established. It is generally assumed by scholars that it was the author(s) of Proverbs who drew on the Ahiqar text or tradition. Although the Aramaic manuscript dates from the fifth century BCE, it is now generally agreed that the composition dates from the seventh or sixth century BCE, so it may be earlier than Proverbs 1-9.[190] McKane, in speaking of *Ahiqar*, comments on the deliberate literary use of imagery in praise of wisdom in lines 95ff.[191] Ginsberg claims that Wisdom is personified here. He observes that the way the text speaks of Wisdom is reminiscent of other personification passages (Prov 8:22-31; Job 28; Sir 1:1; 24:3) where Wisdom is present presiding over the creation of the world, and informs the created world as a principle of order. While the text never explicitly mentions Wisdom's status or function, it does affirm her exalted role and power. The Lord of Holiness or "holy ones" have exalted her, she is established in heaven and she exercises sovereignty in perpetuity. Donner also claims that Proverbs 8 draws on the personification of Wisdom in Ahiqar and regards it as a parallel development to Ma'at.[192] Day's comprehensive study provides convincing textual evidence from *Ahiqar* to support his claim for foreign Semitic influence on the wisdom of Israel. Besides evidence of a possible relationship between the Israelite figure of Wisdom and verses 94b-95 in *Ahiqar*, he distinguishes such features as the contrast between the righteous and the wicked, graded numerical proverbs, animal proverbs, the use of "my son", and "your mother's teaching".[193]

Conclusions

Given the generally accepted notion that relevant Mesopotamian texts originated before Proverbs 1-9 a search through Mesopotamian literature for likely influences on personification of Wisdom texts in Proverbs should prove fruitful. Surprisingly, evidence of any direct influence is elusive. Identifiable traces and fragments of Mesopotamian traditions in Proverbs 1-9 suggest the following outcomes, a creative use by the Israelite wisdom writers of some Mesopotamian material, a strong official monotheistic system in Israel reflected in Proverbs 1-9, and a consciously independent development of an Israelite identity in response to an imminent crisis.

---

[189] J.A. Emerton, review of B. Lang *Wisdom and the Book of Proverbs* in *VT* 37 (1987): 127; see Murphy, *Tree of Life* 2nd ed. (Grand Rapids, 1996): 158-159, and *ANET*: 428.

[190] See Lindenberger, *Proverbs of Ahiqar* (1983): 20; Kottsieper, *Die Sprache* (1990): 241-246.

[191] McKane, *Proverbs* (1970): 161; *ANET*: 428, n.6.

[192] H. Donner, "Die religionsgeschichtlichen Ursprünge," *ZÄS* 82 (1958): 8-18.

[193] J. Day, "Foreign Semitic Influence" *WAI* (1995): 55-70; Day's hypothesises that the Proverbs of Ahiqar predates the sections of Proverbs, which exhibit similar characteristics (Ahiqar lines 167-168; 171-173 Proverbs 10-15). A further possibility is that both may have used a common source.

The search for Wisdom's origins and emergence within the Israelite tradition has engaged and tantalised many scholars.[194]   In a hymn of self-praise (Prov 8:22-31) Wisdom speaks of YHWH "creating" her before creating the world, and twice uses the expression "brought forth". The biblical writers consider Wisdom, like all else, to be of divine origin (Jer 9:11; Job 32:8; Prov 8:22; Sir 24:3; Wis 7:25-26). Personified Wisdom upholds this belief. She claims to be neither great nor old, but to be "the first of his works of old" (Prov 8:22). This is clear in the six ways emphasised in Prov 8:23-29.[195]   This claim appears to be a metaphorical portrayal of Wisdom as the first of YHWH's works in the sense of "the best" of creation, that is "brought into being" by YHWH before all else. Proclamations attributed to the Wisdom figure (Prov 1:20-33; 8:1-36; 9:1-6) startle because of their unique claims made in a feminine voice. Thus Biblical language, which generally images God in masculine terms, is imbued with the feminine voice of Wisdom.

Through the wisdom writers' artistry and poetic imagination Wisdom becomes more than merely a simple description of a person's mode of thought and conduct; she is a unique character taking on a variety of expressions.[196] This poetic imaging of Wisdom draws on and transforms imagery from other ancient Near Eastern traditions to extend and develop insights within its own traditions. It focuses on Wisdom as a gift of the primordial creative power of YHWH. The introduction of personified Wisdom as a speaking figure gives a feminine voice to claims that traditionally came from God or from prophets of masculine gender. While hypotheses about Wisdom's origins abound, her introduction into the biblical text remains a matter of conjecture. Despite foreign influences and possible copying of "foreign goddesses", the Wisdom figure as the Hebrew tradition portrayed her is a unique figure within the biblical tradition.   Scholars have attempted to show that the originators of this figure drew on Ma'at, Asherah, Isis, Anat, or Gula from Egyptian and on Mesopotamian wisdom. All such studies remain inconclusive. Questions about why the wisdom authors created the Wisdom figure, how she functioned and was understood in the Israelite tradition continue to engage scholars and prompted this study. Wisdom's origins, it seems, cannot be adequately explained by invoking Egyptian, Mesopotamian, or other influences. Therefore, in chapter 2, I shall examine Proverbs 1-9 in an attempt to address the question: what situation made it necessary and acceptable in the Israelite tradition to personify Wisdom as a female figure who speaks for God?

---

[194] Keel, *Die Weisheit spielt vor Gott* (Freiburg, 1974):69-74; Lang, *Wisdom* (1986): 147-164; Murphy, *Tree of Life* (1990): 133-149.

[195] Sir 24:9 "created from the beginning, before the world".

[196] In Sir 24:10, Wisdom is in Jerusalem in the Holy Tent, possibly leading worship, and in Wis 7:25 Wisdom is described as an emanation of God.

Chapter 2

Wisdom Responds to a Crisis

Response to Exile: Israelites' Situation after 587 BCE

Personified Wisdom's origins and development within Proverbs 1-9 cannot be explained by invoking influences, or adaptations of possible prototypes, such as Egyptian Ma'at or Isis, or Mesopotamian Astarte or Gula. Investigations into Wisdom's origins so far have failed to yield conclusive evidence that the biblical Wisdom figure replicates an earlier, or contemporary figure in the literature of the ancient Near East. The emergence of this phenomenon in the Israelite tradition raises two crucial questions. What brought about or led to the personification of Wisdom in the Israelite tradition, and how did the tradition understand the role and function of this Wisdom figure?

Several assumptions underpin my claim that the creation of the Wisdom figure was a response to the events of 587 BCE. The first is that the Israelites' understanding of how YHWH acted for them, before the fall of Jerusalem (587 BCE), could not effectively address the crisis resulting from the loss of Jerusalem, the Temple, the Davidic kingship, control over the land, and the exile. A second point takes into account my arguments regarding the dating of Proverbs 1-9 suggesting an exilic to post-exilic dating because of the similarities with the Priestly account in Genesis. My third point is that Wisdom's appearances in public places that are never named suggest either places of no significance, or places in foreign territory. A fourth consideration is that in Wisdom's speeches prophetic motifs and styles, particularly from the exilic period, are common. A brief sketch of what is understood by Exile in this chapter follows.

From the first decades of the sixth century BCE the Exile—dated 597-587 BCE cf. 2 Kgs 24:1-25:26; Jer 52:30—became a pivotal event in the history of Israel, and occupies a major place in many Old Testament texts.[1] Although the number of those exiled may have been small, the memory and interpretation of the Exile became a key motif moulding the faith, thinking and communal understanding of all Jews.[2] The destruction of the Jerusalem Temple, which

---

[1] Comprehensive coverage of the exile is presented in among others in J. Maxwell Miller and John H. Hayes, *A History of Ancient Israel and Judah* (Philadelphia, 1986): 416-436; J. Bright, *A History of Israel* (Philadelphia, 1981): 343-372.

[2] D.L. Smith, *The Religion of the Landless: The Social Context of the Babylonian Exile* (Bloomington, 1989), proposes a contrary view on numbers exiled; J. Neusner, *Understanding Seeking Faith: Essays on the Case of Judaism* (Atlanta, 1986): 137-141; P. Joyce, *Divine Initiative and Human Response in Ezekiel* (Sheffield, 1989): 12-17; W.

guaranteed YHWH's presence in the land, as corroborated by Deuteronomic, prophetic and hymnic literature (Deut 12:5, 11; 2 Sam 24:16; 1 Kgs 8:12-13; 2 Kgs 18:4; 19:14; Pss 5:7; 11:4; 18:6; 27:4; 48:9; 68:17; 74:5-6; 79:1; 84; Amos 1:2; Isa 2:2-3; 6:1-4; Hab 2:20; Ezek 8; Jer 8:28; Lam 1:4, 10; 2:1, 6-7; 20) raised questions for the Israelites concerning YHWH's presence with them. With the removal of the king from Jerusalem questions and doubts arose about the Davidic monarchy's divine election as recounted in 2 Sam 7:1-15, and celebrated in the Jerusalem cult (Pss 2, 45, 89, 110, 132).

For the Israelites whose earlier understandings of YHWH were based on tangible evidence of his promises, divine election, sacredness of Zion, the Temple, the Davidic monarchy, the land of Israel, the Yahwistic symbol system, the Exilic crisis called the very foundations of their traditional beliefs, understandings, and assumptions into question.[3] It could be claimed that it was YHWH who became problematic rather than the issue of their sufferings. This, however, was not the only problem confronting Israel's wisdom writers. Causing more consternation was a face of God that signified indifference to the universe for which God was responsible. Proverbs 1-9 confronts this perceived impassivity of YHWH with the figure of personified Wisdom who makes claims that are made by YHWH in other contexts. Thus, a crisis of faith concerning YHWH was inevitable. In using the term 'crisis' I do not mean to suggest that the event called the Exile was a single event in the history of Israel that differed significantly from all other disasters faced by the Israelites. I use it more in the sense that the emergence of post-exilic Judaism is itself essentially one prolonged response to a crisis. This was the crisis of the dissolution of what remained of the nation of Israel in 587 BCE, the destruction of the Jerusalem Temple and the loss of autonomy over the land of Judah. With the Babylonian disaster, the political and intellectual life of Israel was demolished and the surviving Israelites had to work out a new way of living their traditions or accept assimilation by their neighbours. As the great civilizations of the ancient Near East, in their myths and rituals, had struggled with the threats and changes of nature and history, the Israelites similarly had to address the central issue of the meaning of the disaster that had befallen them (Isaiah 24-27; 65:17-25; Zechariah 14). In the face of a questioning or denial of divine justice, its defence was imperative.

Brueggemann, "A Shattered Transcendence? Exile and Restoration" in *Biblical Theology: Problems and Perspectives* (Nashville, 1995): 170.

[3]   It was not that their history had been free of other catastrophes, since their geographical location between Egypt and Mesopotamia meant frequent attacks on both their northern and southern borders; P. Ackroyd, *Exile and Restoration: A Study of Hebrew Thought of the Sixth Century B.C* (London, 1968); R. Klein, *Israel in Exile: A Theological Interpretation* (Philadelphia, 1979); E. Janssen, *Juda in der Exilszeit* (Göttingen, 1956); Joyce, *Divine Initiative* (1989).

Wisdom's Resources for Coping with Exile

Authoritative and established traditions in the Deuteronomic and Deuteronomistic literature incorporated pre-exilic traditions—that YHWH had made a covenant with Israel as a nation (Exod 19:5-6); had given them the Davidic monarchy (2 Sam 7:1-15); and that the Temple in Jerusalem ensured YHWH's presence with them—which the Jews of the Diaspora carried with them. Such convictions presupposed the existence of the community of Israel in their own land with the freedom to govern themselves. However, following the events of the Exile all such teachings required reinterpretation. Jewish existence among the nations called for a way of life that was authentic to Israel but possible in their changed circumstances. "For Jews these conditions could most readily be met by the wisdom tradition, which had ancient roots in Israelite life, and yet did not appeal for the authority and truth of its teachings to a unique revelation bestowed on Israel as a nation at the decisive moment of its origin".[4]

Wisdom, by providing the basis for a thorough revival of the Israelite world-view, offered vital resources for coping with the situation of Exile. It was in this transformation of the Israelite view of their relationship with YHWH that the role and function of personified Wisdom began to be shaped. To counteract the imminent danger of becoming absorbed by neighbouring peoples, wisdom writers drew on the idea that God created the world through wisdom (Prov 3:19), rather than relying on traditions restricted to the land of Israel. Such revisioning is clear in the figure of Wisdom who discourses at length (Prov 8:1-31) on her primary position in and presence at creation from the very beginning. A compelling tone characterises this speech, in which Wisdom celebrates, not so much her role in unlocking the mysteries of creation, as the belief that creation itself authenticates the truth of her claims. This is shown in the ascription to Wisdom of the goodness of the natural world, the order of human society, and gifts of prosperity and happiness. Wisdom claims to be the principle of harmony and goodness pervading all things, and weaving all aspects of life into a seamless unity with the Creator. Thus, she assures the Israelites of her role in their lives no matter where they are living. "By me kings reign, and rulers decree what is just" (Prov 8:15-16). Wisdom—the gift-giver—claims to be the source of just political power and wisdom thus evoking the qualities associated with the messianic king in Isaiah 1-5, and with God in Job 12:13-16.[5] Her claim to have been created as the first of creation suggests that she is the source of the justice and good order that are integral to the order of creation. The divine qualities of counsel, strength, and understanding are the basis for royal rule according to Job 12:13 and Isa 11:2 says they are the gift of YHWH's spirit to the messianic figure.

Contrary to the notion of an indifferent God, Proverbs 1-9 suggests YHWH is intrinsic to creation and simultaneously transcends all of creation.

---

[4]   R.E. Clements, *Wisdom in Theology* (Carlyle, 1992): 26.
[5]   R.E. Murphy, "Wisdom's Song: Proverbs 1:20-33", *CBQ* 49 (1986): 456-460.

Wisdom's presence and invitation in Proverbs 1-9 are not tied to the land of Israel, the Temple or the monarchy, nor is YHWH's presence in the world limited to the beliefs of his people in Babylon or Egypt or in the land of Israel. Wisdom above all portrays a God who acts for his creation. His presence and action convey the opposite of divine indifference on a large scale. The choice offered in Proverbs 1-9 between Wisdom and Folly draws attention to, and is framed against, the background of Israel's history of unfaithfulness. The issue is one of life or death, fidelity to YHWH or infidelity that leads to death. Personified Wisdom, in her claim to be the first creation and to her presence at creation, introduces a greatly expanded image of YHWH. In attributing the creation of the world and of herself to YHWH, she challenges the apparent indifference of God to the plight of the Israelites/Jews suffering the effects of their defeat by the Babylonians. YHWH, however, had not been overcome by a more powerful god, such as Marduk. Rather the survivors had misconstrued the covenant and what YHWH's care of them involved. In their expectations of YHWH they limited him and lost sight of the God of creation, the God of the universe, the God of the covenant with Noah (Gen 9:17). By focussing their relationship with YHWH on the covenant of land, Temple and monarchy they had not only restricted their view of God's actions, but were forgetting or ignoring their experience of YHWH's care for them as evidenced in the created world and in the many other events of their heritage.

In order to integrate their religious beliefs with the realities of the experienced world it was crucial that the survivors envisaged their lives as dependent on YHWH, their Creator, and addressed the crucial question of the justice, power and wisdom of YHWH. Thus, they revisioned their way of understanding YHWH and their relationship with him in such changed circumstances. The wisdom writers' portrayal of the Wisdom figure gives pride of place to the notion of a world shaped and governed by an all-wise, all-seeing, all-powerful Creator.[6] They endeavour to grapple intellectually with the problems posed by a belief system that proved inadequate when faced with the collapse of institutional structures and symbols viable only within very restricted parameters.[7] When the pre-exilic religious world-view, centred on the land, the Jerusalem temple, and the monarchy was confronted and undermined or destroyed, wisdom's adaptability to address the changed circumstances of the survivors enabled the fashioning and teaching of a tradition and way of life that were not dependent on Temple, monarchy or land.

Israel's dramatically changed sociological and political positions had a profound impact upon the wisdom writers' articulation of their tradition that now became markedly different from that which had earlier prevailed. In contrast to the Deuteronomic historians, who emphasised the saving interventions of YHWH, the wisdom writers deal directly with everyday life. Beliefs, and behaviour that were crucial for survival, were all to be found in the wisdom tradition as it dealt with

---

[6]   C. Westermann, *Theologie des Alten Testaments in Grundzügen* (Göttingen, 1978): 85-86.
[7]   L. Boström, *The Gods of the Sages. The Portrayal of God in the Book of Proverbs* (Stockholm, 1990); Clements, *Wisdom* (1992): 15.

everyday life. Wisdom could be applied outside the land of Israel in the Diaspora as its teaching was not confined to Israel, but was based on insight, experience, observation of behaviour and consequences, nor was its way of life dependent on a formal cult centre. All these requirements were present within the wisdom tradition, and were based on the belief that the world was the artistic handiwork of the benevolent Creator who sustained all of creation.

A significant factor in the wisdom writers' repertoire was the development of the figure of Wisdom as a personal mediator for the people of Israel, rather than relying on Israelite covenantal presuppositions.[8] Such a creative approach to Israel's inheritance led to the reformulation and reordering of ancient Israel's religious symbolism, mythology and ideas.[9] As noted by Clements, the worshipper's attitude of mind and intention came to be accounted more important than actual performance of ritual. Fundamental abstract notions such as "the fear of the Lord" and "the way of wisdom" were used to coordinate and integrate a variety of inherited traditions.[10] Personified Wisdom in Proverbs 1-9, in addressing the people in the open—the market places, the city, the pathway, city walls—and in inviting all to a banquet in her house, suggests a situation removed from formal cult or royal settings. A dispersed people could be reached by Wisdom no matter how hostile or foreign the environment. Her teaching, admonitions and invitations do not require a cult for their setting or legitimation. So by vividly portraying and expressing aspects of wisdom that spoke to the contemporary situation in the figure of Wisdom, the wisdom writers sought to reinterpret and creatively present Jewish tradition with a new voice in a variety of settings. Significantly, this process of reinterpretation was effected most distinctively in areas where previously the cult and monarchy were foremost. With the loss of the monarchy and the Temple, a new focus had to be found for reinterpreted Jewish beliefs, practice and traditions. Wisdom, personified as the voice of YHWH—the designer and Creator of the world—was conceived as the focus for Israelite/Jewish tradition in this time of transition.

Whether Wisdom consequently contributed to the erosion and ultimate displacement of the earlier wisdom world-view, depends on the view held concerning Wisdom's origins.[11] As discussed in chapter 1 there is no conclusive evidence to support claims that personified Wisdom had her origins as a goddess. Nor is there convincing evidence that Wisdom was conceived of in opposition to the cult. However, it seems most likely that the wisdom writers in exilic times were obliged by their circumstances to extend the margins of the earlier cultic views

---

[8] R.E. Clements, "Wisdom and Old Testament Theology" in *WAI* (1995): 273; H. Cazelles, "Les débuts de la sagesse en Israel" *SPOA* (1963): 27-40.

[9] H.-J Hermisson, *Sprache und Ritus im altisraelitischen Kult: zur 'Spiritualisierung' der Kultbegriffe im Alten Testament* (Neukirchen-Vluyn, 1965).

[10] Clements, "Wisdom and Old Testament Theology" in *WAI* (1995): 274; M.E. Barré, "Fear of God and the World of Wisdom" *Biblical Theology Bulletin* 11 (1981): 41-43.

[11] Clements, *Wisdom in Theology* (1992): 52-64, makes the claim that the early wisdom world-view had fundamentally mythological foundations, centred in the cult.

concerning worship, sacred space, land, work, social structure and human behaviour. Wisdom addresses aspects of human relationships pertaining to living a good life as having a universal application. Legitimating this realisation is the fundamental tenet of wisdom, the 'fear of the Lord'. The Wisdom figure demands commitment to the truths she proclaims. Reverence for YHWH, Creator and designer of all creation, is proclaimed as the 'beginning' of wisdom. To accept Wisdom as a trustworthy guide in life demands an attitude of reverential fear, the indispensable first step of commitment without which the voice of Wisdom cannot be heard. Such an appeal to God, the divine source of wisdom and its personification means that Wisdom becomes an outstanding and integral feature of Jewish life and of the Bible.

Wisdom's Role in Proverbs 1-9

After 587 BCE, the Israelites' effective survival and development as a religiously distinct group, required either adaptation to being in the land without structures previously in place (Temple, monarchy, leadership), or a transition to becoming a scattered Diaspora among many nations. Central to considerations concerning recovery was the identification of beliefs and practices that would sustain the Israelite religious heritage. It is no accident that the literature of the exilic and post-exilic era often addresses the notion of chaos and creation as in Psalm 74, Proverbs 1-9, and Job.

Wisdom Justifies the Ways of YHWH

To develop and express their Jewish tradition, identity, and beliefs in new and different settings survivors had to reinterpret their tradition. Pre-exilic teaching was inadequate in this new situation as is evident in the Deuteronomistic allusions to the suffering of the people and the dissolution of their hopes (2 Kgs 23:29; 25:1-3, 9).[12] Transformation of the religious tradition was imperative to counteract the prospect of assimilation or extinction (Jer 44:16-18).[13] Such reconstruction demanded that the envisioning of a new world in which YHWH would continue to be the God of the Israelites and they YHWH's people, even if living in foreign lands. The dimension of the unique pre-exilic identity claimed by Israel was now almost wholly subsumed as part of a prophetic eschatology.[14] This phenomenon

---

[12] S.B. Frost, "The Death of Josiah: A Conspiracy of Silence," *JBL* 87 (1968): 369-382.

[13] D.F. Morgan, *Between Text and Community: The "Writings" in Canonical Interpretation* (Minneapolis, 1990) on the power of the exilic experience.
H.G.M. Williamson, "The Concept of Israel in Transition" in R.E. Clements, ed., *The World of Ancient Israel* (Cambridge, 1989): 141-162, discusses this development; E.M. Meyers, "The Persian Period and the Judaean Restoration: From Zerubbabel to Nehemiah" in P.D. Miller, P.D. Hanson, and S. D. McBride, eds. *Ancient Israelite Religion [AIR]* (Philadelphia, 1987): 509-521, gives the political background.

appears, among others, in Jeremiah, Ezekiel, and Isaiah 40-65. Each of these texts articulates the faith and experience of exilic and post-exilic Judaism by invoking Exile as the governing metaphor.[15] The concept of Torah also came to be developed (Deuteronomy 4 & 30; Sir 24:1-34; Bar 3:9-4:4), with a marked wisdom influence, to provide a basis of teaching which could be observed both in Judah and in the dispersion.[16] In time, this restoration focused upon the notion of a written Torah and its development throughout Jewish life. Wisdom's central role in this development can be seen in both the Wisdom of Ben Sira and Baruch, not just in the bringing together of Wisdom and Torah, but also in their identification.[17]

It is not surprising that theodicy became an issue of pressing concern following 587 BCE when both the justice and providence of God at work in creation came under serious questioning in the wisdom tradition,[18] as it did, for example, in Jeremiah (12:1-13),[19] Habakkuk (3:17-19),[20] and Psalm 89.[21] Some would agree with Crenshaw's claims that "such salvaging of God's honour at the expense of human integrity resulted in a grandiose interpretation of history that

---

[15] R.P. Carroll, *Jeremiah* (Philadelphia, 1986). W.A. McKane, *A Critical and Exegetical Commentary on Jeremiah: Jeremiah I-XXV* (Edinburgh, 1986); J. Lust, "'Gathering and Return' in Jeremiah and Ezekiel", in M. Bogaert, ed. *Le Livre de Jérémie* (Leuven, 1981): 119-142; T.M. Raitt, *A Theology of Exile: Judgment and Deliverance in Jeremiah and Ezekiel* (Philadelphia, 1977); K. Carley, *The Book of the Prophet Ezekiel* CBC (Cambridge, 1974); J. Lust, *Ezekiel and his Book* (Leuven, 1986); B. Lindars, "Good Tidings to Zion: Interpreting Deutero-Isaiah Today," *BJRL* 68 (1985-6): 473-497; P.D. Miscall, *Isaiah* (Sheffield, 1993); Williamson, "Israel in Transition" *The World of Ancient Israel* (1989): 141-161.

[16] E. Würthwein, "Der Sinn des Gesetzes im Alten Testament" in *Zeitschrift für Theologie und Kirche* 55 (1958): 255-270.

[17] G. Sheppard, *Wisdom as a Hermeneutical Construct* (Berlin, 1980); R.E. Clements "Wisdom" in D.A. Carson and H.G.M. Williamson, eds. *It is Written. Scripture Citing Scripture. Essays in Honour of Barnabas Lindars* [*It is Written*] (Cambridge, 1988): 75ff.

[18] Schmid, *Wesen und Geschichte* (1966) argued that Israelite wisdom responded to historical developments within the life of the community. R.E. Murphy, "Assumptions and Problems" *CBQ* 29 (1967): 102-112, and "Wisdom Theses" (1976): 187-200, claim that Schmid did not succeed in demonstrating links between the development of Israelite wisdom and history; cf. J.W. Jenks, "Theological Presuppositions of Israel's Wisdom Literature," *HBT* 7/1 (1985): 43-75.

[19] Jeremiah's poignant cry for justice begins with a confession of YHWH's righteousness (Jer 12:1), is followed by a prophetic accusation that YHWH prospers the wicked, and a divine oracle of hatred for a covenanted people (12:5-13).

[20] Habakkuk affirms God's justice in the face of all evidence to the contrary. The magnificence of faith in his final hymn despite the bleak situation suggested is a rare occurrence in the Old Testament. He vows that even the failure of all food crops, which presumably would mean famine, would not prevent him from rejoicing in God.

[21] Psalm 89 reads like a liturgical lament agonizing over the failure of God to keep his promise to David. In the listing of the mercies of YHWH as seen in his victory over chaos and the election of David, a prophetic oracle promising the permanence of the Davidic dynasty, and a lament over the collapse of that dynasty.

amounted to a monumental theodicy".[22] Davidson provides a brief history of the
use of the term 'theodicy' and discusses the conditions necessary for a problem of
theodicy to arise. He claims that texts such as Job portray God as too mysterious to
be the object of human scrutiny and thus emphasise the mystery and transcendence
of God as an essential element in Israel's faith.[23] This point is also explored by
Nicholson, who in a discussion of theodicy in Job, maintains that the task of
theodicy is to acquit God of any evil that may befall the righteous, thereby giving
meaning to misfortune.[24]

Clements, who addresses the issue of theodicy in wisdom, makes a crucial
point when he says, "The very fact that wisdom offered the most universal and
international body of teaching about life, morality and the nature of reality, made it
the natural resource for coping with the new situation. For a time, wisdom held a
unique key to understanding the new world in which Jews found themselves".[25] In
tracing theodicy in the Old Testament—through its vivid delineation in Job and its
challenge in Qoheleth—Crenshaw notes that only the wisdom tradition explores
the full range of this most central of theological problems in the Old Testament.[26]
He contends that the questioning of divine justice resulted in a theological
restructuring of the tradition's understanding of God and the world. He locates
theodicy within creation and outlines its distinctive features as the threat of chaos
in the cosmic, political, and social realms, thus initiating a response through
creation theology.

Crenshaw sees creation functioning primarily as a defence of divine
justice; and the centrality of God's integrity to Israelite literature placed creation
theology at the centre of the theological enterprise.[27] In the midst of chaos, an
appeal to creation by Wisdom affirms the ongoing possibility that her audience can
discover meaning in their present situation. This defensible doctrine of theodicy, is
suggested in the textual settings of Wisdom's speeches, which are located in the
midst of series of instructions, prayers, and prosaic advice concerning everyday
life, such as the avoidance of sinners (Prov 1:8-19), and of Folly, and the strange or

---

[22] J.L. Crenshaw, "The Shift from Theodicy to Anthropodicy" in J.L Crenshaw ed. *Theodicy in the Old Testament* (Philadelphia, 1983): 7.

[23] R. Davidson, *Wisdom and Worship* (London, 1990): 65-81.

[24] E.W. Nicholson, "The Limits of Theodicy" in *WAI* (Cambridge, 1995): 71-82.

[25] Clements, *Wisdom* (1992): 25.

[26] J.L. Crenshaw, "Popular Questioning of the Justice of God in Ancient Israel" *ZAW* 82 (1970): 380-395 went on to expand and nuance this theme in later publications, such as, "In Search of Divine Presence" *Review and Expositor* 74 (1977): 353-369; "The Human Dilemma and Literature of Dissent" in D.A. Knight, ed. *Tradition and Theology in the Old Testament* (Philadelphia, 1977): 235-258; see also, W. Brueggemann, "A Shattered Transcendence? Exile and Restoration" in *Biblical Theology: Problems and Perspectives* (Nashville, 1995): 169-182; R.E. Friedman, *The Exile and Biblical Narrative* (Chico, 1981); J.D. Levenson, *Creation and the Persistence of Evil* (San Francisco, 1988).

[27] J.L. Crenshaw, "Prolegomenon" in *SAIW* (New York, 1976); "Method in Determining Wisdom Influence upon 'Historical' Literature" *JBL* 88 (1969): 130-133.

foreign woman, who bring death (Prov 2:1-22; 6:20-7:1-27; 9:7-12).[28] Scholars investigating the final editing of Old Testament texts have observed that the principal motive underlying the question of the justice of God as fundamental to understanding some biblical texts (Jeremiah, Habakkuk, Job, Qoheleth, Psalm 73, Wisdom of Ben Sira) was theodicy in connection with the Exile.[29] Crenshaw, however, may be alone in suggesting, "Perhaps the personification of wisdom deserves mention, inasmuch as this intriguing figure functions in God's stead, thus ensuring divine presence and power to an age that saw no visible evidence of such."[30]

Wisdom in Harmony with Monotheism

Clearly, Wisdom in Proverbs 1-9 is in accord with monotheism. The wisdom writers insist that there is but one God and that this deity is known by the name YHWH. Over recent decades history of religion scholars have insisted that the popular religion of pre-exilic Israelites featured widespread reverence for other deities, besides and sometimes instead of YHWH.[31] Wisdom writers do not

---

[28] J.L. Crenshaw, "In Search of Divine Presence" *Review and Expositor* 74 (1977): 364, proposing anthropology as the key to understanding wisdom notes, "The way of looking at things begins with humans as the fundamental point of orientation . . . It believes that all essential answers can be learned by experience".

[29] Perdue, *Wisdom and Creation* (1994): 47; R.C. Van Leeuwen, "The Sage in the Prophetic Literature" in *SIANE* (1990): 295-306; R.E. Clements "Patterns in the Prophetic Canon" in G.W. Coats, et al., eds., *Canon and Authority* (Philadelphia, 1987): 42-55; "Prophecy as Literature: A Re-Appraisal" in D.G. Miller, ed., *The Hermeneutical Quest* (Allison Park, 1986): 59-75; M. Fishbane, *Biblical Interpretation in Ancient Israel* (Oxford, 1985); J.L. Crenshaw, *Whirlpool of Torment* (Philadelphia, 1985); "The Shift from Theodicy to Anthropodicy" (Philadelphia, 1983): 1-16; "Popular Questioning of the Justice of God" *ZAW* 82 (1970): 380-395 claimed "in essence theodicy is the search for a solution to the problem of meaning" but made no reference to the personification of Wisdom at this point; "In Search of Divine Presence" *Review and Expositor* (1977): 353-369; R.N. Whybray, "Prophecy as Wisdom", in R. Coggins, A. Phillips, and M. Knibb, eds., *Israels's Prophetic Tradition. Essays in Honor of Peter R. Ackroyd* [*IPT*] Cambridge, 1982): 181-199; D.F. Morgan, *Wisdom in Old Testament Traditions* (Oxford 1981): 76-83; J.M. Roberts, "Of Signs, Prophets, and Time Limits: A Note on Ps 74:9" *CBQ* 39 (1977): 474-481; "The Human Dilemma and Literature of Dissent" in D.A. Knight, ed., *Tradition and Theology in the Old Testament* (Philadelphia, 1974): 235-258; R.W. Klein, "A Theology for Exiles: The Kingship of Yahweh" *Dialog 17* (1978): 128-134; Mack, "Wisdom Myth" *Int 24* (1970): 46-60; A. Jäger, "Theodizee und Anthorpodizee bei Karl Marx" *Schweizerische Theologische Umschau* 37 (1967): 14-23.

[30] Crenshaw, "Shift from Theodicy" in *Theodicy in the Old Testament* [*TOT*] (1983): 12.

[31] The question of monotheism in Israelite religious tradition is a complex one when set against the wider Near Eastern background. M.S. Smith, *The Early History of God* (1990) notes that wisdom's assumption of a unifying order that prevailed throughout the experienced world assisted in promoting a monotheistic world-view appears very likely. At the same time, a monotheistic religious position fostered the intellectual perspectives

conceive of the divine realm as the nation of Israel alone. YHWH is not merely "the God of Israel", but God who pervades all. Wisdom is with YHWH who works through her, but the figure of Wisdom is in no sense another deity alongside YHWH. Attempts by scholars to find, in the claims of Wisdom in Proverbs 8, remnants of an underlying earlier belief in some ancient Near Eastern goddess, or Israelite goddess of wisdom, misread the significance of this important passage. Personified Wisdom as depicted here is clearly in no sense intended as 'other than' or equal to YHWH. Rather, she is the first of the creation uniting the Creator's design in her regard with God's ongoing creative expression in the world. Through Wisdom, the created world can know God and discover the purpose and grandeur of God. Encompassed by this figure are aspects of the immanence and transcendence of the deity.

In Proverbs, the use of the divine name implies the presence and action of the divine. Therefore, it is not surprising that the distinctively Hebrew 'YHWH' is the most commonly used title for the deity in Proverbs, with the less distinctive 'God' occurring infrequently.[32] Such usage marks the most decisive feature of the assimilation of the wisdom tradition to the religious ethos of Israel. The invocation of the name of YHWH carries with it implications about the nature and intentions of the One to whom it is addressed. This title is clearly Israelite but does not have the specific cultic or national tenor suggested by such titles as 'the God of Israel' or 'the God of Jacob'.[33] As noted earlier, the absence from wisdom teaching of any reference to Israel's occupation of a special land, its distinctive genealogical origin, the covenant, the election of Israel, its royal dynasty, or the Temple, can hardly be mere oversight, but more likely an indication of the irrelevance of these traditions for the audience. Wisdom's universal claims promote the view that YHWH is a universal God. Contributing to the notion of Israel as a unique people is that the 'fear of the Lord', which enables them to respond to YHWH through the dictates of Wisdom pervading all creation. Thus Israel's uniqueness is in the uniqueness of Wisdom who is one with the Creator, a notion affirming Judaism's monotheistic faith.

Since personified Wisdom has universal influence, she transcends national barriers, and functions throughout time and space. The positing of Wisdom's pre-temporal origin 'before creation' (Prov 8:22) serves to reinforce her transcendent divine quality. As Wisdom is with YHWH from the beginning, attempts to find a goddess of wisdom in the figure portrayed in Proverbs 8 are unproductive.[34] Any suggestion that the Creator needed or had an assistant to help

---

adopted by wisdom. See J.S. Holladay "Religion in Israel and Judah under the Monarchy: An Explicitly Archaeological Approach" in *SIANE* (1987): 249-299.

[32] The word YHWH appears at least 85 times in Proverbs, and the word God 7 times.

[33] Both these titles appear, for example, in several Psalms and in Isaiah and Jeremiah.

[34] Whybray, "Proverbs 8:22-31 and its Supposed Prototypes' *VT* 15 (1965): 504-514; Camp, *Wisdom and the Feminine* (1985): 13, claims "personified Wisdom is a literary figure built up of literary images".

him create and govern the universe is absent from the Old Testament.[35] Wisdom's insistence on YHWH as sole Creator coincides with the thought in Isa 40:13-14.

> Who has directed the Spirit of the Lord or as his counsellor has instructed him?
> Whom did he consult for his enlightenment,
> and who taught him the path of justice, and taught him knowledge,
> and showed him the way of understanding? (Isa 40:13-14)

The created works of God enable the Wisdom of God to be seen and understood by human beings, particularly in the order of the universe (Prov 3:19-20; 8:22-36; Ps 104:24).[36] Whybray claims that verses 19-20 depict Wisdom as an attribute of God, with whom she was associated in the creation.[37] It is in the realm of monotheistic belief that the basic insights of Wisdom for understanding and mastering life are most vividly portrayed. Such emphasis on YHWH as sole Creator and on Wisdom's presence at creation may also be a polemic against Mesopotamian creation accounts in which the task of creation was shared by different deities, and may suggest that Wisdom is speaking out of an exilic context.

Because wisdom teaching, which was usually anonymous, lacked any specific historical context, and did not deal with the *Heilsgeschichte* narratives, it could concentrate on other timeless truths. On a functional level, the figure of Wisdom manifests the wisdom writers' remarkable facility in incorporating new ideas to revitalise old religious rites and institutions. This is evident in Wisdom's calling, inviting, and celebrating with all who attend to her, and her threats against those who show no interest in her teachings. In this figure, YHWH comes to meet his creatures. Those who wish to be Wisdom's disciples must reject all the attractions of Wisdom's competitor, Folly, whose power to destroy is masked by her likeness to Wisdom.

Choosing Between Life and Death

Wisdom's appearances in Proverbs 1-9 with her emphases on the choice of life in opposition to death may suggest an exilic context for these portrayals and an Israelite theodicy to deal with the losses sustained at the hands of the Babylonians. Wisdom alternates with, and is thrown into relief by, a series of contrasting "wicked/foolish" female characters against whom the Instructions in chapters 2, 5, 6, 7, and 9 counsel. The author offers a stark choice between Wisdom, the life-giver; and Wisdom's antitheses, the bringers of death, (Prov 2:16; 5:3a; 5:20; 6:24; 7:5a); מֵאִשָּׁה זָרָה מִנׇּכְרִיָּה "the strange/loose woman"; "the adventuress/foreign woman"; "the evil woman" אֵשֶׁת רָע (6:24); "the harlot" אִשָּׁה זוֹנָה (6:26a); "a

---

[35] Whybray, *Heavenly Counsellor* (1971).
[36] Wisdom's function in the creation of the world in Prov 3:19-20 seems to foreshadow the description in 8:22f.
[37] See R.N. Whybray, Wisdom *in Proverbs* (1965): 98-100. For Wisdom's claims regarding creation favour a monotheistic interpretation of the divine activity.

woman dressed as a harlot" אִשָּׁה שִׁית זוֹנָה (7:10); "another's wife" (6:26b; 6:29a).[38] Wisdom's prophet-like utterances (1:20-33; 8:1-36; 9:1-6) are set against the "smooth words" of the "foreign/wicked woman" and Folly's persuasive speeches (2:16-19; 5:3-5; 6:24ff. 7:5-27; 9:13-19).[39] Wisdom offers her followers the gift of life, while her opposites offer their followers pleasures that will take them to Sheol. Vivid depictions of the dangers of falling into the clutches of immoral strange or foreign women whose seductions lead to death suggest a kind of xenophobia inspired by the perceived dangers of association with "foreign" women. This teaching may have been directed to Israelites generally, and not only to the exiles in Babylon, warning them about the dangers of association with foreign women, the risk of becoming assimilated into surrounding or prevailing cultures, and generally of being seduced by "foreign" wisdom. Prov 2:16-19 introduces the contrasting theme of the "strange woman" or "adventuress/foreign woman" by painting a graphic picture of a female figure who lures the young to her house, which is the anteroom to death (Prov 2:16-19).[40]

In recent writings, Blenkinsopp claims that personified Wisdom was created in reaction to the "strange woman". He begins with the assumption that the Wisdom figure of Proverbs 1-9 was conceived as a counter to the influence of the Outsider Woman. This figure he regards as the primary symbolic persona in these chapters, and holds that she represents alien cults, especially those with a strong sexual component.[41] Behind this symbol are the goddess cults, especially those of

---

[38] A persistent feature of Proverbs is a preoccupation with female figures, not only with Wisdom and Folly but also with, "wife of your youth" (5:18) "neighbour's wife" (6:29); "a good wife" (12:4; 31:10); "a wife" (18:22); "a wife's quarrelling" (19:13); "a prudent wife" (19:14); "your mother's teaching" (1:8; 6:20); "mother" (4:3; 10:1; 15:20; 19:26; 20:20; 23:22,25; 28:24; 29:15; 30:11,17; 31:1); "gracious woman" (11:16); "beautiful woman without discretion" (11:22); "contentious woman" (25:24; 27:15); "a woman who fears the Lord" (31:30). See Humbert, "La 'Femme étrangère' du livre des Proverbes" *Revue des Études Sémitique* 6/2 (1937): 49-64 and "Les adjectifs 'Zâr' et 'Nokri' et la 'Femme Étrangère' des Proverbes Bibliques" in *Melanges Syriens* (1939): 259-266.

[39] R.E. Murphy, "Wisdom and Eros in Prov. 1-9" *CBQ* 50 (1988): 600-603; B. Lang, *Die weisheitliche Lehrrede* (Stuttgart, 1972): 87-88, sees four female figures in Prov 2-9, Wisdom, Folly, the immoral woman, foreign woman, and the wife, and considers the overtones peculiar to Israelite Instructions. Some scholars see Wisdom as the hierodule who looks out of her latticed window at foolish youths too easily seduced by the wiles of Folly (Prov 7:6-23); Albright, "Canaanite-Phoenician Sources" *VTSup* 3 (1955): 1-15; Boström, *Proverbiastudien* (1935); The first major section of Wisdom of Ben Sira concludes with a discussion of sexual sins (Sir 23:16-27), and the adulterous woman appears as a foil or counterpart to personified Wisdom who is celebrated in Sir 24:1-34; 51:13-22.

[40] The contrast between personified Wisdom and the foreign/wicked woman of Prov 1:20-2:19 may be echoed in 4Q184. Investigation of this possibility is beyond the scope of the present work. See J. Allegro, *Discoveries in the Judaean Desert of Jordan* [*DJDJ*]: 5:82-84, and the review by J. Strugnell in *RevD* 7 (1970): 263-268; the two women in Revelations chapters 12, 17 and 18 make an interesting contrast.

[41] J. Blenkinsopp, *Sage, Priest, and Prophet* (Louisville, 1995): 43-44; "The Social Context

Asherah. Undoubtedly, levels of meaning are embedded in both the figure of Wisdom and in the foreign/outsider/adventuress women figures. However, undisputed conclusions are impossible since no clear evidence of the direction of influences has been produced. The outsider woman continues to provoke discussion as the recent work by Maier suggests.[42] She analyses the pertinent texts, presents some new insights and situates this figure in a post-exilic context to which she clearly belongs.

Obedience to Wisdom's instructions (2:2-4, 9-15) ensures an attachment to Wisdom who sets the seeker on the right path (2:8-11), and saves him from the temptation to consort with purveyors of death, alliances that lead irrevocably to death. The admonitions concerning the pursuit of Wisdom and the seductions of the "strange/foreign woman" in Proverbs 1-9 are couched in the language of erotic love.[43] Some regard these texts as a warning against sexual immorality, a stock theme of ancient Near Eastern wisdom, particularly in Egyptian Instructions. However, such an interpretation overlooks the allusion to the woman as "strange" or "foreign". Avoidance of death by faithfulness to one's present or future wife, "the wife of your youth", and thus to Wisdom is more likely at the heart of all these warnings: "Her feet go down to death; her steps follow the path to Sheol" (Prov 5:5). "Drink water from your own cistern, flowing water from your own well" (5:15).[44]

An urgent warning against the "smooth-talking adulteress" is picked up again in 6:20-35 with a listing of the negative results to be expected by those who indulge in adultery or illicit sex. Can fire be carried in the bosom without burning one's clothes? Or can one walk on hot coals without scorching the feet? (6:27-28) Comparable to the invitation to listen to the female figure of Wisdom is seduction by the female figure of Folly.[45] Israel's history of unfaithfulness in her readiness to be seduced by other gods—Baals and Asherahs—is attested often. Some identify the "strange woman" as a devotee of a Canaanite fertility cult that attracted so many Israelites, but this identification is difficult to establish.[46] The warnings concern fidelity to the pursuit of Wisdom by the avoidance of all that is "foreign", "foolish", or untrue to the Israelite heritage. Wisdom will preserve the young "from the loose woman" מֵאִשָּׁה זָרָה מִנָּכְרִיָּה אֲמָרֶיהָ "from the adventuress" (Prov 7:5) if they "say to Wisdom 'you are my sister' and call insight your intimate friend" (Prov 7:4). In depicting a young man's meeting with "a woman dressed as a harlot" (Prov 7:7-10), the writer envisages the seduction of the young by the smooth-

---

of the 'Outsider Woman' in Proverbs 1-9" *Biblica* 72 (1991): 457-472.
[42] C. Maier, *Die "Fremde Frau" in Proverbien 1-9* (Göttingen, 1995).
[43] References to sexual conduct are rare in the rest of Proverbs.
[44] A case could be made here that "the wife of your youth" is Wisdom.
[45] The use of sexual imagery in the Bible to express fidelity or infidelity to God is well known as in the theme of the unfaithful wife in Hosea 1-3.
[46] Boström proposes such an identification in *Proverbiastudien* (1935): 42; see J. Day, "Yahweh and the God and Goddesses of Canaan," in *Ein Gott Allein* (1994): 181-196.

talking woman.[47] A striking feature of this vivid scene (Prov 7:14-20) where the "smooth-talking" woman speaks at length, is the emphasis upon speech, almost as if the seduction were verbal not sexual (6:24; 7:5). The power of the word to persuade, even to seduce, is highlighted as much as sexual involvement itself.[48]

Interestingly images of Wisdom as a giver of life appear in Prov 3:16-18 where Wisdom has "long life in her right hand, in her left, riches and honour" (3:16), "she is a tree of life to those who lay hold of her; those who hold her fast are called happy" (3:18). In this vivid turn of a Genesis metaphor Wisdom is the "tree of life" that gives her fruit, which is life.[49] Ironically in Genesis this image portrays a contrasting view "lest he [Adam] put forth his hand and take also of the tree of life and eat, and live forever, therefore YHWH sent him forth from the garden" (Gen 3:22-23). The notion of the foreign woman in Proverbs is examined in a recent article by Cook, who claims that in Proverbs the figure of the "loose woman" (2:16a; 5:3a; 5:20; 7:5a) functions as a metaphor for Folly, the adversary of Wisdom. He finds, in the Septuagint version of Proverbs, enlightening perspectives on the essence of this figure. She is depicted by the Septuagint translator as a foreign woman and, more specifically as foreign wisdom in Proverbs 2, 5, 6, 7, 9. The Jewish concepts of good and evil inclinations that are the so-called היצר הטוב and היצר הרע are rendered by the Greek βουλὴ καλὴ "the good", those who are guided by good counsel (Prov 2:11), and βουλὴ κακὴ "the bad", those who follow bad counsel (Prov 2:16).[50] The foreign woman is identified as βουλὴ κακὴ "bad counsel", so it is foreign wisdom that misleads, rather than sexual transgression. Cook claims that the translator stresses this interpretation in chapters 1-9. Foreign entities, waters, rivers and fountains, are used as metaphors for foreign, or dangerous wisdom, to warn the audience against Greek or foreign wisdom of the Hellenistic period, ca. 200 BCE.[51]

Washington claims that women so designated were not only outsiders in the community, but represented a genuine danger to its system of land holdings. He examines economic factors that led to the polemic against "foreign" women in Proverbs 1-9. Corporate survival was put at risk when such women took advantage

---

[47] M. Heijerman, "Who Would Blame Her? The 'Strange' Woman of Proverbs 7," in F. van Dijk-Hemmes and A. Brenner, eds. *Reflections on Theology and Gender* (Kampen, 1994): 21-31 presents a reader-response analysis of Proverbs 7 in which she develops three portraits of the woman described here: A Mother's Rival, A Man's Scapegoat, and A Needy Woman. She concludes that the "strange woman" teaches that chaos and creativity are closely linked.

[48] See J.-N. Aletti, "Séduction et parole en Proverbes I-IX," *VT* 27 (1977): 129-144.

[49] In addition to its appearance in Prov 3:18, "tree of life" occurs several times in Proverbs 11:30; 13:12; 15:4, and once in Ezek 47:12 with imagery of health-giving trees, while the idea of a just person being like a green tree occurs in Ps 52:8; Prov 11:13; Sir 24:13-20. However, none of these uses equates Wisdom with "the tree of life" as in Prov 3:18. See R. Marcus, "The Tree of Life in the Book of Proverbs" *JBL* 62 (1943): 117-120.

[50] J. Bowker, *The Targums and Rabbinic Literature* (Cambridge, 1969): 116.

[51] J. Cook, "'Iššah Zara' (Proverbs 1-9 Septuagint): A Metaphor for Foreign Wisdom?" *ZAW* 106 (1994): 458-476.

of their increasing ability to hold land during the Persian period. Thus, Washington views the prohibition of exogamous marriage not just as a religious matter, or an element of a patrilineal system but also as an attempt to maintain communal claims in a land where the Jews lived at the pleasure of the Persians.[52] Blenkinsopp also claims that in Proverbs 1-9 Wisdom and her opposite, the Outsider Woman, were created during the early second-temple period as a cautionary instruction to discourage exogamous marriages among returned exiles. The personification of Wisdom is, he suggests, "a secondary elaboration, a counter to the 'Outsider Woman' in the context of the exogamy-endogamy issue".[53] Bonora takes a different view and regards the figure of the "foreign woman" as a metaphor for all deviations from home and tradition, including foreign customs, prostitution, and other kinds of evil, but does not think that she always represents something literally foreign.[54] He regards the appearance of the "foreign woman" in Proverbs 1-9 as reflecting the beginning of the Diaspora, when a great need to preserve traditions existed, and does not see the metaphor as suggesting a negative view of women, since Wisdom is also a woman in Proverbs.[55]

Boström also investigated the "strange woman" rather than personified Wisdom,[56] and argued that the key text in Proverbs 1-9 is the "woman dressed as a harlot" אִשָּׁה שִׁית זוֹנָה (Prov 7:10), whom he equated with the "strange woman" אִשָּׁה זָרָה (Prov 2:16) and the "adventuress/foreign woman" נָכְרִי.[57] He noted that the Wisdom figure, whom he viewed as a summary of the wisdom teacher's instruction brought into intimate relationship with YHWH religion, is a replacement for and protection against the love goddess.[58]

Implied in the final two contrasting vignettes of Wisdom (9:1-6) and Folly (9:13-18) in their distinctive settings and roles is a choice between life and death. The close similarity between the two scenes serves to highlight the perception and discernment needed to make the 'right' choice. Both Wisdom and Folly invite the "simple" to their banquets in their respective houses (9:1-5, 14-17).[59] This pericope has echoes of Isa 25:6 where an equally rich banquet is described. The detailed

---

[52] H.C. Washington, "The Strange Woman of Proverbs 1-9 and Post-Exilic Judaean Society," in Athalya Brenner, ed., *A Feminist Companion to Wisdom Literature* (Sheffield, 1995): 157-184.

[53] J. Blenkinsopp, "The Social Context of the Outsider Woman in Proverbs 1-9" *Bib* 72 (1991): 457, 467.

[54] A. Bonora, "La 'donna straniera' in Pr 1-9," *RSB* 6 (1994): 101-109.

[55] Bonora cites Jezebel as the best biblical example of a foreign woman incarnating all evil.

[56] Boström, *Proverbiastudien* (1935): 42, 135; P.A.H. DeBoer, "The Counsellor" *VTSup* 3 (1955): 42-71.

[57] This character may be the "strange woman/loose woman" (Prov 2:16; 5:3, 20; 7:5); "adventuress/foreign woman" (Prov 2:16; 6:24; 7:5); "evil woman" (Prov 6:24).

[58] Boström, *Proverbiastudien* (1935): 174; DeBoer, "The Counsellor," (1955): 42-71.

[59] Wisdom's preparation of and invitation to her banquet combines the human image of a feast and the image of the divine banquet as described in Isa 25:6; One may ask whether the need was to bring perspective into an association of Wisdom with feasting, or with feasts that lacked the participation of the "simple" as modelled by Wisdom.

portrayal of Wisdom's provision of a banquet of rich food may place her on a par with God who is the host in Isaiah 25.

Marked differences between Wisdom and Folly include contrasting consequences: Wisdom builds her house, prepares her feast, and dispatches her servants to issue invitations (9:1-3); Folly is noisy, wanton, does not know anything and calls to those who pass by (9:13-16). Wisdom offers her guests the way of insight: "Leave simple ones and live and walk in the way of insight" (9:4-6), while Folly offers: "stolen waters are sweet and bread tastes better when eaten in secret".[60] By closing Proverbs 1-9 on a warning note: "her [Folly's] guests are already in the vales of Sheol", the redactor suggests that Wisdom teaches the way of life and all else is Folly. Wisdom offers life to the simple in the course of their everyday lives; Folly—in her many guises—operates in similar fashion. Clearly implied in the recurring theme of the choice between life and death in Proverbs is Moses' dramatic presentation to his followers of the choice between life and death: "I am offering you life or death blessing or curse" (Deut 30:15-30). In the Wisdom of Ben Sira and Baruch the association of Wisdom with the Torah, becomes central to the depiction of Wisdom. In addition to Wisdom's offering of life to her audience is her reprimanding speech (*Mahnrede*) reminiscent of the prophets, particularly of Isaiah and Jeremiah, while the Folly figures use "smooth words", not a description that could be applied to Wisdom's speech. Prophetic motifs in Wisdom's teaching in Proverbs are considered in the next section.

Wisdom's Prophetic Echoes in Prov 1:20-33

This section of the chapter examines the Wisdom speech in Prov 1:20-33 from the viewpoint of its likeness to prophetic writings—a similarity to which I have alluded already—in order to discover what the presence of such motifs in Wisdom's speeches may suggest about her role and function in Proverbs. Prov 1:20-33 exhibits the distinct form of the prophetic oracles in Isaiah and Jeremiah as can be seen in the following breakdown of the poem: verse 20-21 introduction of the speaker; verses 22-23 denunciation; verses 24-25 reproach; verses 26-28 punishment; verses 29-30 judgement; verses 31-33 promise. The poem begins with an introduction by a narrator who reports Wisdom's presence in public as an ongoing event: "Wisdom cries aloud in the street in the markets she raises her voice; on the top of the walls she cries out; at the entrance to the city gates she speaks" (1:20-21). A similar introduction using a rhetorical question appears in 8:1-3: "Does not Wisdom call, does not understanding raise her voice?" While the first denunciation (vv.24-25) addresses "the simple" in the second person (you), the second (vv.28-31) uses the third person (they), an inexplicable switch. Wisdom begins her speech by berating the simple for loving being simple, scoffers for

---

[60] Interestingly the advice is one-sided. While the speaker warns the young man against enticement by the "strange woman," there is no mention of his own responsibility.

delighting in their scoffing and fools for hating knowledge (v.22). Despite their lack of eagerness to attend to Wisdom's teaching, she launches into denunciation, reproach, threats, judgement and finally offers a choice to those who wish to survive the calamity she forecasts. Wisdom's condemnations follow the form of some prophetic judgement speeches:

Wisdom's Condemnations
Prov 1:24-25
Because I have called and you refused . . . .
no one heeded . . . because you have ignored all my counsel and would have none of my reproof.

Prov 1:28-30
They will call upon me, but I will not answer, they will seek me diligently but they will not find me . . . they did not choose the fear of YHWH. They would have none of my counsel, they despised all my reproof.

Prophetic Condemnations
Isa 50:2
Why was no one there when I came? Why did no one answer when I called?
Isa 65:12
When I called, you did not answer, when I spoke, you did not listen.
Isa 66:4
When I called, no one answered, when I spoke, they did not listen.
Jer 7:13
When I spoke to you . . . you did not listen . . . when I called you, you did not answer.
Jer 17:23
Yet they did not listen or incline their ear; and would not hear or receive instruction.
Jer 29:19
Because they did not heed my words . . . they would not listen, says the Lord.
Hos 5:6
They shall go to seek the Lord, but they will not find him; he has withdrawn from them.
Mic 3:4
Then they will cry to the Lord, but he will not answer them.
Isa 1:15
When you stretch out your hands, I will hide my eyes from you . . . I will not listen.
Isa 66:4
I also will choose to mock them . . .
because, when I called, no one answered, when I spoke, they did not listen.
Jer 11:10-11
Though they cry out to me, I will not listen
Zech 7:13-14
When I called, they would not hear . . . .
so, when they called, I would not hear, I scattered them with a whirlwind.

Wisdom's threats are couched in the harsh language that characterises similar threats in prophetic oracles attributed to YHWH

Wisdom's Threats
Prov 1:26-27
I also will laugh at your calamity; I will mock when panic strikes you, when panic strikes you like a storm,
Prov 1:31-32
They shall eat the fruit of their way and be sated with their own devices . . . . waywardness kills the simple, and the complacency of fools destroys them.

Prophetic Threats
Hos 5:6
With their flocks and herds they shall go to seek the LORD, but they will not find him; he has withdrawn from them.
Jer 11:11
Therefore, thus says the LORD, assuredly I am going to bring disaster upon them that They cannot escape; though they cry out to me, I will not listen to them.
Isa 1:15
When you stretch out your hands, I will hide my eyes from you; even though you make many prayers, I will not listen; your hands are full of blood.
Ps 2:4
He who sits in the heavens laughs; the LORD has them in derision.

Phrases used in prophetic texts are echoed in Prov 1:20-33, for example:

Prov 1:22: עַד־מֹתַי "how long?"	Hos 8:5; Isa 6:11; Jer 4:14, 21, 12:4, 3:27; 23:26, 31:22, 47:2; Hab 2:6; Zech 1:2; Dan 8:13, 12:6
Prov 1:23: תָּשׁוּבוּ "turn /return"	Hos 6:1; Jer 3:19; Lam 3:40; 5:21
Prov 1:23: אַבִּיעָה "I will pour out"	Jer 14:16; Zech 12:10; Joel 2:28, 29 (Heb) 3:1
Prov 1:24: יַעַן קָרָאתִי "because I have called"	Hos 11:2; Isa 50:2; Jer 7:13; 65:12; 66:4; Zech 7:13

"How long?" appears many times throughout the Old Testament and particularly in the Psalms and Jeremiah, to indicate endless waiting on the part of the questioner, who is sometimes YHWH. Verse 22 suggests that the audience has rejected or not paid attention to Wisdom's teaching for a long time. Now she is giving them another chance to "turn/return to" to her words (v.23) which will result in her promise "I will pour out my spirit/thoughts on you".[61] Implied in this promise is

---

[61] Commentators have variously rendered אַבִּיעָה as "spirit", "thought", "thoughts", "heart" (cf. LXX; Vulgate; REB; RSV; NRSV; NJB), Ringgren, *Word and Wisdom* (1947): 96;

Wisdom's close relationship with YHWH, whose prerogative she appears here to exercise, going beyond even the prophets' claims to speak for YHWH.[62] "Pour out" is often used for the verbal expression of a person's thoughts as in: "they pour out their arrogant words" (Ps 94:4); "the mouths of fools pour out folly" (Prov 15:2). Ringgren supposes that this may be an echo of the prophetic promise of the pouring out of the spirit (Isa 44:3), and McKane mentions passages where wisdom is considered to be the fruit of the spirit.[63] This expression also suggests an abundant spring whose waters gush in abundance, and by analogy implies that Wisdom will lavishly reward those who acknowledge her authority and attend to her invitation.[64] An image of personified Wisdom as a fountain appears in Bar 3:12 (cf. Prov 18:4) "because you have forsaken the fountain of wisdom", where the exiles are accused of forsaking Wisdom. A similar notion appears in Jer 2:13: "they have forsaken me, the fountain of living waters". "Because I called". (v.24, 28) is reminiscent of Isa 65:1-2 that is the beginning of a judgement speech by YHWH discussed in more detail below.

Wisdom Speaks on her own Authority

Wisdom's reproofs and threats call to mind what appear to be two contradictory aspects of the relationship between YHWH and his people. One version is that of YHWH, speaking through the prophets, calling the audience to turn from their evil ways. They however, do not answer, and so bring disaster on themselves (Jer 35:17). A second version is that of the distressed who call on YHWH for help, suggesting they are confident that God will answer their prayer: "O my God, I cry . . . but you do not answer" (Ps 22:2, Heb 3), but apparently they are not heard. A third variation appears where YHWH's response in Psalm 22 is echoed in Wisdom's threat "They will call upon me, but I will not answer, they will seek me, but they will not find me" (Prov 1:28). Prov 1:26-28 appears to resemble a prophetic judgement scene as shown above, but the formulation of the threat is very different. Unlike the prophetic threat in which YHWH threaten to execute judgement,[65] Wisdom here says she will laugh at what befalls those who refuse her admonishment and reject her advice. Wisdom is not the agent of the calamity but a mocking observer (v.28) rather than the one who carries out the judgement. Kayatz argues that such motifs as the laugh of Wisdom, calling on and not-hearing, seeking and not-finding, were not originally at home in the wisdom literature.[66] Her claim cannot be supported by the text as in its wider context this section is

---

McKane, *Proverbs* (1970): 212; Plöger, *Sprüche Salomos* (1984): 12, 18; Scott, *Proverbs, Ecclesiastes* (1965): 34, 40; Whybray, *Heavenly Counsellor* (1971): 10-13.

[62] However, a different verb is used in Isa 44:3 and in Isa 11:2 the spirit of wisdom is an aspect of the Spirit of YHWH. See R.N. Whybray, *Proverbs* (1994): 47.

[63] W. McKane, *Prophets and Wise Men* (London, 1965): 110.

[64] Kayatz, *Studien* (1966): 127. "I shall divulge my words to you".

[65] Zimmerli, "Zur Struktur" *ZAW* 51 (1933): 187. n.i; Kayatz, *Studien* (1966): 120-25.

[66] Kayatz, *Studien* (1966): 24-27.

rhetorical, and is part of the wisdom style of persuasion. Some have seen it as a condemnatory approach, but this cannot be substantiated as at the end of the speech (v.33) an escape route is still open for those who listen to Wisdom. Wisdom's harangue here has characteristics of both the wisdom teacher, who gives advice and reproof, and of the prophet in the expression "I stretched out my hand" echoing Isa 65:1-10. This is a judgement speech implying the presence of an unperceptive and negligent audience.[67] "I will laugh" אֶשְׂחָק and "I will mock" אֶלְעַג (v.26) are words used to describe YHWH's response to the attackers of his faithful (Pss 2:4; 59:8 [Heb 9]; 37:13). This can also be an expression of confidence in one's own superior strength and immunity from harm or defeat as in Prov 31:25 where the "woman of worth" "laughs at the time to come".

However, in verses 26-28 the mockery suggests indignation at being disregarded. Implied in the stern tone of these verses is a form of negative persuasion in the sense that the wish of the audience to avoid ridicule will persuade them to change. Wisdom "called" (v.24), and was ignored, but now the situation is to be reversed, and those who ignored Wisdom will in turn cry out to her for help but she will not answer them. Echoing Isa 65:1-2 Wisdom's judgement speeches (Prov 1:24, 28-30) suggest the notion of a time when it will be too late to turn to Wisdom for instruction. "Because they hated knowledge" (v.28) is equated with failing to submit to God's authority and discipline and thus missing the opportunity for repentance by not choosing the "fear of the Lord" (1:28-30). "The fear of YHWH" is the framework for this passage. Clearly, the search for Wisdom cannot begin without the "fear of the Lord", as all wisdom and illumination come from YHWH, who is the fountain of wisdom. Failing to choose the fear of YHWH thus ignoring Wisdom's counsel, and refusing to "seek diligently" (echoing Judg 6:29; Amos 5:14; 8:12) means that Wisdom will not be found. In Deuteronomy 4:29 and Jeremiah 29:13, YHWH promises that when the people seek God in times of distress, they will find God, but in Hosea 5:6 and Amos 8:12 the sinful are warned in oracles of judgement that even if they seek YHWH they will not succeed because YHWH has withdrawn his presence from them.

Prov 1:29-30 details Israel's failures, "Because they hated knowledge and did not choose the fear of YHWH, they would have none of my counsel".[68] Such judgement and promises also come from YHWH in prophetic speech as is also seen in the notion of suffering the repercussions of one's way of life (cf. Prov 18:21; Isa 3:10), whether as an individual or as a people. Thus, "the turning away of the simple" and the "complacency of fools" (v. 32; Isa 59:13; Hos 11:7), which denote unfaithfulness to YHWH (Job 22:16; Isa 59:13; Jer 50:6; Hos 11:7; Sir 8:5; Bar 2:8), here characterise unfaithfulness to Wisdom.

Wisdom makes it clear that her audience's attitude towards her, like the

---

[67] Some scholars believe that the similarities are not sufficiently close to suggest a direct relationship between the two passages. Whybray, *Proverbs* NCBC (1994): 46-48, claims that the language is imaginable in other circumstances.

[68] The use of the perfect tense here may suggest that those addressed have already rejected Wisdom's teaching, and are thus already judged.

audience's attitude towards YHWH, is a matter of life and death. Evil רָעָה (v.33), in this context, denotes the "evil" that will be the lot of those who ignore Wisdom's teaching. The promise of reward in verses 31-33 (cf. Deut 33:2; Pss 16:9, 37:3; Sir 4:15), for those who heed Wisdom, balances the threat to those who will eat the fruit of their way. Wisdom likens the relationship between action and consequence to that between seed and fruit, where the action initiates what is seen as an organic process of growth culminating in the effect. A switch of metaphor in verse 31b compares the pleasures, which "the simple" get out of their gratification, and "fools" get from their complacency, with the loathing that follows over-indulgence in food. Both lead to the "turning away" ascribed to the "simple" who fail to accept the discipline imposed, while those who listen to Wisdom will "dwell secure" (v.33, cf. Jer 23:6).[69]

Appeals to Wisdom and Prophecy

We can but surmise how the relationship of the Wisdom figure to the prophetic tradition was perceived. Traces of prophetic sayings in Wisdom's speeches may suggest a relationship between the function of this figure and that of the exilic prophets in particular.[70] Unlike the prophets whom she echoes, Wisdom speaks on her own authority and claims her right to attention. However, attempts to explain the similarity between the speech of Wisdom and prophetic speech, which begin with an underlying presupposition that wisdom and prophecy were two static and isolated traditions, presume that what we regard as specifically wisdom or prophecy existed in isolation, and therefore we can know what is proper to each. If, on the other hand, these boundaries are regarded as not so rigid and impermeable, comparisons do not throw much light on the identifiable differences of form, theological outlook, emphases, and instances of interchange in both traditions.[71]

It is not surprising to find some shared influences between prophetic and

---

[69] See R.E. Murphy, "Religious Dimensions of Israelite Wisdom" in *AIR* (1987): 458 n. 17, asserts, "only in Israel do we find an explicit and intimate association of wisdom with 'fear of God'".

[70] Individual prophets have been studied for evidences of wisdom influences, see J.A. Soggin, "Amos and Wisdom" 119-123; A.A. MacIntosh, "Hosea and the Wisdom Tradition" 124-132; H.G.M. Williamson, "Isaiah and the Wise" 133-141; W. McKane, "Jeremiah and the Wise"142-151 in *WAI* (1995); R.N. Whybray, "Prophecy and Wisdom," in *Israel's Prophetic Tradition* (Cambridge, 1982): 181-199; J. Jensen, *The Use of tôrâ by Isaiah* (Washington, 1973): 122, 135; H.W. Wolff, *Amos the Prophet* (Philadelphia, 1973); J.W. Whedbee, *Isaiah and Wisdom* (Nashville, 1971); J. Fichtner, "Jesaja unter den Weisen" in K.D. Fricke, ed. *Gottes Weisheit* (Stuttgart, 1965): 18-26.

[71] Study of the scribal literary aspect of wisdom influence in the prophetic corpus is relatively new, see C. Van Leeuwen, "The Sage in the Prophetic Literature," in *SIANE* (1990): 295-306; Fishbane, *Biblical Interpretation* (1985); R.E. Clements, "Patterns in the Prophetic Canon" in G.W. Coats, ed., *Canon and Authority* (Philadelphia, 1987): 42-55; "Prophecy as Literature: A Re-appraisal" in D.G. Miller, *The Hermeneutical Quest* (Allison Park, 1986): 59-75.

wisdom writings, but contentions concerning the influence of one tradition on
another can only be proved if the texts being discussed can be dated definitively,
and clear divisions between wisdom and prophecy be made. Some features
adduced by Wolff and Whedbee as specifically wisdom forms or methods of
argumentation, are in reality more like stylistic didactic devices, likely to be
employed by public speakers, and not restricted to any one teaching situation, than
fixed oral forms. Treating such stylistic forms as indications of direct dependence
or imitation would be misleading, since shared characteristics, rather than pointing
to the influence of one tradition on another, may suggest that both texts show
reliance on a common source. In any case the focus for this study is personified
Wisdom, and the concern here is to discover possible explanations for the
similarities between Wisdom's speeches and prophetic speeches, and what this
tells us about the personification of Wisdom.

Marked correspondences between Proverbs 1:20-33 and some prophetic
literature suggests the combination and reapplication of earlier ideas by one or both
of the traditions. In recent years, scholars have investigated the reworking and
integration of various expressions of the Israelite traditions and the incorporation
of non-Israelite materials into the biblical tradition. The movement from the early
stages of the written tradition to its final form in the canon of scripture continues to
be a field of research.[72] Robert and his followers, using lexical evidence, have
repeatedly contended that a style defined as *procédé anthologique* "re-employs,
literally or equivalently, words or formulas of earlier Scriptures",[73] that is, that the
earlier biblical texts are exegetically reused, "reactualised" in new contexts.
Sometimes "the author preserves the literal meaning of his predecessor (texts) but
applies it to another object".[74] In other instances, older terms are extended,
transposed, or otherwise given new significance.[75] Consequently, Robert calls the
texts created through *procédés anthologiques—"ecrits midrashiques"*, and defines
"Midrash" in line with what has been called aggadic exegesis. He says, "One may
call *Midrash* every study of the sense of Scriptures . . . Midrash [may be found]
where the sacred text puts us in the presence of meditations on the divine word,
with a concern for practical applications".[76]

In principle, a controlled comparison of biblical sources is the
methodological ideal of this approach. Robert states, "The only significant
references are those in which identical or synonymous terms contextually treat an

[72] Fishbane, *Biblical Interpretation* (1985): 286.
[73] A. Robert, "Littéraires (genres)," *DBSup* 5 (1957): 410-411.
[74] M. Delcor, "Les Sources du Deutéro-Zecharie et ses procédés d'emprunt," *RB* 59 (1952): 407-411.
[75] A. Robert, "Les Attaches littéraires bibliques de Prov 1-9", *RB* 44 (1935): 345-350; A, Deissler, *Psalm 119 (118) und seine Theologie: Ein Beitrag zur Erforschung der anthologischen Stilgattung im Alten Testament* (Munich, 1955): 277-278.
[76] In the summary of a conference paper given by Robert on "Midrash Biblique," *ETL* 30 (1954): 283; A.G. Wright, *The Literary Genre Midrash* (New York, 1967).

identical or positively analogous thought".[77]   However, the achievements and contentions of this school are subject to different evaluations. Thus, for example, Robert claimed that the wisdom teacher of Proverbs 1-9 uses words and phrases from Deuteronomy, Isaiah, and Jeremiah as the basis of theological speculations.[78] Indeed, the textual references supposed to derive from earlier sources are generally so vague and disconnected, with virtually no clusters of parallel terms or analogous contexts, that little is gained by calling them exegetical or "midrashic".

Comparable to the situations mentioned above, in which similar narratives with strategic differences may not be so much exegetically as typologically related, instances where apparent verbal echoes of earlier texts occur in late sources may not constitute a *traditum-traditio* dynamic, but rather point to a shared stream of linguistic tradition. In such cases, a common *Wortfeld* provides a thesaurus of terms and images shared and differently employed by distinct, though occasionally allied, literary circles. Thus, in consideration of Robert's own proposition that Proverbs 1-9 reflects a reworking of material in the book of Deuteronomy, it could be argued that wisdom terms are coincidently used completely independently by the wisdom writers who produced the Book of Proverbs; by writers who contributed to the Book of Deuteronomy; and by the authors of Isaiah, Amos, Jeremiah, and Ezekiel.[79] This theoretical possibility does not invalidate any specific instance of haggadic exegesis in principle. However, it does serve as a guard against imprecise theories about literary *exegetical* interdependence.

Whatever the starting point, focus, or approach, the frequent appearances of similar phraseology in some prophetic writing and in personification of Wisdom texts, particularly Proverbs 1-9, and Bar 3:9-4:4 must be regarded as more than coincidence. Equally unlikely as the sole explanation is the possibility of a shared source. While the search for an explanation is hampered by the limitations of our knowledge concerning both prophecy and wisdom, particularly regarding dating, earlier sources, and the worlds of those who produced both kinds of literature, the fact remains that such a high level of correlation between the two types of literature must reveal an intention by the writers—or at least the writers of wisdom or prophecy—to reflect and include such references as would emphasise particular ideas that were already present in the Israelite tradition.

Investigations of the scribal and literary aspects of wisdom in the prophetic corpus are relatively new. The occurrence of wisdom language, forms, and ideas considered characteristic of wisdom literature proper, may merely show that the biblical writers were familiar with, and proficient in, the use of a general wisdom mode of thinking common to the Israelite tradition. Whybray in claiming that "wisdom is a general term denoting superior intellectual ability whether innate or acquired, in God, men or animals" ignores the cultural specificity of חׇכְמָה. He overlooks the import of Isa 31:2 in asserting that this passage means only that

---

[77]   A. Robert, "Littéraires (genres)," *DBSup* v. 410.
[78]   See Robert, "Les Attaches littéraires bibliques," *RB* 43 (1934): 42-68.
[79]   Crenshaw, "Wisdom Influence" *JBL* 88 (1969): 132-3.

"these politicians . . . claimed . . . superior intelligence".[80] For such intelligence is not some universal "reason" possessed by all humans; rather, the wisdom in question is precisely that inculturated style of thought most adequately expressed in Proverbs, and in the later wisdom books. However, it may mean more. With the prophet Isaiah, strong verbal and thematic parallels to the proverbs attributed to the court of Hezekiah exist (e.g. Isa 5:21 and Prov 26:5, 12, 16; 28:11).[81] Ben Sira sees Wisdom as literary and learned in character, with her primary sources in the Law, the prophets, and "other books" (Sir 24:23, 33; 38:24; 39:1-3; 44-50).

Sheppard argues that literary sages or scribes undertook the latest stage in the redaction/composition of the canon, including the prophetic literature. Fishbane, on the contrary, asserts that similar sapiential scribal activity began in the pre-exilic era.[82] Since the advent of Sheppard's findings in which he presented the case for a wisdom hermeneutic underlying the final redaction of the Hebrew Bible, several scholars have adopted and advanced this theory.[83] Evidence for this perspective of Torah-Wisdom cum eschatology links the Torah, the prophets, and the Writings by identifying key junctures in the *Tanak* (Deut 34:9-12; Jos 1:5-9; Mal 4:4-6/Heb 3:22; Psalms 1-2). Reindel notes that Ben Sira is a model for the sage who is concerned with prophecies (Sir 39:1, cf. 44-50).[84] In the Hebrew canon the last verses of Malachi (4:4-6/Heb 3:22-24) form a bridge to Psalm 1, and are increasingly recognised as the redactional introduction to the Psalter and to the Writings. Hosea, the first book of the Twelve, also carries a wisdom admonition to the reader (Hos 14:9/Heb 14:10), and Isa 1:2-3 opens the latter prophets with YHWH's accusation against the unwise:

> I reared children and brought them up, but they have rebelled against me.
> The ox knows its owner and the donkey its master's crib;
> but Israel does not know, my people do not understand. (Isa 1:2-3)

Wisdom: A New Messenger

Personified Wisdom in Prov 1:20-33 exhibits characteristics of a wisdom teacher and of a prophet.[85] However, on closer inspection some of these likenesses are more apparent than real. Whatever view is adopted, disagreement persists as to the

---

[80]   Whybray, *Intellectual Tradition* (1974): 11, 20.
[81]   Whedbee, *Isaiah and Wisdom* (1971).
[82]   Fishbane, *Biblical Interpretation* (1986): 23-43.
[83]   Sheppard, *Wisdom as a Hermeneutical Construct* (Berlin, 1980); Van Leeuwen "The Sage in the Prophetic Literature" (1990): 295-306; "Scribal Wisdom and Theodicy in the Book of the Twelve" in *In Search of Wisdom* (1993): 31-49.
[84]   J. Reindel, "Weisheitliche Bearbeitung von Psalmen," *VTSup* 32 (1981): 340-341.
[85]   Wisdom's prophet-like, vehement speech inviting her hearers to listen to her teaching, or to ignore it at their peril, belies Fontaine's notion that this speech could be seen to be a mother's instruction to her son; see C. Fontaine, "Proverbs" in *HBD* (1988):495-517.

message and tenor of her preaching.[86] The figure portrayed in this poem cannot be identified as an empirical wisdom teacher who gives instruction based on what has been learned from teachers, distilled through mature experience of life, and has an aptitude for the skills required of those who "teach" wisdom. Wisdom claims her personal authority, noted first in her appeal for attention (Prov 1:24; 8:5, 32), for promulgating wisdom, advice, and admonishment with the authority of YHWH, and the fear of YHWH, which is the new "instruction/discipline", that she would have her audience accept. Neither can this figure be identified fully as a prophet, for although Wisdom's appeals for the attention of her audience and her condemnations bear a close resemblance to prophetic teaching, and reflect the urgency of prophetic oracles, her message differs in several ways from prophetic teaching.[87]

Wisdom speaks her message on her own authority and demands that individuals must decide for and choose life over death, Wisdom over Folly. What she is demanding would entail an exacting reinterpretation of antecedent traditions and a thorough transformation of traditional assumptions and beliefs. Whoever refuses to listen to her will be struck with disaster and destroyed, while those who attend will dwell in security without fear of evil.[88] In each case, her authority exceeds that of the figures she appears to resemble. In declaring herself the norm for salvation and destruction, she echoes claims that the prophets understood to be from YHWH alone.[89] While intimately associated with YHWH and here endowed with his authority, personified Wisdom is not envisaged as a second god in a theological sense, but neither is she reduced to the position of a wisdom teacher as McKane argues.[90] Wisdom's divine claims suggest that she could be understood as YHWH's intermediary, speaking in his name. It is most improbable that the claims made by Wisdom in her speech could be made by a wisdom teacher, when one considers the rarity of claims similar to those of the Wisdom figure in Proverbs.

The particular correspondences between Prov 1:20-33 and prophetic teachings suggest that Wisdom's declarations might be intended to function prophetically, but her teachings transform the prophetic material, and present it from a new perspective. The most striking feature of this innovation is that Wisdom makes claims for herself that elsewhere are made only by, or for, God, as in Wisdom's direct claim to divine authority for what she teaches—a characteristic

---

[86] McKane, *Proverbs* (1970): 276-77, regards Wisdom as a preacher, but hesitates to call her a preacher of repentance; Gemser, *Sprüche* (1963) and Ringgren, *Word* (1947): 96 see this as a penitential sermon with the positive elements of exhortation to conversion and the promises attached to it.

[87] In Prov 8:32-34 "listen" occurs three times.

[88] P. Trible, "Wisdom Builds a Poem: The Architecture of Proverbs 1:20-33", *JBL* 94 (1975): 509-518, sees this poem composed of three parts and with a chiasmic pattern.

[89] Kayatz, *Studien* (1966): 120-126, describes 1:20-33 as a Wisdom sermon into which prophetic modes of address are taken up and modified.

[90] McKane, *Proverbs* (1970): 277, claims that Wisdom is probably a charismatic wisdom teacher and no more.

most frequently associated with prophetic teachers—which she presents in what has come to be regarded as wisdom language. However, this language, subordinated as it is to the demand for submission to the authority of YHWH, is no longer set in an empirical educational discipline, but in religious discipline and illumination. So Wisdom is depicted as a new kind of messenger who does not have an exact predecessor. She appears as a combination of a prophet and wisdom teacher, and incorporates aspects not found in either teacher or prophet.

In her use of reproof and threat, both of which are prophetic forms of address, but are not specific to prophetic speech alone, Wisdom does not so much speak about repentance as about attentiveness to her message and recognition that her invitation holds the power of life or death depending on her hearers' choices (cf. Bar 3:9:4:4). As noted by Zimmerli, a peculiar inherent inconsistency is evident in the way this section is composed.[91] The discordance may, at least in part, arise from the merging of prophetic forms with the vocabulary and ethos of wisdom. As is common in any such innovation the early stages of a merging of two different traditions reveal traces of joins and partial integrations. In addition the speaker is personified Wisdom, a female character, not the traditional male speaker of prophetic literature.

If Wisdom were really a prophet, verse 26, "Therefore I will punish your disobedience, I will bring disaster on you", would be a judgement from YHWH, but instead Wisdom says: "I will laugh at your calamity; I will mock when panic strikes you". In Zimmerli's view, this would not accord with the idea of an order that maintains itself without outside intervention, and it is this thought that dominates the remainder of the passage. Therefore, Zimmerli observes that verses 26-31 constitute a very lame threat, since the passage is not concerned with "once-for-all decisive words such as obedience, repentance, judgement, but with general, universally valid considerations".[92] Zimmerli's claim that biblical wisdom was based on a notion of world order cannot be regarded as absolute, although throughout Wisdom's speeches order is clearly a given in her invitations to live an ordered life, so as to receive the wealth that is available to those who seek her.[93]

Wisdom Affirms the Presence of YHWH

Wisdom's threat about the advent of the "panic like a storm, calamity like a whirlwind, distress and anguish", and her threats about the "complacency of fools"

---

[91] Zimmerli, "Ort und Grenze" (1964): 146-158.

[92] Zimmerli, "Zur Stuktur" *ZAW* 51 (1933): 187.

[93] Zimmerli, "Zur Struktur" (1933): 177-204 writing on Qoheleth argues that the question: "Who knows what is good for human beings while they live?" is central to the whole wisdom corpus. For Zimmerli "wisdom is radically anthropocentric". Thirty years later in "Ort und Grenze" (1964): 146-158, esp. 149, he describes anthropology as central to wisdom thinking, but notes the search for wisdom in creation, stressing humanity's role and place in the world under the idea of creatio continua. He sees the goal of the sage is "to master life" through knowledge of the world which illuminates proper existence.

seem to suggest that to expect order and predictability in life is a clear indication of foolish complacency. If this text is, as I have proposed in the first section of this chapter, an exilic text, it is very likely that Wisdom is urging her audience to deal with the uncertainty with which they are surrounded by putting their trust in wisdom teaching which can be appropriated in an alien setting for the reasons already outlined above. Wisdom in her speeches consistently teaches and implies the notion of the presence of YHWH in the lives of the Israelites as affirmed throughout the Old Testament. Such teaching in Proverbs 1-9 suggests ordinary/temporal settings and times, as there is no reference to sacred time or space. Gemser proposes that the image of Wisdom in public places, seeking to engage the attention of those there, may reflect the actual practice of wisdom teachers. He claims that they did their teaching where a ready-made audience was assured—marketplace, and city gates—where all manner of political, legal, and commercial business was transacted. This can be interpreted as Wisdom making an appeal to the audience in the very streets in which they are also tempted to listen to the voices of the foreign woman, the strange woman, the adulteress, and where at the close of Proverbs 1-9 Wisdom will compete with Folly for partakers in her banquet (Prov 9:1-6, 13-18). Wisdom's portrayal as teaching in public suggests that she wishes to reach the widest possible audience and asserts her relevance to the mundane reality of the marketplace. As a poetic image the marketplace or public square, centre of public life in the ancient Near East, expresses the fascination of the wisdom writers with ordinary human existence. It represents the arena where human beings contend with the business of daily living, and where Wisdom and Folly compete for human loyalties. Both characters are indigenous to the world of economic and social exchange, so the realm of Wisdom is ordinary human life.

Considering the similarities between this poem and prophetic modes of address, one wonders if it were not primarily the practice of the biblical prophets that lies behind this representation.[94] Descriptions of Wisdom's actions and settings recall similar references in the prophetic texts, as in "to make a noise or to be tumultuous" used as a noun, meaning the thronged or noisy places in the city, such as the "entrance to the city gates". Similar phrases occur in some prophetic texts (Isa 51:20); "at the head of every street" (Lam 2:19; Ezek 16:25); "at every street corner" (Jer 7:2) "stand in the gate of YHWH's house and proclaim there this word"; "Go and stand in the gate of the children of the people, by which the kings of Judah enter and by which they go out, and in all the gates of Jerusalem" (Jer 17:19-20).[95] Prophets had to be speakers who could address the people in the marketplace and compete with the noise, traffic and concerns of everyday activities for their audience's attention. They would have been prepared to be in the public forum and to win an audience by the force of their speech. The use of this phrase in

---

[94] Ringgren, *Word* (1947): 96; Robert, *RB* xliii, (1934): 172-76; Kayatz, *Studien* (1966): 120-25.

[95] Gemser, *Sprüche* (1963): 23; Whybray, *Wisdom* (1965): 77; Murphy, *Tree of Life*, (1990): 98; "Wisdom's Song: Proverbs 1:20-33," *CBQ* 49 (1986): 456-60.

the biblical account places Wisdom, like the prophets, in a place through which all entering and leaving the city had to pass.

McKane and Whybray find traces of Instruction in 1:20-33.[96] While Wisdom's speeches in Proverbs 1-9 have some features that are characteristic of the Instruction genre, emphasis on attentiveness, vocabulary, motive clauses in Prov 1:32; 8:5-6, 32-33, they lack some salient characteristics associated with this genre in wisdom literature. A complete absence of imperatives marks Prov 1:20-33, while chapter 8, with two very brief examples of Instruction, hardly qualifies as Instruction. Personified Wisdom expands and focuses wisdom instruction by identifying that teaching with the source of wisdom and with the prophetic tradition. The underlying Instruction, wisdom, and prophetic traditions evident in the personification texts are expressed in the variety and complexity of the images, figures of speech, and overall treatment of Wisdom, which suggest an extraordinarily flexible figure.

Wisdom Brings a New Theodicy

In Deuteronomic and prophetic teaching, the people's response to YHWH's commands determines their fate. This is clear in Isaiah and Jeremiah, (Isa 65:12; 66:4; Jer 7:13, 26; 17:23; 34:14; 44:5), where the pattern, "Because you did not listen . . . therefore", takes the form of a theodicy in which the refusal of Israel to listen has become the "reason" for the destruction of the Temple, Jerusalem, the loss of the monarchy and exile from the land. In Proverbs it is the reception or rejection of Wisdom's teaching which will bring good or ill (1:29-33). Even Wisdom's speech about herself is the same as that used elsewhere about YHWH. This is particularly clear in "they will call upon me, but I will not answer" (1:23), and "they will seek me diligently but will not find me" (1:28). These lines recall many passages in the Psalms and prophets that speak of calling upon and seeking YHWH. Whybray finds the single reference to "fear of the Lord" (1:29b) a surprise in a poem where otherwise Wisdom speaks exclusively and with authority about herself.[97] However, it would be even more surprising if "fear of the Lord" were omitted in a poem where this virtue is the underpinning of Wisdom's teaching.

Wisdom's command to choose life over death is concentrated in Proverbs 1-9 in personified Wisdom. Here the transformation of the earlier wisdom tradition is accomplished by way of an appeal to both wisdom and prophetic themes with the addition of new features, enunciated by the figure of Wisdom, whose speeches combine prophetic threats and wisdom teaching. Concluding what is probably the earliest speech attributed to Wisdom, is her invitation to the simple ones to choose between the way of Folly and the way of Wisdom (Prov 1:32-33).

---

[96] McKane, *Proverbs* (1970): 275-277, and Whybray, *Wisdom* (1965): 93-95, see 1:20-33 as Instruction, and maintain that personified Wisdom is an aspect of the "nationalisation" of the wisdom tradition.

[97] "I", "my", "me", occur sixteen times in twelve verses. See Whybray, *Proverbs* (1994): 49.

This is the message underlying Proverbs 1-9 and it is dramatically presented in chapter 9 as invitations by Wisdom and Folly respectively to their feasts. Invitation is the keynote of Prov 9:1-6, and in some ways, direct or implied invitation is the keynote of all the personification passages. Whatever may have been the reason for presenting the voice of Wisdom in such personal terms, in the present context Wisdom is depicted as speaking with the authority of YHWH.

Although personified Wisdom's teaching recalls prophetic teaching in its form, her teaching is not merely a repeat of prophetic teaching, but has taken another turn. It is as if the lessons have not been learned, so the teacher must find a new and different approach and formulation. Repeating teaching of another time and situation, even if it is relevant in the new situation, is not effective as it recalls past failure and the disaster that followed. Wisdom—the new messenger who puts things in a new light—uses familiar phrases and assumes that the underlying laws are known. Her message, with all its prophetic connotations, is that her audience are to listen to her teaching. For her teaching, she claims the authority that the prophets associated with YHWH. This teaching demands that her audience choose Wisdom not Folly, and in so deciding, they opt for the fear of the Lord, which is fundamental for all who seek Wisdom.

Wisdom Transforms the Idea of YHWH

Wisdom in Proverbs exhibits a notion of individual responsibility and a questioning tone, which is characteristic of Jeremiah and Ezekiel. Such a transformation of the earlier wisdom tradition is accomplished by way of an appeal to both wisdom and prophetic themes, combined with a new perspective gained from experience of everyday life resulting in a unique adaptation of earlier traditions. Wisdom claims much that traditionally had been regarded as found only in YHWH. Thus, the Wisdom figure manifests the presence of YHWH in a new voice and a new guise to a people who saw no traditional evidence of YHWH's presence with them in their changed circumstances. The wisdom tradition perhaps was best suited to address this predicament, as their primary concern was the created world in which they lived. Underpinning biblical thought is a belief that the world and the life that inhabits it manifests divine activity, and must be viewed in relation to the Creator.[98]

Wisdom writers are unique in the biblical tradition. Rather than beginning from the events of sacred history they begin with the events of ordinary life in the world created by YHWH, and insist that the world does not work mechanically (Prov 8:22-31; Psalms 23; 104; Job 10:8; Bar 3:35).[99] YHWH, the Creator, is also

---

[98] Von Rad, *Wisdom* (1972): 6, 10, 17, 10, 59, 62, 287, 301, was probably the first to focus on Wirklichkeitsverständnis "understanding of reality", and noted that "the most characteristic feature of her (Israel's) understanding of reality was . . . that she believed man to stand in a quite specific, highly dynamic, essential relationship with his environment"; C. Link, *Die Welt als Gleichnis* (Munich, 1976): 268-285.

[99] Although the early wisdom writers do not explore the saving events of the Israelite

the God of Sinai, and the God who acts in Israel's history. While experience of change—destruction, loss, exile, life in a devastated land—raised questions about traditionally accepted beliefs and demanded some response, Israel's idea of itself and its history in relationship with YHWH remained unique even when one allows for such parallels as those presented by Albrektson.[100] The historical sequence of the Israelites' understanding of YHWH, and of themselves as a people, is reflected in the notion of a relationship between YHWH and the Israelites as ongoing, consistent, or fraught with vicissitudes, and unfaithfulness, but always viable.[101] This view pervades personified Wisdom's teaching about God's active presence in creation, and in the lives of all who pay attention to Wisdom.[102] YHWH's dominion over the created world was at the core of wisdom, since a reality not controlled by YHWH was inconceivable.[103] The authors/redactors of Proverbs, and other wisdom writers, proclaimed trust in and reliance on God by their portrayal of Wisdom as the "first" creation and as witness of YHWH's creative activity. Her prophetic sounding speech (1:20-33) connects her with the tradition surrounding the Sinai covenant, and other acts of YHWH in Israel's history. While wisdom teachings were rooted in everyday life, they associated their experience of creation with what they learned from their historical traditions, as they too believed in YHWH as Israel's Creator and Redeemer.

Through the personification of Wisdom the authors of Proverbs 1-9 created a new model for understanding the relationship between YHWH and Israel apart from the historical mode (salvation history) in which it was usually cast. Issues of life, salvation, and continuity of the people are addressed in Wisdom's teaching (Prov 1:33, 8:35; 9:1-6). On this level, the Israelites encountered YHWH in a dynamic relationship that was as valid as the liturgical experience in the Temple, or the Exodus event, an imperative in the face of the Exile. The most developed personification of God's presence and activity in the Old Testament, the acutely drawn Wisdom figure provides an explicit way of speaking about God's relationship with Israel. Proverbs 1-9 describes Wisdom in specifically female roles, sister, mother, beloved, host, and in roles unlikely to be seen as female, teacher, judge, liberator, establisher of justice, but in these roles she is unmistakably a female figure. Never a passive figure, she signifies transcendent power present in the world of human beings. Consistent in all her appearances is

---

tradition, this does not imply that they view life other than historically. Both Wisdom of Ben Sira and the Wisdom of Solomon invoke Israel's saving history.

[100] B. Albrektson, *History and the Gods* (Lund, 1967): 81-86.

[101] J.J. Collins, "Proverbial Wisdom and the Yahwist Vision," *Semeia* 17 (1980): 1-5, illustrates a basic trait that Wisdom shares with Yahwism in claiming that both "contained within themselves the seeds of a debunking tendency".

[102] Like prophecy, the wisdom writers also raised questions as is clear in Job and Qoheleth. J.J. Collins, "The Biblical Precedent for Natural Theology" *JAAR* 45/1 (Supplement, March 1977): 35-67 notes "Wisdom is consistently presented as a revelation which is beyond human control and is experienced as gift".

[103] Von Rad, *Wisdom* (1972): 64.

her power to be an active agent who pervades the world of human beings and invites them to choose the path to life.

Wisdom Envisages a Future for Israel

Personified Wisdom's creation in Proverbs 1-9, I believe, attests to Israelite wisdom's response to the crisis following the events of 587 BCE and the reinterpretation of earlier traditions which gave voice to, and made available, a new possibility—an alternative world—in which Wisdom spoke of her pre-creation origins, claimed to be the source of life, and warned of how she would regard those who failed to listen to her teaching. Wisdom's invitations to her hearers to be her disciples are depicted as a choice between two captivating female figures— Wisdom who gives life, or Folly who brings death—on which their very life depends. Israelite/Jewish life was possible without the physical symbols of election but not without Wisdom whose teaching is given in public places and to whose banquet all are invited. Ultimately, Wisdom is a multivalent expression of God, whose demands on her disciples echo demands made by God on his people. Her speeches and actions engage her audience by subtle means of suggestions, allusions, associations, and relationships. In using various styles of characterisation, the authors make claims for Wisdom that are elsewhere made only for God and attribute to her roles that are ascribed elsewhere to YHWH.

Strong and effective characterisation makes Wisdom a figure of authority, suggesting that by heeding her in a time of crisis, and by following her teaching, which is the teaching of YHWH, life is guaranteed. Incorporating portrayals ranging from a prophet-like figure (1:20-33), to YHWH's first creation and witness to his creative activity (8:1-36), to a house builder/hostess (9:1-6), Wisdom appears against the social background of the Exile, and points to a synthesis of various traditions—particularly wisdom and prophetic. She speaks at times in prophetic tones, claims intimacy and community with God and humanity, and images the God of everyday experiences as YHWH involved in Israel's history. Thus, the Israelite image of YHWH is expanded and faithfulness to him in a changed situation is possible.

Proverbs 1-9 gives a new dimension to YHWH's involvement in the lives of the Israelites. While the Decalogue proposed certain ideals to be pursued by the people of YHWH, some areas of human life, no less important, also required actions and decisions, which ultimately affected peoples' lives profoundly. Proverbs, in portraying Wisdom as a female figure, who reinvokes the command to choose life, as enunciated in Deut 30:16-20 (cf. Prov 8:34-35; 9:11), makes this basic commandment applicable to all aspects of life, whether in exile or in the land. Prophetic motifs and themes in the portrayal of this figure, along with the attribution to her of claims understood and proclaimed by the prophets as coming from YHWH, suggest changed perceptions of YHWH and reveal the way in which some traditional beliefs were transformed.

Transformation of the earlier wisdom tradition was accomplished by way of an appeal to both wisdom and prophetic themes, combined with a reinterpretation of the traditional wisdom outlook and theology. This process of reinterpretation resulted in the personification of Wisdom texts that exhibit remarkable similarities with some prophetic texts. The correspondences are particularly evident in the frequent occurrence in Prov 1:20-33; 8:1-36 of motifs and styles that have their closest parallels in the exilic and post-exilic prophetic literature. However, while personified Wisdom speaks with authority, and her speeches and settings bear distinct resemblances to some prophetic writings, she surpasses the role of prophet, since she claims as her own the words of salvation and destruction that she speaks and the authority for these words. Speaking in public in the first person singular, she calls for attention to her words of truth (8:7); acceptance for her gifts, knowledge, insight, strength; her hatred of the ways of arrogance and evil (8:13), recognition for her role in establishing just rule on earth, "By me kings reign, and rulers decree what is just" (Prov 8:15); assures those who seek her that they will find her (8:20); and claims that she is the first creation (8:22). This self-portrait of Wisdom, who loves, hates, demands, promises, all in the interest of the ways of justice, truth, and life evokes the voice of YHWH as proclaimed through the prophets.

Depicted in the personification (objectification) of Wisdom is a figure who is not tied to human knowledge, skill, or experience, all qualities of the wise person, but is portrayed as a phenomenon so closely associated with God, that she has been in existence before the creation of the world at which she was present. All of this is related by Wisdom herself, who speaking in first person singular, issues invitations, threats, and judgements, elsewhere uttered by God (1:20-33; 8:22-31; 9:4-6). Thus, the authors of the personification texts effected a transformation of the gift of wisdom, a gift of wise persons, or a skill to be acquired through education and practice, to that of a figure who speaks directly to those in public places. This figure appropriates and transforms prophetic speeches of judgement and salvation so that she is speaking the words of YHWH. This the wisdom writers achieve, not through philosophising or seeking to use appropriate abstractions, but by personifying Wisdom thus expanding the Israelite perception of YHWH by introducing into the tradition perspectives on God not previously expressed or imagined.

Ultimately, the portrayals of Wisdom in Proverbs 1-9 imply that this figure is a multivalent expression of God. Her speeches and actions engage her audience by subtle means of suggestions, allusions, associations, and relationships. In using various styles of characterisation, the authors make claims for her that are elsewhere made only for God and attribute to her roles that are ascribed elsewhere to YHWH. Her demands on her disciples echo demands made by God on his people. In combining this figure and many "God" qualities, an expanded image of God is created which revisioned, generated, and evoked faithfulness to Israel's God in the face of the crisis following the Babylonian victory. From the emphasis on Wisdom's intimate connection with creation, "the Lord by wisdom founded the earth" (Prov 3:19), to Wisdom's unfolding in Prov 8:22-31, "the first of his acts of long ago", to her being beside him as אָמוֹן, this figure is inseparable from YHWH, whose authority over the whole world is the core of wisdom. However, while the Israelites believed that all reality was governed by YHWH, who was present throughout their history and had been their redeemer (Exod 15:13) in times past, they faced the defeat and loss brought about by the Babylonians. If faith in YHWH's presence and power were to be revitalised a reinterpretation of how YHWH was present in their situation was imperative.[104] Personified Wisdom's constant offer of "life" and "insight" was perhaps the most powerful revisioning offered. This is illustrated in her words of invitation to choose life, words which recall her earlier promise.

> Give heed to my reproof; I will pour out my thoughts to you;
> I will make my words known to you. (Prov 1:23)

> Come, eat of my bread and drink of the wine I have mixed.
> Lay aside immaturity, and live, and walk in the way of insight. (Prov 9:5-6)

Wisdom Ensures Divine Presence

As discussed above, events preceding and following 587 BCE were decisive for the emergence of the figure of personified Wisdom in the Old Testament. However, the concern of this work is not to describe these happenings as historical events, but to propose that 587 BCE signified for the people of Israel the end of a known world, and the break down of their system of meaning and power. Two major tasks faced the Israelites who longed to sustain their identity either in an alien world as a remnant in the land now controlled by others or in a strange land. The first of these tasks was to envisage a new world in which the old world of king and temple had disappeared and the second required the recreation of a way of life that would sustain them and their heritage in a world of other traditions. The wisdom writers' articulation and development of the figure of personified Wisdom began, as a response to the theological crisis generated by the Babylonian victory over the Israelites and all that it entailed. This character was one means by which the theological crisis was addressed, and a new theological notion affirmed.

By personifying Wisdom, the wisdom tradition fashioned a character who was, as it were, "the first-person voice of wisdom", and gave expression to a way of regarding wisdom that exceeded human knowledge, skill, and experience. She was a paradoxical figure, a public presence and was clearly accessible in Proverbs 1-9. This image is in sharp contrast to her hiddenness and elusiveness in Job 28 and Bar 3:14-37, a contrast, which also applies to the presence of YHWH whom the Israelite tradition perceived as accessible but hidden. Since the Wisdom figure portrayed aspects of YHWH it is not surprising that this figure is elusive yet

---

[104] J. Marböck, *Weisheit im Wandel* (Bonn, 1971), captures this unity of theology and the everyday when he notes in the Wisdom of Ben Sira the mixture of theological and religious interpretation of Wisdom (Sir 4:11-19, 23-24).

accessible, a multifaceted character, who is never explained, who speaks her own message, is spoken about, but never refers to the cult or to salvation history.[105]

That the figure of Wisdom emerged in the wake of the destruction of the Temple seems most likely. The loss of the cult centre meant that the salvation history paradigm had broken down. Israel had to cast about for a way out of the chaos, believed by some to have been caused by their own behaviour. If a society sees itself as having some responsibility for its own situation, then it must also find a way through the disorder. So they looked to a way of thinking and acting in the wider tradition that was not totally dependent on the cult or on the salvation history tradition. Personified Wisdom's speaking in public places, in keeping with the wisdom tradition's view of everyday life as lived in relation to YHWH, is a strong indication that the Temple does not exist. Wisdom offers the choice and the invitation in the marketplace, not in the Temple, or Holy Place setting.

Texts in which Wisdom is personified are couched in imaginative speech that is rooted in the memory of Israel's heritage and address the current situation. This new perception of Israelite teaching is not personal invention. Wisdom writers explore and search their earlier traditions, and initiate a "revisioning" of that tradition. It is very likely that the new articulation took shape primarily in the people's liturgical celebrations, as it is in celebrations and rituals that the people of Israel would seek to give meaning to their lives by "re-membering" YHWH's deeds on their behalf in the past and celebrating them in the present. Wisdom, by enshrining the choices available to "the simple", gives her audience direction about their losses in ways that required them to face the reversals of fortune that they and their ancestors had suffered.[106] Thus, emerge themes, metaphors, and powerful associations that give new life to the tradition, by imaging the presence of God in a new way, and bringing hope to a people in crisis.

Wisdom, a female speaker, addresses survivors by presenting a choice between life/Wisdom, and death/Folly in the marketplace, not in the Temple, or Holy Place setting. Her claims, which are those the prophets regarded as YHWH's claims, are not connected with past claims of the Davidic dynasty, the rituals of the Jerusalem Temple, or the power invested in the king, but are presented as a dynamic source of hope, inviting the simple, the scoffers, and those who hate knowledge (1:21) to listen to her words. Wisdom appears in human situations making spectacular claims because of her intimate association with YHWH. She echoes YHWH's threats and promises, ensures that one-sided and unbalanced claims for Wisdom are avoided. Wisdom writers juxtapose and transform established understandings of YHWH and through the reinterpretation and transformation of earlier traditions; they show that YHWH can act in new ways. Thus, they envisage the emergence of a new community, obedient to Wisdom and her teaching, in which life can begin anew.

---

[105] In Sir 24:1-34 Wisdom's presence in the sanctuary connects her with the cult.

[106] A.N. Wilder "Story and Story World" *Int* 37 (1983): 353-364, on the way language creates worlds. The sociological dimensions of this power of language are made clear in P. Berger and T. Luckmann, *The Social Construction of Reality* (Garden City, 1966).

Personified Wisdom's emergence and development attest to Israelite wisdom's response to the crisis following the events of 587 BCE and the search for a viable interpretation of that crisis. The transformation of earlier traditions gave voice to, and made available, a new possibility, an alternative world in which Wisdom spoke of her pre-creation origins, claimed to be the source of life, and warned of how she would regard those who failed to listen to her teaching. Invitations to her audience to be her disciples—a goal presented as the ultimate destiny for the human being—involves choices, and one's very "life" depends on a choice depicted in Proverbs in terms of two captivating female characters between which the audience must choose: Wisdom who gives life, or Folly who brings death. Therefore, life was possible without Jerusalem, the Temple, the Davidic monarchy or residence in the land of Israel, but not without Wisdom. Cast largely in the forms and images of Israel's longstanding tradition, discernment and presentation of the new depends profoundly on knowledge of the old. Images of YHWH's dealings with human beings are illustrated through the figure of Wisdom who speaks with the authority of YHWH, gives her message in public places, issues invitations to accept her teaching and participate in her banquet. Thus, God continues to speak of salvation and destruction to the people of Israel but they must hear a new voice, the voice of Wisdom personified.

Personified Wisdom was a response to the crisis following the events of 587 BCE, usually called the Babylonian Exile. This involved alienation of the land, the loss of Jerusalem including the temple and the Davidic monarchy and exile of some from the land.[107] The Wisdom figure by her appeals to prophecy and her transformation of Israelite traditions 'justifies' the ways of God in the exilic situation, and instructs her audience on how to deal with the crisis attendant on the Babylonian destruction. Wisdom in Proverbs 1-9 expanded and shaped the Israelite understanding of YHWH's presence in exilic and post-exilic 'foreign' settings, and so contributed directly to the survival and revitalisation of the Israelite faith in YHWH.

---

[107] R.W. Klein, *Israel in Exile* (Philadelphia, 1979): 1-9; P.R. Ackroyd, *Exile and Restoration* (Philadelphia, 1968): 17-38; *Israel under Babylon and Persia* (London, 1970): 1-59; "Archaeology, Politics and Religion: The Persian Period" *IR* 39 (1982): 5-24; B. Oded, "Israelite History" in J.H. Hayes and J.M. Miller, eds. *Israelite and Judaean History* (Philadelphia, 1977): 469-488.

Chapter 3

Wisdom, Where Shall She Be Found?

Introduction

In marked contrast to portrayals of Wisdom in Proverbs Job in a beautiful Wisdom poem twice asks, "But where can wisdom be found; where is the source of understanding?" (Job 28:12), "But whence does wisdom come? Where is the source of understanding?" (Job 28:20). Paradoxically, Wisdom in Proverbs is eloquent, dynamic, vibrant, a public loving figure, prophet-like, a host, a public speaker who threatens, persuades and talks about herself, while Wisdom in Job and Baruch emerges as mysteriously elusive, inaccessible, and incomprehensible. "Wisdom cannot be found in the land of the living" (Job 20:13), "She is hidden from the eyes of all living" (Job 28:21). "No one knows the way to her, or is concerned about the path to her" (Bar 3:31) suggest Wisdom's remoteness from human beings in Job and Baruch. As the questions above illustrates wisdom eludes the keenest of searchers. In this chapter, I examine how the wisdom poems in Job 28 and Baruch 3:9-4:4 portray Wisdom particularly in terms of Wisdom's relationships with God, with the created world and with human beings, the issues and situations addressed by Wisdom and how Wisdom functions in these poems.

"God understands the way to it and God knows its source" (Job 28:23) may be a declaration of acceptance that Wisdom is beyond the reach of human beings or on the contrary, it may imply that Wisdom is God's business, so why search! A corresponding stance characterises, "The one who knows all things knows her, he found her by his understanding" (Bar 3:32). The introduction of these two popular Jewish motifs, woven through Old Testament wisdom, of the search for Wisdom and Wisdom's elusiveness, surely intimates an ongoing search and desire for wisdom in the Hebrew tradition.[1] The classic perception of Wisdom's inaccessibility appears in Job 28, and it is to this text that commentators

---

[1] Some scholars claim that wisdom is personified in Job 28, while others regard it as a divine attribute, but the statement that "only God knows where wisdom is" (Job 28:20-23) implies a more clearly defined identity than that of an attribute or quality of God. "She" and "her" appear to be more in keeping in Job 28 with the references to wisdom, which is feminine gender in Hebrew and Greek. The translator or interpreter decides whether the most appropriate pronoun is "it" or "she". If "she" is used the account reads like a personification text, and as the poetic language of Job 28 intensifies the depiction beyond simple narrative, it may suggest that the author intended to personify Wisdom.

invariably refer; claiming usually that the Baruch poem is dependent on Job 28.[2] Nevertheless, a small number of scholars believe that Job 28 and Baruch 3:9-4:4 share certain similarities but also have quite distinct characteristics. Küchler systematically compared Job 28 with Bar 3:15-38 and more recently Steck has produced a very comprehensive analysis of these two texts.[3] Both of these commentators argue convincingly that the whole of the Wisdom poem in Baruch is not dependent on Job 28. To discuss this issue some discussion of the possible dating of these two works is necessary.

Dating Job 28 and Baruch 3:9-4:4

There is substantial agreement that the book of Job was composed sometime during the period from the mid sixth century to mid fourth century BCE.[4] This agreement is based on the number of Joban references that reflect the exilic and post-exilic Isaiah 40-55 and the use of the Hebrew *ha-satan*, "the Adversary" (cf. Zechariah 3). Characteristics such as references to kings, princes and counsellors, caravans from Teman and Sheba (6:19) also point to the Persian Period (539-332). Other factors such as similarities with Psalm 73, 107, Lament Psalms, Jeremiah, and Deuteronomy, also support a date around this period.

The book of Baruch is in the main considered a later composition than the book of Job. Although set during the Babylonian Exile of the early sixth century BCE, and purporting to be the work of Baruch, Jeremiah's secretary (Jer 32:12-16; 36:4-32; 43:1-7; 45:11-12), the variety of literature in Baruch suggests that this work has had a complex redaction history.[5] Much of the book consists of pastiches of biblical passages copied or paraphrased from Daniel 9; Job 28; Isaiah 40-66 and Psalm 11 of Psalms of Solomon.[6] While the prose section of Baruch (1:1-3:8) has long been viewed as translated from a lost Hebrew original, recent research

---

[2] M. Küchler, *Frühjüdische Weisheitstradition* (Stuttgart, 1979): 49-55.

[3] O.H. Steck, *Das apokryphe Baruchbuch* (1993): 116-163.

[4] A. Hurvitz, "The Date of the Prose Tale of Job Linguistically Reconsidered" *HTR* 67 (1974): 17-34.

[5] Scholars have failed to resolve the issue of the historicity of the character of Baruch. See W.L. Holladay, *Jeremiah 2: A Commentary on the Book of the Prophet Jeremiah, Chapters 26-52* (Philadelphia, 1989): 215-216, follows a long-established consensus in taking what appear to be historical allusions to Baruch at face value. R.P. Carroll, *Jeremiah: A Commentary*, OTL (Philadelphia, 1986): 665, 722-724, challenge this view, and suggests that Baruch is a fictional character, whereby the "tradition created and developed a subsidiary figure to accompany Jeremiah". J.A. Dearman, "My Servants the Scribes: Composition and Context in Jeremiah 36" *JBL* 109 (1990): 404 n. 2 claims "there is no good reason historically or culturally to doubt the existence or the actuality of Baruch"; Most scholars agree that the book of Baruch had a complex history and is unlikely to have been the work of Jeremiah's secretary; C.A. Moore, "Towards the Dating of the Book of Baruch" CBQ 36 (1974): 312-320.

[6] E. Tov, *The Book of Baruch* also called *I Baruch* (Greek and Hebrew) (Missoula, 1975), which is a translation of Bar 1:1-3:8 into Hebrew, illustrates this point well.

suggests that the poetic sections also derive from Hebrew originals. R. Martin who applies a method he terms "syntax criticism" to help determine whether a Greek document was originally written in Greek or translated from Hebrew or Aramaic concludes that 3:9-4:4 is from Aramaic.[7] Burke, by skilful analysis of the Greek text—the earliest extant version of the work—effectively argues that 3:9-5:9 is most likely a translation from a Hebrew original, now lost.[8] According to biblical tradition (Jer 43:1-7) Jeremiah and Baruch were taken to Egypt in 582 BCE after the Babylonian destruction of Jerusalem. However, Bar 1:1-4 tells us that Baruch, like many others, was taken prisoner to Babylon, and it is from here that he sends the gift of money and atonement texts to Jerusalem. Baruch's historical or fictional origins do not alter the work's prophetic and exilic connections. My argument follows a generally accepted view that the work is late post-exilic, probably written/redacted sometime between 200-60 BCE. This view is based on conclusions about the relationship of parts of Baruch to other biblical texts, for example, Bar 1:15-2:19 employs phrases and ideas similar to those in Dan 9:7-19, dated to 164 BCE.

Whether the Baruch text borrowed from the Daniel text or both authors had access to a common text is difficult to know. If Bar 1:15-2:19 is largely Dan 9:4-19 rewritten, and if the book of Daniel was composed in the first half of the second century BCE, Baruch may have been written sometime after 150 BCE.[9] Those who regard the book as the work of Jeremiah's scribe date Baruch to the time of the Exile.[10] Scholarly opinions range from those favouring an exilic date to those opting for a date sometime around 100 CE. Steck considers the book to be a literary unit put together by a group of writers/redactors in the years 163-62 BCE. He places it in the period between The Wisdom of Ben Sira and the Psalms of Solomon.[11] Similarities between Bar 3:37-4:2 and Sir 24:8-11, 23 do suggest that either one of these texts was known to the other author or both authors used the same source. Otzen's proposal that the various parts of Baruch were brought together after the rebellion against the Romans in 70 CE is well substantiated by textual evidence.[12] He argues, correctly, I believe, the Baruch figure experienced the destruction of Jerusalem. Thus, the retrieved Baruch's reflections regarding the city's fate and future could, in the shape of a prophecy, be invoked to comfort those who in Roman times were experiencing the same kind of destruction as that in the Exile. In this way, the figure of Baruch views both destructions from one perspective.[13] Moore argues that the five sections of Baruch were probably written

---

[7] R. Martin, "The Syntax Criticism of Baruch" *IOSCS* Congress VII Vol. 31 (1988): 361-371.
[8] D.G. Burke, *The Poetry of Baruch* SBLSCS 10 (Atlanta, 1982): particularly 20-23.
[9] O.H. Steck, *Das apokryphe Baruchbuch* (1993): 285-303, offers a useful summary of attempts to date the book of Baruch.
[10] E. Kalt, *Das Buch Baruch* (Bonn, 1932): 1-8.
[11] See Steck, *Das apokryphe Baruchbuch* (1993): 119-139; 285-303.
[12] B. Otzen, "Lov og Visdom I Baruks Bog" in E.K. Holt, J.L. Hans, K. Jeppesen, eds., *Lov og Visdom* (Frederiksberg, 1995): 36-48.
[13] Otzen, "Lov og Visdom" (1995): 36-48.

sometime between the fourth and second centuries, the sections being assembled as a book in the second century BCE. He hesitates over the dating of the final composition noting, "the evidence is too scanty and ambiguous to permit greater precision or certainty".[14] If Bar 3:9-4:4 emerged in its final form in late post-exilic times, it may have been addressed to Jewish communities in Judah and in the Diaspora during the Seleucid and later eras of suffering and repression.

Elusive Wisdom in Job 28 and Baruch 3:9-4:4

Contrary to the common perception that Job 28 is a hymn in praise of Wisdom, the poem teaches that Wisdom is very difficult to acquire. Here, as in Ps 111:10 and Prov 1:7; 9:10, we find praises of the two crucial gifts, fear of the Lord and wisdom. In the Old Testament God's bestowal of these gifts was demonstrated in the lives of the "wise ones" of the Hebrew tradition. They were enabled to surpass what their human abilities could have allowed them to achieve.[15] In Job, as in Proverbs, the fear of the Lord is presented as superior to elusive Wisdom. The poem functions as an interlude allowing the audience time to reflect on what has passed so far and perhaps prepare for what is ahead.

Job 28 in composition and theme consider the inaccessibility of Wisdom. Human beings who are able to search out the hiding places of precious stones and metals, (vv.1-6, 9-11, 13), animals who see things never seen by human beings (vv.7-8, 21), the ocean (v.14), and Sheol (v.22) do not know the way to Wisdom. Only God knows (v.23) and the only way to Wisdom is "the fear of the Lord, that is wisdom; and to depart from evil is understanding" (v.28). Fear of the Lord is crucial for attaining wisdom and fearing God and shunning evil are the attributes par excellence of Job. Structurally the poem falls into three sections, (verses 1-11, 12-19, 20-28), and four key words, "place", "way" "to search" "to see", anchor the theme. This poem functions in the book to announce that no human being can know the way to Wisdom. In addition, it implies that the audience already knows that the dialogues between Job and the friends will not effectively resolve the problem raised by Job. The poem suggests that if a resolution is forthcoming it will not come from the friends' present search. Thus, the search is directed forward to chapters 38-41. Wisdom in this poem is cosmic wisdom (vv.25-26) which is a breakthrough from the historical and personal viewpoints pervading the debates of Job. The cosmic perspective also points forward to the divine speeches at the end of the book.

The book of Baruch falls into three distinct parts: 1:1-3:8, a prose section consisting of the prayer of the exiles preceded by an introduction setting the historical context; 3:9-4:4 a hymn in praise of Wisdom; 4:5-5:9 a section that describes Jerusalem consoling her children and receiving consolation. Like Job 28, the wisdom poem in Baruch falls into three sections (3:9-13; 3:14-4:1; 4:2-4).

---

[14] C.A. Moore, *Daniel, Esther, and Jeremiah, the Additions* (1977): 304, 260.
[15] Some wise ones are the woman of Tekoa, Ruth, Joseph, Solomon, Job, Daniel.

Steck describes these three parts as: 3:9-13 exhortative introduction influenced by Deuteronomy; 3:14-4:1 the middle section influenced by Jeremiah and Deuteronomy but clearly in the wisdom tradition, mainly Job 28; Prov 3:13-26; 8:22-31; Sir 24:1-34, where creation is emphasised; 4:2-4 the concluding section mainly influenced by Deuteronomy.[16] Otzen sees the poem organised under themes as follows. The first theme appears in 3:9-13 and emphasises that the people are in exile because they abandoned the fountain of Wisdom. The second theme appears in 3:14-19 and asserts the futility of searching for the rulers of the past, or for the house of Wisdom. A third theme in 3:20-23 highlights the hopelessness of seeking the path to Wisdom, since throughout history the generations have not found it. The fourth theme in 3:24-36 emphasises that only God knows the path to Wisdom. The fifth and final theme in 3:37-4:4 stresses that Wisdom is in the Law of Moses, which only Israel knows. Such a collection of themes highlights the multivariate nature of the poem's structure, and the range of its nuances. Another fascinating aspect of this poem is its many parallels and echoes with Deuteronomy 30.[17]

Baruch 3:9-11
Hear the commandments of life, O Israel; give ear and learn wisdom! Why is it that you are in the land of your enemies, that you are growing old in a foreign country that you are defiled with the dead, that you are counted among those in Hades?

Deuteronomy 30:1-5
Even if you are exiled to the ends of the world, from there the Lord your God will gather you, and from there he will bring you back. The Lord your God will bring you into the land that your ancestors possessed and you will possess it. . . .

Baruch 3:12-14
You have forsaken the fountain of wisdom. If you had walked in the way of God, you would be living in peace forever. Learn where there is wisdom . . . . so that you may at the same time discern where there is length of days, and life, where there is light for the eyes, and peace.

Deuteronomy 30:18-20
I call heaven and earth to witness against you today that I have set before you life and death, blessings and curses. Choose life so that you and your descendants may live, loving the Lord your God, obeying him, and holding fast to him; for that means life to you and length of days . . . .

Baruch 3:29-31
Who has gone up into heaven, and taken her, and brought her down from the clouds? Who has gone over the sea, and found her, and will buy her for pure gold? No one knows the way to her, or is concerned about the path to her.

Deuteronomy 30:12-14
It is not in heaven, that you should say, "Who will go up to heaven for us, and get it for us so that we may hear it and observe it?" . . . . No, the word is very near to you; it is in your mouth and in your heart for you to observe.

Baruch 4:1-4
She is the book of the commandments of

Deuteronomy 30:15-20
See, I have set before you today life and

---

[16] G.W.E. Nickelsburg, *Jewish Literature between the Bible and the Mishnah* (London, 1981): 111, 153, n. 31, sees this section as an editorial connection; see O.H. Steck, *Das apokryphe Baruchbuch* (1993): 129-135.

[17] O.H. Steck, *Das apokryphe Baruchbuch* (1993): 133-4 supports this notion with his discussion of the similarities between Bar 3:9-4:4 and Deuteronomy.

God, the law that endures forever. All who hold her fast will live, and those who forsake her will die. . . . Do not give your glory to another or your advantages to an alien people. Happy are we, O Israel, for we know what is pleasing to God.

prosperity, death and adversity. If you obey the commandments of the Lord your God that I am commanding you today, by loving the Lord your God . . . . then you shall live and become numerous, and the Lord your God will bless you. . . .

Baruch 3:9-4:4 is set between the confession and prayer (Bar 1:15-3:8), which explains the Exile as Israel's punishment for abandoning Wisdom, and three addresses (the first by a prophet, 4:5-9; the second by Jerusalem 4:10-29; and the third by a prophet 4:30-5:9), to the Diaspora and to Jerusalem promising the exiles' return.[18] Although this poem begins with the notion underlying Baruch's confession and prayer (Bar 1:15-3:8) that Israel's exilic punishment was caused by her failure to obey YHWH's commandments, the Law of Moses (Bar 2:28-35 cf. 3:10; Deut 30:17-18), it does not address the concerns about exile, repentance, and return to the land of Israel of the preceding prose text. An abrupt change of mood begins at 3:9 with the switch from prose to poetry, from confession and petition to praise of Wisdom, and to evocations of Deuteronomy 4, 9, 30; Proverbs 1-9, Job 28; and the Wisdom of Ben Sira 24.

Wisdom is God's Gift to Israel

Beginning with a call to repentance and an appeal for attention, Bar 3:9-4:4 makes two immediate associations (3:9-14): life with the commandments (3:9), the dead with defilement (3:10), while at the conclusion the poem associates Wisdom with the Law and with the choice between life and death: "all who hold her fast will live, and those who forsake her will die" (4:1).[19] References to a choice between life and death at the beginning and end of the poem set the principal theme.[20] Verses 9-14 outline the problem and its solution and verses 15-31 offer a discourse pinpointing elusiveness as Wisdom's hallmark (3:15-31). The poem concludes with a response lauding God the Creator as giver of Wisdom to the Israelite people (3:32-38) and an exhortation to the audience to embrace Wisdom/Torah (4:1-4).[21]

---

[18] The first section (Bar 1:1-3:8) includes an introduction (1:1-14), a confession to compatriots in Jerusalem (1:15-2:10), and a prayer to the Lord to save his people Israel (2:11-3:8).

[19] This clear choice is also offered by Wisdom in Prov 8:35-36: "For he who finds me finds life and obtains favour from the Lord; but he who misses me injures himself; all who hate me love death" (cf. Sir 1:10; 4:12).

[20] One of the links between the first (1:1-3:8) and second, (3:9-4:4) sections of Baruch are references to the dead, "Lord Almighty, God of Israel, hear now the prayer of the dead of Israel . . . who did not heed the voice of the Lord their God" (Bar 3:4); "you are defiled with the dead" (v.10b). A choice between life and death also features in Deuteronomy 4; 30; Proverbs 1-9.

[21] J. Anoz, "Estudio Sobre Baruch 3:9-4:4" *Mayévtica* 7 (1981); 161-177, sees this poem as

The Shema, "Listen, O Israel, to the commandments", serves a multiple purpose here. Evoking the "Hear, O Israel, the statutes and the ordinances that I speak in your hearing this day" (Deut 5:1; 6:4; 30:15-20) suggests that Deuteronomy has been infringed, and introduces the characteristic preface to advice in the wisdom genre, "Hear my child(ren) . . . and be attentive" (Prov 1:8; 4:1, 10; 5:7; 8:32-33). This age-old biblical command to "listen" or "be attentive" is addressed to the Jews, descendants of the people first addressed by Moses at Sinai with this cry. It details their unfaithfulness and its consequences. They are "in the land of their enemies" (Bar 3:9-13; cf. 3:4); they abandoned "the fountain of wisdom" (3:12; cf. Jer 2:13);[22] they failed to "walk in the way of God" (v.13); they abandoned the privilege of "living in peace forever".[23]   The author links Wisdom and the commandments in the opening verse (3:9) and categorically proclaims this affinity in the final section of the poem (4:1). Thus, the author links the identification of Wisdom with the Law and by coupling the identification with a choice between life and death enjoins the audience to make a choice.

Having demanded the attention due to a reading of the Law, the author next directs a series of accusatory questions to his hearers in "the land of your enemies". He confronts his audience, who "are growing old in a foreign country" (v.10) with their unfaithfulness, reminds them of their lengthy "exile", being "defiled with the dead" (v.10b), and "counted among those in Hades". Thus, he suggests association with pagans, who are "dead" because they do not know and observe the Law, the source of life.[24] A prophetic tone appears in the accusation of pollution by idolatry (cf. Jer 2:23 "I am not defiled; I have not gone after the Baals"; Ezek 20:31, "you defile yourselves with all your idols to this day"; Mic 6:10-14, "Can I forget the treasures of wickedness in the house of the wicked?"). The poet contrasts the negative images of "enemies", "dead", "Hades" associated with the exiles (vv.10-11) with the image of "the spring of Wisdom" (v.12) that they in their waywardness have "forsaken". Following this accusation is the regretful plea, "if only you had walked in the way of God, you would be living in peace forever" (v.13). Here we have an image of God as the abandoned one who could lead and teach that is reminiscent of Jer 2:13, "they have deserted me, the spring of living waters". It also evokes Sir 1:5 (a verse added by some ancient authorities such as the expanded translation Greek II), "the source of wisdom is God's word in the highest heaven, and her ways are the eternal commandments", which emphasises the notion of Wisdom as one with the Law of Moses.[25]   The

---

a strict unity whose essential theme is praise of the laws of God. He claims that the pericope is organised in a concentric and ternary structure, following a three-member schematic: call to attention, questioning, and answer.

[22] Jer 2:13: "My people have committed two evils: they have forsaken me, the fountain of living waters, and hewed out cisterns for themselves, broken cisterns, that can hold no water".

[23] This verse recalls Isa 48:18 "O that you had listened to my commandments! Then your peace would have been like a river, and your righteousness like the waves of the sea."

[24] This may be a literary device used to create a setting for the poem.

[25] See *NRSV 102 Apocrypha*, note c; P. Skehan and A. Di Lella, *Wisdom of Ben Sira* (New

reference to "eternal commandments" reflects a belief held by the Rabbis.[26] The *Gemara* knows an old tradition that Prov 3:18 also speaks of the Torah, although the scriptural text refers to Wisdom (Ber. 32b).[27] In a contrasting tone, the author now focuses on how the audience must change so that they will enjoy the fruits of Wisdom, "learn where there is Wisdom, where there is strength . . . where there is length of days . . ." (3:14).[28] "Length of days" μακροβίωσις a neologism in Baruch recalls μακροημέρευσις (a neologism) in Sir 1:20, "the root of Wisdom is fear of the Lord; her branches are length of days" (also Sir 1:12, 30:22). These fruits of faithfulness to Wisdom are reminiscent of Prov 3:13-18, "Happy is the one who finds Wisdom and the one who gets understanding," and Job 12:13, "With God are wisdom and might; God has counsel and understanding". To sum up, Bar 3:9-31 announces the subject as the commandments of life/Wisdom; pinpoints the audience's failure to observe Torah as forsaking Wisdom; names the consequences of this failure, and exhorts the audience.

Bar 3:32 effects a smooth transition to the main body of the poem. Having categorically established the futility of seeking Wisdom by means of knowledge, wealth, power, or in locations regarded as places of wisdom, the poet begins the third section of the poem, (3:32-38) by leading the audience into a litany of praise for God the Creator, who "found" Wisdom:

> But the one who knows all things knows her (Wisdom). . . .
> The one who prepared the earth for all time . . .
> the one who sends forth the light, and it goes . . .
> the stars shone in their watches and were glad;
> he called them, and they said, "Here we are!" (Bar 3:32-34)

Multiple images of God as creator and of creation's joyous response characterise this section. By speaking metaphorically of the stars as sentries keeping watch during the night, the poet evokes the intimate relationship between the Creator and the created universe. Surely, the Creator has as much concern for the human part of

---

York, 1987) notes that in GII, an expanded Greek translation of The Wisdom of Ben Sira, this verse may be a gloss on v.4 (cf. Bar 3:12; Jer 2:13; John 1:1-2).

[26] *Midrash Rabbah I Genesis* I2, ET: H. Freedman and M. Simon (London, 1951): 56, In the *Midrash Bereshith Rabbah VIII*: 2-3, Rabbi Simeon Ben Lakish, commenting on Gen 1:26, states that the Torah preceded the creation of the world by two thousand years. "Then I [The Torah] was with Him, as a nursling, and I was his delight day after day (Prov 8:30)".

[27] See S. Singer and M. Adler, *The Authorized Daily Prayer Book* (1962): 69, "It is a tree of life to them that grasp it" identifies Wisdom with Torah; also Aboth 6:10; G.F. Moore, *Judaism in the First Centuries of the Christian Era* (Cambridge, 1927-30): 263-269, deals with the relationship between Wisdom and the Law and gives other examples of the development of this idea by the rabbis.

[28] Three synonyms for Wisdom σοφία (Bar 3:12); φρόνησις "understanding", "intelligence" (Bar 3:14); σύνεσις "prudence", "discretion" (Bar 3:9, 14), appear in the introductory section, and recur throughout this wisdom poem. Although σοφία is the most comprehensive, these words seem to be interchangeable.

the creation as for the stars. Integral to this image is the Hebrew notion of creation where the stars are brought out, rather than come out, a sharp contrast to the Greek view of an ordered universe where law or secondary causation prevails.[29] Crowning this panoply of praise is a proclamation of God's uniqueness, "no other can be compared with him" (3:35). This is reminiscent of Isaiah 40-66 in particular: "Before me no god was formed, nor shall there be any after me" (Isa 43:10-11); "I am the first and I am the last; besides me there is no god" (Isa 44:6); "I am the Lord, and there is no other" (Isa 45:18). God's uniqueness is inseparable from God's association with Wisdom and from God's gift of Wisdom to Israel (v.36b). God alone found the way to Wisdom (vv.29-37), and it is God who gave Wisdom to Israel alone among humanity (v.36). "This is our God . . . he found the whole way to knowledge, and gave her to Jacob his servant and to Israel whom he loved" (Bar 3:36-37).

In Job 28 it is not clear just what God did with Wisdom, but in Bar 3:37-4:2 "[God] gave her to his servant Jacob, and to Israel." The notion of God "choosing" a people is prominent in Isaiah and the designation of the "chosen" people as Jacob in parallel with Israel is frequent (Isa 41:8, 9; 43:10; 44:1, 2; 48:10; 49:7). This is precisely the portion of Isaiah that deals with Babylon.[30] Isaiah's perspective is that the fall of Babylon is inextricably linked with the salvation of Israel as is clear from the first mention of it in 43:14 "For your sake I will send to Babylon" plus the combination of the two themes in chapters 46-47 and in the closing section of chapter 48 and of 45:1-4. It seems very likely that the author of the wisdom poem is prompting his audience to appropriate the sentiments expressed by Isaiah in their own "exilic" situation and to see their circumstances are inextricably linked with their salvation. The homing in on Jacob/Israel serves to pinpoint Wisdom's inextricable connection with the audience's true heritage and to highlight the futility of the search for Wisdom just outlined.

Bar 3:36 answers the question "Who has found her place?" (3:15), and features a distinct divergence from Job 28 in claiming that Wisdom was given exclusively to the people of Israel. "After that she appeared on earth and lived among human beings" (v.38), has provoked more comment, and caused more controversy, than any other verse in Baruch.[31] One source of ambiguity in the Greek is the absence of a subject apart from the verb μετὰ τοῦτο ἐπὶ τῆς γῆς ὤφθη καὶ ἐν τοῖς ἀνθρώποις συνανεστράφη, thus leaving the interpreter some leeway in how the line may be understood. Interestingly, the *Vulgate* has, "post haec in terris visus est et cum hominibus conversatus est". Several Greek and Latin Fathers, especially during the Arian controversy of the fourth century saw this verse as a prediction of the incarnation (John 1:14).[32] Simonetti notes that Bar 3:38, "Only

---

[29] In the Hebrew view of nature, "natural" events were immediately dependent upon divine activity as expressed here in Baruch.

[30] Isa 40:27; 41:8, 14; 42:24; 43:1, 22, 28; 44:1, 5, 21, 23; 45:4; 46:3; 48:1, 12; 49:5-6. See H.G.M. Williamson, *The Book Called Isaiah* (Oxford, 1994):165-166.

[31] "He" is used in Latin and Syriac. See C.A. Moore, *Daniel, Esther, and Jeremiah, the Additions* AB 44 (New York, 1977): 301.

[32] F.H. Reusch, *Erklärung des Buches Baruch* (Freiburg, 1853) provides an exhaustive list

then did she appear on earth and live among human beings." and Isa 45:14, "They will make supplication to you, saying, "God is with you alone, and there is no other; there is no god besides him," were taken up by the Monarchians in order to emphasise the identification of the Son with the Father.

Hippolytus and Tertullian interpreted 3:38 to underline the distinction of the Son from the Father.[33] They interpreted the two texts differently in opposition to the Arians, because both could easily be used to underline the unity of the nature of the Son with the Father.[34] Kneucker and Schürer regarded this verse as a Christian interpolation, and some more recent scholars continue to insist on this, considering the phrase μετὰ τοῦτο "after that" as a clumsy introduction to v.38.[35] Sheppard summarily dismisses this verse as "well attested in Greek texts . . . but generally suspected by commentators to be a later Christian gloss . . . for our purposes, it is not essential to the analysis and has, therefore, been dropped".[36] As no specific denomination is applied to ἀνθρώποις "human beings" this text may be read to say that following the giving of Wisdom to the people of Israel she takes up her abode on earth and is available to all human beings. The context of verses 36-38 clearly suggests that Wisdom is the referent for αὐτὴν the "her" of "he gave her" (v.37) and "the she" of "she is the book" (4:1), and "she appeared" rather than "he" of the Latin, is intended. Such a reading is consistent with other wisdom texts such as, Sir 24:10-12; Wis 9:10; Prov 8:30-31. Some hesitate to call Wisdom "she" in this context even though the poet used three different Greek terms for "Wisdom" each of feminine gender. The close resemblance between this poem and Sir 24: 1-34, where Wisdom is a female figure, suggests that the author of Bar 3:9-4:4 must also have intended Wisdom to be understood as a female figure.[37]

Bar 4:1-2 makes explicit the identification of Wisdom and Torah hinted at in 3:9,12-13, 29-30 (cf. Deut 30:11-13; Sir 24:22-23; Isa 60:3).[38] By presenting adherence to Wisdom/Torah as a choice between life and death (4:1b)—death awaits those who forsake Wisdom—the poet again calls to mind a pivotal choice offered throughout wisdom teaching and particularly by personified Wisdom in Proverbs 1-9. He shows that in faithfulness to Wisdom the "exiles" will return to

---

of Church Fathers who discussed Bar 3:36-38; M. Simonetti, *Biblical Interpretation in the Early Church* (Edinburgh, 1994): 129, 135-6 n. 41.

[33] Hippolytus, *Contra Noetum* 2; 4:5 ; Tertullian, *Adv. Praxean* 13:2; 16:3.

[34] Athanasius, *Ad. Serap.* 2:4; Hilary, *De Trin.* IV 38-40, 42; V 39.

[35] J.J. Kneucker, *Das Buch Baruch: Geschichte und Kritik* (Leipzig, 1879); E. Schürer, *A History of the Jewish People in the Age of Jesus Christ.* 2. Translated by G. Vermes (Edinburgh, 1970): 29-183.

[36] Sheppard, *Wisdom* (1980): 97 n. 19.

[37] Ringgren, *Word and Wisdom* (1947): 114, observes that calling Wisdom "she" is not without its dangers, since, "Wisdom is depicted in 2:9-4:4 as an independent entity, but is not very clearly shaped as a personal being".

[38] R.H. Pfeiffer, *History of New Testament Times with an Introduction to the Apocrypha* (New York, 1949): 421, and others suggest that προσταγμάτων "commandments" represents the Greek translator's misreading of the Hebrew "law of" as tôrôt "laws of" that will last forever.

the ageless Israelite tradition of faithfulness to the Torah. In this exhortation to his audience to be faithful to Torah, the poet offers a tripartite invitation consisting of a command, a prohibition, and a beatitude. A beseeching and hopeful tone accompanies his personal (we) plea to the audience to recognise the uniquely Israelite character of Wisdom.

> Turn, O Jacob, and take her; walk towards the shining of her light.
> Do not give your glory to another or your advantages to an alien people.
> Happy are we, O Israel, for we know what is pleasing to God. (Bar 4:2-4)

The shining of "her light" (4:2) reflects such images as "the commandment is a lamp and the teaching a light" (Prov 6:23a); "your word is a lamp to my feet and a light to my path" (Ps 119:105; cf. Wis 7:26; 18:4); "nations shall come to your light, and kings to the brightness of your rising" (Isa 60:3), the poet suggests that those returning from "exile" will be a light to the nations. A shadow side is also highlighted with the warning "do not give your glory to another or your advantage to an alien people" (Bar 4:3) recalling the warning about the danger posed by the strange/loose woman (Prov 7:25) "Do not let your heart turn aside to her ways", whose house is the way to Sheol. In identifying "your glory" with Israel's possession of Wisdom/Torah, the author recalls Israel's "glory" described in Deut 4:8 where a rhetorical question implies the Israelite character of Wisdom: "What great nation is there, that has statutes and ordinances so righteous as all this law which I set before you this day?" (Deut 4:8; Bar 3:32-37).

"An alien people" may refer to Hellenists and their claims for their wisdom as expressed in Greek philosophy, and to Jews who have rejected the Law of Moses.[39] The poet's threat that continuing unfaithfulness to the Torah will result in God's abandonment of Israel and the giving of the Torah to another people (cf. Exod 32:10; Num 14:12; Deut 9:14) reads like a biblical exaggeration, as it is never suggested in the Old Testament that Israel was given the Torah because of her faithfulness. In liturgical fashion the accolade to Wisdom concludes with the offering of a final blessing/prayer of thanks for the blessed state in which poet and congregation are one (v.4 cf. Deut 33:29).[40] The poet by depicting the grandeur of God's creative power presents the audience with a Wisdom figure who is Torah, the Israelite heritage throughout their history. He assures them that their blessed state is a cause for rejoicing in Wisdom/Torah, and declares them a people, unique and blessed above all others.

---

[39] Tov, *The Book of Baruch* (1975): 557; Kneucker, *Baruch* (1879); J.T. Marshall, "The Book of Baruch" *HDB* I (1901): 251-254, and others see this line as being directed to Christians who have rejected the Torah. This notion depends upon their assigning to the poem a date in early Christian times.

[40] Wis 9:18b expresses a similar notion in, "Thus the paths of those on earth were set right, and human beings were taught what pleases you, and were saved by Wisdom."

How the Poems Function

Many observations have been made about how I see these two poems functioning in the contexts I have assumed for them. While I am aware that any discussion of how texts function is open to many pitfalls I shall nevertheless attempt to present a more specific account of how these texts may have functioned. The questions raised in Job, "Where can wisdom be found? From where does wisdom come?" (Job 28:12); and the question in Baruch "who has found her place? And who has entered her storehouses?" (Bar 3:15) highlight themes of the way to Wisdom, and the mystery of Wisdom's location.[41] In Job 28:27 God רָאָה "saw" Wisdom and יְסַפְּרָהּ "appraised" or "numbered" her (cf. Sir 1:9-10). Of all created things, Wisdom is the most closely associated with God, so if Wisdom is sought, other than with God, failure to find her is inevitable. She is at large in the created world, and is not aligned specifically with any one part of creation. Clearly, knowledge of her whereabouts rests with the Creator. Job 28 implies that Wisdom is not with God but God can appraise her so knows where she is. The authors of Job 28 and Bar 3:14-27 by focussing on Wisdom's transcendence highlight Wisdom's inaccessibility to human beings. Both state with certainty that no human being knows the "way" to her (28:13 LXX), only God knows the "way" (Job 28:23-27; Bar 3:14-37).[42] Bar 3:20-21, 23, 27, 31 specifies some sources of ancient wisdom known to Israel as places where Wisdom is not to be found. Paradoxically, the poet also echoes Deut 30:12-14, which teaches that the Torah is "very near to you".

Bar 3:29-31	Deut 30:12-14
Who has gone up into heaven, and taken her, and brought her down from the clouds? Who has gone over the sea, and found her, and will buy her for pure gold? No one knows the way to her, or is concerned about the path to her.	Surely, this commandment that I am commanding you today is not too hard for you, nor is it too far away. It is not in heaven, that you should say, "Who will go up to heaven for us, and get it for us so that we may hear it and observe it?" Neither is it beyond the sea. . . No, the word is very near to you; it is in your mouth and in your heart for you to observe.

This paradox also enters Job 28 where ultimately "fear of the Lord" is the litmus

---

[41] In the Wisdom of Ben Sira God alone knows the subtleties of Wisdom, and "he created her, has seen her and 'numbered' ἐξηρίθμησεν her. He 'poured out' ἐξέχεεν Wisdom on the works of creation" (Sir 1:9-10).

[42] Thus, within the context of the Book of Job, this poem functions as an indicator of the futility of human probing into the mystery of God as exemplified in Wisdom; neither Job nor the three friends can fathom God's ways; see W. Harrelson, "Wisdom Hidden and Revealed according to Baruch (Bar 3:9-4:4)," in *Priests, Prophets and Scribes*, E. Ulrich, ed., (Sheffield, 1992): 158-171.

test for Wisdom. Both poems provide striking illustrations of the obstacles encountered in the pursuit of Wisdom. Job 28 begins with a sustained image of ancient mining techniques to find precious stones and metals. Bar 3:15 alludes to treasuries or storehouses. Begg, investigated the question of access to heavenly treasuries or storehouses (Bar 3:15; Job 28:2-6; 38:22) against its ancient Near Eastern background. Proposing a fascinating scenario for the texts that speak about hidden wisdom, he claims that the rhetorical questions of Job 38:22 and Bar 3:15 and their expected negative answers as based upon the ancient Near Eastern motifs of "entry into a royal treasury".[43] Entrance was given as a privilege or a right of conquest. That interpretation of the two biblical texts would corroborate the sense that no human being, however powerful or privileged, could expect to enter the heavenly/sapiential "storehouse" θησαυπους.[44] Following on from that reading the same or a related notion may also lie behind Isa 45:3 "I will give you the treasures of darkness and riches hidden in secret places." The author of Isaiah 45 may have been aware that Cyrus had looted the vaults of Croesus at Lydian Sardis, which contained the "treasures of darkness".

Interestingly, a wide range of other Old Testament texts also use this image, for example, Deut 28:12; 32:34; Job 9:9; 37:9; Pss 33:7; 135:7; Prov 8:21; Jer 10:13; 51:16; Ezek 28:4; Sir 43:14, suggesting that such episodes were familiar or at least known in the Hebrew tradition and in the Ancient Near East. The great cost and difficulty of gaining entrance to "treasuries" illustrates by analogy the inaccessibility and elusiveness of Wisdom as portrayed in Baruch and Job.[45] Moreover, both these portraits bring to mind the paradoxical claim in Deut 30:11-15 where the speaker declares that the Torah is "in your mouth and in your heart". The author of Job 28 in comparing the search for Wisdom to that of mining for precious and rare metals in the depths of the earth highlights the insurmountable obstacles confronting the searcher for Wisdom who is searching in the wrong places. "Only God knows the way" (Job 28:23) to Wisdom, and only God, "saw Wisdom and appraised her, gave her her setting, knew her through and through" (Job 28:27). The exclusiveness of God's knowledge of wisdom embraces both her abode and her origins—an inauspicious situation for the one who wishes to find Wisdom. While it is clear that Wisdom's origins and existence are closely associated with God, the question of "where?" breaks into other wisdom texts also (Qoh 7:23-24; Wis 6:22).

---

[43] C.T. Begg, "Access to Heavenly Treasuries: The Traditionsgeschichte of a Motif" *BN* 44 (1988): 15-20, notes that several Old Testament wisdom literature passages contain rhetorical questions emphasising human inability to gain entry to supra-terrestrial storehouses or treasuries.

[44] Begg, "Heavenly Treasuries" (1988): 15-20 notes that this motif has considerable currency in later apocalyptic literature (cf. Col 2:1-3).

[45] According to 2 Baruch, Moses in the course of all he witnessed saw, "the treasuries of the light" (2 Bar 59:1-12). 1 Chr 26:15, 17; Neh 12:25 both speak of storehouse. These may have been the house of stores for the priests.

Responses in Job and Baruch to "Where shall wisdom be found?"

Job 28:13-19	Bar 3:13-32
Mortals do not know the way to it, and it is not found in the land of the living. The deep says, "It is not in me," and the sea says, "It is not with me". It cannot be gotten for gold, and silver cannot be weighed out as its price . . . . the price of wisdom is above pearls . . . nor can it be valued in pure gold.	They have not learned the way to knowledge, nor understood her paths, nor laid hold of her . . . . they have not learned the way to wisdom, or given thought to her paths . . . . No one knows the way to her, or is concerned about the path to her.

In 28:13-19 the search for Wisdom includes human beings, the land, the deep, the sea, and concludes that it cannot be purchased or exchanged for any price, and cannot be valued. Baruch 3:16-32 enumerates people and places (Canaan and Edom) renowned as sources of ancient wisdom (v.22);[46] Ishmaelites (3:22-23 cf. Gen 16; 21);[47] rulers of the nations; Canaanites and Arabs;[48] seekers after wisdom; writers of sayings; and the giants of old who "perished because they had no wisdom" (Bar 3:26-28; cf. Gen 6:4; Num 13:33; Wis 14:6) as of no avail.[49] Not surprisingly, the quest yields no fruit as Wisdom is not to be found in any of these settings.[50] Even impressive stature or mysterious origins do not guarantee the possession of Wisdom. An extension of the quest to the heavens, and the sea as in Bar 3:29-31 and Job 28:13-14, fails to bring success. More surprising news appears in the announcement that Wisdom cannot be bought for "pure gold" (Bar 3:29-30; Job 28:14-19, 24; cf. Prov 8:10-11). The cryptic line "No one knows the

---

[46] H.W. Wolff, *Amos' geistige Heimat* WMANT 18 (Neukirchen-Vluyn, 1964); *Joel und Amos* BKAT 14/2 (Neukirchen-Vluyn, 1967): 53-55, presents arguments for folk wisdom influence on Amos. Incidental factors include Amos's family origin from Tekoa, where Wolff believes a distinctive tradition of skill in wisdom was kept alive. In 2 Sam 14:1 Joab sends to Tekoa, for a wise woman who could use her verbal skill to persuade David to allow Absalom back at court. Wolff connects this with the view that a special pride in the nurture of wisdom was current among the Edomites and may have been present in neighbouring parts of Judah.

[47] Ishmael, son of Hagar, was the traditional ancestor of 12 tribes. Gen 25:12-16 identifies Ishmaelites as nomads on the borders of Palestine from the Sinai to Syria. Midianites were traders from Midian, a region south of Edom and east of the Gulf of Aqabah, mentioned in Gen 37:25-28.

[48] These places were also mentioned in prophetic oracles as examples of the uselessness of human wisdom (Jer 49:7; Ezek 28:12; Obad 8-9; Zech 9:2).

[49] D. Hillers, "A Study of Psalm 148," *CBQ* 40 (1978): 323-334, successfully disputes a claim by von Rad that the Egyptian onomastica ultimately underlie such passages as Job 28, and Psalm 148.

[50] Otzen, "Log og Visdom" (1995): 41-42 finds some similarities between the two poems, but, I believe, correctly claims that the entire wisdom poem is not dependent on Job 28; see also Steck, *Baruchbuch* (1993): 128, for tabulation and analysis of parallels between Job 28 and Bar 3:9-4:4; Küchler, (1979): 49-55 for a systematic comparison of Job 28 and Bar 3:9-4:4 in which he finds eight close parallels.

way to her" (3:20-21, 23, 27, 31) encapsulates the mystery surrounding Wisdom in these texts. A contrasting motif appears in references and allusions (Bar 3:32-36 and Job 28:23-28) to God's knowledge. Clearly, in these texts God is the omniscient Creator and Lord of creation. By depicting the vastness of the created universe, "how great is the house of God, how vast the territory that he possesses!" (Bar 3:24-25) the poet presents an image of a God whose "gaze is all-encompassing, capturing the entire scope of creation",[51] and suggests that while Wisdom is distinct from the works of creation, she is not separate from them. She is present and visible to God.

Job 28:23-27	Bar 3:24-37
God knows the way to it; it is God who is familiar with its place. For God beholds the ends of the earth and sees all that is under the heavens. God has weighed out the wind, and fixed the scope of the waters; When God made rules for the rain and a path for the thunderbolts. Then God saw wisdom and appraised her, gave her her setting, knew her through and through (cf. Sir 1:9-10).	. . . . the one who knows all things knows her, he found her by his understanding. The one who prepared the earth for all time filled it with four-footed creatures; the one who sends forth the light, and it goes; he called it, and it obeyed him, trembling; the stars shone in their watches, and were glad; he called them, and they said, "Here we are!" They shone with gladness for him who made them. This is our God; no other can be compared to him.

Wisdom is manifest in creation because God has lavished her upon creation. Those who fail to recognise Wisdom as God's mystery in all of creation will not find her.[52] In the concluding verse of Job 28 a deft lens change transforms what was a futile quest for Wisdom into a viable enterprise to be embraced, "Behold, the fear of the Lord, that is Wisdom, and to depart from evil is understanding" (Job 28:28). Likewise, Baruch 4:1 announces, "She is the book of the commandments of God, the Law that endures forever. All who hold her fast will live, and those who forsake her will die".[53] Interestingly, the concluding verses pinpoint a significant difference between the poems. Job 28:28 advocates "Fear of the Lord and avoidance of evil" to attain Wisdom, while Baruch 4:1 declares: "She is the book of the commandments of God, the law that endures forever. All who hold her fast will live, and those who forsake her will die."[54] "Wisdom appeared on earth and lived with humankind", underpins the linking of Wisdom with Torah and so

---

[51] D. Bergant, *Job, Ecclesiastes* OTM 18 (Wilmington, 1982): 140.

[52] N.C. Habel, *The Book of Job* (London, 1985): 393, notes the final word which God 'says' stands in antithesis to what Sea, Deep, Death, and Abaddon have 'said' in verses 14 and 22 and reinforces its opposition to the preceding poem. God has direct access to Wisdom; mortals only gain Wisdom indirectly through submission to God.

[53] Verse 28 recalls Job 1:1 where Job is described as God-fearing and avoiding evil.

[54] "Fear of the Lord" appears in many wisdom texts as the principal characterization of the wise person (Job 1:1, 8; 2:3; Prov 3:7; 28:14; 31:30), and as a description of wisdom in action.

prompts the audience to recall, "The word is very close to you, it is in your mouth, it is in your heart for you to put into practice" (Deut 30:14).

Unique teaching about Wisdom in each of the poems surely point to interesting possibilities for how Wisdom was intended to function in these poems and in their respective communities. Bar 3:9-4:4 reveals several unique characteristics that are not found in other wisdom poems. One of the most noticeable is the way the author has combined new features and emphases, with wisdom features from Job 28, Proverbs 1-9, The Wisdom of Ben Sira 24; prophetic connections with Isaiah 40-66 and with Baruch, Jeremiah's disciple; Torah connections with Deuteronomy 4 and 30. This weaving together of these features and connections contributes to the creation of a Wisdom figure that is a rich tapestry of features old and new.[55]

Syntheses of new features with traits familiar from earlier texts, suggest that the author of Baruch 3:9-4:4 is using a composite approach to problems besetting his Jewish audience who may be suffering alienation and oppression. His teaching functions, on the one hand, to recall for his hearers their traditional beliefs and unique situation, as seen in the use of familiar texts or paraphrases of these, and on the other, the introduction of new perspectives on Torah and Exile. Burke produced a study confirming Baruch as an example of the characteristic anthological style of the post-exilic period in which earlier portions of the Hebrew Bible are reused and a pastiche of biblical phrases results. Sheppard also presented a careful analysis of the wisdom poem, pointing out that it has many biblical antecedents and while it is particularly reliant on Genesis, Deuteronomy, and Job, the text exhibits some counterparts of prophetic speech and concerns.[56] Although both poems deal with the inaccessibility and elusiveness of Wisdom, there is a startling contrast between the exclusive claim made in Baruch and the much more inclusive claim in Job 28.

Bar 3:36-37	Job 28:26-27
[God] gave Wisdom to his servant Jacob and to Israel whom he loved.	God alone understands her path and knows where she is to be found. Then God saw Wisdom and appraised her, gave her her setting, knew her through and through.

In Bar 3:36-37 the poet appears to claim that the gift of Wisdom was given only to the people of Israel, a claim that seems akin to Sir 24:8-11. However, Ben Sira names the land of Israel as Wisdom's setting, stating that Wisdom's abode is in Jerusalem, while Baruch announces that Wisdom was given exclusively to the people of Israel but does not tie Wisdom to the land of Israel.[57] This crucial distinction highlights the unique gift of personified Wisdom to Israelite/Jewish

---

[55] A. Rahlfs, ed., *Septuaginta* 2. 5th ed. (Stuttgart, 1952) for Baruch references.

[56] Sheppard, *Wisdom* (1980): 84-99.

[57] Cf. Isa 44:1, "But now hear, O Jacob, my servant, Israel whom I have chosen!" Similarities and differences between Sir 24:8-11 and Bar 3:36-37 are discussed in chapter 4.

communities. It also serves to harmonise with the exilic setting of Baruch, and address Diaspora audiences. Arguably the author of Bar 3:9-4:4 used the historical setting of the Babylonian Exile metaphorically in the second century BCE, not to advocate return to the land so much, as to persuade his audience to recover full identity as a people faithful to their Jewish traditions. Another distinctive feature of the Baruch wisdom poem is the fact that among texts featuring personified Wisdom, this text is alone in not alluding to the much lauded wisdom requirement of "fear of the Lord", that is essential for Wisdom in Job 28, "Behold, the fear of the Lord is wisdom; and avoiding evil is understanding" (Job 28:28). Such a requirement may have been supplanted by the linking of Wisdom with Torah in Baruch. This raises the interesting question as to whether the author of Baruch has subsumed "fear of the Lord and avoidance of evil" into fidelity to Torah. Wisdom's identification with Torah in Baruch is the culmination of the poem that consistently evokes the gift of the Torah and its availability to all Israelites/Jews as expressed in Deuteronomy 4 and 30.[58]

Exilic Setting for Baruch and Job 28

Bar 3:9-4:4 is distinctively exilic in its tone and content. "Exile" in this poem is, I believe, used as a metaphor for alienation from one's heritage and the consequent loss or confusion of identity associated with actual exile from one's native land. The poet suggests that the confusion and loss of identity besetting his audience was the result of a failure to focus on Wisdom, whose time-honoured teaching required a return to the sources of their Jewish heritage. In making "exile" the backdrop for his teaching, the author, writing probably some centuries after the fall of Jerusalem, and the Babylonian Exile, uses a historical experience of the ancestors to address his audience, in an attempt to awaken in his contemporaries a sense of their historic roots at a time when the Jewish communities were in danger of being absorbed by neighbouring peoples. This he does by calling them to renew their allegiance to the Law—evoking the motif of liberation associated with the Exodus—and invoking the teaching of Deuteronomy chapters 4 and 30 which explicitly presumes an exilic situation. Thus, he calls them, on the one hand, to recognise the unfaithfulness that led to their downfall in the past, and on the other, to return to the fountain of Wisdom, that is, to walk in the way of the Lord.

Prophetic Connections

An intriguing feature shared by both poems is how their respective descriptions of Wisdom contrast with the texts preceding and following. In Bar 3:9-4:4 the prophetic prose address preceding it (1:1-3:8), and the prophetic psalms following it (4:5-5:9), share a prophetic stance, along with an "exilic" setting and viewpoint.

---

[58] While both Baruch and Ben Sira identify Wisdom with Torah, certain distinctions are evident between the two poems. At the climax of Wisdom's song in the Wisdom of Ben Sira 24, another speaker proclaims that Wisdom is the Torah, the book of the covenant of the Most High God.

Moore correctly concludes that the Baruch poem is a clear and coherent statement on the nature and importance of Wisdom. It breathes a different spirit and has a different point of view from that of the rest of the book of Baruch and its wisdom character undoubtedly contrasts with the prophetic tone of the surrounding materials.[59] Each section speaks of Israel's unfaithfulness to the Torah and exhorts the audience to return to the observance of the Law. This bringing together of prophecy and wisdom has already been demonstrated in Proverbs 1-9 as discussed in chapter two of this book. Gunneweg notes that the talk of penance at the beginning of Baruch and of the Wisdom poem is a question of "a consciously shaped composition".[60] Steck, to a much greater extent sees the book of Baruch as a literary unit, and does not call 3:4-4:4 a "wisdom poem" but an "admonitory speech" (*Mahnrede*). He focuses on the framework of the imperatives, "Listen, Israel, to the commandments of life!" (3:9); "Turn back Jacob!" (4:2-4), which he calls, "the essential assertions of the admonitory speech". The long middle section 3:14-4:1 about the inaccessibility of Wisdom he regards as a motivation for the penance emphasised at the beginning of the book. Wisdom and thereby the Law is reserved for Israel; therefore, the Jews must turn to the Law. He underscores the influence of Deuteronomy and Jeremiah but underestimates, I think, the influence of wisdom literature. In his recent comparative study of Bar 3:9-4:4 and its source in Job 28, he investigates the structure of these texts, their individual formulations and overall messages. He judges, correctly, I believe, that contextually, the Baruch poem differs from its *Vorlage*, above all in its conception of Wisdom as an attribute inherent in God alone, which God makes known to Israel exclusively as the Law whose purpose is to enable Israel to attain life. He also argues strongly for one author for the book of Baruch.[61] This is a puzzling claim as the initial chapters (1:1-3:8), which are a tapestry of quotations, particularly from Deuteronomy, Jeremiah and Daniel 9, enjoin penance, and contrast sharply with the Wisdom poem. Bar 3:9-4:4, which shows links with Job 28 and Wisdom of Ben Sira 24, is a harmonious discourse on personified Wisdom with a clear conclusion that Wisdom is God's Law, the Torah.

Whatever its origins Bar 3:9-4:4 surprises, because of its placement in the centre of the book of Baruch, where its wisdom character is in sharp contrast with, but not in conflict with, the prophetic emphases of the prose and psalms surrounding it. Its position in the book signifies its centrality to the total text, and emphasises its pivotal role. Celebrating the Mosaic Law as Wisdom (cf. Deut 4:6; Pss 19:8; 119:97-98), the poem links the confession of the prophet and the prayer for the people with a prophetic address to the "exiles". While biblical echoes, particularly Job 28:12-28; Wisdom of Ben Sira 24; Deuteronomy 4 and 30; Isaiah 40-49 resound at particular points of the poem, it is not a mere amalgam or

---

[59] C.A. Moore, "I Baruch," in *Daniel, Esther and Jeremiah: The Additions* AB 44 (New York, 1977): 255-316.
[60] A.H.J. Gunneweg, "Das Buch Baruch" in W.G. Kümmel, ed., *Historische und legendarische Erzählungen* 3 (Gütersloh, 1975): 169.
[61] O.H. Steck, *Das apokryphe Baruchbuch* (Göttingen, 1993): 116-163.

pastiche of other biblical texts. On a literary level, wisdom and prophecy come together in the frequent echoes of Isaiah in the poem, and in its attribution to the prophet Baruch a character who has biblical links with Jeremiah. Therefore, it is not surprising to find many echoes of prophets—as already noted in the analysis of the poem above—alerting the reader to the wider implications of the poem.

While the poem's wisdom character is sharply contrasted with the prophetic prose address preceding it (1:1-3:8), and the prophetic psalms following it (4:5-5:9), all the texts share a prophetic stance and a similar exilic setting and viewpoint. This is illustrated in the references to Israel's unfaithfulness to the Torah, and in the exhortations to the audience to return to the observance of the Torah. Such bringing together of prophecy and Wisdom has already been exemplified in Proverbs 1-9, and is well described by J. Barton ". . . a question which has been linked to the alleged demise of prophecy: the question of the replacement of prophecy by the increasing authority of the Torah as a written scripture in post-exilic times. That prophecy died out *because* the Law came to carry the divine authority prophecy once had is widely believed."[62]

Murphy observes that the "identification of Wisdom and Torah is clearly giving an unambiguous answer to the question that always lurks in the mind of the reader. By the same token one can fail to appreciate what a strange and in a sense forced identification this is".[63]   In identifying Wisdom as "the book of the commandments of God, and the law that endures forever" (Bar 4:1), a notion generally envisioned in the post-exilic period (cf. Sir 24:23; Deut 4:6; Pss 19:8; 119:97-98; Ezra 7:6, 14, 25), the poet makes explicit the identification of Wisdom and the Torah, hinted at in the wording of 3:29-30 (cf. Deut 30:11-13).[64] He created an ingenious tapestry by incorporating both new and familiar threads into an exilic background. Some familiar sounding strands are realigned so that a different perspective is achieved. We see this in the identification of Wisdom with Torah, and in the Wisdom of Ben Sira 24. On closer analysis Baruch makes an explicit claim that the people of Israel alone were given Wisdom by God (3:36-38, cf. Job 28:23-28). In the Wisdom of Ben Sira, the gift is associated with the land of Israel and Jerusalem. This thinking also appears in the distinctions made between the people of Israel and the Gentiles along with explicit references and direct address to Israel (Bar 3:9, 24, 36, 4:2, 4). It has, in common with the other personification of Wisdom texts, its poetic form, and references to God as Creator. Although the figure of Wisdom in Bar 3:9-4:4 is not as clearly delineated as she is in Proverbs 1-9; Sir 24: 1-34; Wis 6:20-9:18, in her unique characterisation in this poem she is the object of a search rather than the one who searches the universe. She is the subject of a verb of action just once (4:1). As in Job 28 and Wis 6:12-

---

[62] See J. Barton, *Oracles of God* (London, 1986): 110.

[63] Murphy, *Tree of Life* (1990): 141.

[64] In the expanded Greek translation (GII) of the Wisdom of Ben Sira verse 5 appears: "The source of wisdom is God's word in the highest heaven, and her ways are the eternal commandments" (Sir 1:5). This much-disputed text is considered by some to be a gloss on, "Wisdom was created before all other things, and prudent understanding from eternity" (Sir 1:4); see Skehan and Di Lella, *Wisdom of Ben Sira* (1987): 136-137.

9:18, she is spoken about while in Prov 1:20-33; 8:1-36; 9:1-6; Sir 24:1-34, Wisdom is the main speaker.

Bar 3:9-4:4 is not a replica of Job 28, or Deuteronomy or Sir 24:1-33. Job 28 insists links fear of the Lord and avoidance of evil with Wisdom. Deuteronomy teaches that Israel is to hear and do the Law. Baruch suggests that Israel enjoys a privileged status vis-à-vis the nations in having access to the Law. Wisdom's oneness with the Torah also means that she is a life-giver (Bar 4:1, cf. Deut 30:11-13), a feature that also appears in Sir 24:23.[65] Wisdom in Proverbs 1-9 emphasises the crucial choice between life and death, and the consequences of failing to choose Wisdom, a choice echoed in Bar 4:1. Sheppard aptly describes the development of the Wisdom figure thus: "An older connection between the goals of Torah and the wisdom literature is fully exploited by the author. Traditionally, wisdom literature offered "life" (e.g. Prov 3:18; 4:13, 22, 23; 13:14; 16:22), even "the way of life" (e.g. 2:19; 5:6; 6:23; 10:17; 15:24) in a manner fully compatible with the same promise based on obedience to the Torah (cf. Deut 30:15 with Prov 3:1-6). This symbiosis of Torah and Wisdom, apparent already in Proverbs, has in the time of Ben Sira and Baruch led to a more aggressive reunion of the different parts of the canon".[66]

Wisdom was not acquired by Israel but God bestowed Wisdom/Torah on the Israelite/Jewish people. Although Israel abandoned Wisdom in the past, the poet offers this gift anew to the Jewish "exiles". She is to be a source of deliverance from their present difficulties, their means of freedom from "exile", and their return to being descendants of Jacob/Israel, their heritage. Set in the midst of texts concerned with exile, repentance, and return, this poem invites its audience to seek their liberation by following "the way of Wisdom", the "way of the Lord". Prophetic echoes pervading the poem suggest an integration of Wisdom/Torah and prophetic teaching, thus presenting the audience with the combined fruits of their Israelite heritage, in effect with the three divisions of the canon, if these were already assembled. This view is proposed in *Seder 'Olam Rabbah 30*: "Until then, the prophets prophesied by means of the Holy Spirit. From then on, 'Give ear and listen to the words of the sages'" (Prov 22:17, was probably understood to mean 'listen to interpreters of the Torah'). That the Torah did come to have a status that eliminated the need for fresh prophetic revelation there can be little doubt.

The use of the appellative "God" ὁ θεὸς the God of Israel, in Job 28:23 and in Bar 3:13, 24, 27; 4:1, 4 is significant. While this name is used for the deity in numerous passages throughout the book of Job (3:23; 29:2, 4; 31:2; 35:10; 37:15; 39:17; 40:1) in Baruch its use is confines overall to the poem. Bar 1:15-3:8, regularly uses "Lord" κύριος, and Bar 4:5-5:9 "the eternal" ὁ αἰώνιος.[67] The name preferred for the deity is significant, for in both poems "God" is the universal sole creator, whose is inseparable from wisdom. Anthropomorphisms occur elsewhere (Bar 2:11, 16f, 29; 3:4), but not in these poems on Wisdom; the same is true of

---

[65] C. Larcher, *Études sur le livre de la Sagesse* (Paris, 1969): 342.

[66] G. Sheppard, *Wisdom as a Hermeneutical Construct* (1980): 99.

[67] Despite this difference, the poem is an integral part of Baruch.

human feelings and mental functions attributed to God (Bar 1:13; 2:13, 20; 3:5; 4:9, 25, 27; 5:5).[68] God who bestows Wisdom on Israel is the God who created the world and holds it in being, "It is great and has no bounds; it is high and immeasurable" (3:25); "God looks to the ends of the earth, and sees everything under the heavens (Job 28:24). As the created world is clearly God's sanctuary, constant holiness is imperative, just as the Creator's relationship to the heavens is etched in the stars that shine "in their watches . . ." (cf. Isa 40-26; Ps 147:4).[69]

In bringing together God's power to create both authors focus on God's creative activity in the very fashioning and sustaining of the cosmos, (cf. Isa 42:5; 44:24; 43:1-7). However, Job 28 while permeated with this distinctive language of creation does not combine it with combined with references to the Israelite tradition of to the ancestors as does Bar 3:9-4:4. Here the author highlights the idea of God's long established relationship with Israel expressed in the gift of Wisdom, given specifically to the people of Israel, and recalls God's redeeming actions in the past. (A similar reflection appears in Wis 10:1-21). Baruch promises that the "exiles" will be restored to their heritage: "He found the whole way to knowledge, and gave her to Jacob his servant and to Israel whom he loved"; "Hear O Jacob my servant, and Israel whom I have chosen" (Bar 3:36, cf. Isa 44:1).[70] By combining obligation and kinship, this reference to God's special relationship with Israel highlights God's bond with those in "exile". Their deliverance will be one of restoration of what they have alienated by their own unfaithfulness. A return from "exile" is possible if they remember, "This is our God; no other can be compared to him" (v.35).[71] Job 28 offers no such assurances. The high point of the poem proclaims and warns the audience, "Truly, the fear of the Lord, that is wisdom; and to depart from evil is understanding". However, like Baruch, the poet advocates active rather than passive behaviour. The figure of Job surely is the prototype for the exilic audience addressed here.

Personified Wisdom also functions in Baruch to focus on, and centralise the issues threatening the Jewish audience with the loss of their heritage and identity. They are called to, repent for forsaking "the fountain of Wisdom", and for failing to walk "in the way of God" (3:12-13), for allowing Israel's Wisdom, the Law, to become the gift of "an alien people" (4:3), and for seeking Wisdom among alien peoples. However, in true wisdom mode the poem concludes by inviting the audience to be among the blessed, "for we know what is pleasing to God" (Bar 4:4 cf. Deut 33:29). Therefore, Wisdom in Baruch is not inaccessible. By recognising

---

[68] R. Pfeiffer, *A History of New Testament Times* (New York, 1949): 423-424.

[69] This same notion appears in Sir 24:2-6 where Wisdom, speaking in the sanctuary, describes her cosmic journey, before God commanded her to "make your dwelling in Jacob".

[70] E. Schuller, *Post-Exilic Prophets* MBS 4 (Wilmington, 1988): 64-70, explores the notion of "redeemer" and "redeem" invoking a metaphor based on Israelite family law in which the next of kin was obliged to the duty of redemption when something of value has been lost or some duty not fulfilled, because of death, debt or injury.

[71] It seems likely that Isa 45:14, "They will make supplication to you, saying: 'God is with you only, and there is no other, no god besides him'", informed the author of Bar 3:35.

Wisdom as the Torah, they will hold her fast and live, rather than join those who forsake her and die. This polemic suggests that Wisdom/Torah in Baruch addresses the Jews in physical and metaphorical exile from their heritage, to inspire them to return to their rich tradition and thus to God.

Chapter 4

Wisdom: An Enduring Heritage

Introduction

Ben Sira in a poem in praise of Wisdom asks "To whom has Wisdom's root been revealed? Who knows her subtleties"? (Sir 24:28). This perennial question has many formulations in Israelite/Jewish tradition. The preceding chapter discussed two poems that address this question. Jews of Second Temple times undoubtedly pondered questions such as those voiced in Job 28:12, 20. These Jewish questions, posed in the Hebrew tradition were inevitable and more insistent with the arrival and establishment of Greek outposts and communities in the land of Israel and throughout the region following Alexander's conquest of the Near East. Integral to Hellenistic culture was a long–established engagement in philosophy.[1] Such a "love of wisdom" was deemed essential for anyone aspiring to be a person of learning. Contemporary Jews, no doubt, faced claims that the Greeks had access to real wisdom in the works of their great philosophers, "lovers of wisdom", Plato, Aristotle, Pythagoras, Zeno, and their followers. Answers to Job's dilemma and other questions raised in Israelite wisdom were surely proffered by Greek philosophers. No doubt such teaching was viewed as relegating Jewish tradition and teaching to second place, or at least diminishing its validly and ultimate importance. The centrality of the Torah in the lives of Jews could soon become rare if Greek philosophers provided all the teaching and answers needed for life.

    Jews loyal to their tradition could argue that their wise ones had pondered questions about how and where to find wisdom and had arrived at some answers. Proverbs 2:6 states, "For the Lord gives wisdom; from his mouth comes knowledge and understanding. Job 28:28 concludes "And he said to human beings, 'Truly, the fear of the Lord, that is wisdom; and to depart from evil is understanding'." However it seems likely that Jewish teachers could not find in their tradition answers for all the questions about wisdom raised in their time. Prov

---

[1] "Philosophy" is a Greek word, from φιλεῖν, "to love," and σοφία, "wisdom". For Hellenistic Culture during Second Temple times see E. Schürer, *The History of the Jewish People in the Age of Jesus Christ* 2, translated by G. Vermes, F. Miller, and M. Black (Edinburgh, 1979): 29-183. For Greek education, philosophy and the Jews see M. Hengel, *Judaism and Hellenism*, 2 vols. (London, 1974), vol. I: 65-102; L, Grabbe, *Judaism from Cyrus to Hadrian* 1 (Mineapolis, 1992): 147-170. For Diaspora Jews see J.J. Collins, *Between Athens and Jerusalem: Jewish Identity in the Hellenistic Diaspora* (New York, 1883).

3:13 "blessed is the one who finds wisdom", and Prov 8:35 "whoever finds me finds life" intimate that wisdom could be found. However, exact information about wisdom's location was not available in the literature, so questions continued. Ben Sira's, "The first human never knew wisdom fully, nor will the last succeed in fathoming her" (Sir 24:28) suggests that the search is ongoing, as is very clear in his work.

One of the most fruitful and significant developments of Israelite wisdom, the conception of personified Wisdom, was foundational for Ben Sira's work. He transforms this Wisdom figure from the earlier Israelite Wisdom figure in Proverbs to an Israelite/Jewish Wisdom figure who reveals Hellenistic features, and is one with the Torah. Marböck found significant dependence in Ben Sira's Wisdom hymns on Greek aretalogies in the use of "He is all", "the Most High", the hymn to heroic figures, and superscriptions. As discussed in preceding chapters, attempts to identify personified Wisdom with likely prototypes or with certain mythological and philosophical conceptions, such as Ma'at, Isis, Astarte or other goddess figures, Stoic "world law", or Platonic world soma, remain inconclusive.[2] It is as if personified Wisdom refuses to be obscured by such comparisons. This chapter focuses on the central Wisdom poem (Sir 24:1-34) with particular concentration on Wisdom's distinctive relationship to God, to the created universe and its inhabitants. I begin with an investigation of the probable dating and historical and literary contexts for the Wisdom of Ben Sira. This is followed by a literary study of the text of Sir 24:1-34 and a discussion of relationships, and roles attributed to the Wisdom figure in this text.

Di Lella, who considers Proverbs to be one of Ben Sira's principal sources, argues that Proverbs provided a legitimate precedent for borrowing from Gentile wisdom literature.[3] His textual study of the poem illustrates heavy reliance on portrayals of Wisdom in Proverbs 1-9, particularly 8:1-36. Ben Sira's grandson wrote in his prologue to the Greek translation: "so my grandfather Jesus [Ben Sira], who had devoted himself especially to the reading of the Law and the Prophets and the other books of our ancestors, and had acquired considerable proficiency in them, was himself also led to write something pertaining to instruction and wisdom" (Sir Prologue *NRSV*). The Wisdom figure in Sir 24:1-34, like the rest of the book, was undoubtedly tailored to the time and setting in which it was created.

Historical and Literary Contexts of Sir 24:1-34

The book of Ben Sira can be dated fairly accurately, since the author's grandson, the Greek translator of the Prologue in giving details about Ben Sira and his times, mentions that he (the grandson) arrived in Egypt in the thirty-eighth year of the

---

[2] O. Keel, *Die Weisheit spielt vor Gott. Ein ikonographischer Beitrag zur Deutung des mesahäqät in Sprüche* 8:30f. (Freiburg, 1974); Lang, *Wisdom* (1986): 147-164; Murphy, *Tree of Life* (1990): 133-149.

[3] Ben Sira's dependence on Proverbs can be detected in almost every portion of his book, see Skehan and Di Lella, *Wisdom of Ben Sira* (New York, 1987): 43-45.

reign of King Euergetes. The epithet "Euergetes" was given to two Lagid kings, Ptolemy III Euergetes I (246-221 BCE) and Ptolemy VII Physkon Euergetes II (170-164 and 146-117 BCE). Since Ptolemy reigned only twenty-five years, he cannot be the Euergetes in question. Ptolemy VII, however, began to rule in 170, conjointly with his brother, Ptolemy VI Philometor (181-146), and he died fifty three years later, in 117. Calculating from 170, the official year of accession of Ptolemy VII, the thirty-eighth year would be 132 BCE. So it seems that Joshua Ben Eleazar Ben Sira probably wrote his work in Hebrew between 198 and 175 BCE.[4] The year 198 BCE is set by the death of the high priest Simon "the Just", the last of Ben Sira's "men of renown" (50:1-24), who is described as a figure of the past, and is given a long panegyric. This priest named Simeon, son of Jochanan (Onias in some Greek MSS), is generally believed to be Simeon II, who served as High Priest from 219 to 196 BCE. It is credible that Ben Sira witnessed Simeon celebrating the rituals of the Daily Whole Offering in the Jerusalem Temple. His reference to the High Priest implies that he is already dead, and he does not allude to the horrifying events that occurred in Palestine during the reign of the Seleucid Antiochus IV Epiphanes (175-164), who figures in Daniel 7-12.

Seleucids before Antiochus IV had pursued a policy of Hellenisation. Antiochus who went further than any of his predecessors by insisting on total Hellenisation surprisingly gained the support of some Jews. Notable among them was Jason (174-171 BCE), son of Simeon II, probably the High Priest whom Ben Sira praises, who introduced a vigorous Hellenisation process (1 Macc 1:11-15; 2 Macc 4:7-17). With Antiochus IV's assistance he ousted his brother from the office of High Priest and built a Greek gymnasium in Jerusalem (2 Macc 4:7-16). In 167 BCE Antiochus set about ending the practice of the Jewish religion in his realm. As Ben Sira makes no mention of Antiochus IV's policy, it seems likely that he had died or that his manuscript was completed before 175 BCE, the year of Antiochus's accession to the throne. If Ben Sira had written after that time, his deep concern for the Torah would certainly have provoked him to make some references to these events. It is generally agreed that 132 BCE is the date when Ben Sira's grandson went to Egypt, and translated his grandfather's work in the years following. Some scholars maintain that the work was published before 117 BCE.[5] Wilcken proposed a different theory as to the date of publication, but both Smend and Di Lella refuted his argument.[6] It is generally agreed that the book of Ben Sira can be dated to the first quarter of the second century, the work having been composed during the process of Hellenisation carried out in Jerusalem (1 Macc 1:11-15; 2 Macc 4:7-17) under Jason the high priest (174-171 BCE).

In his ground–breaking study of the encounter of Judaism and Hellenism in the early Hellenistic period, fourth to second centuries BCE, Hengel

---

[4]   The form of his name differs in the Hebrew and Greek texts of 50:27.

[5]   G.H. Box and W. O. E. Oesterley "Sirach," in *Apocrypha and Pseudepigrapha of the Old Testament* [*APOT*] (Oxford, 1913): 293, 317.

[6]   See U. Wilcken, *Archiv für Papyrusforschung* 3 (1906): 321; 4 (1907): 205; R. Smend, *Die Weisheit des Jesus Sirach erklärt* (Berlin, 1906): 3-4; Skehan and Di Lella, *Wisdom of Ben Sira* (1987): 8-10; A.H. Forster, "The Date of Ecclesiasticus" *ATR* 41 (1959): 1-9.

acknowledges extraordinary difficulty in demonstrating direct Hellenistic influences in Jewish (Hebrew and Aramaic) literature of the period.[7] Granting the Hellenistic "spirit of the times", as a factor in the literature under consideration, he suggests that all Judaism must be designated Hellenistic Judaism in the strict sense, from the middle of the third century BCE. He recommends a differentiation being made between the Greek–speaking Judaism of the Western Diaspora and the Aramaic/Hebrew–speaking Judaism of Palestine and Babylonia. Even this distinction, he says, is one–sided, as Jerusalem from the time of the Ptolemies, was a city in which Greek was spoken to an increasing degree.[8] If Hengel's suggestion is correct, and no evidence has been put forward to deny it, it seems likely that the Israelite tradition was influenced considerably by Hellenism. Whether Ben Sira related to this Hellenistic world and its culture by becoming immersed in it or by keeping apart from it is much debated.

Ben Sira marks the end of the first encounter between Judaism and Hellenistic civilization, and initiates a new era, which is characterised by critical repudiation. Writing about 180-175 BCE, immediately before the Hellenistic reform attempt, he is involved in a controversy with those Jews who because of their assimilation into Hellenism have become almost completely alienated from the traditions of their ancestors. For him they are apostates from the Torah and no longer believe that God works recognisably in this world, and makes demands on individuals. Against this thinking he proposes justification of divine retribution: human beings are free and receive the reward that is their due. Alongside his view about retribution is his teaching that God created the world for the sake of human beings with minute attention to detail and harmony; Israel with its unique and miraculous history guided by God is the centre point of humanity. In the Torah Israel is entrusted with Wisdom, the power which orders all creation. In the threatening situation in Jerusalem, Ben Sira came forward with prophet–like claims: he admonishes the sons of the High Priest Simon, intercedes for the oppressed poor, and in the style of some prophets prays for the dawn of national eschatological salvation for Israel.

While the Wisdom of Ben Sira is clearly Jewish, it is the product of a Hellenistic age, and the Wisdom figure in Ben Sira's text exhibits unmistakable Hellenistic influences. Middendorp traces evidence for such influences even listing about one hundred parallels between Ben Sira and various Greek authors.[9] Snaith in commenting on this work notes: "It is puzzling how Middendorp can detect so many quotations by Sirach of Greek works in the largely non–extant Hebrew. Detecting Greek quotations in the original Hebrew of a work much of

---

[7]   Hengel, *Judaism I* (1974): 115-126.
[8]   Hengel, *Judaism I*: (1974): 104.
[9]   Th. Middendorp, *Die Stellung Jesu Ben Siras zwischen Judentum und Hellenismus* (Leiden, 1973): 8-24, surveys evidence gathered by scholars who investigated parallels between the Wisdom of Ben Sira and various Greek authors. He finds the greatest number of parallels in Theognis with fewer from Euripides, Xenophon, Hesiod, Homer and Sophocles.

which is extant only in Greek translation seems an oddly unreliable method."[10]
However, Snaith's own claim that Ben Sira showed a positive attitude towards
Hellenistic culture, "to show pious Jews how to live with Greek culture positively,
not rejecting it altogether",[11] does not fit easily with the traditional call to fidelity
issued throughout The Wisdom of Ben Sira. Indications of Ben Sira's Jewishness
are: insistence on the importance of the Torah (Sir 6:32-37; 15:1; 19:20; 21:6;
23:27; 24:23, 33, 39:8), frequent reference to "fear of the Lord" (Sir 1:11-30; 2:15-
17; 6:16-17; 19:20-20-31; 24:23-29; 25:12), praise of the Israelite heroes (Sir 44-
50), and a tirade against the nations (Sir 36:1-22).

As Kieweler, in his detailed study of the Wisdom of Ben Sira, provides a
detailed survey of Greek authors and Hellenistic writers, I shall mention here only
works that impinge directly on the matter of Hellenistic influence on Ben Sira.[12]
Both Kieweler and Sanders take issue with Middendorp's overstatement of Ben
Sira's dependence on Greek authors, his belief that Ben Sira deliberately chooses
portions of Greek works resembling Jewish proverbial literature to show his Jewish
readers the value of Gentile wisdom and his Hellenistic readers "the great
similarities between Hellenistic and Jewish thought."[13] Sanders prefers to consider
Ben Sira's "unconscious use of Hellenic material that has entered the mainstream
of Hellenistic thinking and speech".[14] Sanders' thesis that Ben Sira had read the
work of Theognis seems very likely.[15] The practical advice of Theognis in a
gnomic setting is very similar to the advice provided by Ben Sira even though Ben
Sira may have been addressing a wider group than Theognis. Middendorp in his
claim that certain passages were "lifted" from Theognis may have inflated his case,
as the use of familiar expressions, phrases, or verses does not always mean that the
user is so much borrowing as recalling such material or using information that is
current in a particular community. He may not even be aware of the origin of the
expression or line when using biblical quotations or paraphrases, as Ben Sira does
so frequently. It seems more likely that Ben Sira was using Greek literature in a
similar way to harmonise and integrate Hebrew and Greek literature, because of
the increasing Greek influence in Palestine in the early second century.
Comparisons of the text of Ben Sira with that of such writers as Theognis may

---

[10] J.G. Snaith, "Ecclesiasticus: a tract for the times" in *WAI* (1995): 174.
[11] Snaith, "Ecclesiasticus" (1995): 172.
[12] See H.W. Kieweler, *Ben Sira zwischen Judentum und Hellenismus* (Frankfurt, 1992): 69-
      262.
[13] See Kieweler, *Ben Sira* (1992): 69; J.T. Sanders, *Ben Sira and Demotic Wisdom* (Chico,
      1983): 29.
[14] See Sanders, *Ben Sira* (1983): 23-49; R. Pautrel, "Ben Sira et le Stoïcisme" *RSR* 51
      (1963): 530-555, identifies Stoic influence in, "The end of the matter is this: God is all"
      (Sir 43:27). However, the notion of the unity of creation and of all humanity under one
      God appears throughout the Old Testament so can hardy be regarded as a specifically
      Stoic idea.
[15] Theognis was a Greek elegiac poet, born about 540 BCE.

eventually throw more light on borrowings and influences. Hengel claims that Sir 24:3-7 exhibits "unmistakable parallels" to statements in Hellenistic Isis aretalogies.[16] Under Ptolemaic rule this Egyptian goddess is known to have been worshipped at Acco in Phoenicia, and Hengel suggests that she may have been known in Jerusalem.

Marböck, like many others, found motifs from Isis aretalogies in Sir 24: 1- 34.[17] He claims that Ben Sira on realising that he was a member of a particularistic religion that has come into competition with the universal religion of Hellenism (Sir 1:1-10; 24:1-36), reached a conclusion that resulted in a new departure for wisdom thought. Twin notions of creation and wisdom were the means by which he extended the horizons of Jewish faith. Ben Sira, using Wisdom to hold the two poles in creative tension, portrays Wisdom as active both in creation and in the "fear of the Lord"; moreover, creation is a continual process, so that Wisdom is at work in every creative act and in the pious deed. This view appears in Zimmerli who claimed, "Wisdom thinks resolutely within a theology of creation".[18] Since the cosmos is the product of divine wisdom, it bears the imprint of that impetus; therefore, the intellect can search out the hidden mysteries of the universe. Other scholars who understand wisdom to be the human search for mastery of life reflect this notion.[19]

Ben Sira's historical position, near the dividing line between the Egyptian and Greek periods in Palestine, is evident in close parallels in his work with Egyptian literature. In a detailed study of Ben Sira's relations with Egyptian traditions, Sanders gives considerable space to the *Papyrus Insinger*, a demotic instruction, composed by someone before the time of Ben Sira's, probably in the pre–Ptolemaic era.[20] Several topics discussed in the two works are similar, and

---

[16] Hengel, *Judaism* (1974):158-159; 284-288.

[17] Mack, Marböck and Reese also detect Hellenistic influence and a dependence on Greek aretalogies in the Wisdom of Ben Sira, see Mack, *Logos und Sophia* (1973): 20-26, 63-107. Marböck, *Weisheit* (1971): 100-104; J.M. Reese, *Hellenistic Influence on the Book of Wisdom* (Rome, 1970): 36-50; These parallels were already seen by Knox "The Divine Wisdom" *JTS* 38 (1937): 230-237; *St. Paul and the Church of the Gentiles* (Cambridge, 1939): 55-89; cf. H. Conzelmann, "The Mother of Wisdom" in *The Future of our Religios Past* (1971): 230-243; J. Kloppenborg, "Isis and Sophia in the Book of Wisdom" *HTR* 75 (1982): 57-84.

[18] W. Zimmerli, "Ort und Grenze der Weisheit im Rahmen der Alttestamentlichen Theologie", *SPOA* (1963): 121-138; (ET in *SAIW* 314-326).

[19] W. Brueggemann, *In Man We Trust* (Atlanta, 1972); J.F. Priest, "Where is Wisdom to be placed?" in *SAIW* (1976): 275-282; J.F. Priest, "Humanism, Skepticism, and Pessimism" *JAAR* 36 (1968): 311-326; O.S. Rankin, *Israel's Wisdom Literature* (Edinburgh, 1936); Zimmerli, "Ort und Grenze" (1963): 121-138.

[20] *AEL*: 184-217; M. Lichtheim, "Observations on Papyrus Insinger" in E. Hornung and O. Keel, eds., *Studien zu Altägyptischen Lebenslehren* (Fribourg, 1979) 283-305; *Late Egyptian Literature in the International Context* (Fribourg, 1983). Papyrus Insinger, written in demotic script and probably from the pre-Ptolemaic period is named after the Dutchman who purchased it for the Leiden royal museum in 1895. Sanders, *Ben Sira* (1985): 68-77; Skehan and Di Lella, *Wisdom of Ben Sira* (1987): 47-50 for a discussion of Sanders' conclusions regarding Greek and Egyptian influences on Ben Sira.

follow the same order, usually a clear indication of borrowing. It seems very likely that Ben Sira had read this Egyptian work plus the Greek work of Theognis. Sanders claims that the Egyptian author, "is more like Ben Sira, in both style and content, than any other collection of proverbs, Theognis included, save only the book of Proverbs itself."[21] Besides *Papyrus Insinger* and Egyptian aretalogies, Ben Sira may have used *The Instruction [or Maxims] of Duauf*, also known as *The Satire on Trades*, which was probably the source of many ideas and expressions found in 38:24-39:11.[22] If he used Egyptian wisdom literature, Ben Sira continued the precedent set in Proverbs, which in 22:17-23:11, drew on the Egyptian *Instruction of Amenemope* composed probably in the thirteenth century BCE.[23]

Mack found the relationship between Egyptian and Old Testament wisdom a fruitful direction from which to launch his investigation into the complex relationship between Sophia and Logos mythology in Hellenistic Judaism.[24] In working out the objectification of wisdom, the myth–ology, Mack produced his own threefold typology of Wisdom.[25] He claims that personified Wisdom is not a myth, but the result of a reworking of mythic materials as theological categories of thought. He considers the three "types" of wisdom in Ben Sira, and other wisdom books, to have been developed with the Isis–Osiris mythology in mind.[26] Several decades before, Smend stated, "Ben Sira heightens the statement in Prov 1:7-10, that the fear of the Lord is the beginning of Wisdom . . . by asserting that all wisdom comes from the Lord and that it has been with him from eternity; and that in these words, which he sets at the head of his work, he formulates a Jewish declaration of war against Hellenism".[27] Fidelity is given greater significance by the threat from outside and becomes the primary condition of wisdom, as do the all–embracing definitions of Ben Sira "the whole of wisdom is fear of the Lord", and "in all wisdom there is the fulfilment of the law" (Sir 19:20), which bring new

---

[21] Sanders claims regarding the likelihood that Phibis was the author of Papyrus Insinger is challenged by J. Ray, in: Review of *Ben Sira and Demotic Wisdom* by J.T. Sanders *VT* 35 (1985): 383 where he claims that "he [Sanders] misleads by calling the text Phibis which is probably the name of the copyist, and is usually read Phebhor" See also Sanders, *Ben Sira* (1985): 105.

[22] *ANET* 432-434.

[23] *ANET* 421-424.

[24] Mack *Logos* (1973): 20, says his purpose is to pursue Conzelmann's opinion regarding the distinction between myth and mythology (the employment of myth for theological reflection).

[25] Mack's typology may be summarised as: *nahe*, "near" (Prov 8:22-31; Sir 24:6) has analogies in Egyptian mythology in Ma'at, Isis; *verbogen*, "hidden" (Job 28, Bar 3:16-21, Wis 9:13-18, Sir 1:1-8); *entschwunden*, "disappeared" (1 Enoch 42; 2 Esdras 5:9-10; 1 Apoc Bar 48:36). This may have resulted from Jewish thinkers taking Egyptian Isis mythology as a way of constructing its own "mythology". Mack situates the development of this wisdom typology against the background of the trauma of exile, seeing Wisdom's promises as a response to the post-exilic questions of faith.

[26] Mack, *Logos* (1973): 47-48; "Wisdom Myth and Mytho-logy," *Int* 24 (1970): 46-70.

[27] R. Smend, *Die Weisheit des Jesus Sirachs erklärt* (Berlin, 1906): 33; Pfeiffer, *Introduction* (1948): 371f.

insights to the view of wisdom teaching.[28] Ben Sira exhorts his audience to practise constraint with regard to the search for knowledge (3:17-23), possibly a warning about the free critical questioning of Greek "wisdom," which must have been very attractive. As Eissfeldt notes, "Much more strongly than in Proverbs or even in Qoheleth the element of universal and general human interest retreats behind the specifically Jewish".[29] Fichtner too alludes to "controversy with Hellenism" in which wisdom and pious observance are identified, and the possibility of a profane wisdom dissociated from piety is excluded.[30]

Interestingly, Larcher claims that the wisdom writers sought to universalise the idea of the Jewish God under the impact of the wider Hellenistic culture of the time.[31] In his study of suffering and justice, Schrader argues that Ben Sira was influenced by the *Lebensgefühl* "sense of life" of the Hellenism of his day,[32] so placed no great value on strict observance of the Torah. This surprising conclusion seems to be at odds with the text where Wisdom's identification with the Torah is the climax and hinge of the whole composition. Certainly, details of law do not receive much attention from Ben Sira, but the Torah is lauded by him.[33] Wischmeyer, in her study of the culture of Ben Sira, describes his religious orientation: "the depths of the soul were filled out with a religious intellectual/erotic and aesthetic point of view; with love of God through Wisdom and with the love of Wisdom herself."[34]

In addition to studies of the Wisdom of Ben Sira, with particular emphasis on Hellenistic influences noted above, Di Lella has provided a valuable collection of information and critical reflections about a wide range of resources and recent studies.[35] He includes evaluations of these for study of the Wisdom of Ben Sira, editions of the Hebrew MSS, of the Greek, Syriac and Latin versions and some helpful tools. This recent collection serves as a supplement to his earlier bibliography which is very detailed.[36] Harrington has also produced a valuable

---

[28] See J. Becker, *Gottesfurcht im Alten Testament* (Rome, 1965); P.C. Beentjes, "'Full Wisdom is fear of the Lord' – Ben Sira 19:20-20:31: Context, Composition and Concept" *Estudios Biblicos* 47/1 (1989); : 27-45; Smend, *Die Weisheit* (1906): index 189; cf. Sir 1:27; 2:8, 10, 13; 14:16; 15:15.

[29] Eissfeldt, *The Old Testament* (1965): 598.

[30] J. Fichtner, *Die Altorientalische Weisheit* (1933): 82-94, 125-130, discusses the fundamental differences between the Wisdom of Ben Sira and the Book of Proverbs.

[31] Larcher, *Études* (1969): 342, 365.

[32] L. Schrader, *Leiden und Gerechtigkeit. Studien zu Theologie und Textgeschichte des Sirachbuches* (Frankfurt, 1994): 303-304.

[33] Murphy, *Tree of Life* (1996): 215, observes on this point that Schrader "fails to reckon with variations in Torah observance. . . Sirach approaches the traditions of the Law from the point of view of Wisdom, but this seems like an inner-Jewish development and does not owe anything substantial to Hellenism".

[34] O. Wischmeyer, *Die Kultur des Buches Jesus Sirach* (Berlin, 1995): 247; 285, emphasises Wisdom's elevated linguistic expression in the Wisdom of Ben Sira.

[35] A. Di Lella, "The Wisdom of Ben Sira: Resources and Recent Research" in *Currents in Research: Biblical Studies* 4 (1996): 161-181.

[36] Skehan and Di Lella, *Wisdom of Ben Sira* (1987): 93-127.

survey of books and monographs which appeared since 1965.[37] In view of these recent surveys of critical works on Ben Sira, I do not provide further discussion of these works, but proceed to an analysis of the text of Sir 24:1-34 24. Few recent commentaries on the Wisdom of Ben Sira have been produced, probably because of the difficulties involved in establishing a critical text on which to base the study. Skehan and Di Lella's scholarly work remains the most recent of its kind.[38]

A Study of the Text of Sir 24:1-34

Forming the centre and the climax of the book the Wisdom of Ben Sira is the hymn to Wisdom. Several scholars have undertaken detailed studies of this eulogy to Wisdom.[39] While each study has enriched our reading and study of the chapter, the role and function of the Wisdom figure in this poem has not attracted much detailed investigation. In the following pages, I aim to investigate the literary aspects of Sir 24:1-34, with a view to understanding how the personification of Wisdom functions in the text. Di Lella and Gilbert both provide detailed discussions of editions of texts and versions of the Wisdom of Ben Sira plus comprehensive overviews of the current situation.[40]

The original Hebrew of the poem has not been found, therefore the versions are used. Among them is the Greek that has come down to us in two redactions: the short redaction—found in the big uncial MSS, *Vaticanus* IV[e], *Sinaiaticus* IV[e], and *Alexandrinus* V[e], which are generally followed in modern editions of the poem and the long redaction, which is found in MS 248, written in minuscule.[41] This text adds a passage between verses 17 and 19 and between

---

[37] D.J. Harrington, "Sirach Research since 1965: Progress and Questions" in J.C. Reeves and J. Kampen, eds., *Pursuing the Text: Studies in Honor of Ben Zion Wacholder* (Sheffield, 1994): 164-176.

[38] Skehan and Di Lella, *Wisdom of Ben Sira* (1987)

[39] Smend, *Die Weisheit* (1906): 216-224; N. Peters, *Das Buch Jesus Sirach oder Ecclesiasticus* (Münster, 1913): 194-206; C. Spicq, *L'Ecclésiastique Translation and Commentary* (Paris, 1943): 684-693; P.-E. Bonnard, La Sagesse en personne annoncée et venue: Jésus Christ (Paris, 1966): 69-79; Larcher, *Études* (1969): 340-348; Marböck, *Weisheit* (1971): 34-96, S. Pié Y Ninot, *La Palabra de Dios en los libros sapienciales* (Barcelona, 1972): 176-183; O. Rickenbacher, *Weisheitsperikopen bei Ben Sira* (Göttingen, 1973): 111-172, is concerned mainly with the letter of the text, and seeks to determine the sense of the words used in the light of Hebrew fragments, and the Greek, Syriac and Latin versions; Gilbert, "L'Éloge" *RTL* 5 (1974): 326-348; Skehan and Di Lella, *Wisdom of Ben Sira* (1987): 327-338.

[40] A. Di Lella, "The Wisdom of Ben Sira" in *Currents in Research 4* (1966): 178-181; Skehan and Di Lella, *Wisdom of Ben Sira* (New York, 1987): 51-62, provide a detailed account of the Hebrew text and ancient versions; M. Gilbert, "L'Éloge" *RTL 5* (1974): 326-328.

[41] H.P. Rüger, *Text und Textform im hebräischen Sirach. Untersuchungen zur Textgeschichte und Textkritik, der hebräischen Sirachfragmente aus Kairoer Geniza* (Berlin, 1970): VIII-117, claims that the short Greek text represents the translation made

verses 23 and 25.[42] The state of texts may indicate two editions of the Hebrew at different periods. The Vulgate was translated from the Greek, but has varied additions in the same places as MS 248. The Syriac version was established from the Hebrew text and is very close to the short Greek text, except for verse 23. I used Ziegler's 1980 critical edition of the LXX along with the *NRSV* and Skehan's translation for this work.[43]

Sir 24:1-34 as a literary work has drawn a number of scholars to identify and describe its literary structure. Fritzsche, Smend, Rickenbacher, Marböck, Gilbert, Skehan and Di Lella have all attempted to determine an underlying structure in this poem.[44] Rickenbacher in his exhaustive exposition, used the structure proposed by Smend, according to which chapter 24 consists of six strophes each one of six distiches.[45] Gilbert settles on thirty six verses with verse 23 presenting difficulties because in the short Greek version it exists as a triptych. It is equally true that vv. 23-29 and 30-34 form two distinct unities, each of six verses, the first speaking of Wisdom and the second of the author or sage himself. But as the first two verses serve as an introduction to the discourse on Wisdom (24:3-22), can they also be included as part of the first strophe of the chapter (24:1-6)? The fourth strophe (24:12-15) is clearly distinguished from verses 10-11 with which verse 12 is connected, and thus presents a further difficulty in Smend's tidy pattern.

Marböck's arguments are literary and thematic, with particular emphasis on the forms of words, and the themes evoked.[46] He and Gilbert concur that the proposed structure presents a difficulty, as v. 9 presents one of the sharpest divisions of the text.[47] Fritzsche observed that the discourse on Wisdom (24:3-22) was composed of twenty distinct diptychs, and he put, in addition, a caesura between verses 12-13.[48] The first observation is important, as the biblical authors sometimes used acrostics in poetic texts.[49] Di Lella notes that Ben Sira, like many other Hebrew poets, employed the technique of composing units of twenty-two or twenty-three lines to signal the opening or closing of a major part of his book. He

by the grandson of his grandfather's text; It is generally agreed today that Sir 24:1-34 in the Greek version in its short redaction is a unity.

[42] J.H.A. Hart, *Ecclesiasticus. The Greek Text of Codex 248 edited with a Textual Commentary and Prolegomena* (Cambridge, 1909): XVIII-378.

[43] J. Ziegler, *Sapientia Iesu Filii Sirach*. Septuaginta Vetus Testamentum Graecum XIII/2 (Göttingen, 1980); Skehan and Di Lella, *Wisdom of Ben Sira* (1987).

[44] See Gilbert, "L'Éloge" (1974): 326-7; Skehan and Di Lella, *Wisdom of Ben Sira* (1987): 51-62.

[45] Rickenbacher, *Weisheitsperikopen* (1973): 113-118.

[46] Marböck, *Weisheit* (1971): 44-47.

[47] Gilbert, "L'Éloge" (1970); Marböck, *Weisheit* (1971): 45.

[48] O. Fritzsche, *Kurzgefasstes exegetisches Handbuch zu den Apokryphen 5* (Leipzig, 1859); Rickenbacher, *Weisheitsperikopen*, (1973): 114.

[49] Alphabetic (acrostic) poems are found in several parts of the Bible, for example, Psalms, Lamentations, Prov 31:10-31, Sir 51:13. On Sir 51:13 see M. Delcor, *Le texte hébreu du cantique de Siracide 51:13 (19) et les anciennes versions: Textus 6* (Paris, 1968): 27-47; Rickenbacher, *Weisheitsperikopen* (1973): 197-213.

draws attention to other examples of this usage, but does not include 24:3-22 among them.[50] The process does not necessarily mean that each verse begins with the letter of the alphabet which corresponds to its place—that is, that verse one begins with *aleph*, verse two with *beth*, and so on—but it is possible that the sequence of twenty-two verses is sufficient to draw attention to the entity about which the author speaks. The process itself goes beyond the literary skill that it imposes. To sustain an argument for seeing Sir 24:3-22 as an acrostic, with each verse beginning with the corresponding letter of the Hebrew alphabet, is difficult, as only the first verse of the discourse (24:3) where ἐγώ points to the likelihood of אֲנִי seems to support this notion. The caesura which Fritzsche saw between verses 12-13 is not there either in the sense or in the words. Perhaps 24:13 begins with a *lamed* to mark the beginning of the second part of the alphabet (as in Prov 2:12), but in the Greek version that would be impossible. Interestingly, in Sir 24:1-34 two distinct uses of σοφία (24:1, 25), each having a different sense, frame the discourse on Wisdom (24:3-22), and introduce the two sections of the poem. In view of the many interesting structures proposed for this poem by eminent scholars I hesitate to provide a new structure but offer a study of the poem as a series of vignettes.

Vignette One: Introducing Wisdom Sir 24:1-2

In introducing personified Wisdom as singing her own praises to her own people (24:1), in "the assembly of the Most High" (24:2), the author seems to place Wisdom in the heavenly court. However, commentators disagree on the question of Wisdom's location in these verses.[51] Although 24:1-2 suggest that Wisdom begins her speech in the heavenly court, it becomes clear, as the poem progresses, that she is addressing the people of Israel, and is located in the Temple in Jerusalem, "leading the liturgy" ἐλειτούργησα (v.10), in the "Holy Tent".

Vignette Two: Wisdom's Journey Sir 24:3-8

Wisdom begins her song by focussing on her journey from God to earth (24:3-8). It takes her through the vault of heaven and to the abyss v.5 (cf. Job 22:14; Prov 8:27), as depicted in her claim to have come from the mouth of God (24:3), and in her acknowledgement that it was God's command that installed her in Israel

---

[50]   Skehan and Di Lella, *Wisdom of Ben Sira* (1987): 74.
[51]   Smend, *Die Weisheit des Jesus Sirach erklärt* (1906) considers that Wisdom is speaking in an academy assembly; also Rickenbacher, *Weisheitsperikopen* (1973): 118-120; Spicq, *L'Ecclésiastique*, (Paris, 1951): 684-685; Bonnard, *La Sagesse en personne annoncée et venue Jésus-Christ*, (Paris, 1966): 69, and others see her in an assembly of the people of Israel; Pie Y Ninot, *La Palabra de Dios en los Libros sapienciales*, (Barcelona, 1972) : 176-177, following P. Tena, *La Palabra Ekklesia* (Barcelona, 1958): 41-47 sees in the Wisdom of Ben Sira a progression with the people, reunited in the assembly in the presence of YHWH in the Temple; Marböck, *Weisheit* (1971): 58, finds in Sir 24:1 a reference to Israel and in Sir 24:2 to the celestial assembly.

(24:8).[52] The relationship between the two extremes is heightened by the repetition of the verb κατασκηνόω "to pitch one's tent" (24:4, 8), and the accumulation of verb compounds of kata- (24:3-4, 8) emphasising a descent. Wisdom issues from the mouth of God (Gen 1:2); Wisdom covers the earth like a mist (24:3). Here she is equated with the life–giving mist that waters the earth in Gen 2:4b-6.[53] The Massoretic text says: "a mist rose up from the earth and watered the whole surface of the soil".[54] It seems likely in this section that Wisdom is being portrayed as a creature and her role is to sustain the fruitfulness of the earth. Thus, she does not exercise a creative function so much as an enabling one in ensuring the fecundity of the earth (24:5-6). By forming such links, Ben Sira anchors Wisdom and the wisdom tradition in the beginnings of the universe. This means that from Wisdom can be learned the secrets of the universe as well as a knowledge of God, and from Wisdom abundant life can be obtained (cf. Wis 7:15-22).[55] A reference to her dwelling in the heights (24:4) echoes the earthly heights mentioned in Prov 1:20-21 while her presence in the pillar of cloud recalls the glory of YHWH's presence in the cloud, mentioned in the Pentateuch (Exod 13:21-22; but not in Genesis) and in the Temple of Solomon, "the cloud filled the house of YHWH" (1 Kgs 8:10). It filled the pre–existing Temple in the heavens (Exod 25:8-9, 10; 26:30; Wis 9:8c), which YHWH showed to Moses, and in the image of which was built the Jerusalem Temple.

Wisdom's domain encompasses the entire universe, as intimated in the invocation of the four dimensions, two verticals and two horizontals, of the Jewish cosmos: the heavens and the abyss, the sea and the land (24:5-6a).[56] She, like God, has dominion over sea, land, peoples, and nations. Although her domain is universal, in that all the peoples of the earth are included under her sovereignty (24:6b), Wisdom journeys in search of a resting place, not in the sky (24:4) but among people (24:7), until the Fashioner/Creator of all gave his command, and chose the spot for her tent instructing her to establish herself in Israel (24:8).[57] So, she is to be located in a precise place among the people of Israel. This situation harmonises with her dwelling in heaven, as the use of the verb κατασκηνόω refers to the dwelling of Wisdom in the heavenly court and in Israel. Sir 24:1-34 and the Book of Enoch describe a descent of Wisdom into this world. The notion of a more intimate contact between Ben Sira and apocalyptic literature has recently been explored by Argall, who considers the author of 1 Enoch to be contemporary with Ben Sira.[58] He examines the themes of revelation, creation, judgement, plus

---

[52] In Job 22:14 God journeys through the vault of heaven.

[53] This connection is rejected by Larcher, *Études* (1969): 342.

[54] For the state of the question see C. Westermann, *Genesis* (Neukirchener-Vluyn, 1970): 273-275; J. Lévêque, *Job et son Dieu*, ÉBib (Paris, 1970): 588.

[55] Isaiah teaches clearly that the word of God exercises a role in the creative act (Isa 55:11), and Sir 42:15 takes this view while Sir 24:3a is not explicit.

[56] Larcher, *Études sur le Livre de la Sagesse* 342, contrary to C. Spicq, refuses, correctly, I believe, to read Sir 24:6 in the sense of "to create".

[57] Sir 24:7 describes the people and the nations mentioned in the preceding verse.

[58] R.A. Argall, *1 Enoch and Sirach* (Atlanta, 1995): 7, n.15.

literary features, that both share. Enoch has a revealed Wisdom from heaven (1:1-3; 82:1-2), and in Sir 24: 1-7 Wisdom comes down from heaven. Despite the similarities, Argall concludes that these two traditions are opposed to each other.[59]

Vignette Three: Wisdom Pitches Her Tent Sir 24:9-12

A change of focus is introduced in 24:9 with the Wisdom figure claiming her ancient origin, which goes back to the beginning of time "before the ages," and stretches beyond the future, "will not cease to be". Wisdom's relation to time is now correlated with her association with space in 24:2-8. Verse 9 envisages the future as a time when Wisdom will have no limits.[60] Yet verses 10-12 depict Wisdom's apparent geographical/symbolic location, by referring to Wisdom's connection with the "Tent", recalling the Ark of the Covenant in the Temple in Zion. However, Ben Sira was writing in Second Temple times when the ancient Ark, YHWH's throne, had disappeared, presumably, but not demonstrably, because of the Babylonian destruction of the Temple and Jerusalem. As a new ark had not been constructed (Jer 3:16-17), it seems likely that he is portraying Wisdom as the substitute for the Ark.[61] The Ark/Tent sheltered the "Ark of Testimony" (Exod 26:33: 40:21), as the two "tables of the testimony" given at Sinai (Exod 31:18) were kept inside it (Exod 25:16; 40:20). In Deut 10:8 the term "Ark of the Covenant" is used, and in Deut 31:9, 26, we read that the scroll containing the Deuteronomic version of the Law was given an honoured place alongside the Ark. Wisdom here identifies herself as the Ark in relation to YHWH. In her ministering she is the presence of YHWH "leading the liturgy" ἐλειτούργησα (24:10) in the "Holy Tent". Jerusalem the "the city God loves" is Wisdom's domain (v.11). Wisdom takes root in an honoured people, who are the Lord's inheritance, which suggests she resides in the whole people of Israel (v.12).

Vignette Four: Wisdom Flourishes Like a Tree Sir 24:13-15

By using "like" to link verses 13-15 the author emphasises the physical locations named or alluded to in the text and forms a unity with important geographical notations. From the literary point of view, the triple repetition of the verb ἀνυψώθην "I grew tall" suggests growth to an impressive size and maturity. Wisdom proclaims her excellence and desirability by attributing to herself the qualities of some magnificent indigenous trees. The "cedars of Lebanon" (v.13a) are the most majestic and celebrated trees in Syria–Palestine and are frequently mentioned in the Bible. They are used as a metaphor for strength and beauty (see Ps 92:13; Num 24:6; Cant 5:15). The "cypress" (v.13b) was noted for its great

[59] Argall (1995): 98, 250.
[60] Totality or unity is often expressed by the use of extremes.
[61] H. Gese, "Die Weisheit, der Menchensohn und die Ursprünge der Christologie als konsequente Entfaltung der biblischen Theologie" in *Alttestamentliche Studien* (Tübingen, 1991): 218-248, esp. 226-228.

height (cf. Sir 50:10). "Mount Hermon" (v.13b) which is located on the north-eastern border of Palestine, very close to Lebanon, overlooks the ancient city of Dan and is the source of the Jordan. It remains to this day a sight of great beauty in the Middle East (cf. Ps 133:3; Cant 4:8).

En–gedi (v.14a) is a place in the wilderness of Judah (Josh 15:62) on the western shore of the Dead Sea (Ezek 47:10), and about equidistant from both its extremities. This city of the Amorites (Gen 14:7) was originally called Hazezon-tamar, "Hazezon of the palms". It was famous for its date palms that produced excellent fruit.[62] The vineyards of En–gedi were celebrated in Solomon's time (Song 1:4). The "fountain" from which it derives its name rises on the mountain side about 600 feet above the sea, and in its rapid descent spreads luxuriance all around it. Jericho (v.14b), the city of Benjamin in the Jordan Plain west of the river Jordan, was a luxuriantly fertile area, also called "the city of palm trees" (2 Chr 28:15) and noted for its magnificent rose gardens (Sir 24:14; 39:13).[63] Olive trees, "beautiful in appearance", the main fruit–bearing trees of the Mediterranean region, flourish in the foothills, in the area known as the Shephelah (v.14c; cf. Josh 10:40; 12:8) the foothills of the Judean mountain region. Plane trees are found in small numbers mainly in the northern part of the Holy Land (v.14d) Gen 30:37 and Ezek 31:8 also refer to the plane tree. The inclusion of the phrase "beside the water" (v.14d restored in GII and in the Syriac but omitted in GI), while possibly emphasising the source of the trees' growth in an arid land, may simultaneously be linked with similar references in Pss 1:3; 63:1; 65:9; 107:35; Sir 39:13; Jer 17:8.

Ben Sira, through a series of comparisons with indigenous trees and shrubs, familiar from earlier biblical texts and known for such qualities as beauty, strength, provision of nourishment, and attractiveness, attributes their qualities to personified Wisdom. In this same section (vv.13-15) the sites mentioned are located near or on the borders of Israel. Gilbert surmises that, even if we take into account the difficulties surrounding the transmission of the text, we cannot escape the impression that the author intends to mark out the frontiers of the country occupied by a people for whom he was writing.[64] It is clear that Wisdom claims to have grown tall, and flourishes in the whole of the land of Israel. However, these lines also evoke the imagery of the Garden of Eden planted by God (Gen 2:8-9).

Vignette Five: Wisdom in the Liturgy Sir 24:15-17

A definite switch to images and vocabulary suggesting the cult appears in verse 15 when the author introduces the imagery of perfumes and incense used in the service of the Meeting Tent in the wilderness.[65] "Cinnamon", "fragrant cane" and "precious myrrh" (v.15a) were combined with cassia, (tree bark used as a spice),

---

[62] Chr 20:2; Josephus, *Antiquities*, xiv 4, 1.
[63] A. Vaccari, "'Quasi plantatio rosae in Iericho' (Eccli 24:18)" *Verbum Domini* 3 (1923): 289-94.
[64] Gilbert, "L'Éloge" (1974): 332.
[65] Exod 30:23, 34, treat of the making of chrism and incense, and both commodities appear again in Exod 37:29 [LXX 38:25].

and blended with olive oil to make a precious sacred perfume that was used in the anointing of Aaron and his sons, the Tent, the ark of the commandments, and other sacred appurtenances.[66] It was also with chrism that the Temple was consecrated by anointing the Ark, the furniture in the sanctuary, and the priests. "Galbanum" (v.15c) a bitter, aromatic gum; "mastic", an aromatic gum from the mastic tree; and "onycha", the calcareous plate on the foot of some molluscs, were blended with pure frankincense to produce the incense used in the liturgical services in the Tent. In verse 15d Wisdom compares herself to "the odour of incense in the Holy Tent" thereby identifying herself as sacred, sweet smelling, and pleasing to God. Added to these qualities seems to be the requirement that she is indispensable in liturgical celebrations authorised by the cult.[67] Wisdom also gives pleasure similar to that of a sweet–smelling perfume.

Sir 24:15 draws on Exod 30:34 for the composition of the perfume that is for the exclusive use of the cult of YHWH according to the LXX.[68] This perfume was placed in the meeting tent ἐν τῇ σκηνῇ τοῦ μαρτυρίου (LXX). In these two references, the author suggests a liturgical and priestly role for Wisdom; she is an intermediary between God and human beings. The text also focuses our attention on the Temple, after the extensive journey around the whole territory of Israel. Conceivably, the author may be condensing and compressing the scene in order to set up another focus similar to that in 24:3-8; or he may be suggesting that the whole territory of Israel, in which Wisdom flourishes, is in a certain way like the Temple. This interpretation seems more likely, as in the next two verses (16-17) symbols of Israel, rather than of the Temple, appear.

Just as the opening stanza (v.3) of the discourse uses "I" as the first word of the first two bicola, so too do verses 16-17 and 19-22. The imagery here returns to flora, as in verses 13-14. Wisdom likens herself to the "terebinth" in verse 16a, a deciduous tree with red berries that was noted for its luxurious and expansive branches.[69] In Israelite history the terebinth was associated with non-Yahwist worship and cultic prostitution. Terebinth is also mentioned several times in the Old Testament as one of the trees which characterises holy places. Among these one must include the high places, where the terebinth trees gave delight to the people. Some of Isaiah's harshest prophesies use the image of the terebinth to address the apostasy and unfaithfulness of the Israelite people "it will be burned again, like a terebinth or an oak whose stump remains standing when it is felled" is addressed to the kingdom of Judah, symbolized by the terebinth, which is doomed to destruction (Isa 1:29; 6:13; 57:5; cf. 1:30; Hos 4:13).

---

[66] Chrism in Exod 30:23-24 (LXX) consists of σμύρνης ἐκλεκτῆς "liquid myrrh"; κινναμώμου εὐώδους "sweet-smelling cinnamon"; καλάμου εὐώδους "aromatic cane"; ἴρεως "cassia" ἔλαιον ἐξ ἐλαίων "olive oil". Ben Sira may have this text in mind in 24:15, particularly if one accepts the reading ὡς κάλαμος suggested by MS 248 (ὡς πάλαθος), instead of ἀσπάλαθος hapax in the Septuagint.

[67] See Num 16:6-7, 17-35; 2 Chr 26:16-19. The pleasant smell of incense is also referred to in Prov 27:9; Cant 3:6.

[68] It consisted of stacte, onyx, galbanum, mingled with "pure incense".

[69] In Judg 6:11 the angel of YHWH speaks with Gideon under the terebinth.

Wisdom, who "buds forth delights", is paralleled with the vine (v.17a) which produces grapes for wine. The vine is also used in many texts as an image of Judah destined for destruction (Isa 5:1-7). But while Judah is symbolized by the terebinth with flourishing foliage, Wisdom in 24:16 is presented as a terebinth with marvellous branches, and while the vine representing Judah gives only bitter juice, the vine symbolizing Wisdom produces delicious fruit. The image of the vine in Psalm 80 (79) is also evoked by Ben Sira, when it is introduced in verse 12 with Wisdom saying, "I have struck root among the glorious people". This image is developed in the theme of Wisdom as a vine extending over the whole countryside from the sea (the coast boundary) to the river (inland). Wisdom here is depicted clearly by the coherence of the images of the terebinth and the vine, both in the extending branches of the Terebinth, and in the growth and spreading abilities of the vine once it strikes root. This expression also appears in Psalm 84 to describe the gifts of YHWH to the faithful who come to the Temple. Wisdom produces fruits fair and rich, fruits of honour and wealth, classical fruits of Wisdom (v.17b).[70] Wisdom's domain is God's holy city, wherein she addresses the people directly (24:19). The location of Wisdom's speech in the Jerusalem Temple highlights the centrality of the Temple to the poem. It is from a Temple perspective and in a Temple setting that references and allusions to the liturgical cult are appropriate and to be expected.[71]

Vignette Six: Wisdom's Banquet Sir 24:19-22

Ben Sira having had Wisdom speak in self–praise and describe herself as possessing the riches of marvellous fruits and wine, now has her extend an invitation (Sir 24:19-22) to the people to share in her banquet. This well–established Old Testament image (Prov 9:1-6; Isa 25:26; 55:1-3), carries with it distinct liturgical implications (Sir 1:16-17; 6:19).[72] In Isa 55:2-3 a banquet of "what is good" is given so that "your soul may live". It is also within the context of a banquet that the divine promise is given: "I will make with you an everlasting covenant, my steadfast, sure love for David" (Isa 55:3). Contrary to every appearance, the permanent, everlasting covenant made with David is to endure, but now the covenant will be with "you" (in Hebrew this is clearly a plural pronoun). As David was "a witness to the peoples" (Isa 55:4) in that his victories over the nations testified to them of the power of the Lord rather than of other gods (Ps 18:43-45a), so now the whole people are to be witnesses to the nations "you are my witnesses" (Isa 43:10, 44:8). The steadfast sure love (2 Sam 7:15, Ps 89:28) granted to the Davidic line is now for all. Isaiah turned to an old tradition and adapted it in a radical and creative way to give hope to the people of Israel. Here

---

[70] Similar fruits are alluded to in Prov 3:16 "Long life is in her right hand; in her left hand are riches and honour," and Prov 8:18, "Riches and honour are with me, enduring wealth and prosperity" cf. Sir 4:21b; Prov 8:21.

[71] Gilbert, "L'Éloge" (1974): 330.

[72] See A. Feuillet, "Thèmes bibliques majeurs du discours sur le pain de vie (Jn 6)" *Nouvelle Revue Théologique* 82 (1960): 814-819; 918-922.

Ben Sira utilises the notion of re–membering associated with acts of worship, in a variety of contexts, throughout the poem and the entire book.[73]

Using wisdom vocabulary Sir 24:20 recalls the notion of blessings on the earth thus evoking images of a land flowing with milk and honey, and of geographical expansion producing an abundance of the fruits of the earth (cf. Neh 9:25). The blessings of the earth are the ingredients for Wisdom's banquet, both those remembered and those of the future. The memory of Wisdom, "You will remember me as sweeter than honey, better to have than the honeycomb," (24:20) draws attention to the all-pervading presence and endurance of Wisdom.[74] Many wisdom expressions appear in verses 19-22, for example, acceptance of Wisdom's invitation is essential in order to "be filled with her fruits," which are "fair and rich" (v.17).[75] Wisdom offers an invitation to "you that yearn for me" (v. 19). She describes herself, "the memory of me is sweeter than honey and the possession of me sweeter than the honeycomb" (v. 20),[76] and affirms that anyone who eats and drinks of her delights "will hunger" and "thirst for more" (v.21 cf. John 4:14; 6:35). She proclaims that the one who "obeys" Wisdom (cf. Prov 8:32a) "will not be put to shame", while the fool—the person who does not keep the Law—will experience shame and disgrace (v. 22; cf. Ps 22:6). The final promise/threat of this vignette, "those who work with me will never fail", inspired an interesting observation by Skehan who notes: "Perhaps the most interesting lexical link between Proverbs 8:36 וְחֹטְאִי, "the one who misses me" and Sir 24:22 ἁμαρτήσουσιν "will not sin" is the *NRSV* reading of the only two cases in biblical literature in which this basic physical sense of falling short, missing the mark, appears" (cf. *NAB* "will not fail"). Although sustainable, Skehan's perception of this text is open to a different interpretation in the light of the following text which identifies Wisdom with the Torah (Sir 24:23).[77]

In defining Wisdom as the Torah, Ben Sira places her clearly within the Israelite tradition that stretches back to the Mosaic covenant, "a heritage for the community of Jacob", and to Israelite origins. References to Exod 24:7 "the book

---

[73] See Rickenbacher, *Weisheitsperikopen*, (1973): 164-165; Images in 24:20 resemble those used in Sir 49:1. Other liturgical references occur in Sir 35:9; 38:11; 45:16. These comparisons suggest that Ben Sira is invoking the place of memory in the cult. Another aspect of memory emphasised by Ben Sira is the memory of the former acts of God (42:15); of illustrious men: Moses (39:9; 48:8-9; 45:1); Judges 46:11. He also invites his readers to reflect on the last hour of life. Once (Sir 15:8), it is a question of remembering with Wisdom (Sir 15:8); another time it is to remember the commandments and the covenant (Sir 28:7).

[74] Sir 24:20 is probably an inclusion antithetical to 23:26 "She will leave an accursed memory; her disgrace will never be blotted out", said of the memory of the adulterous woman, who would be cursed.

[75] Sir 6:18-38; Prov 8:4-10, 32-36; 9:4-6, 11.

[76] See Ps 19:11, where the "ordinances of YHWH" are said to be "sweeter than syrup or honey from the comb"; see also Ps 119:103; Prov 16:24; 24:13-14.

[77] P. Skehan, "Structures in Poems on Wisdom: Proverbs 8 and Sirach 24" *CBQ* 41 (1979): 365-379.

of the covenant" and to Deut 33:4 "the law which Moses commanded", link personified Wisdom with the whole of the Hebrew tradition. A linking of creation with the Law (Ps 19), and of observance of the Law with giving evidence of wisdom to the nations (Deut 4:6-9) assigns a wisdom twist to the Torah.[78] He argues that the centre of attention is consistently on Wisdom who is, or becomes the Torah, in the possession of Israel. There is a selective application to Wisdom of some Torah traditions which can be associated with the divine presence in Israel. Ben Sira perceives Torah as a continually rising flood (vv.25-29), and in relation to it, his own teachings are a minor stream.

Vignette Seven: Wisdom and the Torah Wis 24:23-29

In this vignette we see that Ben Sira's reflection on the role of Wisdom (vv.23-29) is composed of six verses of two lines each, except for verse 23 which has three lines. This stanza, in which the author is the speaker, identifies Wisdom with the Torah, thus providing a key to Wisdom's discourse.[79] As this is a pivotal text a brief review of how the text is structured is in order here. In Sir 1:1-10 and 24:1-33 Ben Sira portrays the Wisdom figure as created from the beginning (Prov 8:22-31; Sir 1:4; 24:9), and being present in all of creation (1:9).[80] He describes her as traversing the entire cosmos, and finally, at YHWH's behest, she pitches her tent in Israel, in God's beloved city of Jerusalem (24:3-12). Going back to and beyond Deuteronomy, which identified the laws of the Torah with wisdom (4:6), Ben Sira identifies Wisdom with the Torah (24:23), "as a result of which both were conceived together as a heavenly element which descended from heaven to take up its abode among the children of Israel".[81] Thereby he creates a scenario in which Wisdom, who pervades the cosmos, also maintains a resolute focus in Zion and by being identified with the Torah achieves a new universal significance.[82]

   In contrast to the preceding and following verses, verse 23 is in prose, beginning with an emphatic statement that Wisdom is the Torah of Israel.[83] It presents several unusual features and has given rise to much debate. Rickenbacher, Smend, and Peters claim that it is overloaded, and propose reducing it to two lines

---

[78] G. von Rad, *Wisdom* (1972): 246, speaking of this poem, notes: "It is Wisdom who speaks here, not Torah, and this is where Sirach's heart beats"; Sheppard, *Wisdom as a Hermeneutical Construct* (1990): 61, describes Sir 24:1-22 as "plainly a recital of the history of Wisdom who resides in Israel as the Torah"; see also Marböck, *Weisheit* (1971): 81-96;

[79] Gilbert, "L'Éloge" (1974): 336-338, discusses various readings of this stanza; Skehan, "Structures in Poems" *CBQ* 41 (1979): 365-379; Skehan and Di Lella, *Wisdom of Ben Sira* (1987): 336.

[80] See Skehan and Di Lella, *Wisdom of Ben Sira* (1987): 35.

[81] M. Weinfeld, *Deuteronomy and the Deuteronomic School* (Oxford, 1972): 256.

[82] J.C. Rylaarsdam, *Revelation in Jewish Wisdom Literature* (Chicago, 1946): 18-46; Hengel, *Judaism* (1974): 157-162.

[83] G.T. Sheppard, "Wisdom and Torah: The Interpretation of Deuteronomy Underlying Sirach 24:23," in G.A. Tuttle, ed. *Biblical and Near Eastern Studies* (Grand Rapids, 1978): 166-178.

by removing βίβλος διαθήκης θεοῦ ὑψίστου νόμον which they consider to be a gloss.[84] The arguments for this include claims that Ben Sira would not have written a triptych, and that the term διαθήκης represents the covenant with Noah, Abraham, the priests, and David, but not with Israel or with Moses, therefore it does not belong here. Although modern biblical theologies understand covenant as the Sinai covenant—the central core of Israel's religious experience—biblical tradition knows of other and very different covenants, such as the covenant made with Noah, "The waters shall never again become a flood" (Gen 9:15); with Abraham, "I will establish my covenant between me and you, and your offspring after you throughout their generations, for an everlasting covenant, to be God to you and to your offspring after you" (Gen 17:7); with David, "Your house and your kingdom shall be made sure forever before me; your throne shall be established forever" (2 Sam 7:16); with Phinehas, "Behold, I give to him my covenant of peace" (Num 25:12); with David and the Levites (Jer 33:19-22); "I will not remove from him my steadfast love, or be false to my faithfulness" (Ps 89:33). In these instances, God enters into an agreement which is much more in the nature of a promise which is unconditional, rather than a contract which lists terms and obligations for both parties. These covenants will not be revoked or the promises changed even in the face of transgressions and violations. God's eternal fidelity, expressed in promises that endure forever, is their focus. In each case such everlasting covenants are not dependent on the fidelity of human beings. Precisely how the tradition held on to two very different understandings of covenant as condition and as promise, is just one of the many paradoxes of the Old Testament.[85]

Exod 24:7 speaks of "the book of the covenant" βιβλίον τῆς διαθήκης with reference to the code of the Sinai covenant, as does 2 Kgs 23:2, 21; 2 Chr 34:31; 1 Macc 1:57. However, it is not clear whether βιβλίον τῆς διαθήκης refers to the Sinai or Deuteronomic code.[86] Sir 24:23bc cites the LXX version of Deut 33:4, which differs slightly from the Massoretic text.[87] Rickenbacher and Peters consider "the book of the covenant of the Most High God" to be influenced by Bar 4:1 "she is the book of the commandments of God, the law that endures forever".[88] In the Latin version *Testamentum* is used (Pss 24:10, 14; 49:5; 54:73; Sir 14:22; 24:32; 38:38; 44:21, 25; Bar 2:35; Wis 18:22; Dan 3:24). Gilbert argues that διαθήκης represents, "the law which Moses enjoined on us as a heritage for the congregation of Jacob"; not the covenant with Noah, Abraham, the priests, or

---

[84] Rickenbacher, *Weisheitsperikopen* (1973): 111-172; Smend, *Die Weisheit* (1906): 216-224; N. Peters, *Das Buch Jesus Sirach oder Ecclesiasticus* (Münster, 1913): 194-206.

[85] J.D. Levenson, "The Davidic Covenant and its Modern Interpreters," *CBQ* 41 (1979): 205-219.

[86] In Hellenistic Judaism letter 316 of Ariesteas speaks, as does Sir 24:23, of the βίβλος and not of βιβλίον.

[87] The reference to Deuteronomy is signalled in mss 248. The plural συναγωγαίς instead of the singular of the Massoretic text of Deut 33:4 is probably an allusion to the synagogue cult.

[88] Rickenbacher, *Weisheitsperikopen* (1973): 113; Peters, *Jesus* (1913): 202; Marböck, *Weisheit* (1971): 40, rejects their hypothesis.

David.[89] Sir 24:23 cites Deut 33:4 (LXX) with "the assembly of Jacob", thus Ben Sira brings the ancient tribal assembly—the inheritors of the Mosaic Law—into line with the "assembly of Jacob" in his own day.

Fishbane's work in uncovering and analysing of cases in which earlier/older biblical texts or traditions are taken up into later texts for purposes of authoritative reference, reinterpretation, and clarification raises several issues. One that is pertinent to this study is the issue surrounding the methodological difficulty inherent in the assumption of a demonstrable dependence of one text on another, since actual literary dependence is very difficult to prove.[90] The sense of v.23 clearly indicates that what has just been proclaimed by Wisdom corresponds to the Torah and Prophetic texts. In these we hear about the creation of the world, the choice of Israel, and the bestowal of the land, in the centre of which stands the Jerusalem Temple where the liturgy in honour of YHWH is celebrated, and from which comes the word of YHWH (Genesis 1-2, 12; Isa 2:4; Micah 4:2).[91]

Verses 25-27 arranged in parallel diptyches, detail the benefits of νόμος. These include the overflowing of Wisdom of which Torah is the expression.[92] So those who listen to Wisdom are filled with what she is herself. Ben Sira further illustrates Wisdom's abundance by alluding to six rivers associated with the history of Israel and referred to in the Bible: "brimful, like the Pishon with wisdom" (v.25a); "like the Tigris at the time of the new crops" (v.25b); "running over like the Euphrates with understanding" (v.26a); "like the Jordan at harvest time" (v.26b); like the Nile that "floods with knowledge" (v.27a); "like the Gihon at vintage time" (v.27b).[93] In likening Wisdom/Torah to the four branch rivers that flowed out of Eden, Pishon, Gihon, Tigris, and Euphrates (Gen 2:10-14), the author makes an unmistakable connection with the Garden of Eden, and with the land of Israel. Perhaps there is also a suggestion that a complete union of Wisdom and Torah would ensure the blessed setting depicted in Genesis 2.

Ben Sira by invoking images of the Nile (Exod 1:22-2:14) and the Jordan

---

[89] Gilbert "L'Éloge" (1971): 336-338 also claims that the Syriac version, taken from the Hebrew, uses a text similar to the Greek version. Whatever conclusion one reaches it must be noted that διαθήκη "covenant" appears at least eleven times in the Wisdom of Ben Sira (11:20; 14:12, 17; 16:22; 42:2; 44:20; 45:5, 7, 17, 24; 47:11); Exod 24:7 speaks of "he (Moses) took the book of the covenant", referring to the Sinai covenant. In 1 Macc 1:57 "the book of the covenant" may denote the Mosaic or Deuteronomic code.

[90] Fishbane, *Biblical Interpretation in Ancient Israel* (Oxford, 1985): 286.

[91] L. Monsengwo, *La notion de NOMOS dans le Pentateuch grec.* (Rome, 1973): 246-50, claims that the term νόμος need not be given a legalistic interpretation. However, he does not discuss Sir 24:23, so his argument has limited value for this text; both תּוֹרָהT and νόμος denote the whole of God's teaching in actions and in words; interestingly, Sir 24:3-22 seems to be devoid of legalistic considerations.

[92] See Skehan and Di Lella, *Wisdom of Ben Sira* (1987): 336, note "The Torah, like Wisdom in verse 3, is perceived as a spirit".

[93] The Pishon was the first of the four rivers of Paradise to flow from Eden (Gen 2:11); Gihon was the second river from Eden, and is identified with the Nile in the LXX of Jer 2:18, cf., Gen 2:13; the Tigris was the third river out of Eden (Gen 2:10-15) and the Euphrates was the fourth river out of Eden (Gen 10-15).

(Josh 3:14-4:18) to describe Wisdom/Torah, recalls pivotal "events" in Israelite history. The Nile recalls the fate of first-born Hebrew male children in Israel and the saving of Moses from the water to become the one who leads the Hebrews out of bondage and to receive the covenant at Sinai. Mention of the Jordan recalls the crossing of the Israelites with the Ark of the Covenant into the land of promise. The Gihon links Eden, Jerusalem and the Temple. Di Lella notes that perfect balance is achieved in verses 25-27 by having one river in each of the six lines.[94] The linking of the Jordan and the Nile to the four rivers of Paradise also recalls Gen 13:10, "the Jordan Plain was well watered everywhere like the garden of YHWH, like the land of Egypt".[95] A similar balance is reflected in "YHWH made a covenant with Abram, saying, 'To your descendants I give the land, from the river of Egypt to the great river, the river Euphrates'"(Gen 15:18).[96] Ben Sira circumscribes the land by the Tigris, the Euphrates, and the Nile, and nominates the two rivers of Paradise as its boundaries. His paralleling of the Jordan, the river of entry to the Promised Land, with the Nile, the river flowing out of Egypt, implies a harmonization of the creation of Eden with the gift of the land. This matching may suggest that Ben Sira views the land of Israel as the Garden of Eden.

According to Ben Sira it is in this land that Wisdom/Torah is abundant. He continues to sketch Wisdom's territorial expansion to the point of her "pitching her tent" in the Temple, and spreading over the entire land, the land of Paradise (cf. Isa 54:2-3). Sir 24:28-29 reiterates this in parallel and antithetical phrases highlighting the total incomprehensibility, and immensity of Wisdom. "The first human being never knew Wisdom fully" (v.28a), because the Torah, which is Wisdom, was not yet revealed, and even the "last human being" on earth will not "succeed in fathoming her" (v.28b). This merism—first human and last human— emphasises that Wisdom is beyond all human understanding and human attempts to attain her. Likewise the comparison of the sea with the abyss expands the image of Wisdom's total incomprehensibility. The image of water in, "For her thoughts are more abundant than the sea, and her counsel deeper than the great abyss" (v.29), uses a particularly apt symbol for Wisdom. This well-established image of divine munificence and goodness appears in many other biblical texts (Isa 12:3; Jer 2:13; 17:13; Ps 36:9-10). The chiastic structure of v.29 emphasises Wisdom's vastness and at the same time brings this section to a conclusion, effecting a smooth transition to the next vignette which retains the water imagery by equating Wisdom with a great river.

Vignette Eight: Role of the Wisdom Teacher Sir 24:30-33

In verses 30-34 Ben Sira reflects on the task of the wisdom teacher, who is both an "expositor of the Torah" (Sir 3:15), and one who "will pour out teaching like

---

[94] See Skehan and Di Lella, *Wisdom of Ben Sira* (1987): 336-7.
[95] See G. Lambert, "The Drama of the Garden of Eden", *Nouvelle Revue Théologique*, 76 (1954): 925.
[96] In the Massoretic text the "river" of Egypt is the Nile.

prophecy", ὡς προφητείαν (24:33). Sounding a humble note, he claims he will leave his instruction to all future generations (24:32-34).[97] His language in verses 30-34 features some prophetic echoes, and according to the Syriac version, it is prophecy.[98] Other sections of the Wisdom of Ben Sira offer instruction to the wisdom teacher but in a markedly different vein. Sir 39:1-3 uses similar terminology but emphasises that the wisdom teacher: "Seeks out the wisdom of all the ancients, and is concerned with prophecies; preserves the sayings of the famous and penetrates the subtleties of parables; seeks out the hidden meanings of proverbs and is at home with the obscurities of parables" (Sir 3:20-22; 39:1-3).[99]

Ben Sira uses the first person "I" to focus his reflection on the two images of river and sea. In likening himself, as a wisdom teacher, to "a rivulet from her stream" (v.30a), he sustains the imagery of verses 25-29. Among the readings proposed are: the Latin version which identifies "I" with Wisdom, not with Ben Sira; the Greek version, followed by many contemporary translators, reads "I am like a canal issuing from a river, like a watercourse I flow towards paradise". This reading links the stanza with the preceding verses, suggesting that the Torah, the expression of Wisdom, makes Wisdom abundant in the same way as a river is abundant.[100] However, Ben Sira is not a river, and he does not identify himself with Wisdom, but claims to be but a tributary. The wisdom teacher compares himself to a rivulet issuing from Wisdom's stream. This rivulet channels its waters into a garden to irrigate plants and flowers and in the process becomes a river and eventually a sea. Ezek 47:1-12 is echoed here in the imagery of a meagre watercourse, which grows to be a river and finally overflows like a sea. In Ezekiel, the water flows from the eastern side of the Temple, thus calling to mind the Gihon under the same name as the fourth river of paradise. Ben Sira, resident in Jerusalem (Sir 50:27), may be describing himself as spreading Wisdom which he has already located in the Temple at Jerusalem (Sir 24:10).

In Ezekiel the water from the Temple enables the desert land of Judah to be fruitful and blossom and thus transform it into the garden of paradise. Ben Sira also locates the paradise theme in this context (Sir 24:25-27, 30). Wisdom's development, as depicted in the antecedent verses, is mirrored in the activity of the author, who may be claiming the role of sustaining the fruitfulness of the earth, in the sense of being a bearer of Wisdom, at least according to the way the Greek translator understood Sir 24:30b. Here the link with Gen 2:6-10, "A river flowed

---

[97] Smend, *Die Weisheit* (1906): 224; Skehan and Di Lella, *Wisdom of Ben Sira* (1987): 330-338.

[98] See Gilbert, "L'Éloge" (1971): 336-338, who sees the same view of Wisdom in Wis 7:7; 8:21; 9:17-18. Hengel *Judaism 1* (1970):134-35, stresses that on a literary level wisdom and prophecy come together in the "prophetic" wisdom poem in Bar 3:9-4:4.

[99] Fishbane, *Interpretation* (1985): 541, n. 28, and H.P. Rüger, *Text und Textformen im hebraischen Sirach* (1970): 30-39 both comment on the text form of this unit.

[100] See P. Faure, "Comme une fleuve qui irrigue: Ben Sira 24:30-34, Critique textuelle" RB 102 (1995): 5-27; interestingly Sir 24:30 in the Syriac version can be translated to read: "And I, I am like an irrigation canal, like a tributary/arm of water watering the garden". This coheres with the following verses, apart from the plural "gardens" in the Syriac, as the singular seems more in keeping with the entire passage which refers to Genesis 2.

out of Eden to water the garden," is rather striking. Ben Sira does not envisage the wisdom teacher as the source, the gushing spring, but likens the teacher to a canal into which the source pours, and takes the water to the garden to irrigate it. The teacher's role is to water the garden with the water from the source, for which he is the vehicle. As a channel of Wisdom, he proclaims his message so that it spreads abroad. Sir 24:32b suggests a view extending beyond the borders of Israel, despite the focus on the land earlier in this poem. The image of Wisdom spreading beyond the borders may point towards a hope that the work of Ben Sira in the Greek version will be welcomed in the Diaspora.

Wisdom in Sir 24:1-34 demonstrates the author's multidimensional approach throughout the text. He also applies this approach in his self-portrait as Wisdom's disciple, who by expanding his teaching synthesizes the two aspects of time and geography for all who look for Wisdom (24:9b). Here we see how, by using imagery associated with the Garden of Eden, the author gradually leaves the land of Israel in order to develop his theme. He finally integrates the notions of location/place, and time/seasons, which he delineates so vividly throughout this hymn. In identifying Wisdom as Torah, Ben Sira seeks to reinterpret and present Wisdom anew in his day so that the rich tradition of Wisdom would not be discarded or become outmoded in the face of Hellenism. As he brought together the riches and heritage of Wisdom and Torah the role and function of this greatly enriched figure took on a more varied expression.

Wisdom's Role and Function in Sir 24:1-34

As noted earlier Ben Sira's grandson probably translated his grandfather's work into Greek near the end of the second century in the Hellenist city of Alexandria. This great city was indisputably a place of religious and philosophical ferment, in which questions about Jewish beliefs and traditions and their continuing relevance in the Hellenistic world were current. Such questioning resulted in turmoil and division among Jews, and increased Judaism's suspicious attitudes towards the surrounding world. It exacerbated the obstacles already testing the allegiance of those faithful to Judaism, and for Jews for whom the universal appeal of Hellenism, with its Greek culture and learning, proved very attractive it was the deciding factor. Some embraced Hellenism, adopting Greek thinking, customs and names, but others resisted assimilation by Hellenism maintaining some or all of their Jewish traditions, modes of thinking and customs in a hostile environment.

Hellenism, considered by its adherents to be a superior and civilizing culture, exalted the human, valued learning, and speculated about wisdom and the divine world. While the classical Greek philosophies of Plato and Aristotle may have been disintegrating, many varieties of religious speculation sprang up. The Hellenists searched for human perfection, for wisdom, and for the all-embracing powers and deities of the universe.[101] Proposals to achieve happiness ranged from

---

[101] J. Reese, *Hellenistic Influence on the Book of Wisdom and Its Consequences* (1970),

Stoicism to Epicureanism, to the worship of Isis, the mother goddess of Egyptian religion. To the Hellenists, Judaism was an unwelcome and "foreign" religion, given to strange rituals and the worship of a national deity. Consequently, Jews were dealt with as outsiders in Hellenised Alexandrian society, and such treatment undermined their confidence in the power of their own traditions. Their God also seemed unable, or unwilling to save them from ridicule, and persecution.

Ben Sira Responds to Hellenism

Addressing the question of how to live in a Hellenistic world Ben Sira spells out a way of life based on the traditions of Israel, and directed towards the problems raised by Israel's confrontation with Hellenism. While he relies on the ancient teachings of Israel, he does not do so in order to recapture the past, but rather to reinterpret the earlier traditions and integrate them in new ways.[102] Using the past to illumine the situation of the Jewish community for whom he is writing, he presents anew the power of the ancient traditions of Israel to challenge the claims Hellenism is making upon Jewish believers. Ben Sira neither attacks nor belittles the culture that threatens Judaism. Rather, he regards Hellenism as another and more recent culture, accepts some of its values, and takes its questions with great seriousness. In his teaching he confronts questions raised by Hellenism: the quest for the meaning of life, devotion to learning, speculations about the divine, a desire for wisdom. However, he rejects Hellenism's answers to these questions, and proposes answers that are grounded in, and embrace the sacred traditions of Israel. He insists that only in communion with the God of Israel can one gain Wisdom, which is neither a human achievement, as some Greek philosophers promised, nor a goddess of the ancient world, but is the creation and the gift of the God of Israel.

Wisdom, as the creation of YHWH, bestowed on the people of Israel, is explored and developed through a variety of themes and metaphors in the Wisdom of Ben Sira.[103] His major themes, fear of YHWH, Torah, and Wisdom, often blend into each other, so that one cannot separate them, or distinguish them one from another. This technique enables Ben Sira to examine Wisdom from many perspectives, and in this way to create a new synthesis of wisdom thought. Personified Wisdom stands at three key points in the book's architecture: the

---

provides a comprehensive examination of the pervasive influence of Hellenistic thought and literary forms upon the Book of Wisdom.

[102] A. Di Lella, "Conservative and Progressive Theology: Sirach and Wisdom," in *SAIW* (1976): 401-426, described his work as a "conservative" response to Hellenism.

[103] E. Jacob "Wisdom and Religion in Sirach," in *Israelite Wisdom* (1978): 247-260; Von Rad, *Wisdom* (1972): 240-262, claim that wisdom is Ben Sira's main idea; but Crenshaw, *Old Testament Wisdom* (1981): 143-173, and J. Haspecker, *Gottesfurcht bei Jesus Sirach* (Rome, 1967): 87-105, argue that "fear of YHWH" is the principal theme; Smend, *Die Weisheit des Jesus Sirach erklärt* (1906): xxiii, wrote: "Subjectively, wisdom is fear of God; objectively, it is the Law Book of Moses"; Skehan and Di Lella, *Wisdom of Ben Sira* (1987): 75-76; 143 claim the purpose of the poem is to provide identification of "wisdom" as Ben Sira understands the concept as "the fear of the Lord", and see the two concepts interwoven throughout the poem, especially in vv. 25-27.

beginning (Sir 1:10-20), the middle (Sir 24: 1-34), and the end (Sir 5: 1-30). Thus she is portrayed as integral to the structure of the book and bearing Ben Sira's theology. These organising passages contain the core of the author's message as stated in Sir 1:9-10, where Wisdom is "numbered" ἐξηρίθμησεν (the Greek equivalent of "appraised" in Job 28:27) and poured out on the works of creation.[104] Wisdom was created before "the sand of the sea, the drops of rain" so she too is beyond human understanding (Sir 1:1-4).

Wisdom in New Settings

Wisdom is portrayed in Ben Sira in new situations: singing her own praises from the assembly of the Most High (24:1-2); coming forth from the mouth of the Most High (v.2); covering the earth like a mist (v.3); having dominion over everything (v.6); taking root in Jacob/Israel (v.9); settling in Jerusalem and leading the liturgical service in the "Holy Tent" (v.10); and as one with Torah (v.23; cf. Bar 4:1-2). These new images of Wisdom recreate for the audience new ways of perceiving the presence of God in their midst. Just as the creation and development of the Wisdom figure in Proverbs 1-9 signalled the emergence of a theodicy in response to the crisis surrounding the events of 587 BCE, so too, in a Hellenistic world, whose dominant culture posed a threat that bore similarities to the situation following 587 BCE, Wisdom in Ben Sira reinterprets earlier traditions and makes available a new possibility, an alternative world, in which Wisdom speaks and offers a way of life based on the Torah.

　　Although no recorded historical disaster occurred, Hellenism's all-pervasive effects presented a serious challenge to the survival and identity of Judaism. As argued in chapter two regarding the crisis precipitated by the events following 587 BCE, it was particularly in the portrayals of the Wisdom figure that Proverbs 1-9 outlined a way. Evidence of the disorientation caused by the encroachment of Hellenism on Judaism may similarly be gleaned from the books whose writers addressed the problems besetting the Jewish communities living in the midst of a Hellenistic culture. Hengel's assessment of this evolution perhaps captures a salient issue involved in the development, "Without question there is an inner logic in this development in Jewish wisdom speculation, but we should ask whether a movement in this direction would have developed at all if it had not been furthered by the necessity to ward off foreign influences. We must therefore agree with J. Fichtner, who sees the decisive motive force in the controversy with Hellenism".[105] However, Sir 24:1-34 does not bear out Fichtner and Hengel's claims that Hellenism was the motive force responsible for the developments in later wisdom writing.[106] Hangel claims: "Over against Hellenism and its wisdom, Judaic wisdom could only assert itself if it approximated to the factor which played the decisive role in this struggle on the side of the Jews: the Law. The significance

---

[105] Hengel, *Judaism* I (1974): 157-162.
[106] J. Fichtner, *Die altorientalische Weisheit in ihrer israelitisch-jüdischen Ausprägung* (1933): 127 claimed that the decisive motive force was the 'controversy with Hellenism'.

of *hokmah* for the shaping of Jewish religion in the struggle against Hellenism and its σοφία is not to be underestimated."[107]

Faithfulness to Wisdom/Torah

According to Sir 24:23 everything that Wisdom proclaims in her discourse corresponds to the Torah. As Wisdom's discourse has nothing legalistic in it, one could ask in what sense is the claim to be understood? No specific mention is made of any commandment of the Law, nor is a list of authorized injunctions provided. The Sir 24: 30-34 are couched as an invitation to become a disciple of Wisdom. So the Torah is not presented as a legal code or list of commandments binding on all who seek to be faithful to their heritage. In the time of Ben Sira the Pentateuch, the Torah, was already familiar to the Jewish people. So it seems likely that Sir 24:23 in referring to the Torah is speaking of the Pentateuch. These five books do contain laws, but they appear in a story covering Israel's sacred history from creation to the death of Moses on Mount Nebo in sight of the Promised Land on the eve of the conquest. It is not surprising that Sir 24:3 echoes Gen 1:1-3 and Deut 33:4 in evoking the history of the origin of the world, while Sir 24:7-8 highlights the election of Israel from among all the peoples of the earth.

Sir 24:10-12 recalls Deuteronomy on the centralization of the cult, while descriptions of incense and perfume refer back to Exodus. All these strands are woven together and form the tapestry that is the Wisdom figure in Sir 24: 1-34.[108] Ben Sira's intellectual heritage as a wisdom teacher may be a clue to his breakthrough to the innovation that is Wisdom identified with Torah. Important features about the wisdom tradition itself may serve to clarify the way in which such a creative transformation could have been brought about. While wisdom writing was familiar in various forms throughout the ancient Near East, Israel had developed its own tradition in this field, and obviously had developed ways of nurturing its pursuit. By the time of Ben Sira the Wisdom figure was already a feature of the Jewish heritage (at least in Proverbs 1-9). Although the international flavour of biblical wisdom has posed a problem for some biblical scholars I believe that this was the very feature of Israel's wisdom that gave it the ability to deal with crises, which called other biblical traditions into question.

Wisdom writers sought to address their audiences as people who shared the experiences of the physical world, and called on them to understand the world as they perceived it. They were aware that the world taught them something that was beyond it—something which in no way opposed the revelation of YHWH in their history—but was the experience which life taught them. However, the personification of Wisdom cannot be reduced to the notion of a primordial order immanent in the world, and yet distinct from God, to the point that one can describe it or experience it. This idea has been postulated by several scholars with regard to Proverbs 8, a figure that is far more than a personification of primordial

---

[107] Hengel, *Judaism* I (1974): 115-126; 161-162.

[108] G. von Rad, *Wisdom* (1972): 241-44 suggests that Ben Sira had more admiration for Wisdom than for the Torah itself.

order.[109] From the introduction of the Wisdom figure in Proverbs 1-9—probably in
the time of the Babylonian Exile—this figure had been elevated to being the bearer
of the covenant; the image of true faithfulness to YHWH; a figure who speaks with
the voice of YHWH, and at times recalls prophetic teaching but announces a
different outcome.

Sir 24:3-23 was clearly inspired by Prov 8:22-31.[110] On the other hand
Deut 4:5-8, which is close to v.23, acclaims the commandments of the
Deuteronomic Law as showing "your wisdom and discernment to the peoples"
who when they hear all these statutes, will say "Surely this great nation is a wise
and discerning people" (Deut 4:6). The community of Israel is situated in a world
created by God which is, at the same time, the world shared by all humanity. The
Deuteronomic Law is a privileged expression of a way of life given only to the
Israelites /Jews. But the Law is received by Israel as the Word of God transmitted
by Moses. Ben Sira makes the affirmation of Deut 4:5-8 explicit, by understanding
it as valuable for all peoples. No doubt he has Proverbs 8 in mind when he
portrays personified Wisdom present in creation and understands the first part of
Genesis to speak implicitly of the same Wisdom as the Wisdom in Proverbs 8. If
this view is accepted it is possible to consider the rest of the Pentateuch as a
description of the work of Wisdom.

At the beginning of his work Ben Sira sets out the basic principle for his
readers: "If you desire wisdom, keep the commandments" (1:26). In practice,
Wisdom and the Law have already become one, and he expresses this by putting
the great hymn of Wisdom, in chapter 24, in which this fusion is achieved, in the
centre of his work. With this step Wisdom becomes the exclusive gift of God to
Israel. This provides the possibility of repudiating an alien autonomous ideal of
wisdom which declines any association with the Law, which for Ben Sira would
mean idolatry. Accordingly, he warns against false "striving for wisdom" (3:21-
24). He takes up earlier ideas, but modifies them, and he does so in order to gain a
contemporary starting point for his argument. Transgression of the Law and
apostasy bring certain punishment from God in this life, while fear of God and
obedience to the Law lead to all the good things which are worth striving for, even
to his opponents: "honour and praise", "happiness, joy and a long life", "well-
being and flourishing health", and not least an "abiding remembrance after death"
(39:9-11). The polemic force in Ben Sira's work arises from the presupposition of
an unbreakable link between human action and divine retribution. While in
Proverbs, action and consequence are to some extent directly related, Ben Sira
portrays God as the one who initiates and implements punishment. God repays

---

[109] D. Harrington, "The Wisdom of the Scribe according to Ben Sira" in J.J. Collins, ed.
Ideal Figures in Ancient Judaism (Chico, 1980): 183, claims that Ben Sira never
attributes a mythological dimension to Wisdom, thus shows his "conservative" character.

[110] P. Skehan, "Structures in Poems on Wisdom: Proverbs 8 and Sirach 24" *CBQ* 41 (1970):
365-379, Skehan reconstructs the Hebrew original of chapter 24 on the basis of Proverbs
8. He also notes that although chapter 24 is closely related to Proverbs 8, it is unique in
several aspects.

(35:13), "The Lord alone is to be declared righteous" (18:2).[111]

Torah as the Focus of Reflection

It is clear from the evidence in chapter 24 that Ben Sira is speaking as a wisdom teacher throughout the poem. His description of himself as the generic wisdom teacher suggests that the Torah itself has become the object of reflection for the wisdom writers. Wisdom identified with the Torah is here integral to wisdom teaching and writing. The application of wisdom approaches to the Torah must have shown that portrayals of personified Wisdom could also be used in portrayals of the Torah. Transformations were necessary, as can be seen in the earlier portrayals of the Wisdom figure in Proverbs. In her speech and locations (Prov 1:20-33) Wisdom brings to mind some of the prophets, and she manifests the prophetic spirit mentioned in Joel. Likewise, Ben Sira depicts Wisdom/Torah as emanating from the one source, God, who is the Creator and giver of everything. Implicit in this teaching, as in Proverbs 1-9, is that ultimately wisdom demands a choice of life over death, Wisdom over Folly. Ben Sira puts it succinctly: "Before each person are life and death, and whichever one chooses will be given" (Sir 15:17).

For Ben Sira, personified Wisdom and Torah are inseparable and become a unity in Israel. It is possible that Ben Sira, who was living in Jerusalem at a time when Judaism was encountering Hellenism, would have sought to defend the patrimony of Israel by showing its grandeur and long standing credentials. While chapter 24 does not exhibit any specific examples of anti-Hellenism, or censure Hellenistic teachings or practices, he lauds Judaism's ancient heritage and magnificence. Absence of references to Hellenism could indicate a deliberate ignoring of a movement so widespread and powerful.[112] Ben Sira illustrates, develops and enriches the figure of personified Wisdom identified with the Torah, by demonstrating the coherence of these two arms of Israel's sacred traditions. He enhances Israel's heritage for the Jews by showing that they can legitimately understand and accept the Torah in a wisdom context. His teaching aims to persuade his audience not to lose faith in the Torah or regard their Wisdom or Law as in any way inferior to that of the Hellenists. They must treasure Wisdom/Torah as God's special gift to them and so it is their enduring heritage and a categorical response to those who do not know or appreciate the sacred traditions of Judaism.

In the Wisdom of Ben Sira the Torah is perceived as the expression of two of the author's deep convictions on the subject of Wisdom. In one sense he insists on the tent as the cornerstone from which Wisdom shines. Here he applies to Wisdom what Isa 2:3 and Micah 4:2 say of the Torah: "For from Zion will come the Torah and from Jerusalem the Word of YHWH". For Ben Sira the Torah is

---

[111] Hengel, *Judaism I* (1974): 143-145.

[112] The lauding of Judaism's claim to a grander, better, and more ancient heritage than that of Hellenism can be seen clearly in the Wisdom of Ben Sira chapters 44-50 in the "Praise of Israel's great ancestors" where there is much implied denigration of Hellenism and its values.

not a simple code of laws but the privileged expression of Wisdom coming to dwell with human beings. In the Torah is the revelation of God present to the people of which the Temple is the location *par excellence*. A dual movement of the concentration and expansion of Wisdom pervades the structure of chapter 24 as illustrated in: "From the mouth of the Most High I came forth, and like mist covered the earth", a reinterpretation of Gen 2:6 "as a stream rising from the earth and watering the whole face of the ground", thus confirming Wisdom as the element which ensures the vitality and fruitfulness of the Torah.

Wisdom/Torah Extends Jewish Horizons

Ben Sira draws attention specifically to the role of Wisdom in creation in Sir 24:9 by having Wisdom proclaim, "Before the ages, from the first, he created me, and through the ages I shall not cease to be" (cf. Prov 8:23). In this Wisdom is distinct from God, her Creator, and while seeming to share the state of creature with the rest of creation, she is unique in being the first of creation, "before the ages", and thus different from everything that is created after her.[113] Sir 24:3 describes the origin of Wisdom by allusion to Gen 1:1-3: "Wisdom came out of the mouth of God." Here Wisdom seems to be depicted as the first creative word in the priestly version of the creation.[114] In her hymn of self-praise, Wisdom is commanded by God to "pitch her tent" in Israel, and thus becomes identified with the Temple service and the Law of Moses.[115] The image of creation by word negates any view of the Creator as a Deus absconditus, but rather portrays a God who is intimately involved with creation. Furthermore, the image of God as Creator by word invalidates any view of God as capricious.

The authors of Bar 3:9-4:4 and Sir 24: 1-34 conceptualize God as speaking through Wisdom/Torah, which is the embodiment of the creative, life-giving word of the Creator. Ben Sira initiates this new departure for wisdom thought, by bringing into harmony the twin notions of Torah and Wisdom as the means by which the horizons of Israelite faith are extended.[116] Through a series of parallels, Wisdom, the first of all creation, is shown to be one with the Torah, "the book of the Most High's covenant" which also highlights creation by YHWH. In

---

[113] An interesting parallel is the chiasmus in Sir 24:8ab.

[114] The Latin version adds two further lines to 24:3a; transition from creation by word to the Torah as the incorporation of the divine commandment is skilfully expressed in Ps 119:1-4a, which describes, in majestic terms, the revelation of God in creation through the "speech" of nature. In vv. 3-4 the psalmist praises the incomparable value of the Law in leading away from evil and breaking the dominion of sin.

[115] Whether "Israel" here means the people or the land of Israel is unclear. Land seems likely as the hymn mentions Jerusalem and the Temple. Bar 3:30 makes the point that the Covenant was given to the people of Israel. This means that the gift of the Law is to the people of Israel regardless of where they are living. Baruch probably intends the Diaspora Jews. If the land is the focus for Wisdom a question concerning the location and the origin of the Torah follows.

[116] I am presuming a later date for Bar 3:9-4:4.

The Wisdom of Ben Sira we see a transformation of the prophet-like Wisdom figure of Proverbs into a Wisdom figure identified with the Torah. The Divine Wisdom exists in Israel in concrete form, in the Torah, which is Israel's Wisdom before the nations and is in essence a restatement of its election: "All this is the book of the covenant of the Most High God, the law which Moses commanded us, as an inheritance for the congregations of Jacob" (Sir 24:23).[117]

All the preceding statements are included in the "all" of verse 23a. In this way the many-layered conception of cosmic wisdom was indissolubly associated with the history of Israel and conversely, the Law which was under attack in Jerusalem and may have become a source of embarrassment for some Jews in the time of Ben Sira was given a historical, and a rational basis. While the universality and widespread influence of wisdom thinking of the ancient Near East are evident in Ben Sira's own writing, the emphasis throughout the book is on the uniqueness of the Jewish heritage as expressed in personified Wisdom. In 1:10, we see the alignment of Wisdom with the chosen ones: "and he supplied her to those who love him", a notion picked up and developed in 24:6-8: "Make your dwelling in Jacob, and in Israel receive your inheritance." Ben Sira places Wisdom in the Jerusalem sanctuary, but paradoxically his Garden of Eden imagery emphasises her universality, as does Baruch's sustained metaphor of exile. While the identification of Wisdom with the Torah was not an entirely new idea, as Deut 4:5-8; Pss 19:8; 119:97-98 allude to a similar notion, the portrayal of Wisdom as Torah (Bar 3:9-4:4; Sir 24:23) signals powerful changes in Jewish tradition and teaching.

Torah Locates Wisdom in Israel's History

Universal wisdom becomes the possession of the people of Israel and ultimately of those faithful to the Torah. At the same time, the old mythological notion that Wisdom sought a dwelling place on earth in vain and in disappointment returned to her heavenly dwelling was rescinded. Ben Sira assures his readers that Wisdom has found her abiding place on earth in the Torah, which was entrusted to Israel alone. Whether Ben Sira was the first to make this momentous identification, or whether he took it over from elsewhere is impossible to ascertain. However it came about, it marks the climax in the composition of Ben Sira's writing that has come down to us. It seems likely that this result of a lifetime's work may also have been a presentation of new ideas about Wisdom.

The cult and works of love are included in the Torah. The traditional Jewish belief that the world stands on three things: the Torah, the cult/Temple, and on works of love, was, if it were current in Ben Sira's lifetime, an excellent point of departure for the bringing together of Torah and Wisdom. The beginnings of the integration of Law and Wisdom are already indicated in Deut 4:6, where God's commandments are called the wisdom of Israel against the nations and this becomes even more marked in Psalms 1 and 119, which were probably composed

---

[117] G.F. Moore *Judaism in the First Centuries of the Christian Era* (Cambridge, 1927): 264, n.1, notes the extreme improbability that Sir 24:23 is a later interpolation, as W.L. Knox "The Divine Wisdom", *JTS 38* (1937):230-237 assumes.

in the third century BCE. Psalm 119:118, 158 speak of apostasy and neglect of the commandments, verses 110, 113, 121, 126, 139, 143, 150, 157, 161 speak of oppression of those faithful to the Law. This could be a reference to the conflict which was more evident in Ben Sira's time so the psalm may come from the second half of the third century when the Tobiads were in power. If this were the case, some movement towards the identification of Wisdom and Torah had begun. G. von Rad notes, "Sirach 24 is not a unit. The section that begins in verse 23 'all this is the book of the covenant, the law which Moses gave us' has obviously been added to the self presentation of wisdom. The first person style of the speech breaks off, and now it is the teacher who speaks, interpreting Wisdom's speech. Clearly Sirach is here addressing an already existing tradition."[118] While there may be an inner logic in this development of Jewish wisdom speculation, it is far from certain that such a development would have taken place, even in facing the difficulties arising from the influence of Hellenism, without the perception and knowledge of the Jewish heritage, and the necessary gifts and ability to capture such a powerful insight in language that has enshrined it in the Jewish tradition for later generations.

At the climax of Wisdom's song, Ben Sira makes an unabashed and unparalleled identification of Wisdom as the book of the covenant of the Most High (Sir 24:23; cf. Bar 3:9-4:3). Thus, Ben Sira and Baruch connect universal Wisdom with the history of Israel and its covenant law. In Baruch this emphasises what Wisdom herself declares when she announces that God instructed her to pitch her tent in Israel and dwell among the people. Unfortunately the details of this development cannot be documented but it is a crucial factor within the religious dimensions of biblical wisdom. The combination of Torah and Wisdom is so late that it cannot illuminate the religious dimensions common to all of wisdom. Ben Sira regularly imitates the Hebrew Bible by showing a special predilection for Deuteronomy, even identifying Wisdom with Moses' covenant (Sir 24:1-29).[119]

Although he may be among the earliest witnesses to what became central in Jewish institutions (Sir 51:23, 29), Ben Sira's curriculum included Pentateuch, wisdom collections, and prophecy (Sir 39:1-11). It is interesting that he refers infrequently to the Jewish Scriptures. Most of the Wisdom of Ben Sira is a collection of maxims and poetic essays on proper behaviour, in the style of the Hebrew Bible, but without the citation of it, and presented through the prism of Ben Sira's own theology. His translator and grandson identifies the themes of the book as "discipline/education, and wisdom" (Sir Prologue 1:12). Ben Sira, like the author(s) of Proverbs 1-9 in using the prophetic tradition, cherished what appeared to be irreconcilable traditions of wisdom, prophecy, and Torah. He makes Wisdom and Torah inseparable (24:8-12, 23; 12:23).[120] A question beyond the scope of this study confronts us here with regard to understanding whether Wisdom flowed into

---

[118] G. von Rad, *Wisdom* (1972): 166.

[119] Sheppard, *Wisdom as a Hermeneutical Construct* (1980): 19-83.

[120] J.L. Crenshaw, "Sirach" in *HBC* (1988): 837, claims that these were irreconcilable traditions.

Torah or Torah into Wisdom, or whether the wisdom authors and Deuteronomists were one and the same. Wisdom's relationship to the Torah in Ben Sira and Baruch must be understood against the background of confusion and assimilation of Judaism by Hellenism. Certainly some consideration must be given to the effects on Judaism of living in a predominantly Hellenistic society.

Clearly, Jewish thought was greatly influenced by its Hellenistic environment. In his reinterpretation of Israelite tradition in language that recalls and highlights its unique history and development Ben Sira employs enduring Israelite themes, images, and metaphors in his refashioning of the Wisdom figure and thus gives new expression to the tradition. His "recreated" Wisdom figure enabled the Jewish people to remain faithful to, and to recover their Jewish heritage, when it was in danger of being eroded and assimilated by the prevailing Hellenistic culture. Derivations of individual themes are often difficult to identify, as are chance analogies and real instances of dependence. Overall, however, foreign influences affected the detail rather than the entire picture of the world and of history envisaged by Ben Sira, which still rests on an Old Testament conception of salvation history.

A simple yet astute logic underlies the move to identify Wisdom and Torah. Wisdom and Torah were both the divine way of life; it followed ineluctably that they were the same, as Ben Sira makes clear by placing this teaching in the centre of his composition. Wisdom, as the Torah itself, is the means by which God is revealed to human beings, while on the other hand, they achieve communion with God by means of the Torah, and equally by means of Wisdom. In Sir 24:23 this identification becomes complete with the figure of Wisdom quoting Deut 33:4 and applying the verse to herself. In making Wisdom identical with the Mosaic Law she is clearly declared to be a divine gift, rather than a human acquisition; and thus Ben Sira makes Israelite Wisdom superior in every way to the wisdom of the Hellenists.

Chapter 5

Personified Wisdom as Saviour

Introduction

Unlike Ben Sira, the author of the Wisdom of Solomon, choose to compose his masterpiece on Wisdom in Greek, the language of the culture that threatened the survival of Jewish tradition and belief. Writing, probably in the first century BCE, he addresses his teaching to Jews living in Alexandria, the Hellenistic city that was home to large communities of Jews at the time.[1] His work contains persuasive and compelling apologetic, delicate and complex rhetoric after the fashion of the philosophical argumentation beloved of the Greeks, contemplative poetry with Wisdom as its subject, and reinterpretations of Israel's sacred history reminiscent of some psalms. He is audacious in his teaching on several points. His audacity appears especially in his understanding and expression of Wisdom as a reflection of the Deity and in the way in which he interprets Israel's history and integrates its narrative into his Greek thinking. Personified Wisdom, is on one hand as a figure familiar from other biblical wisdom texts (Job 28; Prov 1:20-33, 8:1-36; 9:1-6; Sir 24:1-33; Bar 3:9-4:4), but on the other hand she is an amazingly new and transformed Wisdom figure (Wis 6:22-10:21).[2]

Faithful Jews caught up in the intersection of Judaism and Hellenism faced demanding and onerous decisions concerning the manner in which they might live in accord with their traditions and nurture their Jewish faith among people who did not share their heritage. Could they survive as a unique and chosen people in such circumstances? How ought they to relate to their Gentile neighbours and culture? How react to the suffering alluded to in Wis 1:1-6:4? The author's appeal to his readers for ethical conduct suggests a shared awareness and endurance of the abuse of power by their Hellenist rulers with the accompanying injustice. Beginning with these assumptions this chapter examines the figure of Wisdom in Wis 6:22-10:21 by investigating the historical and social context of the book, examining how the author, who adopted the mantle of Solomon, fashions the Wisdom figure in Wis 6:12-10:21; and considers how this figure functions in the text.

---

[1] Many Jews seem to have migrated to this region during the reigns of the first two Ptolemies. The earliest Jewish inscriptions in Egypt date from the third century.

[2] The Wisdom of Solomon is well defined structurally, being composed of three clearly delineated, closely interlocking sections: Wis 1:1-6:11 contrasting the way of Wisdom with the way of the impious; Wis 6:12-10:21 presenting personified Wisdom, Wis 11:1-19:22 describing how Wisdom works in the course of history.

Historical and Social Contexts of the Wisdom of Solomon

As mentioned in the introduction the author of the Wisdom of Solomon wrote as Solomon.[3] His book, written in Greek, probably originated in Alexandria, the intellectual hub of the ancient world. Alexandria, with its large Jewish population, was a home to many Jews of the Diaspora, and a centre for the meeting and merging of Jewish traditions and Greek culture. While displaying an explicit concern with life in the Dispersion, the author of Wisdom also shows considerable knowledge of Greek ideas.[4]   In addition, he reveals various concerns and connections with Palestinian Judaism. In different ways Temple and cult are topics of discussion, although sometimes peripherally, and there are indications that he is also familiar with apocalyptic traditions in Palestine. Interestingly, echoes of Homer and Hesiod, allusions to Egyptian religious practices and Greek philosophical vocabulary also appear in the Wisdom of Solomon.[5] The Wisdom of Solomon is first mentioned in Christian references. In the Muratorian fragment, this work is mentioned among the debated Christian writings, either an indication of its extra-canonical status or a sign of its newness.

Despite the Solomonic authorship claim, most scholars agree that the book was written many centuries after Solomon.[6] However, no consensus has so far emerged, with the work being placed anywhere between 220 BCE and 50 CE.[7] It seems likely that it appeared after the completion of the Septuagint of the Prophets and Writings, as there is widespread agreement that the author made use of the Septuagint version of Isaiah. This would bring the date to at least the end of the third century BCE. Horbury considers it a Greek composition by a single Jewish writer working in Egypt in the first century BCE.[8]   While the author appears to be unacquainted with the writings of Philo (20 BCE to 54 CE), the book does belong to the same milieu of thought. This may be reasonable grounds to presume it appeared sometime in the last half of the first century BCE.[9] It is

---

[3]   Solomon, as a literary construct, is clearly a complex symbol, representing both the wise ruler and the wisdom teacher. See E. Lohse, "Solomon" *TDNT* 7 (1971): 459-465. The strategy of attaching a prestigious name to an anonymous work, widespread in antiquity, legitimated the work, and gave it an authority it might otherwise not have enjoyed. Solomon, the wise man par excellence, is credited with several works including, Wisdom of Solomon, Proverbs, Song of Songs, Psalms of Solomon, and Qoheleth.

[4]   Reference to the four cardinal virtues in 8:7 and the philosophical discussion of the knowledge of God in 13:1-9 are examples of this knowledge.

[5]   Larcher, *Études* (1969): 193; 183-185; 208-223; Reese, *Influence* (1970): 12-17; P. Heinisch, *Das Buch der Weisheit* (Münster, 1912) 149-157; G. Ziener, *Die theologische Begriffssprache im Buche der Weisheit* (Bonn, 1972): 142-148.

[6]   In addition to the title, the Wisdom of Solomon the book is called the Book of Wisdom.

[7]   Reese, *Influence* (1970): 8; M. Gilbert, *La Critique des dieux dans le livre de la Sagesse* (1973): 161-164, 172; Winston, *Wisdom* (1979):20-25; *ABD* 6 (1986): 122-123; Larcher, *Études* (1969).

[8]   W. Horbury, "The Christian use and the Jewish origins of the Wisdom of Solomon" in *WAI* (1995): 182-196.

[9]   Larcher, *Études* (1969): 151-178; Winston, *Wisdom of Solomon* (1979): 33, notes that

generally accepted that the work is an original Greek composition, while retaining the parallelism of Hebrew poetry. Publication of the critical edition of the Greek text in 1962 (Ziegler) rekindled an already abundant and long-established tradition of scholarship around the Wisdom of Solomon.[10]

Some Fathers of the Church regarded the Wisdom of Solomon as one of the most important of the Deuterocanonical books. Amongst the earliest references are those by Pope Clement, "by the word of his might [God] established all things, and by his word he can overthrow them. 'Who shall say to him, "What have you done?" or who shall resist the power of his strength?' [Wis 12:12]" *Letter to the Corinthians* 27:5 (ca. 80 CE); The *Letter of Barnabas* "'Let us bind the righteous man because he is displeasing to us' [Wis 2:12]". References also appear in Clement of Alexandria, *Stromata* 6.11 and 14, Tertullian, *De Praescriptione Haereticorum* 7: "What indeed has Athens to do with Jerusalem? What concord is there between the Academy and the Church? What between heretics and Christians? . . . our instruction comes from the porch of Solomon who has himself taught that the Lord should be sought in simplicity of heart"; Adv Valentinianos 2.2; Cyprian, *De Mortalitate* 23; Lactantius, *Divinae Institutiones* 2.2.3.16; 4.29, 4-5; Tatian, *Oratio ad Graecōs* 5; Irenaeus, in *Adversus. Haereses* 4.38.3 alludes to Wis 6:19; John of Damascus, *De Fide Orthodoxa* 4.17; Hippolytus of Rome, *De Septimestri* 4 and 7. St. Augustine quotes from the Wisdom of Solomon several hundred times. In his *De Praedestinatione Sanctorum* 14:26-29, he favoured its inclusion in the Canon of Scripture, and cites apostolic, liturgical and traditional evidence to support his case.[11] St. Jerome regarded the book as a Pseudepigraphon and placed it with the books excluded from the Canon, but used it nevertheless.[12]

Given that the Wisdom of Solomon was probably produced in Alexandria in the late Ptolemaic, or early Imperial period, the Jews being addressed were living in a Hellenised society and were familiar with the Egyptian goddess Isis, in her Hellenised form. Many scholars have observed that the author of Wisdom was also familiar with other aspects of Hellenism, and adopted some of these in his presentation of Jewish theology.[13] A selection of identical terms that appear in both Wisdom and Isis texts may substantiate this claim.[14]

"Stoicising Platonism of Wisdom is a trademark of Middle Platonic scholasticism".

[10] H.B. Swete, *The Old Testament in Greek according to the Septuagint* 3 (Cambridge, 1912); J. Ziegler, ed. *Sapientia Salomonis* (Göttingen, 1962); P.W. Skehan, "The Text and Structure of the Book of Wisdom" *Traditio 3* (1945): 1-12; A.G. Wright, "The Structure of the Book of Wisdom" *Bib 48* (1967):165-184; "Wisdom" in *NJBC* (1990): 510-522; J.M. Reese, "Plan and Structure in the Book of Wisdom" *CBQ* 27 (1965): 391-399; M. Gilbert, "La structure de la prière de Salomon (Sg 9)" *Bib 51* (1970): 301-331; K.G. Sandelin, *Wisdom as Nourisher* (Åbo, 1986); P. Bizzeti, *Il Libro Della Sapienza* (Brecia, 1984).

[11] A.M. La Bonnardière, *Le Livre de la Sagesse* (Paris, 1970): 56-57.

[12] See *PL* 28: 1241; Larcher, *Études* (1969): 58.

[13] A. Di Lella, "Conservative and Progressive Theology" *CBQ* 28 (1966): 135-154.

[14] *Inscriptiones Graecae* 12, fasc. 5 and supplement (Berlin, 1914): Isis Hymns.

Shared Vocabulary in Wisdom and Isis Texts

Wisdom	Isis
Wis 6:14: "throne-companion"	Kyme, 43: "attends" the sun
Wis 7:2: "during a ten-month's space"	Kyme 16: "ten month foetus"
Wis 7:7, 16 "prudence was given to me"	Oxy. Litany 34, 40, 60, 124: "prudence"
Wis 7:10: "radiance" never ceases	Madi 551.32: more beautiful / sun's radiance
Wis 7:15: God is "guide" of Wisdom	Oxy. Litany 122: Isis is the "guide"
Wis 7:17-19: power over elements, years and stars	Oxy. Litany: 172-4, 204, 227-30, 237-9: founded the great year / commands stars
Wis 7:17: knows "structure of the universe"	Kore Kosmou 52: "constitution of world"
Wis 7:17: reliable knowledge	Mesomedes 1.11: has a "reliable" tongue
Wis 7:18: knows beginning / end of seasons	Isis & Osiris, 77: "knows beginning / end"
Wis 7:20: teaches about plants and roots	Madi 548.8, 53: teaches about plants / roots
Wis 7:22: "holy"	P. Oxy. Litany XI 1380, 36, 38, 39: "holy"
Wis 7:22: "beneficent"	Oxy. Litany 247: Isis is "beneficent"
Wis 7:22: Wisdom . . . taught me	Kyme 11; Ios 17; Cyrene 12: taught by Isis
Wis 7:24: permeates all by her pureness	P. Oxy. Litany xi 1380, 175: "purifies"
Wis 7:25: Nothing tainted in Wisdom	P. Oxy. xi 1380, 109: Isis is "undefiled"
Wis 7:27: "is but one"	Cyrene 6: Isis "is but one"
Wis 7:27: "can do all things"	Cyrene 15: "Nothing done without me"
Wis 8:1: extends to the ends of the earth	Madi 550: 20-21, 25; Cyrene 5; Kyme 45: extends to the ends of the earth
Wis 8:1: rules all graciously	Kyme 10; Oxy. 58-159: Isis brings order
Wis 8:2: make her my "bride"	P. Oxy. xi 1380, 30, 85: Isis is bride
Wis 8:4: "initiate" in the knowledge of God	P. Oxy. xi 1380, 111: Isis is "initiator"
Wis 8:4: Wisdom chooses God's works	Kyme 13: Isis founded works of the sea
Wis 8:5: In Wisdom is all wealth in life	Kyme 5, 12: Isis gives all fruits of life
Wis 8:8: Wisdom knows the seasons	Chalcis 3: Isis is all seasons
Wis 8:8: Wisdom solves riddles	Kore Kosmou, 66: Isis solves riddles
Wis 8:9: Wisdom comforts in sorrow	Madi 550.6: Isis frees from sorrow
Wis 8:13-17: Wisdom gives immortality	P. Oxy. xi 1380: goddess of immortality
Wis 8:15: Monarchs fear wisdom	Kyme 1, 23: Isis ends tyranny
Wis 8:15: Wisdom courageous in war	Kyme 39; Oxy. Litany 158: Lady of War
Wis 8:16: With her is gladness and joy	P. Oxy. xi 1380, 19, 31: is gladness and joy
Wis 8:18: Wisdom is delight	Madi 549.4: Isis makes all delight
Wis 8:18: wealth in labours of her hands	Cyrene 9: gained the reward of her labour
Wis 8:20: I entered an "undefiled" body	P. Oxy. xi 1380, 109: Isis is undefiled
Wis 9:4: Wisdom "throne companion"	Kyme 43: I "attend" the sun
Wis 9:11: Wisdom will "guide"	Oxy. Litany 122: Isis is the "guide"
Wis 9:14: Wretched need Wisdom	Mesomedes 1.24: Isis pities wretched
Wis 10:1-21: Wisdom is Saviour - 6 times	Oxy. Lit. 55 Madi 548.13: saviour-11 times
Wis 10:2: Wisdom has power to rule all	Oxy. Litany 239; Madi 548.25, 31: rules all
Wis 10:4: Wisdom directs the righteous	Oxy. Litany 188-189: directs the righteous
Wis 10:17: Wisdom is the light of stars	Oxy. Litany 158-159: light of stars
Wis 10:20: Praise God with one accord	Madi 550.15: Listen to Isis with one accord

Investigations into the influence of the Isis cult on the development of personified Wisdom have yielded positive and negative findings.[15] In 1901, Reitzenstein suggested that portrayals of Wisdom in the books of Sirach and Wisdom were influenced by Egyptian theology.[16] While his study lacked detailed analysis of sources, his proposal provoked interest. Knox considered the claim: "Young Jews, seeking advancement under the Ptolemaic dynasty, might find it hard to resist the attraction of Isis. The personified Wisdom is the answer of orthodox Judaism: the source of order in creation and conduct is not Isis, but the Wisdom of God".[17] Pfeiffer proposed, "All the characteristic epithets of the Old Testament-Jewish Wisdom were lacking in Isis, except that Isis is called the πάρεδρος of Osiris-Helios".[18] This view has not received much support among scholars. More recently, Reese and Mack analysed the relation of Wisdom 6-9 to the Isis Aretalogies. In separate works, they document the extent to which the Aretalogies provide close parallels to the description of Wisdom in the Wisdom of Solomon.[19] Reese investigates the influences of Hellenistic language, ideas, style and literary genre on Wisdom and Mack illustrates the way in which the wisdom tradition continued to be open to Hellenist sources in its use of metaphors from Isis mythology.

Reese identifies Epicurean speculation on immortality, anthropological and ethical teachings in treatises on kingship, vocabulary and presentation from the literature and popular religion of the Isis cult, and numerous epithets and characteristics that appear both in Isis aretalogies and in the Wisdom of Solomon. He makes a strong case for the hypothesis that the portrayal of Wisdom, especially in the motif of union with God, is a conscious effort to offset the appeal of the literature of the revived Isis cult.[20] Reese finding that Wis 6:22-10:21 followed the general structure of Isis aretalogies and Greek hymns; saw the section beginning "what is Wisdom?" (6:22) and especially 7:22-8:1, corresponds to the part of the aretalogies outlining the nature and origin of Isis; secondly, the description of Isis's powers is reflected in the enumeration of Wisdom's wondrous gifts (Wis 8:2-16); third, the list of Wisdom's benefits for the just (Wis 10:1-21) corresponds to the "blessings" section of the aretalogies.[21] Pressing ahead with this analysis he

---

[15] Kayatz, *Studien zu Proverbien 1-9* (Neukirchen-Vluyn, 1966); Conzelmann, "Mother of Wisdom" (1964): 225-234; Marböck, *Weisheit* (1971); Hengel, *Judaism I* (1974): 1.157-162; 2.101-102; Reese, *Influence* (1970): 42-49; Winston, *Wisdom* (1979): 34-38.

[16] R. Reitzenstein, *Zwei religionsgeschichtliche Fragen* (Strassburg, 1901): 104-112.

[17] W. L. Knox, "Divine Wisdom" *JTS* 38 (1937): 230-237.

[18] G. Pfeifer, *Ursprung und Wesen der Hypostasenvorstellung im Judentum* (Stuttgart, 1967): 84; see also G. Fohrer, "Sophia" in *TWNT* (1966): 476-496.

[19] Mack, *Logos und Sophia* (Göttingen, 1973).

[20] Reese, *Influence* (1970): 40, 46-48.

[21] A.-J. Festugière, "A propos des arétalogies d'Isis," *HTR* 42 (1949): 220-228, noted the structure of Isis aretalogies followed Greek hymns which consisted of four parts: (a) nature, origin, and cult centres of the divinity; (b) powers; (c) works, blessings and discoveries; (d) prayer of invocation. Some hymns from *Medinet Madi* follow this pattern, but other Isis hymns deviate from it; see A. Norden, *Agnostos Theos* (Berlin, 1913): 168-176.

demonstrated how the author of Wisdom modified the aretalogy form by including an autobiographical introduction (Wis 7:1-22a) and a prayer for Wisdom (9:1-18). These "distinguish the nature of his quest for Wisdom from the self-sufficient pagan attitude and enable him to engraft new ideas into traditional Jewish piety."[22]

Mack investigating non-biblical elements in Wisdom argues that mythic language from the cult of Isis influenced the author. Her identification with light and "she pervades all things" parallel solar functions of Isis.[23] Similarly, the remarkable description of Wisdom's relation to God and the King, as mother of the king and lover of both, may be accounted for by positing contact with the Isis cult. For Mack, the use of mythic language was not, as others had thought, part of a polemic. Rather, the borrowing of the language and mythologumena of Isis constituted a theologically reflective enterprise that sought to understand Yahwism afresh in the midst of hostility, persecution and death.[24] Winston notes that the earlier optimism of Alexandrian Jews for social and cultural acceptance by the Greeks had been replaced by disillusionment and disappointment.[25] He cites the enumeration of crimes and corruptions connected with idolatry, and attacks on Egyptian practices, as signs of the separation of Jews from Egyptians and Greeks. From this evidence he argues that the author, "is primarily addressing his fellow Jews to encourage them to take pride in their traditional faith, and aims to convince them that their way of life, rooted in the worship of the one true God, was of an incomparably higher order than that of their pagan neighbours whose idolatrous polytheism had sunk them into the mire of immorality."[26]

Undoubtedly, similarities such as particular hymnic forms, vocabulary, lists of names in Isis aretalogies and Wisdom chapters 6-10 are clearly identifiable. However, Wis 10:1-21 can stand alone, and may not necessarily have been composed as an integral part of an aretalogy. Even if Wisdom 6-10 is shown to mirror the literary form of an aretalogy this proves no more than that this text is an imitation of the hymn style generally and not necessarily in the form of an aretalogy. Reese's neat division of the aretalogy is not common to all the extant Isis hymns and aretalogies.[27] A comparison of Wis 7:22-8:1 with the nature-origin strophe of the aretalogy in the *Oxyrhynchus Papyri 1380* shows that both texts consist simply of a listing of names and functions of Sophia and Isis respectively.[28] Reese's comparison of Wis 8:2-21, does not replicate the second part of the aretalogy form, which is a complete list of the virtues of Isis. This is an

---

[22] Reese, *Influence* (1970): 44.
[23] Mack, *Logos* (1973): 34-38, 65-66.
[24] Mack, *Logos* (1973): 186; "Wisdom Myth and Mytho-logy" *Int* 24 (1970): 46-60.
[25] Winston, *Wisdom* (1979): 20-30, 59.
[26] Winston, "Wisdom" in *ABD* (1988): 126.
[27] A.-J. Festugière, "A propos des arétalogies d'Isis," *HTR* 42 (1949): 224-225.
[28] E. des Places, "Epithètes et attributs de la 'Sagesse'" *Bib 57* (1976): 414-419, notes the similarity between the twenty-one epithets of Wisdom in 7:22-23 and Cleantes' description of "the good" (SVF 557 Clement of Alexandria Protrepticus 6.72.2) which consists of twenty-six attributes.

autobiographical reflection by Solomon on his pursuit of Wisdom in which the virtues motivating his search are named.

Kloppenborg also identifies Isis as the model for Wisdom. He argues persuasively that the author of Wisdom drew upon the mythology surrounding the goddess Isis, particularly the Hellenistic version, for his portrayal of the Wisdom figure.[29] He queries Reese's detailed tables and impressive list of shared epithets and characteristics for Wisdom 6-10 and aretalogies of Isis, seeing them as problematic, since he claims many similarities disappear when the context is examined.[30] A claim that the author of Wisdom may have drawn on features in common use for exalted deities (epithets such as "almighty", "beneficent", "pervading all things" were applied to Zeus, Athena and other gods as well as to Isis), Wisdom does not explain why the Wisdom figure in the Wisdom of Solomon has so many characteristics in common with Isis as the table on page 145 demonstrates. Wisdom's attributes in 8:2-9 do show significant correlation with attributes of Isis, and earlier wisdom texts attribute to Wisdom some of these features (Prov 8:14-21).[31] Schroer's interesting feminist study of this book seeks to reconstruct the situation of Jewish women in the first century BCE. Her analysis of Wisdom's attributes in Wisdom 6-10 leads to a comparison of the power of Wisdom with that of Isis.[32] The author of Wisdom possibly adopted, modified and adapted some patterns from Isis texts. Wisdom may be the "mother" γενέτις of all good things (7:12), but she is not named mother of the king, as Isis is of Horus. In addition, despite her powers, Wisdom remains the creation and gift of God, and as such, she is clearly subordinate to God. Rather than transforming the mythic power of Egyptian royal ideology for Judaism, it seems likely that the author of Wisdom worked from biblical sources, and included some strands of current thinking that fitted into his earlier Jewish traditions. He aimed above all to bring his audience to recognise Wisdom as their saviour and their means of remaining faithful to their Jewish tradition.

It seems likely that the author adapted the framework and made remarkable alterations to the structure of the typical aretalogy, as two features found in the aretalogy also appear in the Wisdom of Solomon, the autobiographical introduction (7:1-22a), and the prayer for Wisdom (9:1-18).[33] However, the nature of the quest for Wisdom differs from that of the Hellenists. It provides scope for the inclusion of ideas compatible with the Jewish tradition, thus safeguarding it in

---

[29] Kloppenborg, "Isis and Sophia," *HTR* 75/1 (1982): 57-84, claims that Reese forces the correspondence between Wisdom and the form of an aretalogy.

[30] Kloppenborg, "Isis and Sophia" (1982): 60.

[31] Isis saves Horus from danger and brings about his accession to the throne; she is the associate of Re in creating and regulating the cosmos, and the spouse of the earthly king, conferring upon him the power to regulate human affairs. Kloppenborg claims the author of Wisdom used this pattern.

[32] S. Schroer, "Die personifizierte Sophia im Buch der Weisheit" in *Ein Gott allein?* (Göttingen, 1994): 543-558.

[33] The three parts of a typical Isis aretalogy are: a lyrical expression of praise; a catalogue of her wondrous deeds on behalf of her worshippers; a list of titles proclaiming her benefits for humanity.

an alien milieu. "I will explain or interpret" (6:22) occurs in the Isis hymns in the context of proclaiming her wise and beneficent wonders, as does the reinforcement of the promise with a restatement in the negative, "I will conceal no mysteries from you" (6:22). To spell out the saving power of Wisdom in the lives of believers, and in the deliverance of the Jewish people, the author of Wisdom uses references to weaknesses (7:1-6), the need to be taught by Wisdom (7:7-14), and Solomon's petition that he will communicate well and accurately the gifts that Wisdom has bestowed on him (7:15-22a). Without merging personified Wisdom with Isis, the writer skilfully incorporates elements of the Hellenistic praises of Isis. Thus, he offers his audience a persuasive argument illustrating the idea that while parallels between Wisdom and Isis are possible, they do not constitute identification. Careful scrutiny reveals their shallowness. His Jewish audience must recognise Wisdom, inseparable from the God of their sacred tradition, as their true heritage.

Skilfully including Hellenistic ideas in his development of the Wisdom figure, the author draws on "unerring knowledge of what exists" and on the seven parallels to describe the key features of his learning (7:17-22). In naming the structure of the world and the activity of the elements (v.17) as one section of his knowledge, he uses phraseology that echoes the teaching of Isis in the hermetic hymn *Kore Kosmou*. Isis is a teacher of the "constitution of the universe," that is, the physical makeup of the world. "Activity of the elements" the parallel phrase, expands and specifies that he knows about the fundamental elements constituting the universe. References to the signs of the zodiac and astronomy, "the beginning and end and middle of times, the alterations of solstices and the changes of seasons" (7:18), can be said to show Hellenistic scientific terminology. However, knowledge of such phenomena was also of interest in Judaism. Traditionally, Abraham was regarded as the father of astronomy. Attribution to Wisdom of knowledge of "the cycles of the year and the constellations of the stars," (v.19) reminds readers that for the Hellenists Isis regulated the year, but for the writer Wisdom is more beautiful than "every constellation of stars" (7:29). Demonstrating his encyclopaedic knowledge, he describes Wisdom, his teacher in chapter 7. This is in sharp contrast to the attribution of his knowledge to God in 7:15. Such ambiguity may be a way of asserting that God and Wisdom are identical. Interestingly he gives Wisdom a variety of titles and features usually attributed to God (Wis 8:4; 9:9). In using τεχηνῖτις "fashioner of all" (7:22; cf. 8:6; 14:2), he chooses for her the feminine of the title he gives to God τεχνίτην (13:1; 14:18).

Evidence that many attributes ascribed to Wisdom are also attributed to Isis, do not explain how or why the author of Wisdom may have borrowed features and qualities from Isis or been influenced by such a popular cult. Isis appears to have been an integral part of the religion of Egypt and the Aegean area. She figured in the theology of kingship, as the mythical mother, protector and vindicator of the ruler. The aretalogies credit her with control over agriculture, seamanship, marriage, childbirth, scholarship, and laud her as provider of knowledge, wealth, and immortality for her disciples.[34] Evidence of integration

---

[34] Hellenistic Isis' roles are documented in T.A. Brady, *The Reception of the Egyptian Cults*

into the Jewish tradition of Hellenistic material appears in the way the author introduces into the traditional biblical figure features of style and vocabulary from the cult of Isis. However, the use made of this material is clearly to enhance the portrayal of Wisdom rather than to promote Isis. In picturing Wisdom as the benefactor of humanity, the author of Wisdom illustrates the role she plays, both in the life of the believer, and in the salvation of God's people. While skilfully incorporating elements of Hellenistic religion into the Wisdom figure, he avoids replicating the figure of Isis, but manages to enrich and transform the traditional figure of personified Wisdom who is now portrayed as having the power to save.[35] In this way, by integrating into the Jewish tradition elements of the Hellenistic culture in which the Jews of the Diaspora are immersed he challenges his audience to reflect upon their heritage in a Hellenistic setting, and upon the demands inherent in remaining faithful to their heritage.

A further consideration is the fact that Greek philosophical vocabulary has long been recognised as an influence on the Wisdom of Solomon and technical language used to express ideas show that numerous Greek concepts had become part of Jewish thinking and understanding.[36] Many words used in the Wisdom of Solomon point to such integration.[37] Some examples are: τοῦ θεοῦ ἐνεργείας "the working of God" (7:26); παντοδύναμον "all-powerful" (7:23; 11:17; 18:15); φιλάνθρωπον "benign" (7:23;1:6); φιλάγαθον "loving the good" (7:22); νύμφην "my bride" ἐραστὴς "a lover" (8:2); συναναστροφὴ "companionship" (8:16); πόνοι "pain, suffering, toil" (8:7); δεσπότης "Lord" (6:7; 8:3; 11:26; 13:3, 9);[38] τεχνῖτις "fashioner/architect" (7:22-23, 8:6); τεχνίτην "artificer" (13:1);[39] διοικεῖ "orders" (8:1; 12:18; 15:1); στοιχείων "elements" (7:17; 19:18); πρόνοια "foresight, care, attention" (14:3); συνέχον "hold together, encircle" (1:7). These terms do not occur elsewhere in the Old Testament, although the subjects with which they deal do occur there. The physiology expressed in 7:2 also departs from the Biblical model. The use of words and ideas from Hellenistic learning may have been an attempt to

---

by the Greeks (330 BC) (Columbia, 1935); G. Vanderbeek, *De Interpretatio Graeca van der Isisfigur* (Louven, 1946); F. Dunand, *Le Culte d'Isis dans le bassin oriental de la Méditterranée* (Leiden, 1973). On the aretalogies see: D. Müller, *Ägypten und die griechischen Isis-Aretaloien* (Berlin, 1961); Y. Grandjean, *Une nouvelle arétalogie d'Isis* (Leiden, 1975); J. Bergman, *Ich bin Isis* (Uppsala, 1968).

[35] Healing activities, discoveries, inventions, the control of female fertility and childbirth were roles attributed to Hellenistic Isis but they are not credited to Wisdom.

[36] An example of the author's use of Hellenistic terms and philosophy for the transmission of Jewish thought appears in, "For a perishable body weighs down the soul, and this earthly tent burdens the anxious mind" (Wis 9:15).

[37] Nearly twenty per cent of Wisdom's total vocabulary comes into this category.

[38] δεσπότης denotes the link between God, Lord of everything (6:7; 8:3; 11:26; 13:3, 9), and the universe. The word appears in other biblical texts to describe God's relationship to human beings (Sir 3:7; 23:1); κυριος is used in Wis 1:1 for this relationship.

[39] Wisdom may be understood as "fashioner" in Wis 8:6: 14:2. The term is used also for the human craftsman who makes precious things (2 Kgs 12:12; 1 Chr 22:15; 29:5; Wis 7:2; Sir 9:17; 45:11; Jer 24:1; 29:2), and idols (Deut 27:15; Jer 10:9; Bar 6:45; Wis 14:18).

convince Jewish readers that fidelity to their Jewish heritage did not cut them off from participating in the cosmopolitan knowledge of Alexandria, and that Greek culture could be integrated into their own tradition. Instead of adulterating or destroying their Jewish tradition, the heritage of Jewish believers could thus be reinforced. The background of the author's quest for Wisdom was that of his readers, so he integrated into the Wisdom of Solomon the resources with which they were familiar in their contemporary Hellenistic culture.

Old Testament Echoes in Wis 6:12-10:21

While many identifiable characteristics of Hellenism are evident in Wisdom 6-10, the Wisdom figure is rooted in the Jewish tradition.[40] Despite echoes of Hellenistic philosophy, the author's vocabulary is clearly reminiscent of the Septuagint. He knows the Hebrew of the sacred texts, but mostly draws on the Septuagint version using a style called anthological composition.[41] A heavy reliance on quotations is replaced by a studied use of biblical data as can be seen in 10:1-21. In his portrayal of personified Wisdom we find elements from the Pentateuch, Prophets, Psalter, Prov 1:20-21; 3:15 (LXX); 8:1-36, Job 28, Sir 24:1-24, Genesis, Isa 3 (LXX), Exodus, Isaiah 40-66, Psalms, 1 Kgs 3:5-15; 4: 32-34, 2 Chr 1:8-10. Wisdom is undoubtedly a new synthesis of teaching that is profoundly traditional in substance.

Old Testament References in the Wisdom of Solomon

Wisdom of Solomon	Old Testament Texts
Wis 7:22a: For Wisdom the fashioner of all taught me	Prov 8:30: I was beside him, like a master worker
Wis 7:27: She can do all things, and while remaining in herself, she renews all things	Ps 104:23-31: how manifold are your works . . . you renew the face of the earth
Wis 8:2: Her I loved . . . from my youth and longed to make her my bride	Ps 44 (45):12 (11): The king will desire your beauty
Wis 8:7: She teaches self-control and prudence, justice and courage	Prov 8:14-15: I have counsel and sound wisdom, I have insight, I have strength
Wis 8:8: She has foreknowledge of signs and wonders	Dan 2:21-27: He changes times and seasons . . . . He works signs and wonders
Wis 8:10-12: they will put their hands on their mouths	Job 29:8-10: Princes refrained from talking, and laid their hand on their mouths
Wis 9:3: To rule the world in holiness and righteousness	Ps 71:1-2: May he judge your people with righteousness (cf. Pss 9:9; 95:13; 97:9)
Wis 9:5: For I am your servant, the son of your maidservant	Ps 115:7 (116:16): O Lord, I am your servant, the son of your handmaid.
Wis 9:8: a temple on your holy mountain, and an altar in the city of your abode	Jer 17:12: A glorious throne set on high . . . is the place of our sanctuary

---

[40] The extent of Hellenistic influence is debated; see Reese, *Hellenistic Influence* (1970) for a detailed discussion of the topic.

[41] Wis 2:12 quotes Isa 3:10 of the LXX, which is radically different from the Hebrew, and Wis 15:10; 12:12 quotes Isa 44:20 and Job 9:12, 19.

The Suffering of the Righteous

A blessed "immortality" in God's presence is mentioned here for the first time in the tradition.[42] This gift is Wisdom's reward for the righteous (2:23; 3:1, 15; 6:19). Immortality may be linked to the concern with the suffering of the righteous mentioned so frequently in the first section of the book. Threatened or actual persecution and suffering pervade Wis 1:16-5:23 and suggest that the community being addressed is under attack. Wis 2:10-5:23, which echoes Isa 3:10; 52:13-53:12 (LXX), a text concerned with the sufferings of the righteous wise one seems to emphasise this particularly.[43] In these texts, the author is clearly reactivating the powerful image of the suffering wise and innocent ones who are vindicated by God.[44] In recovering this image, which pervades the Old Testament, he seeks to give meaning to the present sufferings of faithful Jews in Alexandria and elsewhere under Ptolemaic rule. By personifying Wisdom as saviour, he is interpreting their sufferings in the light of the sufferings of their Israelite ancestors. While acknowledging their suffering the author also exhorts his readers to practise righteousness (1:1-12, 15; 3:1-9; 4:1-2; 5:6, 15-23; 8:7; 9:3). He assures them that they will receive the final reward of the righteous, immortality, good reputation and a "beautiful diadem from the hand of the Lord" (5:16). In this way, he emphasises the saving qualities of righteous living. Despite their unhappy position as Jews in a Greek city, living in a hostile environment, they, the righteous, are called to seek Wisdom, as they will ultimately enjoy immortality as their reward.

Adherence to the Torah

Righteousness in the Bible implies an uncompromising adherence to the Law of Moses. This is undoubtedly implied in the Wisdom of Solomon in the midst of a liberal use of the literary forms and philosophical concepts of Hellenism. Personified Wisdom reveals a milieu of Jewish piety that preserves a heritage in which the Torah is the traditional and approved guide to community life, ritual, and observance. Given the general acceptance of a late first century BCE date, Wisdom references to Temple and Torah (Sir 24:23; Bar 4:1) are not an innovation in this

---

[42]   This appears to be the earliest use of this term in the bible.

[43]   The author assumes that his readers have a good knowledge of the Septuagint.

[44]   M. J Suggs, "Wisdom of Solomon 2:10-5:23: A Homily Based on the Fourth Servant Song," *JBL* 76 (1957): 26-33; see subsequent studies of D. Georgi "Der vorpaulinische Hymnus Phil 2:6-11." In E. Dinkler, ed. *Zeit und Geschichte* (Tübingen, 1964): 263-293; and G.W.E. Nickelsburg, *Resurrection, Immortality, and Eternal Life in Intertestamental Judaism* (Cambridge, 1972): 48-66, 88-89, 144-180 qualified this thesis by pointing to an Isaianic (exegetical) tradition that Wisdom took up for its own literary purposes; Reese, *Influence* (1970): 113, rejected Suggs' thesis on the basis of what he understood to be the Greek literary form and didactic intention of the passage; Winston, *Wisdom* (1979): 120-146 is in general agreement with Suggs' thesis; see also C. Larcher, *Le Livre de la Sagesse ou La Sagesse de Salomon* 1 (Paris, 1983): 255-266.

text. However, in Wis 6:12-9:18 these references recall the commands of YHWH to Solomon to build a Temple and altar in Jerusalem. Wisdom herself acts as Torah, not after the manner described in Sirach 24 and Bar 3:9-4:4, but more after the manner of Psalm 119 considered to be a Torah psalm *par excellence*, as it expresses, in many different ways the Psalmist's devotion to the Torah.[45] This psalm uses ten different terms for Torah: commandment; statute;   word; judgement; testimony; precept; law; instruction; and way (two senses), but the Law as such is never detailed. Wis 6:12-10:21 also exhibits this feature, as is evident in, "law" νόμος (6:4; 9:15); "instruction" παιδεία (6:17; 7:14); "word" λόγος (9:1); "judgement" κρίσις (6:5; 8:11; 9:3, 5).[46]

As the descendants of Israelites who had long experience in remaining faithful while "in exile" and under the rule of foreign powers and influences, the Jews in the Diaspora were, no doubt, aware that the survival of their tradition demanded that leaders remained faithful to their heritage, whether in Egypt, Babylon, Alexandria or Jerusalem. Such faithfulness required that they be courageous, creative, pragmatic and eschatological in their orientation. Champions of the Jewish heritage had to focus their hopes on a new way of life wherein that which had been lost of the essential heritage could be recovered and restored. One way to focus attention and restore hope was by using first person evidence. This the author of Wisdom does, in his description of the gifts he received from Wisdom, which are available to all who seek Wisdom.

Thus, the autobiographical section and Solomon's prayer for Wisdom serve to join personified Wisdom with the God of history, the Hebrew YHWH. Human beings are saved by Wisdom (9:18) so Wisdom is somehow identified with God, not distinct from God. In Wisdom God's saving power is put into effect. Wisdom who "knows the things of old and infers the things to come" (8:8) here reflects two aspects of Isis.[47] Her activities (8:2-18) are of this world because human beings achieve immortality and everlasting "glory" (8:16-18) by making use of the things that God has created for their use. Wisdom surpasses Isis, "who dwelt in the rays of the sun," by being "a breath of the power of God, and a pure emanation of the glory of the Almighty; therefore nothing defiled gains entrance into her. For she is a reflection of eternal light, a spotless mirror of the working of God, and an image of God's goodness" (7:25-26).

---

[45] J. Day, *Psalms* (Sheffield, 1992): 56-58 analyses this psalm showing it to be a Torah hymn; Harrington claims that Sofia functions as the "Law" designated by the ten synonyms in Psalm 119.
[46] Interestingly, the author of Wisdom, unlike Ben Sira and Baruch, never explicitly identifies Wisdom with Torah (Wis 6:18 seems to mean general human laws), but he does refer to Israel's task of taking the imperishable light of the Law to the world (Wis 18:4) and claims that Wisdom is the source of prophecy (7:27). Winston, *Wisdom of Solomon* (1979): 42-3, states that the author of Wisdom along with Philo believed that the teachings of the Torah were tokens of the Divine Wisdom. They were in harmony with the laws of the universe and as such implant all the virtues in human beings. Wisdom is the supreme arbiter of all values. She is clearly the archetypal Torah of which the Mosaic Law is but an image.
[47] J. Bergman, *Ich bin Isis* (Uppsala, 1968): 280.

Both God and Wisdom are represented as creating the world (1:14; 7:22; 11:17); being sought by humanity (1:1-2; 6:12-16); granting knowledge and immortality (5:15-16; 7:15-22; 8:13); guiding and protecting Israel (10; 11-19). Wisdom's presence at creation and her function as God's instrument is not an innovation of the author of Wisdom. Prov 8:22-31 portrays Wisdom as a female figure created before the creation and present with YHWH at the creation. While some vocabulary used here to describe Wisdom may have been drawn from the praises of Isis, other characteristics attributed to her, such as her presence throughout the cosmos and her ordering of all things, may witness to Stoic conceptions.[48] Wisdom as delineated in the Wisdom of Solomon is a product of the Hebrew tradition. She remains firmly grounded in the Hebrew tradition while being transformed into a Jewish-Hellenistic figure in keeping with the setting in which she now functions.

The "autobiographical" account of Solomon's interaction with Wisdom provides an effective device to illustrate the apologetic concern of the author to draw upon the popular cult literature of Isis. His aim is to explain to his readers that their own traditions provided a better religious home than the contemporary religious philosophy of Alexandria. By highlighting the ethical powers that Wisdom communicated to the author in his role as King Solomon, he provides a parallel lesson for his readers. Wisdom is the source of ethical behaviour and those who devote their lives to her can become kings in the metaphorical sense. Thus, they will experience the gift of immortality. If they develop the gifts of their heritage, they will reign and enjoy greater happiness than they could ever discover in Hellenistic philosophy or religion. He appropriates for Wisdom the "wondrous powers" of Isis, because his readers are familiar with them. The author's use of technical terms from Hellenistic culture and ethics are new to biblical literature, as is the description of his personal encounter with Wisdom. Despite advocacy of his audience's Jewish heritage, he does not propose a denial or cutting off from Hellenistic learning, but recommends that they use such knowledge, since human culture and true wisdom are God's gifts. He illustrates, in the seven comparisons based on the Exodus in the final section of the book (Wis 10:1-19:22), a sure way to be a faithful adherent to Judaism.

A Jewish/Hellenistic Wisdom Figure

This section of the chapter discusses how the author of Wisdom 6-10 portrays Wisdom in a Hellenistic context. A paradox is presented. Wisdom must be sought (7:1-3) but unlike Wisdom in Job 28, in this text access to Wisdom is not difficult, as she goes about seeking those worthy of her (6:16); "she is easily discerned by those who love her, and is found by those who seek her" (6:12), yet, Wisdom will

---

[48] See J Reese, *Hellenistic Influence* (Rome, 1970): 46-49; Mack, *Logos* (1973): 90-95; Winston, *Wisdom of Solomon* (1979): 182; J.J. Collins, "Cosmos and Salvation: Jewish Wisdom and Apocalyptic in the Hellenistic Age" *History of Religions* 17 (1977): 128-34.

not enter a soul that devises evil, nor will she dwell in a "body" burdened with debt (*RSV* "enslaved to sin") ἐν σώματι κατάχρεῳ ἁμαρτίας (1:4). Therefore, it appears that while Wisdom is accessible, sinners cannot have Wisdom, but those who seek her sincerely will have no difficulty in finding her. It is to this complex figure that the author attributes the role of setting straight the paths of human beings, teaching them what pleases God, and being a saviour (9:18). With such metaphorical language, we see the Wisdom figure intimately associated with God. Of all Solomon's benefits she is "their mother" γενέτιν (Wis 7:12). The gift of the spirit of Wisdom is a gift from God, given in answer to prayer (7:7). Extending the paradox into the unconditional nature of Wisdom's gifts is the image of Solomon praying for the gift to "speak with judgement", so that he may have thoughts "worthy" of the gifts he receives through her (7:15; 6:15). In keeping with the intention he affirms, "Wisdom is an unfailing treasure for human beings; those who receive her, obtain friendship with God" (7:14), and "even if one is perfect . . . without the Wisdom that comes from God they will be regarded as nothing" (9:6). Wisdom's active role in the created universe is part of this paradox, she is the "fashioner" τεχνῖτις of all (Wis 7:22; 8:6; cf. Prov 8:22-31), yet we learn that God is the source of all knowledge of the cosmos. "God gave me unerring knowledge of existent beings" (7:17-20), but Wisdom "the fashioner of all taught me" (7:21-22).[49]

Wisdom and Creation

Just as Wisdom proceeds out of the mouth of God and is the life-giving mist which waters the earth in Sir 24:2 (cf. Gen 2:4b-6), the Wisdom figure in the Wisdom of Solomon is anchored in cosmic beginnings. She becomes the means by which her disciples learn the secrets of the universe, come to a knowledge of God, and obtain life in abundance (Wis 7:15-22). Wisdom orders the cosmos and human society and provides instruction in the knowledge of God. Present in all of God's works, she points the way to the Creator (Wis 1:7; 8:1-4; 9:17-18). Wis 6:12-9:18 affirms that God's gift of personified Wisdom serves to harmonise all levels of creation. Using terminology from Hellenistic religion, the author portrays Wisdom as God's "throne partner" πάρεδρον (9:4). Yet he does not present her as a transcendent being distinct from God, but as a literary figure that portrays the effective and saving presence of God, who is at once transcendent and immanent creation. She unites herself to those who believe in her by offering herself to them as their bride.

It is specifically because God's Wisdom is God's gift to transform human life that the author can personify Wisdom. He perceives that all aspects of life are of God and are within Wisdom's domain, because she "reaches mightily from one end of the earth to the other" (8:1).[50] The Wisdom disciple encounters Wisdom in every element of creation, in the seasons of the year, solstices, cycles of years,

---

[49] God is described as τεχνίτην in Wis 13:1.

[50] This image echoes Psalm 19: "Its (the sun) rising is from the end of the heavens, and its circuit to the end of them." The similarity is evident in the notion of a revitalising presence transforming all human activity.

animal activities, and in powers of plants (7:17-20). Whoever is wise, from a
biblical perspective knows that all workings of the cosmos come under the
guidance and concern of God. She goes before those who seek her, conducting
them to the throne of God. "Wisdom is an unfailing treasure for human beings;
those who receive her obtain friendship with God" (7:14), and "even if one is
perfect . . . without the Wisdom that comes from God they will be regarded as
nothing" (9:6). While the part played by Wisdom in creation may appear
ambiguous in Prov 8:30, in Wis 8:4 "she is an initiate in the knowledge of God,
and an associate in God's works" suggests a higher level of assurance about
Wisdom's role in creation.[51]

Wisdom's New Apparel

Unique to the portrayal of personified Wisdom in the Wisdom of Solomon is the
attribution to this figure of twenty-one properties.[52]

> For within her is a spirit intelligent, holy,
> unique, manifold, subtle,
> mobile, incisive, unsullied,
> lucid, invulnerable, benevolent, shrewd,
> irresistible, beneficent, humane,
> steadfast, sure, free from anxiety,
> all-powerful, overseeing all,
> penetrating all spirits,
> intelligent pure and most subtle (7:22-23)

Wisdom is given a more wonderful role and more dazzling imagery in the Wisdom
of Solomon than in any other book where she is portrayed. Here Wisdom becomes
an expression of God to human beings; an emanation of divine attributes. Besides,
she is Solomon's bride, making it possible for him to be a wise and just king. She
functions in partnership with the divine word, appearing to be identical with God's
Holy Spirit (6:12-9:18). While Ben Sira and Baruch identify Wisdom with Torah
the author of Wisdom brings God and human beings closer describing Wisdom as
"a breath of the power of God . . . a pure effluence of the glory of the Almighty"
(7:25). As such, Wisdom mirrors God's eternal light and activity, for she is an
image of God's goodness (7:26). Using a fivefold succession of metaphors the
author describes Wisdom's essence and efficacy: ἀτμίς "breath"; ἀπόρροια
"effluence" (v.25, cf. Exod 19:18; Lev 16:13; Sir 24:2); ἀπαύγασμα "effulgence"
(v.26; Isa 60:19); ἔσοπτρον ἀκηλίδωτον "spotless mirror" (v.26); εἰκὼν "image"
(v.26).[53] She renews all things, "enters into holy souls to make them friends of God

---

[51] Larcher, *Études* (1979): 391, notes the author of Wisdom, probably because of Greek
influence, goes far beyond his predecessors in the issue of continuous creation, and the
reason for God's special presence in the world by reason of spirit and Wisdom.

[52] Ten adjectives in 7:22-23 are not used elsewhere in the Septuagint.

[53] A. Wright, "Wisdom," *NJBC* (1990): 516, commenting on Wis 7:25-26 says, "The
author, enlarging on Proverbs 8 and Sirach 24, seeks the most immaterial images

and prophets" (v.27), "nothing is pleasing to God but the one who lives with Wisdom" (v.28), she surpasses all of creation (v.29), "over Wisdom no evil can prevail" (v.30), and finally her might is universal (8:1). These attributes portray her relationship to God in terms that border on identity.[54] While "emanation" (v.25) and "effulgence" (v.26) were common in Hellenistic religious vocabulary, the author situates Wisdom in the Jewish tradition in naming her the τεχνῖτις the "artificer" who constructs and orders the world (v.21; Prov 8:32), attributing to Wisdom powers of design and construction like those of God the "fashioner/designer" of the world as a dwelling place for human beings.[55]

Solomon's Relationship with Wisdom

Solomon's account of his relationship with Wisdom (8:1-8) is couched in language rich in sexual imagery, ἐφίλησα "I loved her" (v.2), and "sought her" to lead her away as my "bride" so "enamoured of her beauty" was I.[56] Here the emphasis is on Wisdom's beauty emanating from her "intimacy" συμβίωσιν with God, "the Master of all who loved her" (v.3).[57] Wisdom is "initiate in the knowledge of God" μύστις ἐπιστήμης; "associate of God's works" αἱρετὶς τῶν ἔργων αὐτοῦ; "maker of all things" ἐργαζομένης; "artificer of all that is" τεχνῖτις (vv.3-6).[58] Her uniqueness is highlighted by the enumeration of the traditional human desires: "riches", "understanding", "justice", "wide experience". Wisdom embraces them all (vv.5-8). Progressively the author has fleshed out an image of Wisdom as surpassing all human need, and now elaborates on this figure with seven indirect statements. He arranges the Solomonic motifs that encompass the whole range of human wisdom (8:9b-16a), in two sets of three with 8:12 as their axis (cf. 1 Kgs 3).

For Solomon and by, analogy for human beings, Wisdom the saviour is counsellor in prosperity, comfort in anxiety and grief (v.9), an assurance of honour among the elders (v.10), giver of judgement and immortality. Through her, he is enabled to govern peoples (vv.11-14).[59] "When I enter my house, I shall find rest

---

possible to describe the origin of Wisdom."
[54] There is an echo of these images in Heb 1:3; Col 1:15; 2 Cor 4:4.
[55] This imagery also points to the primal origins of Wisdom, and links the power of design and skill associated with creation to the divine Wisdom of which all artisans partake; *ANEP* 749; see also O. Keel, *The Symbolism of the Biblical World* (New York, 1978): 17; L. Perdue, *Wisdom in Revolt* (Sheffield, 1991): 39.
[56] The Greek verb here means to love as a friend. This is the only appearance of this verb in the Wisdom of Solomon.
[57] The Greek term συμβίωσιν indicating a marriage relationship appears in 8:3, 9, 16, but nowhere else in the Bible.
[58] This reference recalls the much-discussed text of Prov 8:30 in which the debate centres on whether personified Wisdom in this text has a role in creation.
[59] Solomon's catalogue of qualities echoes lists of secret things in apocalyptic literature and hints at later development of a Solomonic literature that recounts his magical and demonological knowledge and his control of nature. See M.E. Stone, "Lists of Revealed Things in the Apocalyptic Literature," in G.E. Wright, F. M. Cross, W.E. Lemke, P.D. Miller, eds. *Magnalia Dei: The Mighty Acts of God* (New York, 1976): 436-437.

with her; for companionship with her has no bitterness, and life with her has no pain, but gladness and joy", expresses the embodiment of these gifts. Sexual imagery is sustained with the image of the bride offering an intimate experience of God's gracious presence to her lover. By repeating the technical term for a marriage partner (8:16; Prov 8:32) and introducing an Epicurean word for sexual intercourse, "find rest", προσαναπαύσομαι the text intensifies the imagery of a man's prolonged courting of a potential bride. Thus, Solomon's pursuit of Wisdom is akin to the love involved in passionate courtship (8:2-18). This is the model for all who wish to be lovers of Wisdom.[60] "I loved her and sought her from my youth, and I desired to take her for my bride, and I became enamoured of her beauty" (Wis 8:2; Sir 51:13-22).

Solomon's relationship with Wisdom issues forth in the four key virtues of Hellenistic piety—self-control, prudence, justice and courage—celebrated in Platonic and Stoic philosophy (Wis 8:7; cf. 4:1; 5:3; 4 Macc 1:3-4).[61] For the Greeks, human beings acquired virtue by self-discipline in developing their four basic powers, will, the appetites for pleasure and for self-preservation. When each of these powers or appetites was fully developed, one had acquired the virtue. While acknowledging the virtues desired by all Greeks, the author of Wisdom presents these as gifts bestowed by Wisdom. They are not to be regarded as mere human resources, which may be acquired by human effort, but must be sought from Wisdom. Human destiny is a gift of God, not an earthly or personal achievement. "In the life of human beings nothing is more useful than these", because they encompass "righteousness" which is "immortal" (8:7; 1:15). In describing virtues as the "labours" of personified Wisdom, the notion of labour pains may be suggested in the sense that Wisdom brings forth "virtues" as her children. With Wisdom as his companion, Solomon claims that these virtues are the fruit of their relationship. She will make these gifts available to those who seek her. Her gifts will enable the Jewish audience to be at home in their Hellenistic setting. These gifts will equip them to discuss "things of old," and anticipate "future events". Thus, they will acquit themselves well when participating in discussions with their contemporaries.

Although the author knows the classical sources, he does not follow them slavishly, but transforms them as he does Old Testament ideas. In describing "justice" as the possession of the four cardinal virtues, he is invoking a Platonic idea taken up by the Stoic Chrysippus (281-206), but adapts it for his own purpose

---

[60] This section is reminiscent of the Hellenistic hymns to the goddess Isis, but with marked departures.
[61] Influence of Platonic and Stoic philosophy on the Wisdom of Solomon has long been recognised by scholars; see Reese, *Hellenistic Influence* (1970); Winston, *Wisdom of Solomon* (1979); P. Menzel, *Der griechische Einfluss auf Prediger und Weisheit Salomos* (Halle, 1889): 41-70; M. Friedländer, *Griechische Philosophie im Alten Testament* (Berlin, 1904): 182-208; P. Heinisch, *Die griechische Philosophie im Buche der Weisheit* (Münster, 1908): 158; I Heinemann, "Die Griechische Quelle der 'Weisheit Salomos'", in *Jahresbericht des jüdischtheologischen Seminars* (Breslau, 1921): 136-156.

by removing the notion of the morality of effort.[62] He insists that these virtues are not the personal achievements of the believer, but are the gifts of the πονοι "pains" of Wisdom (8:7). These virtues are bestowed by Wisdom rather than acquired by the efforts of the seeker of Wisdom. Wis 8:19-21 points to the antithesis between the corruptible body/earthly frame, and the soul/mind, with the former weighing down the latter.[63] "I could not otherwise gain possession of her, except God gave her, and to know the source of this grace was a mark of understanding" (8:21). With this clear proclamation of the one way to "acquire" Wisdom, the audience is instructed to pray for Wisdom as Solomon did (9:1-18), because she enters into the soul that seeks her, and leads in the ways of God's service, which in turn leads to eternal life in God's presence.

It is not surprising that the Wisdom of Solomon presents Solomon praying for Wisdom in the first person. A Jewish audience would already have a traditional image of the king praying at Gibeon (1 Kgs 3:6-9). "Sayings of the Fathers" a later product of Jewish thought collected about 200 CE testifies that the quest for Wisdom continued in the Judaic tradition.[64] The intensity of Solomon's prayer in Wisdom is in marked contrast to its predecessor at Gibeon. Wis 9:1-17 is a didactic prayer that brings together all the points that have so far been made, proclaims that God works through Wisdom, and at the same time, Wisdom is the divine gift without which no human being can please God.[65] Only with grave "difficulty" μόλις can one divine the things that are on the earth; how then can one ever trace the things that are in heaven? (v.16). This prayer introduces subtle complications and is a collection of paradoxes. The doxology lauds God as Creator (vv.1-3) and identifies God's word and Wisdom as the instruments of creation. Solomon acknowledges Wisdom as God's "throne-companion" (v.4) and requests of God

---

[62] J. von Arnim, *Stoicorum Veterum Fragmenta* (Leipzig, 1921-24): vol. 3.60.15; 3.61.32; see discussion of stoic morality of effort in A.J. Festugière, *La Révélation d'Hermès Trismégiste* (Paris, 1944-1954): 2.300-301; Reese, *Hellenistic Influence* (1970): 15.

[63] Wis 8:19-20 has provoked much debate. Winston, *Wisdom of Solomon* (1979): 198, sees here the idea of pre-existent souls; Reese, *Hellenistic Influence* (1970): 81-82 notes pre-existence of the soul exits in Platonic philosophy, but does not suggest direct dependence on Plato; Larcher, *Études* (1969): 270-279, claims the author either excludes or does not know the Platonist or Hellenist ideas concerning life after death.

[64] Murphy, *Tree of Life* (1990); R.B.Y. Scott, "Solomon and the Beginnings of Wisdom," in *SAIW*: 90-101, sees Solomon's connection with the Israelite wisdom movement resting on 1 Kings 5:9-14; 10:1-10, 13, 23-24, and the superscriptions to Prov 1:1; 10:1; 25:1, which affirm its historicity. He finds evidence for an organised literary wisdom movement associated with the monarchy, and dates this to the 8th century BCE (so later than Solomon). No biblical evidence suggests the existence of a school of literary wisdom prior to the 8th century BCE. A. Alt, "Die Weisheit Salomos" *TL* 76 (1951): 139-144, notes that biblical descriptions of the king's knowledge correspond to onomastica found in ancient Egyptian, Canaanite and Mesopotamian texts. The data suggest that the form appeared in Babylon before its counterpart in Egypt.

[65] On the sophisticated structure of this prayer see M. Gilbert, "La Structure de la prière de Salomon (Sg 9)." *BIB* 51 (1970): 301-331; "La volonté de Dieu et donc de la Sagesse (9:17) *NRT* 93 (Rome, 1971): 145-166.

that Wisdom bring him all the gifts he needs, including being "worthy of his father's throne". It seems unlikely that this is to be taken literally, but it may suggest that the audience are being encouraged to pray for the wisdom to be worthy inheritors of their revered Jewish tradition, as is borne out in what follows. A reaffirmation of the unique power of Wisdom appears in "She will guide me wisely in my actions and guard me with her glory" (v.11). This replaces the "listening heart" of 1 Kgs 3:9. The image reflects the divine light and power with which the angel of the Lord "guarded" the people during the Exodus (Exod 23:20), and by association will guard those addressed in their Hellenistic wilderness. In recognising Wisdom's inaccessibility and God's transcendence, the petitioner accepts that God must "send" Wisdom (v.10).[66] The final line of the prayer proclaims Wisdom saviour of the ancestors and by implication saviour of those addressed.

Wisdom's Function and Role in Wis 6:22–10:21

Wisdom, the newly nuanced figure in the Wisdom of Solomon is the product of the retrieval and reapplication to Wisdom of the saving work of God in the lives of the ancestors from the Creation to the Exodus. Wisdom as saviour shows the "way" through the confusion and attraction to Hellenistic culture, beliefs, and practices, experienced by faithful Jews seeking to retain their rich and ancient heritage.[67] Commentators have attributed a variety of roles and functions to this figure. Knox claimed that Wisdom was "the answer of Orthodox Judaism: the source of order in creation and conduct is not Isis, but the Wisdom of God", while Reese sees this figure as an apologetic assertion that Judaism was in no way inferior to paganism.[68] Mack opts for "reflective mythology", the theological use of myth to obtain new understandings of human existence and Winston believes the author chose the Wisdom figure as the mediator of his own message to his contemporaries. By working from this figure, he could invoke images from the traditions of Israel and Hellenism that appealed so strongly to the Jews of Alexandria, and thus fashion a new creation.[69] While each of the above has well-documented support for their conclusions regarding Wisdom's role, it is possible to find considerable evidence in Wis 6:12-10:21 to suggest that Wisdom's function in the Wisdom of Solomon is above all that of saviour as Kloppenborg and Vogels have already noted.[70]

---

[66] Larcher, *Études* (1985): 604, claims that the prayer of Solomon has universal import, as Wisdom here overshadows the Torah.

[67] This development in wisdom thinking is unique to the Wisdom of Solomon.

[68] Knox "The Divine Wisdom" *JTS* 38 (1937): 236; Reese, *Hellenistic Influence* (1970): 50.

[69] Mack, *Logos* (1973): 95; Winston, *Wisdom of Solomon* (1979): 37.

[70] Kloppenborg, "Isis" (1984); W. Vogels, "The God Who Creates Is the God Who Saves: The Book of Wisdom's Reversal of the Biblical Pattern" *EgT* 22 (1991): 315-335

Wisdom Implements God's Saving Plan

Wisdom's function and role are intimately connected with the purpose of the book as a whole, the focal point of which appears in Solomon's prayer for wisdom (Wis 9:1-17). This prayer marks a turning point in the theological unfolding of Wisdom whose role in creation is highlighted in: "by your wisdom have formed human beings" (v.2); "for all were saved by Wisdom" τῇ σοφίᾳ ἐσώθησαν (v.18). The author envisages all of life as caught up into God's saving plan, and exhorts his audience to live their lives under the guidance of God's saving Wisdom. Wis 2:23 attributes creation directly to God but 9:2 attributes the creation of human beings to God's Wisdom, God's "throne partner" πάρεδρον (v.4). She relates God to creation and in particular to human beings. The "God of my ancestors" brings all peoples to their destiny, and empowers them while they are like Solomon "weak and short-lived, with little understanding of judgement and laws" (v.5).

Wis 9:7-12 outlines three tasks given by God to Solomon, to be king, to be judge, and to build a Temple in Jerusalem. Just as the Temple was to be "a copy of the holy tent," which God prepared for the Israelites in the desert, so the king's works are to be copies or reflections of God's works in creation with Wisdom as "throne partner" (v.4). References to their Jewish heritage, must recall for his audience their sacred history and the importance of faithfulness to their traditions. Obviously, the author is not suggesting that they construct the Temple with its altar of sacrifice in the land where they now find themselves. "Temple" here is imaged in a symbolic sense of God's presence in their midst, and is intended to revive memories of the tradition surrounding their election by God. Solomon's prayer recalls that Wisdom "was present when you made the world". She communicates true understanding of physical objects and God's "commandments" (v.9).

The author exhorts his audience to be faithful to the Wisdom of their tradition. This biblical figure was surely familiar to them, but she is being recreated and portrayed in new attire. They are reminded of their responsibility to witness to God's saving power, as "the multitude of the wise is the salvation of the world" (6:24). Developing the idea expressed in, "God created all things that they might endure" (1:14), the author now extends salvation to future life, "for justice is immortal" (1:15). He addresses each member of his audience as "king" in God's universal plan for the salvation of all creatures. In the history of Israel the power to save and its exercise are ascribed to YHWH (Deut 26:5-9; Josh 24:2-13; Psalms 78; 105; 106; 136; Wisdom of Ben Sira 44-50; 3 Macc 2:1-20). Salvation is usually reserved to God, even in earlier wisdom literature. Wisdom grants long life (Prov 3:16; 9:11), counsel, insight, strength (8:14) and divine favour (8:35-36). However, "saving from danger" has not been her function. Nevertheless, it is Wisdom who is indisputably described as saviour in Wis 9:18-10:21.

Wisdom as Saviour of the Ancestors

Wisdom is named saviour in 9:18; 10:4, 8, 8, 21, and the use of anaphora places the focus clearly upon her. Wis 9:18 announces the theme of the author's encomium καὶ τῇ σοφίᾳ ἐσώθησαν "and were saved by Wisdom", the central focus of the book, which is summarised in 10:9: "Wisdom rescued from troubles those who serve her". She strengthened Abraham, rescued Lot, gave victory to Jacob, stayed with Joseph when he went into the dungeon and brought him to triumph and authority. Most dramatically, she worked through Moses to free the people from bondage, leading them over the waters and guiding them through the wilderness. [71] "A holy people and a blameless race. Wisdom delivered from a nation of oppressors . . . She brought them over the Red Sea" (Wis 10:15-16). It is instructive to examine other lists of God's saving deeds or lists of Israelite heroes and compare these with the encomium of Wis 10:1-21. Of the lists in Deut 26:5-9; Josh 24:2-23; Psalms 78; 105; 106; 136; Sir 44-50, only Sir 44:17-18 mentions Noah, but without reference to the guidance of the ark. Similarly, Ps 105:18 refers to Joseph's imprisonment in a Hellenistic setting.[72]

Motifs similar to those of the Isis/Horus cycle in Hellenism are used in chapter 10. Among these are Wisdom's role of guarding and protecting the righteous in the face of opposition (vv.1, 5, 11, 12); her action in exposing false accusations against the righteous (v.14); her role in granting the ability to rule (v.2); a vision of the kingdom of God; "knowledge of holy things" (v.10); the sceptre of kingship and eternal glory (v.14). The author not only portrays Wisdom as saviour, but also attributes to her specific deeds that are very similar to those attributed to Isis in various aretalogies. Kloppenborg points out that most of the deeds mentioned in the Wisdom of Solomon were omitted in earlier biblical lists of deeds attributed to God, but the author of this text uses them to highlight Wisdom's care of the righteous.[73] It is unlikely that he was completely dependent on the Hellenistic Isis cycles for incidents in Wis 9:18-10:21 as all are to be found also in biblical and Intertestamental texts.[74]

Wisdom Saves the Righteous

Wisdom's saving power shows itself actively in history as she brings about the decisive revelatory and liberating events of her people Israel. She is the "fashioner of all things" (Wis 7:22) and the "mother" (Wis 7:12) of all good things who is responsible for their existence and knows their inmost secrets. Arranging the universe harmoniously, "she reaches mightily from one end of the heavens to the other, and she orders all things well" (Wis 8:1). Wisdom knows the structure of the world and its elements, the cycles of the seasons and the stars, the varieties of the

[71] P. Beauchamp, "Le peuple juif et les nations à partir de l'Ancien Testament" *Bulletin, Pontificio Consejo para el Diálogo Interreligioso* 76 (1991): 46-47; A. Di Lella, "Conservative and Progressive Theology: Sirach and Wisdom" *CBQ* 28 (1966): 139-154.
[72] Mack, *Logos* (1973): 91, notes that Wisdom's power to master all things (10:2) recalls Isis's conferral of a similar power on Horus the king.
[73] Kloppenborg, "Isis" (1984): 72; J. Bergman, *Ich bin Isis* (Uppsala, 1968): 289-292; References to the Horus-Seth conflict abound; A.H. Gardiner, *The Library of A. Chester Beatty Chester Beatty Papyri* 1 (London, 1931).
[74] Winston, *Wisdom of Solomon* (1979): 211-223.

animals, plants and roots, the powers of spirits and the ways of human reasoning (Wis 7:17-22). Her power to renew is affirmed "in every generation she passes into holy souls and makes them friends of God, and prophets" (Wis 7:27). Wisdom not only does deeds associated with YHWH, but she speaks words that have God-like qualities. This female personification of the creative and saving power of God in the world, is active and present in creation, all-knowing, all-powerful, omnipresent, renews all things, works in history to save her chosen people, guides and protects them through their struggles and crises, and carries out functions elsewhere attributed to YHWH.

Wisdom also has the power to save the righteous in virtue of her intimate connection with cosmic forces. She can give instruction concerning ontology, cosmology, physics, astronomy, and biology, because she was responsible for their creation (7:17-22). She, like Isis, is responsible for the regulation and oversight of the cosmos (Wis 7:24; 8:1). Although many Stoic terms occur in the description of Wisdom's cosmic activities, she is not portrayed as the Stoic *pronoia* or *logos*, which was devoid of personal aspects, and unlikely to be responsive to the supplications of the righteous. Isis was also believed to have personal aspects such as the power to save her disciples from disaster and to grant blessings to her petitioners.

Wisdom as Guide

A clear connection is made between Wisdom personified as "guide" and Wisdom's guide, the God of Israel, the ὁδηγός "guide" who led the Israelites out of Egypt (7:15).[75] Solomon begs Wisdom to "guide" ὁδηγήσει him in his actions (9:11), she "guided a righteous man . . . on the straight path" (10:10), and "she guided them on a wondrous journey" (10:17).[76] Just as Wisdom is portrayed as "guide", God is also characterised as σοφῶν διορθωτής "corrector of the wise" (7:15). For his Jewish audience the author gives a clear message. They are to recognise the God of their Jewish tradition as the author of all wisdom and human learning. The wonders of nature, so dear to the Hellenist scholars, are seen in this text to derive their order and harmony from the Israelite God of nature and creation. Major areas of Hellenistic scholarship are listed and referred to God's guidance (7:16-21), implying that they all exist for human beings, and are within God's plan for the cosmos. Humanity's total dependence on God is vividly stated: "both we, and our words, are in God's hands" (7:16) and contrasted with, "God made all things by his word" (9:1). Human words only have the power God grants them through Wisdom.

God and Wisdom are one

Through a series of seven comparisons Solomon, the speaker, outlines how God and Wisdom work to fashion events in the cosmos (7:16-22a). In attributing the

---

[75] The word "guide" is not applied to God in the Old Testament. In Greek mythology, Hermes was considered the guide of souls, and Isis was sometimes given this title.

[76] Wisdom is identified with the Ark of the Covenant in Sir 24:10-12.

same saving power to God and to Wisdom, the author proclaims that they represent
the same reality. Clearly, the audience share a common religious milieu, their
Jewish heritage that has developed and sustained their ancestors over the centuries.
However, for those faced with attractive alternatives to faithfulness or return to
their Jewish traditions, persuasive teaching depended on the citing of compelling
evidence for the claims made for this ancient tradition. Whether one understands
the search for Wisdom outlined in the Wisdom of Solomon as didactic exhortation,
protreptic, or encomium, it seems to assume that the audience is sympathetic to
Hellenistic culture and thought and to Jewish traditions and teachings.

     The author of the Wisdom of Solomon is obviously an accomplished
writer.[77] He synthesises the wisdom and apocalyptic traditions of his audience and
an eclectic selection of Greek philosophy and religious thought.[78] By assuming the
identity of Solomon, he specifies Wisdom as his chief concern, and through his
authority as Solomon (1:1; 6:1-11) embeds his newly designed Wisdom figure
totally in the religious tradition of his Jewish audience, while being aware of the
intellectual and emotional attractions of Hellenism for them. He seeks to counter
such temptations by incorporating qualities of Hellenism in a positive way as
essential to the pursuit of Wisdom in their contemporary society.[79]

Wisdom is Saviour

Wis 6:12-9:18, when viewed retrospectively in the light of Wis 10:1-21, gains a
new perspective.[80] Wisdom is acclaimed for having brought salvation to biblical

---

[77] Winston, *Wisdom of Solomon* (1979): 18-20, calls this a didactic exhortation; Reese,
Hellenistic Influence (1970) 117-121, 151-152, a protreptic; P. Bizzeti, *Il Libro Della
Sapienza* (Brescia, 1984) an encomium; see also P. Beauchamp, "Épouser la Sagesse—
on n'épouse qu'elle?" in M. Gilbert, ed. *La Sagesse de l'Ancien Testament* (Louvain,
1979): 347-369; "Wisdom Literature" in M.E. Stone, ed. *Jewish Writings of the Second
Temple* (Philadelphia, 1984): 283-324.

[78] J.M. Reese, "Plan and Structure in the Book of Wisdom" *CBQ* 27 (1965): 391-399;
Hellenistic Influence (1970); *The Book of Wisdom, Song of Songs* (Wilmington, 1983):
59-116; J. J. Collins, "Cosmos and Salvation: Jewish Wisdom and Apocalyptic in the
Hellenistic Age" *HR* 17 (1977): 128-134; A.G. Wright, "Numerical Patterns in the Book
of Wisdom" *CBQ* 29 (1967): 524-538; "The Structure of the Book of Wisdom" *Bib* 48
(1967): 165-184; "Wisdom" in NJBC (New Jersey, 1990): 510-522; Gilbert, "La
structure de la prière de Salomon (Sg 9)" *Bib* 51 (1970): 301-331; Larcher, *Études*
(1969): 179-261; E.G. Clarke, *The Wisdom of Solomon* (Cambridge, 1973); Winston,
Wisdom of Solomon (1979); "Solomon, Wisdom of" *ABD* 6 (1992): 120-127; "Wisdom
in the Wisdom of Solomon" in *ISW* (1993): 149-164; W. Horbury, "The Christian use
and the Jewish origins of the Wisdom of Solomon" in *WAI* (1995):182-196.

[79] This is clear in the use of Hellenistic philosophical vocabulary and ideas.

[80] Contrary to older commentators, contemporary scholars tend to associate ch. 10 with chs.
1-9. Three aorist passives in 9:18 διωρθώθησαν "make straight" ἐδιδάχθησαν "teach"
ἐσώθησαν "were saved", reappear in ch. 10. The anaphora αὕτη appears six times in ch.
10, but disappears in ch. 11, as does Wisdom. Moreover, the emphasis shifts from the
pursuit of Wisdom to a comparison of Jews and pagans and their respective fates. See
Reese, "Plan and Structure in the Book of Wisdom," *CBQ* 27 (1965): 391-399; Wright,

heroes—from Adam to Moses—and for continuing to save those who submit to her guidance. All who dedicate themselves to Wisdom are included in her parade of those saved and enjoy immortality. In urging his audience to entrust themselves to the leadership of Wisdom, who will conduct them to every virtue, the author presents the pursuit of Wisdom as a goal integral to their Jewish heritage. By associating Wisdom with Solomon, he is by implication asserting that the Wisdom to be sought is, that which, throughout their history, has been their birthright. Their ancestors were dedicated from the time of Adam to this Wisdom. The audience is reminded that while they have much in common with Hellenism, the Hebrew wisdom tradition has unparalleled ancient royal origins. Therefore, if they are or become disciples of Wisdom they will be following the example of their blessed ancestors and are assured of immortality. By placing considerable emphasis on humanity, "mortal"; "the first-formed human being" θνητὸς πρωτοπλάστου 7:1; Adam 10:1, the author suggests that human beings are the object of Wisdom's saving activity.[81] Conception and gestation, "moulded into flesh within the period of ten months", sustains the emphasis on humanity. Interestingly, neither the image nor the time duration is biblical, but the notion of a pregnancy of ten months is found in an Isis aretalogy, suggesting that the author adopts a Hellenistic notion here. To regard the birth of a king as no different from that of any other mortal reflects a commonplace understanding both in Jewish and Hellenistic tradition.[82] However, here an added emphasis is given to Wisdom's relationship with an ordinary mortal, and by implication with all human beings.

Traditionally Wisdom had links with royalty, so the author ensures that his audience recognises Solomon as an ordinary mortal who receives Wisdom's friendship. In this way, he emphasises that Wisdom is not to be confused with a kind of royal patron (7:1-6). Solomon's common humanity is detailed further with references to "When I was born, I began to breathe the common air, and fell upon the kindred earth; my first sound was a cry, as is true of all" (7:3).[83] It is at this point that Solomon attributes his exaltation to Wisdom, which is not his due to his birth or noble calling, prestige, advantage, or natural talent, but solely from God to whom he "prayed" εὐξάμην (7:7). This term for a biblical prayer of request echoes Deut 9:26, Solomon's vision (1 Kgs 3:5-15), and prayer (1 Kgs 8:12-53), and anticipates the prayer in Wis 9:1-18 which culminates in the proclamation of Wisdom as saviour.

Wisdom's saving role for human beings continues to be advanced with reference to her as, "an inexhaustible treasure for human beings and those who acquire her attain friendship with God" (7:14); "she enters into holy souls and renders them friends of God and prophets" (7:27); and the "gifts that come from

---

"The Structure of Wisdom 11-19," *CBQ* 27 (1965): 28-34; "The Structure of the Book of Wisdom," *Bib* 48 (1967): 165-184; Winston, *Wisdom of Solomon* (1979): 9-12.

[81] The term is used again in 10:1 "first-fashioned father of the earth".

[82] The humanity of Israelite kings is highlighted throughout the Old Testament.

[83] The allusion to crying at birth (v.3) is in keeping with the traditional belief that all humans cry at birth. There may be a contrast here with Zoroaster who was supposed to have laughed at his birth.

instruction" (7:14c). This dual reference to the discipline of the covenant, living according to the Law of Moses, and to "instruction", which implies that true culture for his Jewish readers embraces Wisdom through which they will "obtain" the wealth that leads to "friendship with God" (7:14).[84] Recalled in this image is, "the Lord used to speak to Moses face to face, as a man speaks to his friend" (Exod 33:11). This is imaged in Solomon's personal attestation to the richness of his friendship with Wisdom, the equivalent of friendship with God, which is salvation.

Certain characteristics of Wisdom, such as her presence at creation, her close relationship with God, and her teaching role, were well established in the Hebrew wisdom tradition so references to them are to be expected in any later wisdom writing. Nevertheless, the Wisdom of Solomon goes far beyond these traditional motifs. Her role as the divine guide of history in 9:18-10:21 is startlingly new, and must have been prompted by the situation in which the tradition was now developing.[85] While this book is firmly based in the biblical tradition, I suggest that this distinctive depiction of Wisdom is the result of a response, by the author, to Hellenism's powerful challenge to Judaism, particularly in the confusion arising from the Isis cult.

Wisdom's Apparent Affinity with Isis

Wisdom's affinity with Isis, who is called σωτήρ "salvation", σώτειρα "saviour", πανσώτειρα "saviour", in dedications recounting her saving deeds, is here unmistakable. Isis's ability to act as saviour stems from her position as mistress of fate, *Heimarmene*. Unlike the Greek gods, she was intimately associated with the powers of the cosmos. The former aspect—clearly the legacy of her Egyptian background—meant that in a time when fatalism was widespread, she was a goddess who was not only loving and faithful to those who served her, but powerful enough to influence the forces that dominated human existence.[86] It meant that success, long life, and wealth were a reward for the worship of Isis. Moreover, this goddess was credited with major roles in creating; she was also regarded as the inventor and patron of maritime trades. Returning to the list of Wisdom's accomplishments in 9:18-10:21, one observes that the events named are precisely those over which Isis had control. Wisdom's "guiding" κυβερνήσασα of the boat, Noah's ark (10:4), corresponds closely to one of Isis's major skills, the protection and guidance of sailors. The specific reference to Wisdom as making the righteous wealthy (10:11) is significant in view of the very frequently encountered notion that Isis confers wealth upon the pious.[87] Similarly, Wisdom's presence

---

[84] Παιδείας "instruction" is a Greek word for "culture", which also appears in 6:17-20, where it is a step towards obtaining the "kingdom".

[85] Ben Sira in his praise of the Ancestors chapters 44-50 does not invoke Wisdom as guide. See R.A.F. MacKenzie, "Ben Sira as Historian" T.A. Dunne, and J.M. Laporte, eds., *Trinification of the World* (Toronto, 1978): 312-327.

[86] For other ways of overcoming Fate current in the Hellenistic world, see H.O. Schröder, "Fatum (*Heimarmene*)" *RAC* 7 (1969): 562-570.

[87] Hymn from *Medinet Madi*: 70.

with the righteous in prison (10:14) is closely paralleled by Isis's promise to save prisoners when they pray to her.[88]

While many such similarities between Wisdom and Isis may be distinguished, personified Wisdom remains within the biblical tradition. The sacred story of Israel, and of the faithful who observe the Law, is central to Wisdom. The writer gives Wisdom's deeds a new expression and shape in a hostile religious situation. He did not co-opt a powerful symbol from the dominant culture to revitalise the Israelite tradition and make it pertinent for Jews who undoubtedly were attracted to Hellenism. On the contrary, he reinterpreted the Jewish Wisdom figure by aligning her more closely with God's saving deeds than any of his predecessors in the tradition had done and in his new conception of this figure made a breakthrough to a vision of Wisdom as saviour.[89]

Conclusions

Personified Wisdom in the role of saviour was a response to the confusion and fear confronting Jews living in a Hellenistic world. The centralisation of the notion of Wisdom as saviour is clear in the distinct shift in emphasis achieved in Wis 6:12-10:21. While in chapters 1-5 the thematic emphasis is on "righteousness", δικαιοσύνην (1:1, 15; 2:11; 5:6, 18), and δίκαιον (2:10, 12, 16, 18; 3:1, 10; 4:7, 15; 5:1, 5), a clear switch to the theme of σοφια appears in 6:12-10:21. The word itself is used at least twenty-five times.[90] Righteousness is highlighted as the quality to be loved and acquired in chapters 1-5, and is shown to be an essential forerunner to the pursuit of Wisdom.[91] Introduced fleetingly at the beginning of the book under a variety of names, such as, "holy spirit", "divine tutor", "benevolent spirit", "spirit of the Lord" (Wis 1:5-7), Wisdom comes fully into focus and holds the central position in the middle section (Wis 6:12-10:21), and moves to a minor role in the third and final section.[92] Wisdom's key position and crucial role throughout 6:12-10:21 is reflected in her central location in the composition (as in other wisdom texts also), and in the emphasis on the need to search for her. She is "found by those who seek her" (6:12), and "she is the first to make herself known to those who desire her" (6:12-16).[93] In addition, she is the means of achieving the virtues

---

[88] As many as are in prison in the power of death . . . having called upon you to be present were all saved. *Medinet Madi* 1. 29, 34.

[89] Kloppenborg, "Isis" (1984): 86.

[90] In contrast to Wis 6:12-10:21, Σοφια occurs five times in the rest of the Wisdom of Solomon (1:4, 6; 3:11; 14:2, 5).

[91] "Righteousness" (8:7) in 6:12-10:21 is mentioned once.

[92] Wis 6:1-21 provides a transition from the theme of justice to that of Wisdom, with imperatives of 6:1-2, listen, understand, learn, give ear, referring both backwards to the theme of justice and forward to 6:9-12 on the pursuit of Wisdom, uses verbs similar to those used of justice. In 8:7 justice is explicitly a gift of Wisdom. See S.A. Geller, "Fiery Wisdom: Logos and Lexis in Deuteronomy 4" *Prooftexts* 14/2 (1994): 107-111.

[93] Reese, *Hellenistic Influence* (1970): 124, 130, shows convincingly that the Wisdom of

and rewards of chapters 1-5, just as in the crucial events from the Creation to the Exodus she is the Saviour.[94]

Displaying a profound knowledge and appreciation of the culture surrounding him, the author integrates historical, philosophical, scientific and cultic elements of Hellenism into a picture of Wisdom as the source of all knowledge, both profane and sacred. He expresses his theological insights through a characterisation already familiar to his Jewish audience, and thus enhances the long tradition of biblical wisdom. He recreates the figure of personified Wisdom, whom earlier wisdom authors had created, invoked and developed in previous crises, to address the current crisis arising from unfaithfulness to the Hebrew tradition on the part of Jews immersed in Hellenism. Such a dilemma will have led to questions regarding identity, the maintenance of the tradition, and above all the validity of the tradition in its foreign cultural environment. Put simply the dilemma confronting faithful Jews is how they are to justify the ways of the God of Israel, the God of their Jewish tradition in this situation. The author's goal is to respond to this challenge.

Wisdom's portrayal as saviour is intended to encourage and persuade his Jewish audience to remain devoted to the essence of their ancestral heritage while living in a Hellenistic milieu. Jews who are wavering, or have reneged on their allegiance, are faced with a compelling conception of their tradition that could persuade them to recognise the richness of their tradition and to return to their heritage. The author recreates a Wisdom figure that incorporates Jewish and Hellenistic features, a familiar but in many ways new and contemporary portrayal of an attractive and rich figure, grounded in Israelite wisdom. Thus, he presents an incentive to Jews in a Hellenistic society to remain faithful to, or return to, their Jewish heritage. The importance of the pursuit of this figure is the overarching theme of Wis 6:12-9:18. It is the last line (9:18) of this section of the Wisdom of Solomon that provides the reason *par excellence* to justify a search for Wisdom. This quest is presented in three sections that purport to detail Solomon's pursuit of Wisdom and at the same time delineate the quest in which the audience are being persuaded to engage. Solomon speaks in the first person of his search for Wisdom (7:1-22); for her God like gifts, for "what Wisdom is" (7:22-8:1), and "how she came to be" in his own life (8:2-18). Demonstrating his faithfulness to tradition, he concludes by praying for Wisdom (9:1-18).[95]

Through this account, the author builds up a picture of Wisdom, which reaches a climax in the closing line of Solomon's prayer with a proclamation of Wisdom's role as saviour of human beings, "Thus it was that the paths of human

---

Solomon is a unity, by identifying forty-five "flashbacks—short repetitions of a significant word, or group of words, or distinctive idea in two different parts pf Wisdom". See the association between 6:12 and 13:5-6 where "to contemplate" is the beginning and the means for one to "seek" and "find" Wisdom and God.

[94] On ch. 10 see A. Schmitt, "Struktur, Herkunft und Bedeutung der Beispielreihe in Weisheit 10" *BZ* 21 (1977): 1-22.

[95] This is an interesting contrast with the first person speech of the Wisdom figure in Proverbs and Sirach.

beings were set straight, and all were taught what pleases you and were saved by Wisdom" (9:17-18). The injunction to "seek God with sincerity of heart" (1:1), is picked up in the promise to readers that they will find God if they take personified Wisdom as spouse (8:2), and thus they will be initiated into the divine gifts (8:4).[96] In outlining Solomon's own relationship with Wisdom (8:2-21), besides recovering the symbol of Solomon as the lover of Wisdom *par excellence*, the author re-actualises other Israelite traditions and includes Hellenistic shadings by echoing patterns characteristic of Isis as a powerful saviour-figure in Hellenism. The achievement of personifying Wisdom in the role of saviour affirms Judaism as a saving religion in the face of Hellenistic claims and promises. The new Wisdom figure portrayed as saviour, and vindicator of the righteous, is the symbol of hope offered by the author of Wisdom to faithful Jews living in the midst of all that a Hellenistic society with its popular Isis cult offered.

Wis 6:12-10:21 deals directly with the temptation to apostasy faced by the Jews living among gentiles, by pinpointing the appeal of Hellenism to those who are facing decisions regarding identity, and allegiance to their heritage. By invoking and developing personified Wisdom, the writer seeks to provide satisfactory answers to the profound religious questions arising in his time. Polemic against political authority is not a priority for him. Rather, he shows that the figure of Wisdom presented in the Jewish wisdom writings is the Wisdom who is to be sought and treasured by the Jewish people. It is by looking to her that they will be saved. This problem approach recognises that his audience have to embark on a transition, and to enable them to find their bearings in the midst of confusion, he offers them the figure of Wisdom as their guide. She will provide all that is necessary to lead them to God. He shows the wisdom of the Hellenists to be but a shadow of personified Wisdom by reinterpreting the figure of Wisdom who was already familiar from earlier biblical texts.

In addressing the confusion and disillusionment besetting Jews in a Hellenistic culture, the author documents and confirms the unique faithfulness of Israel's God, thus showing that Judaism offers a living heritage surpassing the promises of Hellenism. To convince his audience that Judaism could compete with, and even transcend, Hellenism's claims, he pursues debates current in Hellenism and presents answers that display Hellenic form and style but are in keeping with Jewish tradition. His mastery of Hellenistic thinking enables him to present a new interpretation of traditional Jewish teaching, and find in the Hellenistic culture in which he and his Jewish audience are living, a corresponding search for, and similar insights into the saving presence of God. By bringing together Israelite teaching and Hellenistic insights and modes of expression, he articulates Israel's

---

[96] G. Scarpat, "Un Hapax Assoluto: AIRETIS (Sap. 8,4)", in *Scritti classici e cristiani offerti a Francesco Corsaro* (Catania, 1994): 643-647, notes that Wis 8:4 contains the term αἱρετίς (NAB "selector")—hapax in all of Greek literature—as part of the praise of Wisdom attributed to Solomon. Scarpat argues that the use by the Stoics and by Philo, (regarded by Scarpat as contemporaries of the author of the Wisdom of Solomon), of the cognate participle αἱρῶν for the Logos points to Wisdom's role as "guiding/advising" all God's works.

heritage in terms and images viable for the circumstances of time and place in which he and his audience now live. He thus offers, in a new form, the assurance that God is present with them. This new presentation retains teaching integral to Jewish tradition, enables Judaism to adapt and survive in its Hellenistic context, while enabling his audience to develop and nurture new insights into their own tradition.

Chapter 6

Conclusion

Inspiring this study was a series of questions about the figure of personified Wisdom: What or where are Wisdom's origins? What are the characteristics of her relationship with God and with human beings? What issues and situations does she address? What roles and functions does Wisdom fulfil? These questions were like take-off points for the study of a variety of biblical texts in which Wisdom is personified. They helped to focus each study and at the same time, they set constraints, which resulted in large tracts of the fascinating terrain of personified Wisdom being left unexplored. By undertaking a careful exploration of texts, I discovered original creations, expansive metaphors, new and ancient patterns, faint traces of other figures, reinterpretations, and much else. Some of these discoveries contributed to or lay behind the Wisdom figures studied. Engagement with the texts enabled me to hear many voices. The first of these was Wisdom's followed closely by voices of poets and writers who conceived, created, developed and enhanced the personified Wisdom figure in so many guises and in many different locations. Most insistent were and are the hosts of voices from communities where the multifaceted figure of Wisdom spoke, played, eluded searchers, and continues to delight in being with humanity.

Elusive Origins and Diverse Explanations

Views regarding biblical Wisdom's origins, while remaining a matter of conjecture, give rise to much debate in biblical research. Findings of scholars espousing particular theories fall into three fluid groups. Well-represented are those who propose various ancient Near Eastern goddesses, such as Ugaritic Anat, Canaanite Astarte, Mesopotamian Ishtar, or Gula, Egyptian Ma'at, the Semitic mother-goddess in Jewish worship at Elephantine, and the Hellenised form of the Egyptian goddess Isis, as having contributed to the appearance or development of the phenomenon of personified Wisdom. Equally, those who favour literary and theological, or sociological arguments to explain the Wisdom figure's origins produce well-documented arguments. However, none of the findings to date yields conclusive evidence identifying an equivalent, a predecessor, or a contemporary figure in the literature of the ancient Near East, on which the Israelite Wisdom figure was modelled. Although Wisdom may exhibit features common to female characters portrayed in the wisdom literature of other ancient Near Eastern peoples, the unique qualities of this figure in the Old Testament, her claims for herself, and her teaching, give her the appearance of a unique biblical creation. Ironically, interpretations of biblical texts that speak of Wisdom's origins are far from unanimous, as shown in chapter one. Several Hebrew words elude scholars' most persistent attempts at exegesis, perhaps an appropriate semantic option for the elusive figure of personified Wisdom.

Reinterpretation of Prophecy and History

Personified Wisdom, as a new formulation, no doubt served ideological purposes that remain obscured by time. I suggest, in chapter two, that Wisdom's prophet-like appearance, her speech in the marketplace and at the city gates was associated with the crisis initiated by the defeat and destruction suffered by the Israelites. Particularly significant in these scenes in Proverbs is the fact that the female figure of Wisdom delivers teaching that echoes exilic and post-exilic prophets. Moreover, her teaching is proclaimed in public places, with no mention of the Temple, Jerusalem, or the land of Israel. Wisdom's self-description evokes connotations of YHWH speaking through the prophets. In her calls for attention, and announcement of reproach, punishment, and promise (Prov 1:20-33; 3:13-18; 4:5-9; 8:1-36), Wisdom echoes prophetic promises: "I will walk in the way of righteousness, in the paths of justice" (Prov 8:20).

Wisdom's prophet-like qualities are particularly evident in that the words she speaks have the character of divine speech (Prov 1:20-33). In addition, her claims that her words are norms for salvation or destruction are claims made by the prophets but understood to be from YHWH. Sayings such as, "because I have called and you refused to listen" (Prov 1:24) echo, "Because you did not listen . . . therefore . . ." express claims made by YHWH, as proclaimed by Isaiah, Zechariah, and Jeremiah (Isa 50:2; 65:12; 66:4; Jer 7:13; 11:10; 17:23, 22:1-5; 25:4; Zech 7:13). The theological concern underlying this development is clearly that of the Exile. Such a concern is expressed in Jeremiah and Ezekiel where it takes the form of a theodicy, in which the refusal of Israel to listen has become the "reason" for the Exile. Similar conclusions may be reached by a comparison of sayings and motifs of Wisdom's teaching with other post-exilic literature, as shown in chapter 2. This suggests that the wisdom tradition participated in Israel's theological struggle following the Babylonian Exile.

I argued that the development of personified Wisdom in the exilic era was a theological response to the chaos resulting from the destruction of Jerusalem and the Temple, the loss of the land and the failure of the monarchy. What is certain is that the author(s) of Proverbs, by portraying a figure who was part of God's created order from the beginning, and appears in the marketplace as a teacher, affirms the Wisdom of God in the form of personified Wisdom. In what is probably her earliest portrayal in the Old Testament, Wisdom accuses her hearers of not having listened to her in the past and threatens to laugh at their plight, a starkly different outcome from that suggested in the prophetic texts. Speaking in the first person, the Wisdom of God teaches how God's relationship with Israel and the created world is to be understood. The question of theodicy is, I believe, the context for the literary creation and development of the Wisdom figure.

Historical and prophetic texts focus attention on Israel's election by YHWH, thereby creating Israel's identity. Wisdom, on the other hand, turns from this sense of Israel's difference from others, and proclaims the world and its inhabitants as the work of the Creator. Wisdom, who speaks for God, contrasts sharply with figures who speak for God in the prophetic and historical literature. The prophetic voice, almost without exception, is portrayed as male, as is the God of the historical texts. Male speakers using the language of command and reprimand usually deliver YHWH's teachings. They insist that obedience and a change of heart are imperative if Israel's election and unique position of being in covenant with YHWH are to be sustained. In contrasting Wisdom, the fullness of life (Prov 8:35), with the female figures of Folly, bringers of death and destruction, the author may be addressing an associated crisis attendant on the disaster of the Babylonian invasion. It is interesting that, apart from Wisdom, the female figures who receive extended consideration in Proverbs illustrate teaching on sexual conduct. Hosea and especially exilic and post-exilic prophets use sexual imagery to express fidelity or infidelity to God. Many prophetic references attest to Israel's immorality in her pursuit of Baals and Asherahs. However, in Proverbs the issue is a choice between life, which is fidelity to the search for Wisdom, and death, the search for Folly, which is sexual infidelity. Paradoxically, in her personification, Wisdom is elevated beyond correct behaviour to be a God like figure.

Elusive Wisdom

Two popular Jewish motifs, woven through Old Testament wisdom are the search for Wisdom and Wisdom's elusiveness, Wisdom's accessibility and Wisdom's hiddenness. These motifs intimate an ongoing search and desire for wisdom in the Hebrew tradition. While the classic perception of Wisdom's elusiveness and inaccessibility appears in Job 28, the Wisdom poem in Baruch 3:9-4:4 also explores the difficulty of finding Wisdom's "storehouses" (Bar 3:14), and immediately poses the question "who has found the place of Wisdom?" (Job 28:12, 28; Bar 3:15). Both poems emphasise the paradox of Wisdom's hiddenness and inaccessibility. On the one hand Wisdom must be sought with effort and "discipline" (Sir 4:17; 6:18-36; Prov 4:10-27; 6:6; Wis 1:5; 7:14), but on the other hand, Wisdom eludes human searching, because she is a gift from God (Prov 2:6; 8:22-36; Ps 105:22; Sir 1:9-10, 26; 6:37; Wis 7:7; 9:4).

Job 28 by highlighting the difficulty of knowing where Wisdom can be found serves to point the debates between Job and his friends towards cosmic realities (Job 38-41). This is clear in Job 28:28 where the "fear of the Lord" is offered as the solution, while Baruch 4:1 offers the Torah. In Bar 3:36-37 the poet claims that the gift of Wisdom was given only to the people of Israel, a claim that seems akin to Sir 24:8-11. However, Ben Sira names the land of Israel as Wisdom's setting, stating that Wisdom's abode is in Jerusalem, while Baruch announces that Wisdom was given exclusively to the people of Israel but does not tie Wisdom to the land of Israel. This crucial distinction highlights the unique gift of personified Wisdom to Israelite/Jewish communities. It also serves to harmonise with the exilic setting of Baruch, and address Diaspora audiences. Arguably the author of Bar 3:9-4:4 used the historical setting of the Babylonian Exile metaphorically in the second century BCE, not to advocate return to the land so much, as to persuade his audience to recover full identity as a people faithful to their Jewish traditions. Another distinctive feature of the Baruch wisdom poem is the fact that among texts featuring personified Wisdom, this text is alone in not alluding to the much lauded wisdom requirement of "fear of the Lord", and the absolute essential for Wisdom in Job 28, "To human beings God said: Behold, the fear of the LORD is wisdom; and avoiding evil is understanding" (Job 28:28). This requirement may have been supplanted by the linking of Wisdom with Torah in Baruch. This raises the interesting question as to whether the author of Baruch has subsumed "fear of the Lord and avoidance of evil" into fidelity to Torah. Wisdom's identification with Torah in Baruch is the culmination of the poem that consistently evoked the gift of the Torah and its availability to all Israelites/Jews as expressed in Deuteronomy 4 and 30.

Wisdom as Torah

At the high point of Wisdom's song, Ben Sira who regularly imitates the Hebrew Bible by showing a special partiality for Deuteronomy, makes a direct and unrivalled identification of Wisdom as the book of the covenant of the Most High (Sir 24:23; cf. Bar 3:9-4:3). Thus, Ben Sira and Baruch connect universal Wisdom with the history of Israel and its covenant law. This emphasises what Wisdom herself declares when she announces that God instructed her to pitch her tent in Israel and dwell among the people. Jewish thought was greatly influenced by its Hellenistic environment. In his reinterpretation of the Israelite tradition in language that recalls and highlights its unique history and development, Ben Sira employs enduring Israelite themes, images, and metaphors in his refashioning of the Wisdom figure and thus gives new expression to the tradition.

A simple yet astute logic underlies the move to identify Wisdom and Torah. Both are the divine way of life so it followed ineluctably that they were the same, as Ben Sira makes clear by placing this teaching in the centre of his composition. Wisdom, as the Torah itself, is the means by which God is revealed to human beings, while on the other hand, they achieve communion with God by means of the Torah, and equally by means of Wisdom. Ben Sira makes this identification complete with the figure of Wisdom quoting Deut 33:4 and applying the verse to herself (Sir 24:23). In making Wisdom identical with the Mosaic Law, he declares her a divine gift, rather than a human acquisition; and thus Ben Sira makes Israelite Wisdom superior in every way to the wisdom of the Hellenists.

Wisdom as Saviour

The Wisdom of Ben Sira, the Wisdom of Solomon and Baruch bring Jewish wisdom into dialogue with Greek wisdom. All retain a sense of Israel as a chosen people, but borrow from Hellenist culture, address its questions, and seek to engage with its wisdom. While Ben Sira and Baruch, by identifying Wisdom with the Torah, associate her with Israel's history, the author of Wisdom, as shown in chapter 5, by lauding Israel's unique history (Wis 10:1-21), equates Wisdom's care for Israel with her care for all creation. Wisdom is thus universalised, as it is never suggested that Israel alone was God's creation. The author in recounting Wisdom's role in Israel's history, (Adam, Cain, Noah, Abraham, Lot, Jacob, Joseph, Moses), as the story of Wisdom's redeeming power, the author attributes to Wisdom saving deeds elsewhere attributed to YHWH. "A holy people and a blameless race Wisdom delivered from a nation of oppressors" (Wis 10:15-16). Wisdom's initiation of the decisive revelatory and liberating events for her people Israel is but the culmination of the preceding chapters (6:12-9:18) which credit her with numerous divine deeds: (Wis 7:12-8:1). The author describes her with twenty-one attributes and a fivefold densely layered metaphor. The author of Wisdom undoubtedly seeks to persuade his readers that Wisdom is God's presence throughout the created world, and so is an effective saviour.

Personified Wisdom: A Supple Character

Wisdom's portraits show her to be a remarkably flexible character, which is not anthropomorphism, metaphysical description, or static figure, but a symbol characterised by unique energy, scope, and variety. Israelite/Jewish wisdom writers integrated human and divine imagery into their creations of this rich, and mysterious female figure, which they envisaged as intimately associated with YHWH. Wisdom's first person speeches and the poems in praise of Wisdom, highlight Wisdom's intimate association with YHWH. Everything said by or about her emphasises her God like qualities: her divine origin, her presence at creation, "created in the beginning . . . the first of his acts of old" (Prov 8:22-29; Sir 1:4, 9-10; 24:3, 9); "fashioner of all things" (Wis 7:22); "mother" (Wis 7:12); "she orders all things well" (Wis 8:1); knows the structure of the world and its elements (Wis 7:17-22); her delight in being with human beings in the created world (Prov 8:4, 31-36; Sir 24:7, 12, 19-22; Wis 8:2-3); her gifts of life, prosperity, insight, fear of the Lord (Prov 1:32; 3:13-18; 8:1-5, 35; 9:1-6; Sir 1:14-20; 6:18-31; 24:19-33; Wis 7:7-14); her close association with Israel (Sir 24:8-12; 24:23; Bar 4:1; Wis 10:1-21); her location in the sanctuary (Sir 24:10-12); "in every generation she passes into holy souls and makes them friends of God and prophets" (Wis 7:27).

Textually each Wisdom portrait is centralised and is a key motif in the wisdom literature by the positioning of the texts in Proverbs, Job, the Wisdom of Ben Sira, Baruch and the Wisdom of Solomon. These poetic descriptions of Wisdom are also set in the midst of series of instructions, prayers, and prosaic advice addressing everyday human concerns, such as, avoidance of sinners (Prov 1:8-19); warnings about Folly, the adulteress, and the foreign women who bring death (Prov 2:1-22; 6:20-7:1-27; 9:7-12); speeches explaining reasons for Job's sufferings (Job 3-27; 28-37); warnings against specific sins (Sir 22:27-23:27);

warnings against cynics (Wis 9:7-12); warnings about vindication and the final judgement (Wis 5:20-6:11); the gifts that bring happiness (Sir 25:1-12); confession of sins and a prayer of encouragement for an exiled community (Bar 1:16-3:8; 4:5-5:9); a call to repentance for past sins (Wis 1:1-6:11). Wisdom's association with YHWH and with human beings goes hand in hand with her vitality and moral persuasiveness expressed in her practical moral advice, her concern with behaviour, her link with prophecy, her elusiveness; her association with fear of the Lord, her teaching in public, her power to save.

Ranging from the elusive and inaccessible figure in Job 28 to a figure who transcends created limitations, exercising divine power in creative and saving deeds in Wisdom 6-10, personifications of Wisdom are coloured by their settings, the intentions of their authors and their canonical placements. Interestingly, wisdom writers maintained the identity of the Wisdom figure even as each reworked it in new settings and endowed it with new meaning. The flexibility exercised by these authors is evident in the way Wisdom functions in an array of roles. She witnesses to creation (Prov 8:22-32); Wisdom protects, delivers, saves all in distress (Wis 9:18-10:10); a teacher speaking in the marketplace (Prov 1:20-21), and in the highways (Prov 8:1-2); a host in her "house of seven pillars" (Prov 9:1-6); seen and declared, established and searched out by God (Job 28:27); pitched her tent in Israel, in the Holy Tent (Sir 24:7-11); one with the Torah (Sir 24:23; Bar 4:1); poured forth upon all living things (Sir 1:9-10); "comes from the mouth of the Most High and covers the earth like a mist" (24:3); given to his [God's] servant Jacob and to Israel whom he loves (Bar 3:37); "inseparable from God, permeating the world, yet remaining with God" (Wis 7:22b-8:1); making human beings into "friends of God and prophets" (Wis 7:27).

Wisdom: God's Active Presence in the Universe

Given the biblical evidence relating to Hebrew teaching about the deity, one can assume that religious monotheism was the milieu in which the personification texts were produced and treasured. Any notion of a second God would have been untenable. By depicting Wisdom as the fashioner of all things (Wis 7:22); the deliverer of Israel from a nation of oppressors (Wis 10:1-21); the giver of justice and life (Prov 8:35), the wisdom writers portray God's activity and presence in the created world in surprisingly fresh and courageous imagery. Given that Wisdom's activity is akin in all respects to the activity of God, one must conclude that personified Wisdom speaks directly of God, and is an unequivocal expression of the most intense divine presence in the world. I believe that the primary aim of Israelite/Jewish wisdom writers was to assure their audiences of YHWH presence with them. Rather than producing polemic against goddess worship, they used elements of goddess language to speak of Israel's God whose beneficence, power, and transcendence were expressed in Wisdom herself. Personification texts had to harmonise descriptions of Wisdom in female imagery with Israelite/Jewish faith, without introducing a fragmented idea of God. Wisdom teachers and writers, by delineating Wisdom as the first of God's creation, and maintaining her creature status, avoided what would have appeared as false representations of YHWH.

A monotheistic faith functioned to order the creation, by borrowing and integrating new ideas into the figure of personified Wisdom. Wisdom figures in Proverbs, Job, the Wisdom of Ben Sira, Baruch, and the Wisdom of Solomon are expressions of beliefs, expectations and hopes about God's association with the created world and its inhabitants. Such figures surpassed claims made for various goddesses and counteracted their appeals. Personified Wisdom celebrates God's transcendent goodness as Creator, sustainer and saviour of the world and all it contains. This the authors achieved in imagery portraying the divine presence in the female figure of Wisdom. A peculiar characteristic of Israel's monotheistic religion is that the supreme God and the personal God were united in the person of a single deity. In this respect, wisdom literature, like the rest of the Old Testament, represents YHWH as personal God. Israelite/Jewish abhorrence for physical images of YHWH is in marked contrast to the lack of restraint manifested by the wisdom writers when employing verbal images. In the Old Testament, human traits are usually attributed to YHWH.

Personified Wisdom's originators and interpreters carefully blended familiar aspects of YHWH, with neglected images from Israel's earlier traditions, and with newly minted metaphors.[1] With this figure, the wisdom poets also transformed traditional modes of expression, which used masculine terms for God, by portraying Wisdom as a female figure, an astonishing development in the Hebrew tradition. Thus, they enriched the image of YHWH to address situations affecting Jews whose traditions and heritage were under attack in unfamiliar and threatening circumstances. This personification of YHWH's presence in the world replaced the image of YHWH as a God concerned only for the Israelites, with the notion of YHWH as Creator and Redeemer, a notion traditionally seen in the prophets, but now attributed to Wisdom.

Indisputably, Wisdom is the Bible's most fascinating literary figure. It is in the poetic creation of this figure that the wisdom writers capture the notion of God's active presence in the universe. To describe Wisdom as the "fashioner of all things" (Wis 7:22), the deliverer of Israel from a nation of oppressors, is to speak of her in terms usually ascribed to God. To equate Wisdom's activity with that of God, and as having the same effects and attributes, is to depict the Wisdom figure as an expression of the most intense divine presence in the world. The unique figure of Wisdom, bearing distinctive connections with prophecy, creation, the fear of the Lord, the Torah, and salvation, transformed the Israelite heritage in times of dissolution and loss, by ensuring the presence of YHWH with the Israelites/Jews throughout chaos and defeat. This insight is consistent with the insistence of wisdom writers on the inability of human beings to define or confine the deity who remains always beyond the reach of language.

Wisdom's functions are not limited by boundaries of nationality, gender,

---

[1] I. Murdoch, *Existentialists and Mystics: Writings on Philosophy and Literature* (London, 1997), observes in relation to the use of metaphors: "It seems to me impossible to discuss certain concepts without resort to metaphors", a point that is particularly apposite in discussions about personified Wisdom.

or time. Wisdom writing relates to human beings in ways that are different from that of the prophetic and historical traditions. Wisdom portraits proclaim symbolically Israel's experience of God's presence in new and unexpected circumstances. While poetic imagery has a way of turning into philosophic realism at the hands of prosaic theologians, the genius of Judaism kept the most prosaic of its adherents from crystallising Wisdom into a competitor with God. In Judaism Wisdom is personified but never apotheosized. While Wisdom never becomes a god, she does become the next most significant figure in the tradition.

Bibliography

Ackroyd, Peter R. "Archaeology, Politics and Religion: The Persian Period". *The Illiff Review* 39 (1982): 5-24.

_____. *Israel under Babylon and Persia.* Oxford: Oxford University, 1970.

_____. *Exile and Restoration: A Study of Hebrew Thought of the Sixth Century B.C.* London: SCM Press, 1968.

Albrektson, B. *History and the Gods: An Essay on the Idea of Historical Events as Divine Manifestations in the Ancient Near East and in Israel.* Lund: Gleerup, 1967.

Albright, William F. "Some Canaanite-Phoenician Sources of Hebrew Wisdom". *Vetus Testamentum Supplements* 3 (1955): 1-15.

_____. "Islam and the Religions of the Orient". *Journal of the American Oriental Society* 60 (1940): 298.

_____. "The Goddess of Life and Wisdom". *American Journal of Semitic Languages and Literature* 36 (1919): 258-294.

Aletti, Jean-Noël. "Proverbes 8:22-31. Étude de structure". *Biblica* 57 (1976): 25-37.

_____. "Séduction et parole en Proverbes 1-9". *Vetus Testamentum* 27 (1977): 129-144.

Allegro, J.M. *Discoveries in the Judaean Desert of Jordan [Qumrân Cave 4.1 (4Q 158 - 4Q 186) (50, 1325)].* Vol. 5. Oxford: Clarendon, 1968.

Alster, Bendt. *The Instructions of Suruppak.* Mesopotamia. Copenhagen Studies in Assyriology 10. Copenhagen: Akademisk Forlag, 1974.

Alt, Albrecht. "Die Weisheit Salomos". *Theologische Literaturzeitung* 76 (1951): 139-144.

Anderson, Bernard W. "Prov 8:22-36: Moving Beyond Masculine Metaphors". *Bible Review* 10/5 (1994): 22, 57-58.

Anderson, George W. *A Critical Introduction to the Old Testament.* London: Duckworth, 1959.

Anoz, José. "Estudio Sobre Baruch". *Mayévtica* 7 (1981): 161-177.

Argall, Richard A. *1 Enoch and Sirach: A Literary Comparative and Conceptual Analysis of the Themes of Revelation, Creation and Judgment.* 8. Atlanta: Scholars Press, 1995.

Arnim, Hans F. *Stoicorum Veterum Fragmenta.* Leipzig: Teubner, 1921.

Arthos, John. "Personification". In *The Princeton Encyclopedia of Poetry and Poetics.* ed. A. Preminger, F.J. Warnke and O.B. Hardison, London: Macmillan, 1975: 612 cols 1-2.

Assmann, Jan. *Ma'at: Gerechtigkeit und Unsterblichkeit im Alten Ägypten.* Munich: Beck, 1990.

Baltzer, Klaus. *Deutero-Isaiah. A Commentary on Isaiah 40-55.* Translated by M. Kohl. Hermeneia. Minneapolis: Fortress, 2001.

Barré, Michael L. "'Fear of God' and the World View of Wisdom". *Biblical Theology Bulletin* 11 (1981): 41-43.

Barton, John. *Oracles of God: Perceptions of Ancient Prophecy in Israel after the Exile.* London: Darton, Longman and Todd, 1986.

_____. "Natural Law and Poetic Justice". *Journal of Theological Studies* 30 (1979): 1-14.

Barucq, André. *Le Livre des Proverbes.* Paris: J. Gabalda, 1964.

Baumgartner, Walter. "Die Israelitische Weisheitsliteratur". *Theologische Rundschau* 5 (1933): 259-288.

Beattie, James. *Elements of Moral Science*. Edinburgh: Cadell, 1793.

_____. *Essays on Poetry and Music*. London: Dilly & Creech, 1779.

Beauchamp, Paul. "Le peuple Juif et les nations à partir de l'Ancien Testament". *Bulletin, Pontificio Consejo para el Diálogo Interreligioso* 76 (1991): 43-60.

_____. "Epouser la Sagesse ou n'épouser qu'elle? Une Énigme du Livre de la Sagesse". In *La Sagesse de l'Ancien Testament*. ed. Maurice Gilbert, Louvain: Louvain University, 1979: 347-369.

Becker, Joachim. *Gottesfurcht im Alten Testament*. Analecta Biblica 25. Rome: Päpstliches Bibelinstitut, 1965.

Begg, Christopher T. "Access to Heavenly Treasuries: The Traditionsgeschichte of a Motif". *Biblische Notizen* 44 (1988): 15-20.

Bentzen, Aaga. *Introduction to the Old Testament*. 2 vols. Copenhagen: Gad, 1952.

Berger, Peter L. and Thomas Luckmann. *The Social Construction of Reality: A Treatise in the Sociology of Knowledge*. New York: Doubleday, 1966.

Bergman, Jan. *Ich bin Isis: Studien zum memphitischen Hintergrund der griechischen Isisaretalogien*. Acta Universitatis Upsaliensis 3. Stockholm: Almqvist, 1968.

Bizzeti, Paulo. *Il Libro della Sapienza: Struttura e genere letterario*. Supplementi alla Rivista biblica 11. Brescia: Paideia, 1984.

Blenkinsopp, Joseph. *Sage, Priest and Prophet: Religious and Intellectual Leadership in Ancient Israel*. Louisville: Westminster John Knox, 1995.

_____. "The Social Context of the "Outsider Woman" in Proverbs 1-9". *Biblica* 72 (1991): 457-473.

Bonnard, P.-É. "De la Sagesse personnifiée dans l'Ancien Testament à la Sagesse en personne dans le Nouveau". In *La Sagesse de l'Ancien Testament*. ed. Maurice Gilbert, Louvain: Louvain University, 1979: 117-149.

_____. *La Sagesse en personne annoncée et venue Jésus-Christ*. Lectio Divina 44. Paris: Editions du Cerf, 1966.

Bonnardière, A.-M. la. *Le Livre de la Sagesse*. Paris: Etudes Augustiniennes, 1970.

Bonnet, Hans. *Reallexikon der ägyptischen Religionsgeschichte*. Berlin: De Gruyter, 1952.

Bonora, Antonio. "La 'donna straniera in Pr. 1-9". *Ricerche Storico Bibliche* 6 (1994): 101-109.

Borger, Rykle. "Die Beschwörungsserie *bît méseri* und die Himmelfahrt Henochs". *Journal of Near Eastern Studies* 33 (1974): 183-196.

Boström, G. *Proverbiastudien: Die Weisheit und das fremde Weib in Spr. 1-9*. Lund: Gleerup, 1935.

Boström, Lennart. *The God of the Sages: The Portrayal of God in the Book of Proverbs*. CBOTS 29. Stockholm: Almqvist & Wiksell, 1990.

Bousset, W. *Die Religion des Judentums im späthellenistischen Zeitalter*. Tübingen: Mohr, 1926.

Bowker, John W. *The Targums and the Rabbinic Literature: An Introduction to Jewish Interpretation of Scripture*. Cambridge: Cambridge University, 1969.

Box, G.H. and W.O.E. Oesterley. "Sirach". In *Apocrypha and Pseudepigrapha of the Old Testament* [*APOT*], Vol. 1. ed. R.H. Charles, Oxford: Clarendon, 1913: 268-517.

Brady, T. A. *The Reception of the Egyptian Cults by the Greeks (330-30 BC)*. Columbia: Columbia University Press, 1935.

Bright, John. *A History of Israel*. 3rd ed. London: SCM Press, 1981.

Brueggemann, Walter. "A Shattered Transcendence: Exile and Restoration". In *Biblical Theology: Problems & Perspectives*. ed. S. Kraftchick and B. Ollenburger, Nashville: Abingdon Press, 1995: 169-182, 316-320.

_____. *In Man We Trust: The Neglected Side of Biblical Faith.* Atlanta: John Knox Press, 1972.

Brunner, Hellmut. *Altägyptische Erziehung.* Wiesbaden: Harrassowitz, 1957.

Budge, Ernest Alfred Wallis. "Papyrus 10474 in the British Museum, 1923". Second Series of Facsimilies of Egyptian Hieratic Papyri in the British Museum, London.

Burke, David G. *The Poetry of Baruch. A Reconstruction and Analysis of the Original Hebrew Text of Baruch 3:9-5:9.* SBLSCS 10. Chico, California: Scholars Press, 1982.

Camp, Claudia V. "The Female Sage in Ancient Israel and in the Biblical Wisdom Literature". In *The Sage in Israel and the Ancient Near East.* ed. J.G. Gammie and L.G. Perdue, Winona Lake: Eisenbrauns, 1990: 185-203.

_____. *Wisdom and the Feminine in the Book of Proverbs.* BL 11. Sheffield: Almond Press, 1985.

Carley, Keith W. *The Book of the Prophet Ezekiel.* London: Cambridge University, 1974.

Carr, R.H. ed. *Plutarch's Lives of Coriolanus, Caesar, Brutus, and Antonius.* Vol. 35. Oxford: Clarendon, 1906.

Carroll, Robert P. *Jeremiah: A Commentary.* OTL. London: SCM Press, 1986.

Cassirer, Ernest. *Language and Myth.* New York: Dover, 1946.

_____. *The Philosophy of Symbolic Forms.* 2 vols. New Haven: Yale University, 1955.

Cazelles, Henri. "Ahiqar, Ummân, and Amun, and Biblical Wisdom Texts". In *Solving Riddles and Untying Knots. Biblical, Epigraphic, and Semitic Studies in Honor of Jonas C. Greenfield.* ed. Z. Zevit, S. Gitin and M. Sokoloff, Winona Lake: Eisenbrauns, 1995: 45-55.

_____. "La Sagesse de Proverbes 8:22: Peut-elle être considéréée comme une hypostase?" In *Trinité et liturgie.* ed. A. M. Triacca and A. Pistoia, Rome: Centro Liturgico Vincenziano, 1984: 53-67.

_____. "Les débuts de la sagesse en Israël". In *Sagesses du Proche-orient ancien, Colloque de Strasbourg 17-19 Mai 1962 [SPOA].* ed. Jean Leclant, Paris: PUF, 1963: 27-40.

_____. "L'enfantement de la Sagesse en Proverbes 8". In *Sacra Pagina 1.* ed. J. Coppens, A. Deschamps and E. Massaux, Paris: LeCoffre, 1959: 511-515.

_____. "Review of G.R. Driver, *Canaanite Myths and Legends*". *Vetus Testamentum* 7 (1957): 422-430.

_____. "Le Personnage d'Achior dans le Livre de Judith". *Recherches de Science Religieuse* 39 (1951): 125-137; 324-327.

Charlesworth, James H. ed. *Old Testament Pseudepigrapha.* Garden City: Doubleday, 1983-85.

Clarke, Ernest G. *The Wisdom of Solomon.* Cambridge: Cambridge University, 1973.

Clemen, C. *Die phönikische Religion nach Philo von Byblos.* Leipzig: J.C. Hinrich'sche, 1939.

Clements, Ronald E. "Patterns in the Prophetic Canon". In *Canon and Authority: Essays in Old Testament Religion and Authority.* ed. G.W. Coats and B.O. Long, Philadelphia: Fortress, 1987: 42-55.

_____. "Prophecy as Literature: A Re-Appraisal". In *The Hermeneutical Quest.* ed. D.G. Miller, Allison Park: Pickwick, 1986: 59-75.

_____. *Prophecy and Tradition.* Oxford: Blackwell, 1975.

Clifford, Richard J. "Woman Wisdom in the Book of Proverbs". In *Biblische Theologie und gesellschaftlicher Wandel für Norbert Lohfink.* ed. G. Braulik, W. Groß and S. MacEvenue, Freiburg: Herder, 1993: 61-72.

_____. "Proverbs 9: A Suggested Ugaritic Parallel". *Vetus Testamentum* 25 (1975): 298-306.

Coleridge, Samuel T. *The Statesman's Manual; or The Bible the Best Guide to Political Skill and Foresight: A Lay Sermon, addressed to the higher classes of society.* London: J. Duncombe, 1816.

Collins, John J. *Between Athens and Jerusalem: Jewish Identity in the Hellenistic Diaspora.* New York: Crossroads Publishing, 1983.

————. "Proverbial Wisdom and the Yahwist Vision". *Semeia* 17 (1980): 1-17.

————. "The Biblical Precedent for Natural Theology". *Journal of the American Academy of Religion* 45 Supplement 1 (1977): 36-67.

————. "Cosmos and Salvation: Jewish Wisdom and Apocalyptic in the Hellenistic Age". *History of Religions* 17 (1977): 121-142.

Conzelmann, Hans. "The Mother of Wisdom". In *In the Future of Our Religious Past: Essays in honour of Rudolf Bultmann.* ed. Rudolf K. Bultmann and J. McConkey Robinson, New York: Harper & Row, 1971: 230-243.

Coogan, Michael. "The Goddess Wisdom-'Where Can She Be Found'?: Literary Reflexes of Popular Religion". In *Ki Baruch Hu: Ancient Near Eastern, Biblical, and Judaic Studies in Honor of Baruch A. Levine.* ed. R. Chazan, B.A. Levine, W.W. Hallo and L.H. Schiffman, Winona Lake: Eisenbrauns, 1999: 203-209.

Cook, Johann. "'*Iššah Zara* (Proverbs 1-9 Septuagint): A Metaphor for Foreign Wisdom?" *Zeitschrift für die Alttestamentliche Wissenschaft* 106 (1994): 458-475.

Cowley, A. ed. *Aramaic Papyri of the Fifth Century B.C.* Oxford: Clarendon, 1923.

Crenshaw, James L. "Sirach". In *Harper's Bible Commentary.* ed. J. L. Mays, San Francisco: Harper & Row, 1988: 837.

————. "The Shift from Theodicy to Anthropodicy". In *Theodicy in the Old Testament.* ed. James L. Crenshaw, Philadelphia: Fortress, 1983: 1-16.

————. "The Human Dilemma and Literature of Dissent". In *Tradition and Theology in the Old Testament.* ed. Douglas A. Knight, Philadelphia: Fortress, 1977: 235-258.

————. "Prolegomenon". In *Studies in Ancient Israelite Wisdom.* ed. James L. Crenshaw, New York: KTAV, 1976: 1-45.

————. "Method in Determining Wisdom Influence upon 'Historical' Literature". *Journal of Biblical Literature* 88 (1969): 129-142.

Dahood, Mitchell. "Proverbs 8:22-31: Translation and Commentary". *Catholic Biblical Quarterly* 30 (1968): 512-521.

————. *Proverbs and Northwest Semitic Philology.* Rome: PBI, 1963.

Day, John. "Foreign Semitic Influence on the Wisdom of Israel and its Appropriation in the Book of Proverbs". In *Wisdom in Ancient Israel: Essays in honour of J.A. Emerton.* ed. J. Day, R. P. Gordon and H.G.M. Williamson, Cambridge: Cambridge University, 1995: 55-70.

————. "Asherah in the Hebrew Bible and Northwest Semitic Literature". *Journal of Biblical Literature* 105, no. 3 (1986): 385-408.

————. *Psalms.* OTG. Sheffield: JSOT, 1992.

Dearman, J.A. "My Servants the Scribes: Composition and Context in Jeremiah 36". *Journal of Biblical Literature* 109 (1990): 404.

DeBoer, A.H. "The Counsellor". *Vetus Testamentum, Supplements* 3 (1955): 42-71.

Deissler, Alfons. *Psalm 119 (118) und seine Theologie: Ein Beitrag zur Erforschung der anthologischen Stilgattung im Alten Testament.* Munich: K. Zink, 1955.

Delcor, M. "Ecclesiasticus or Sirach". In *The Cambridge History of Judaism,* Vol. II. ed. W. D. Davies and L. Finkelstein, Cambridge: Cambridge University, 1989: 415-422.

————. *Le texte hebreu du cantique de Siracde 51:13 (19) et les anciennes versions: Textus 6.* Paris: Éditions du Cerf, 1968.

————. "Les Sources du Deutéro-Zecharie et ses procédés d'emprunt". *Revue Biblique* 59 (1952): 385-411.

Bibliography   183

Delitzsch, Franz. *Das Solomonische Spruchbuch*. Vol. 2. Leipzig: Dörffling & Franke, 1873.
Des Places, Édouard. "Épithètes et attributs de la "Sagesse" (Sg 7:22-23 et SVF I 557 Arnim)". *Biblica* 57 (1976): 414-419.
Di Lella, Alexander. "Conservative and Progressive Theology: Sirach and Wisdom". *Catholic Biblical Quarterly* 28 (1966): 139-154.
Dijk, J.J.A. van. *La Sagesse suméro-accadienne. Recherches sur les genres littéraires des textes sapientiaux*. Leiden: Brill, 1953.
Donner, Herbert. *Geschichte des Volkes Israel und seiner Nachbarn in Grundzügen*. GAT 4. Göttingen: Vandenhoeck & Ruprecht, 1984.
_____. "Die religionsgeschichtlichen Ursprünge von Prov. Sal. 8". *Zeitschrift für Ägyptische Spraches und Altertumskunde* 82 (1957): 8-18.
Duesberg, Hilaire. *Les Scribes inspirés*. 2 vols. Paris: Desclée de Brouwer, 1938.
Dunand, F. *Le culte d'Isis dans le bassin oriental de la Méditerranée: Le culte d'Isis en Asie Mineure*. Vol. 3. 3 vols. Études préliminaires aux religions orientales dans l'Empire Romain 26. Leiden: Brill, 1973.
Dürr, Lorenz. *Mittleilungen der Vorderasiatisch-aegyptische Gesellschaft*. Leipzig: JC Hinrichs'sche, 1938.
_____. *Das Erziehungswesen im Alten Testament und im Antiken Orient*. MVAG. Leipzig: J.C. Hinrichs'sche, 1932.
Eissfeldt, Otto. *The Old Testament: An Introduction*. Translated by P.R. Ackroyd. New York: Harper & Row, 1965.
_____. *Ras Shamra und Sanchunjaton*. Halle: M. Niemeyer, 1939.
Eliade, Mircea. *Images and Symbols*. New York: Harper & Row, 1969.
Emerton, John A. "Review of *Wisdom and the Book of Proverbs* by B. Lang". *Vetus Testamentum* 37 (1987): 127.
_____. "Wisdom". In *Tradition and Interpretation*. ed. George W. Anderson, Oxford: Oxford University, 1979: 214-237.
_____. "A Note on the Hebrew Text of Proverbs 1:22-33". *Journal of Theological Studies* 19 (1968): 609-614.
Erman, Adolf. "Eine ägyptische Quelle der 'Sprüche Salomos'". *Sitzungsberichte der Preussischen Akademie der Wissenschaften* [*SPAW*] 15 (1924): 86-93.
_____. *The Literature of the Ancient Egyptians: Poems, narratives and manuals of instruction from the third and second millenia B.C.* Translated by Aylward M. Blackman. London: Methuen, 1923.
Ewald, Heinrich. *Sprüche Salomos. Kohélet. Zusätze zu den frühern Theilen und Schluss*. Die Dichter des alten Bundes 4. Göttingen: Vandenhoeck & Ruprecht, 1837.
Faure, Patrick. "Comme une fleuve qui irrigue. Ben Sira 24, 30-34, I. Critique textuelle". *Revue Biblique* 102 (1995): 5-27.
Festugière, A. J. *La Révélation d'Hermès Trismégiste*. Vol. 2. 2 vols. Paris: Gabalda, 1954.
_____. "A propos des aratalogies d'Isis". *Harvard Theological Review* 42 (1949): 220-228.
Feuillet, A. "Thèmes bibliques majeurs du discours sur le pain de vie (Jn 6)". *La Nouvelle Revue Théologique* 82 (1960): 814-819, 918-922.
Fichtner, Johannes. "Jesaja unter den Weisen". *Theologische Literaturzeitung* 74 (1949): 75-80.
_____. *Die altorientalische Weisheit in ihrer Israelischen-Jüdichen Ausprägung: Eine Studie zur Nationalisierung der Weisheit in Israel*. BZAW 62. Giessen: Verlag von Alfred Töpelmann, 1933.
Fishbane, Michael. *Biblical Interpretation in Ancient Israel*. Oxford: Clarendon, 1985.
Fohrer, Georg. *Introduction to the Old Testament*. Translated by D. Green. New York: Abingdon, 1968.

_____. "Sophia". In *Theologisches Wörterbuch zum Neuen Testament* [*TWNT*], Vol. 7. ed. G. Kittel, Stuttgart: W. Kohlhammer Verlag, 1966: 476-496.

Fontaine, Carole R. "Proverbs". In *Harper's Bible Commentary.* ed. J. L. Mays, San Francisco: Harper & Row, 1988: 495-517.

Forster, A.H. "The Date of Ecclesiasticus". *Anglican Theological Review* 41 (1959): 1-9.

Foster, B.R., ed. *Before the Muses: An Anthology of Akkadian Literature.* Leiden: Brill, 1973.

Fox, Michael V. "'Amon Again". *Journal of Biblical Literature* 115 (1996): 699-702.

_____. "World Order and Ma'at: A Crooked Parallel". *Journal of the Ancient Near Eastern Society of Columbia University* 23 (1995): 37-48.

_____. *The Song of Songs and the Ancient Egyptian Love Songs.* Madison: University of Wisconsin, 1985.

Freedman, H., and M. Simon. *Midrash Rabbah: Genesis I.* 12 vols. London: Soncino, 1951.

Friedländer, M. *Griechische Philosophie im Alten Testament.* Berlin: de Gruyter, 1904.

Friedman, Richard E. *The Exile and Biblical Narrative: The Formation of the Deuteronomistic and Priestly Works.* Chico: Scholars Press, 1981.

Fritzsche, O.F. *Kurtzgefasstes Exegetisches Handbuch zu dem Apokryphen.* Vol. 5. Leipzig: Hirzel, 1859.

Frost, S.B. "The Death of Josiah: A Conspiracy of Silence". *Journal of Biblical Literature* 87 (1968): 369-382.

Frye, Northrop. *Words with Power: Being a Second Study of the Bible and Literature.* New York: Harcourt, 1990. 015198462 X.

Galter, Hannes. *Der Gott Ea/Enki in der akkadischen Überlieferung.* Graz: Druck & Verlagsgesellschaft, 1983.

Gardiner, Alan H. *The Library of A. Chester Beatty: Description of a Hieratic Papyrus with a Mythological Story, Love-songs and other Miscellaneous Texts. The Chester Beatty Papyri No. 1.* Vol. I. London: Printed privately by J. Johnson at Oxford University and published by Emery Walker, Ltd., 1931.

_____. "Some Personifications". *Proceedings of the Society of Biblical Archaeology* 37/38/39 (1915-17): 253-262, 43-54, 83-95, 134-140.

Gelin, Albert. "Le chant de l'infante". *Bible et Vie chrétienne* 7 (1954): 89-95.

Geller, Stephen A. "Fiery Wisdom: Logos and Lexis in Deuteronomy 4". *Prooftexts* 14, no. 2 (1994): 103-139.

Gemser, Berend. *Sprüche Salomos.* HAT 16. Tübingen: Mohr, 1963.

_____. "The Instructions of 'Onchsheshonqy and Biblical Wisdom Literature". *Vetus Testamentum Supplements* 7 (1960): 102-128.

Georgi, D. "Der vorpaulinische Hymnus Phil 2:6-11". In *Zeit und Geschichte: Dankesgabe an Rudolf Bultmann zum 80. Geburtstag.* ed. Erich Dinkler, Rudolf Karl Bultmann and Hartwig Thyen, Tübingen: Mohr, 1964: 263-293.

Gerleman, Gillis. *Das Hohelied.* BKAT 18. Neukirchen-Vluyn: Neukirchener Verlag, 1965.

Gese, Hartmut. "Die Weisheit, der Menchensohn und die Ursprunge der Christologie als konsequente Entfaltung der biblischen Theologie". In *Alttestametnliche Studien.* ed. Hartmut Gese, Tubingen: JCB Mohr, 1991: 218-248.

_____. *Lehre und Wirklichkeit in der alten Weisheit: Studien zu den Sprüchen Salomos und zu dem Buche Hiob.* Tübingen: Mohr, 1958.

Gesenius, W., and E. Kautzsch. *Gesenius' Hebrew Grammar.* Translated by A. E. Cowley. Edited and Enlarged ed. Oxford: Oxford University, 1995.

Gilbert, Maurice. "Le discours menaçant de Sagesse en Proverbes 1:20-33". In *Storia e tradizioni di Israele. Scritti in onore di J. Alberto Soggin.* ed. D. Garrone and F. Israel, Brescia: Paideia Editrice, 1991: 99-119.

_____. "Wisdom Literature". In *Jewish Writings of the Second Temple Period : Apocrypha, Pseudepigrapha, Qumran, sectarian writings, Philo, Josephus.* ed. Michael E. Stone, Philadelphia: Fortress, 1984: 283-324.

_____. "La Sagesse personnifiée dans les textes de l'Ancien Testament". *Cahiers Evangile* 32 (1980): 5-36.

_____. "Le discours de la Sagesse en Proverbes 8: Structure et cohérence". *Bibliotheca Ephemeridum Theologicarum Lovaniensium* 51 (1979): 202-218.

_____. "L'Éloge de la Sagesse (Siracide 24)". *Revue Théologique de Louvain* 5 (1974): 326-348.

_____. *La critique des dieux dans le Livre de la Sagesse (Sg 13-15).* AnBib 53. Rome: Biblical Institute, 1973.

_____. "Volonté de Dieu et don de la Sagesse (Sg 9:17)". *La Nouvelle Revue Théologique* 93 (1971): 145-166.

_____. "La structure de la prière de Salomom (Sg 9)". *Biblica* 51 (1970): 301-331.

Goodwin, C.W. "On Four Songs Contained in an Egyptian Papyrus in the British Museum". *Transactions of the Society of Biblical Archaeology* 3 (1874): 380-388.

Gordis, Robert. "The Social Background of Wisdom Literature". *Hebrew Union College Annual* 18 (1944): 77-118.

Gordon, Cyrus H. *Ugaritic Manual: Newly revised grammar, texts in transliteration, cuneiform selections, paradigms, glossary, indices.* Rome: PBI, 1955.

Gordon, Edmund I. "A New Look at the Wisdom of Sumer and Akkad". *Bibliotheca Orientalis* 17 (1960): 122-152.

_____. *Sumerian Proverbs: Glimpses of everyday life in Ancient Mesopotamia.* Museum Monographs. Philadelphia: University of Pennsylvania Museum, 1959.

Grabbe, Lester. *Judaism from Cyrus to Hadrian: The Persian and Greek Periods.* Vol. 1. Minneapolis: Fortress Press, 1992.

Grandjean, Yves. *Une nouvelle arétalogie d'Isis à Maronée.* Leiden: E.J. Brill, 1975.

Greenfield, Jonas C. "The Wisdom of Ahiqar". In *Wisdom in Ancient Israel.* ed. J. Day, R.P. Gordon and H.G.M. Williamson, Cambridge: Cambridge University, 1995: 45-48.

_____. "The Seven Pillars of Wisdom (Prov 9:1)-A Mistranslation". *Jewish Quarterly Review* 76, no. 1 (1985): 13-20.

_____. "Ahiqar in the Book of Tobit". In *De la Tôrah au Messie: Mélanges Henri Cazelles.* ed. M. Carrez, J. Doré and P. Grelot, Paris: Desclée 1981.

Gressmann, Hugo. *Israels Spruchweisheit im Zusamenhang der Weltliteratur.* Berlin: Karl Curtius, 1925.

Griffith, F.L. "The Teaching of Amenophis the Son of Kanakht. Papyrus BM 10474". *Journal of Egyptian Archaeology* 12 (1926): 191-231.

Grimme, Hubert. "Babel und Koheleth-Jojakhin". *Orientalische Literaturzeitung* 8 (1905): 432-438.

Gunkel, Herman. "Ägyptische Parallelen zum Alten Testament". *Zeitschrift der Deutschen Morgenländischen Gesellschaft* 63 (1909): 531-539.

Gunneweg, A.H.J. "Das Buch Baruch". In *Historische und legendarische Erzählungen.* ed. W.G. Kümmel, Gütersloh: Mohn, 1975: 183-192.

Guthrie, H.H. *Wisdom and Canon: Meanings of the Law and the Prophets.* Chicago: Seabury-Western Theological Seminary, 1966.

Habel, Norman C. "The Symbolism of Wisdom in Proverbs 1-9". *Interpretation* 26, no. 2 (1972): 131-157.

Hadley, Judith M. "Wisdom and the Goddess". In *Wisdom in Ancient Israel.* ed. J. Day, R.P. Gordon and H.G.M. Williamson, Cambridge: Cambridge University, 1995: 234-243.

_____. "Yahweh and 'his asherah': Archaeological and Textual Evidence for the Cult of the Goddess". In *Ein Gott allein? JHWH-Verehrung und biblischer Monotheismus im Kontext der israelitischen und altorientalischen Religionsgeschichte.* ed. W. Dietrich and M. A. Klopfenstein, Fribourg: Fribourg University, 1994: 235-268.

_____. "The Khirbet el-Qom Inscription". *Vetus Testamentum* 37 (1987): 50-62.

_____. "Some Drawings and Inscriptions on two Pithoi from Kuntilleth 'Ajrud". *Vetus Testamentum* 37 (1987): 180-213.

Hallo, William W. "On the Antiquity of Sumerian Literature". *Journal of the American Oriental Society* 83 (1963): 167-176.

Harrington, Daniel J. "The Wisdom of the Scribe according to Ben Sira". In *Ideal Figures in Ancient Judaism: Profiles and Paradigms.* ed. J.J. Collins and G.W.E. Nickelsburg, Chico: Scholars Press, 1980: 181-188.

Hart, J.H.A. *Ecclesiasticus: The Greek Text of Codex 248 with Textual Commentary and Prolegomena.* Cambridge: Cambridge University, 1909.

Haspecker, J. *Gottesfurcht bei Jesus Sirach: Ihre religiöse Struktur und ihre literarische und doktrinäre Bedeutung.* AnBib 30. Rome: Biblical Institute Press, 1967.

Heidel, Alexander. *Babylonian Genesis: The Story of Creation.* 2nd ed. Chicago: University of Chicago, 1963.

Heijerman, Mieke. "Who Would Blame Her? The Strange Woman of Proverbs 7". In *Reflections on Theology and Gender.* ed. F. van Dijk-Hemmes and A. Brenner, Kampen: Kok Pharos, 1994: 21-31.

Heinemann, Issac. "Die Griechische Quelle der 'Weisheit Salomos'". In *Jahresbericht des jüdischtheologischen Seminars,* Breslau: Th. Shatzky, 1921: 136-153.

Heinisch, P. *Das Buch der Weisheit.* Vol. 24 EHAT. Münster: Aschendorff, 1912.

_____. *Die griechische Philosophie im Buch der Weisheit.* Münster: Aschendorff, 1908.

Hempel, Johannes. *Die Althebräische Literatur und ihr Hellenistisch-Jüdisches Nachleben.* Wildpark-Potsdam: Akademische Verlagsgesellschaft, 1930.

Hengel, Martin. *Judaism and Hellenism: Studies in their Encounter in Palestine during the Early Hellenistic Period.* Translated by John Bowden. 2 vols. Philadelphia: Fortress, 1974.

Hermisson, Hans-Jürgen. *Sprache und Ritus im altisraelitischen Kult: Zur 'Spiritualisierung' der Kulturbegriffe im Alten Testament.* Neukirchen-Vluyn: Neukirchener Verlag, 1965.

Hiller von Gaertringen, F. *Inscriptiones graecae insularum maris Aegaei praeter Delum.* Vol. 12, facsimile 5 and supplement. 14 vols. Berlin: de Gruyter, 1873-1914.

Hillers, D. "A Study of Psalm 148". *Catholic Biblical Quarterly* 40 (1978): 323-334.

Holladay, J.S. "Religion in Israel and Judah under the Monarchy: An Explicitly Archaeological Approach". In *Ancient Israelite Religion.* ed. P.D. Hanson, S. Dean McBride and P.D. Miller, Philadelphia: Fortress, 1987: 249-299.

Holladay, W. L. *Jeremiah 2: A Commentary on the Book of the Prophet Jeremiah Chapters 26-52.* Philadelphia: Fortress, 1989.

Horbury, William. "The Christian Use and the Jewish Origins of the Wisdom of Solomon". In *Wisdom in Ancient Israel.* ed. J. Day, R. P. Gordon and H.G.M. Williamson, Cambridge: Cambridge University, 1995: 182-196.

Hornung, Erik. "Lehren über das Jenseits". In *Studien zu altägyptischen Lebenslehren.* ed. E. Hornung and Othmar Keel, Freiburg: Vandenhoeck & Ruprecht, 1979: 217-224.

Humbert, Paul. "La 'Femme étrangère' du Livre des Proverbes". *Revue des Études Sémitique* 6, no. 2 (1937): 49-64.

_____. "Les adjectifs 'Zâr' et 'Nokrî' et la 'Femme Étrangère' des proverbes bibliques". In *Mèlanges Syriens offerts à M. René Dussaud*, Vol. 1, Paris: P. Geuthner, 1939: 259-266.

_____. "'Qânâ' en Hêbreu biblique". In *Festschrift für Alfred Bertholet*. ed. W. Baumgartner, Tübingen: Mohr, 1950: 259-267.

_____. *Recherches sur les sources égyptíennes de la littérature sapientiale d'Israel.* Neuchâtel: Éditions de la Baconnière, 1929.

Hurvitz, Avi. "Towards a Precise Definition of the Term *noma* in Prov 8:30 [Hebrew]". In *The Bible in the Light of its Interpreters*. ed. Sara Japhet, Jerusalem: Magnes, 1994: 647-650.

_____. "The Date of the Prose Tale of Job Linguistically Reconsidered". *Harvard Theological Review* 67 (1974): 17-34.

_____. Irwin, William A. "Where Shall Wisdom Be Found?" *Journal of Biblical Literature* 80 (1961): 133-142.

Jacob, Edmond. "Wisdom and Religion in Sirach". In *Israelite Wisdom: Theological and Literary Essays in Honor of Samuel Terrien*. ed. J. Gammie, W. A. Brueggemann, W. Lee Humphreys and J. M. Ward, New York: Scholars Press, 1978: 247-260.

Jäger, A. "Theodizee und Anthropodizee bei Karl Marx". *Schweizerische Theologische Umschau* 37 (1967): 14-23.

Janssen, Enno. *Juda in der Ezilszeit: Ein Beitrag zur Frage der Entstehung des Judentums.* Göttingen: Vandenhoeck & Ruprecht, 1956.

Jenks, Alan W. "Theological Presuppositions of Israel's Wisdom Literature". *Horizons in Biblical Theology: An International Dialogue* 7, no. 1 (1985): 43-75.

Jensen, Joseph. *The Use of Tôrâ by Isaiah: His Debate with the Wisdom Tradition.* Washington: CBA, 1973.

Joyce, Paul M. *Divine Initiative and Human Response in Ezekiel.* Sheffield: Sheffield, 1989.

Jung, C.G. *Symbols of Transformation.* Princeton: Princeton University, 1956.

Kalt, E. *Das Buch Baruch: Ubersetzt und Ercklärt.* Bonn: Peter Hanstein, 1932.

Kayatz, Christa. *Einführung in die alttestamentliche Weisheit.* Neukirchen-Vluyn: Neukirchener Verlag, 1969.

_____. *Studien zu Proverbien 1-9: Eine form-und motivgeschichtliche Untersuchung unter Einbeziehung Ägyptischen Vergleichsmaterials.* WMANT 22. Neukirchen-Vluyn: Neukirchener Verlag, 1966.

Keel, Othmar. *Das Hohelied.* ZBKAT 18. Zürich: Theologischer Verlag, 1986.

_____. *The Symbolism of the Biblical World: Ancient Near Eastern Iconography and the Book of Psalms.* Translated by Timothy J. Hallett. New York: Seabury Press, 1978.

_____. *Die Weisheit 'spielt' vor Gott. Ein ikonographischer Beitrag zur Deutung des mesahäqät in Sprüche 8:30f.* Freiburg: Vandenhoeck & Ruprecht, 1974.

Keel, Othmar, and Christoph Uehlinger. *Göttinen, Götter und Gottessymbole.* Freibourg: Herder, 1992.

Khanjian, John. "Wisdom". In *Ras Shamra Parallels* II. ed. L. Fisher, Rome: PBI, 1975: 371-400.

Kieweler, Hans-Volker. *Ben Sira zwischen Judentum und Hellenismus.* Beiträge zur Erforschung des Alten Testaments und des antiken Judentums 30. Frankfurt: P. Lang, 1992.

Kitchen, K.A. *The Ancient Orient and the Old Testament.* Leicester: InterVarsity Press, 1966.

Klein, M.J. *Anthropomorphisms and Anthropopathisms in the Targumim of the Pentateuch.* Jerusalem: Hebrew Union College, 1983.

Klein, Ralph. *Israel in Exile: A Theological Interpretation.* OBT. Philadelphia: Fortress, 1979.

_____. "A Theology for Exiles: The Kingship of Yahweh". *Dialog* 17 (1978): 235-258.

Klopfenstein, Martin A. "Auferstehung der Göttin in der spätisraelitischen Weisheit von Prov 1-9?" In *Ein Gott allein? JHWH-Verehrung und biblischer Monotheismus im Kontext der israelitischen und altorientalischen Religionsgeschichte.* ed. W. Dietrich and M.A. Klopfenstein, Fribourg: Fribourg University, 1994: 531-542.

Kloppenborg, John S. "Isis and Sophia in the Book of Wisdom". *Harvard Theological Review* 75, no. 1 (1982): 57-84.

Klostermann, A. "Schulwesen im Alten Israel". In *Theologische Studien. Theodor Zahn zum 10. Oktober 1908 dargebracht,* Leipzig: B.G. Teubner, 1908: 193-232.

Kneucker, J.J. *Das Buch Baruch: Geschichte und Kritik.* Leipzig: Deichert, 1879.

Knierim, Rolf. "Cosmos and History in Israel's Theology". *Horizons in Biblical Theology* 3 (1981): 59-123.

Knox, Wilfred L. "The Divine Wisdom". *Journal of Theological Studies* 38 (1937): 230-237.

Koch, K. "Gibt es ein Vergeltungsdogma im Alten Testament". *Zeitschrift für Theologie und Kirche* 52 (1955): 1-42.

Kottsieper, Ingo. *Die Sprache der Ahiqarsprüche.* BZAW 194. Berlin: de Gruyter, 1990.

Küchler, M. *Frühjüdische Weisheitstraditionen: Zum Fortgang weisheitlichen Denkens im Bereich des frühjüdischen Jahweglaubens.* OBO 26. Stuttgart: Kohlhammer, 1979.

Lambert, Wilfrid G. "Ancestors, Authors, and Canonicity". *Journal of Cuneiform Studies* 11 (1957): 11-12.

_____. *Babylonian Wisdom Literature.* Oxford: Clarendon, 1960.

Lambert, Wilfrid G. and Alan R. Millard. *Atra-Hasis: The Babylonian Story of the Flood, with the Sumerian Flood Story by M. Civil.* Oxford: Clarendon, 1969.

Lang, Bernhard. *Die weisheitliche Lehrrede: Eine Untersuchung von Sprüche 1-7.* SB 41. Stuttgart: KBW Verlag, 1972.

_____. "Wisdom". In *Dictionary of Deities and Demons in the Bible.* ed. Karel van der Toorn, Bob Becking and Pieter W. van der Horst, Leiden: Brill, 1995: 1692-1702.

Larcher, C. *Études sur le Livre de la Sagesse.* EBib. Paris: Gabalda, 1969.

_____. *Le Livre de la Sagesse ou La Sagesse de Salomon.* 3 vols. EBib. Paris: Gabalda, 1983-85.

Leclant, J. *Les Sagesses du Proche-Orient Ancien.* Colloque de Strasbourg. Paris: Cerf, 1963.

Leiman, Sid Z. *The Canonization of Hebrew Scripture: The Talmudic and Midrashic Evidence.* Hamden: Archon, 1976.

Levenson, Jon D. *Creation and the Persistence of Evil: The Jewish Drama of Divine Omnipotence.* San Francisco: Harper & Row, 1988.

_____. "The Davidic Covenant and its Modern Interpreters". *Catholic Biblical Quarterly* 41 (1979): 205-219.

Lévêque, Jean. *Job et son Dieu: Essai d'éxègése et de théologie biblique.* Paris: Gabalda, 1970.

Lichtheim, Miriam. *Ancient Egyptian Literature.* 3 vols. Berkeley: University of California, 1973-80.

_____. "The Instruction of Amenemope". In *Ancient Egyptain Literature: A Book of Readings,* Vol. 2. ed. Miriam Lichtheim, Berkeley: University of California Press, 1978: 146-163.

_____. *Late Egyptian Wisdom Literature in the International Context.* OBO 52. Freiburg: Universitätsverlag, 1983.

_____. "Observations on Papyrus Insinger". In *Studien zu altägyptischen Lebenslehren.* ed. E. Hornung and Othmar Keel, Freibourg: Vandenhoeck & Ruprecht, 1979: 283-305.

Lindars, B. "Good Tidings to Zion: Interpreting Deutero-Isaiah Today". *Bulletin of the John Rylands Libary* 68 (1985): 473-497.

Lindenberger, James M. *The Aramaic Proverbs of Ahiqar.* Baltimore: John Hopkins University Press, 1983.

Link, Christian. *Die Welt als Gleichnis: Studien zum Problem der naturlichen Theologie.* Munich: C. Kaiser, 1976.

Loretz, O. *Qoheleth und der alte Orient: Untersuchungen zu Stil und theologischer Thematik des Buches Qohelet.* Freiburg: Herder, 1964.

Lust, Johan. *Ezekiel and his Book: Textual and Literary Criticism and their Interrelation.* BETL 74. Louvain: Peeters, 1986.

_____. "Gathering and Return in Jeremiah and Ezekiel". In *Le Livre de Jérèmie: Le Prophète et son milieu, les Oracles et leur transmission.* ed. Pierre-Maurice Bogaert, Leuven: Peeters, 1981: 119-142.

MacIntosh, A.A. "Hosea and the Wisdom Tradition". In *Wisdom in Ancient Israel.* ed. J. Day, R.P. Gordon and H.G.M. Williamson, Cambridge: Cambridge University, 1995: 124-132.

Mack, Burton L. *Wisdom and the Hebrew Epic: Ben Sira's Hymn in Praise of the Fathers.* Chicago: University of Chicago, 1985.

_____. *Logos und Sophia: Untersuchungen zur Weisheitstheologie im Hellenistischen Judentum.* SUNT 10. Göttingen: Vandenhoeck & Ruprecht, 1973.

_____. "Wisdom Myth and Myth-ology". *Interpretation* 24 (1970): 46-60.

MacKenzie, R.A.F. *Sirach.* Wilmington: Michael Glazier, 1983.

_____. "Ben Sira as Historian". In *Trinification of the World. A Festschrift in Honor of F.E. Crowe.* ed. T.A. Dunne and J.-M. Laporte, Toronto: Regis College, 1978: 313-327.

Maier, C. *Die "Fremde Frau" in Proverbien 1-9.* OBO 144. Göttingen: Vandenhoeck & Ruprecht, 1995.

Man, Paul de. "Anthropomorphism and Trophe in the Lyric". In *The Rhetoric of Romanticism.* ed. Paul de Man, New York: Columbia University, 1984: 239-262.

Marböck, Johann. *Weisheit im Wandel: Untersuchungen zur Weisheitstheologie bei Ben Sira.* Bonner Biblische Beiträge 37. Bonn: Peter Hanstein, 1971.

Marcus, Ralph. "On Biblical Hypostases of Wisdom". *Hebrew Union College Annual* 23 (1950-51): 157-171.

_____. "The Tree of Life in the Book of Proverbs". *JBL* 62 (1943): 11-120.

Marmorstein, A. *The Old Rabbinic Doctrine of God: Essays in Anthropomorphism.* New York: KTAV, 1937.

Marshall, J. T. "The Book of Baruch". In *Hastings' Dictionary of the Bible*, Vol. I. ed. J. Hastings, New York: Scribner, 1901: 251-254.

Martin, Raymond A. "The Syntax Criticism of Baruch". In *VII Congress of the International Organization for Septuagint and Cognate Studies.* ed. Claude E. Cox, Atlanta: Society of Biblical Literature, 1988: 361-371.

Maspero, Gaston. "Les Chants d'Amour du Papyrus de Turin et du Papyrus Harris 500, 1/3". *Journal Asiastique* 8, no. 1 (1883): 18-47.

McKane, William. "Jeremiah and the Wise". In *Wisdom in Ancient Israel.* ed. J. Day, R. P. Gordon and H.G.M. Williamson, Cambridge: Cambridge University, 1995: 142-151.

_____. *A Critical and Exegetical Commentary on Jeremiah: Jeremiah I-XXV.* Edinburgh: T. & T. Clark, 1986.

_____. *Proverbs: A New Approach.* OTL. London: SCM Press, 1970.

_____. *Prophets and Wise Men.* SBT 44. London: SCM Press, 1965.

McKenzie, John L. "Reflections on Wisdom". *Journal of Biblical Literature* 86 (1967): 1-9.

Meinhold, Arndt. *Die Sprüche.* 2 vols. Zürcher Bibelkommentare 16. Zürich: Theologischer Verlag, 1991.

Meinhold, J. *Die Weisheit Israels.* Leipzig: Quelle & Meyer, 1908.

Menzel, P. *Der griechische Einfluss auf Prediger und Weisheit Salomos.* Halle: C.A. Kaemmerer & Co, 1889.

Meyers, Erik M. "The Persian Period and the Judaean Restoration: From Zerubbabel to Nehemiah". In *Ancient Israelite Religion.* ed. P.D. Hanson, S. Dean McBride and P.D. Miller, Philadelphia: Fortress, 1987: 509-521.

Middendorp, Th. *Die Stellung Jesu Ben Sira zwischen Judentum und Hellenismus.* Leiden: Brill, 1973.

Miller, D.G. "Female Language for God: Should the Church Adopt It?" In *The Hermeneutical Quest: Essays in honor of James Luther Mays on his sixty-fifth birthday.* ed. D.G. Miller, Allison Park: Pickwick Publications, 1986: 97-114.

Miller, Douglas B. *Symbol and Rhetoric in Ecclesiastes: The Place of Hebel in Qohelet's Work.* Academia Biblica 2. Atlanta: SBL, 2002.

Miller, J. Maxwell, and John H. Hayes. *A History of Ancient Israel and Judah.* Philadelphia: Westminster Press, 1986.

Miller, Patrick D. "The Absence of the Goddess in Israelite Religion". *Hebrew Annual Review* 10 (1986): 239-248.

Miscall, Peter D. *Isaiah.* Sheffield: JSOT Press, 1993.

Monsengwo, L. *La notion de NOMOS dans le Pentateuch grec.* Rome: AnBib 52, 1973.

Moore, Carey A. *Judith: A New Translation with Introduction and Commentary.* AB 40. New York: Doubleday, 1985.

_____. *Daniel, Esther, and Jeremiah, the Additions: A New Translation with Introduction and Commentary.* AB 44. New York: Doubleday, 1977.

_____. "Toward the Dating of the Book of Baruch". *Catholic Biblical Quarterly* 36 (1974): 312-320.

Moore, G.F. *Judaism in the First Centuries of the Christian Era: The Age of the Tannaim.* 3 vols. Cambridge: Harvard University, 1927.

Morenz, S. *Egyptian Religion.* London: Methuen, 1973.

Morgan, Donn F. *Between Text and Community: The Writings in Canonical Interpretation.* Minneapolis: Fortress, 1990.

_____. *Wisdom in the Old Testament Traditions.* Oxford: Blackwell Publishing, 1981.

Mowinckel, Sigmund. "Hypostasen". In *Die Religion in Geschichte und Gegenwart 2,* Tübingen: Mohr, 1928: 2065-2068.

Müller, D. *Ägypten und die griechischen Isisaretalogien.* ASAW 53/1. Berlin: Akademie-Verlag, 1961.

Müller, Hans-Peter. *Mensch–Umwelt–Eigenwelt. Gesammelte Aufsätze zur Weisheit Israels.* Stuttgart: Kohlhammer, 1992.

Müller, W.M. *Die Liebespoesie der Ägypter.* Leipzig: Hinrichs'sche, 1899.

Murdoch, Iris. *Existentialists and Mystics: Writings on Philosophy and Literature.* London: Chatto & Windus, 1997.

Murphy, Roland E. *The Tree of Life.* 2nd ed. Grand Rapids: Erdmans, 1996.

_____. "Wisdom Literature and Biblical Theology". *Biblical Theology Bulletin* 24/1 (1994): 4-7.

_____. *The Tree of Life: An Exploration of Biblical Literature.* ABRL. New York: Doubleday, 1990.

_____. "Proverbs and Theological Exegesis". In *The Hermeneutical Quest: Essays in Honor of James L. Mays on his sixty-fifth birthday.* ed. D. Miller, Allison Park: Pickwick Pub, 1986: 87-95.

_____. "Wisdom's Song: Proverbs 1:20-33". *Catholic Biblical Quarterly* 48 (1986): 456-460.

_____. "Hebrew Wisdom". *Journal of the American Oriental Society* 101/1 (1981): 21-34.

_____. "Wisdom Theses and Hypotheses". In *Israelite Wisdom: Theological and Literary Essays in Honor of Samuel Terrien.* ed. J.G. Gammie, W.A. Brueggemann, W. Lee Humphreys and J.M. Ward, New York: Scholars Press, 1978: 35-42.

_____. "What and Where is Wisdom?" *Currents in Theology and Mission* 4 (1977): 283-287.

_____. "Wisdom Theses". In *Wisdom and Knowledge. Papin Festschrift.* ed. J Armenti, Philadelphia: Villanova University Press, 1976: 187-200.

_____. "Assumptions and Problems in Old Testament Wisdom Research". *Catholic Biblical Quarterly* 29 (1967): 102-112.

_____. "The Kerygma of the Book of Proverbs". *Interpretation* 20 (1966): 3-14.

_____. "A Consideration of the Classification 'Wisdom Psalms'". *Vetus Testamentum Supplements* 9 (1963): 156-167.

Neusner, Jacob. *Understanding Seeking Faith: Essays on the Case of Judaism.* Atlanta: John Knox, 1986.

Nickelsburg, G.W.E. *Jewish Literature Between the Bible and the Mishnah: A Historical and Literary Introduction.* Philadelphia: Fortress, 1981.

_____. *Resurrection, Immortality and Eternal Life in Intertestamental Judaism.* HTS 26. Cambridge: Harvard University, 1972.

Norden, Eduard. *Agnostos Theos: Untersuchungen zur Formengeschichte Religiöser Rede.* Leipzig: B.G. Teubner, 1913.

Notter, Viktor. *Biblischer Schöpfungsbericht und Ägyptische Schöpfungsmythen.* Stuttgart: KBW Verlag, 1974.

Nougayrol, Jean. *La Mésopotamie.* Paris: Bloud et Gay, 1965.

Nowack, W. *Die Sprüche Salomos.* 2nd ed. Leipzig: Deichert, 1883.

Nyberg, H.S. "Studien zum Religionskampf im Alten Testament". *Archiv für Religionswissenschaft* 35 (1938): 329-387.

Oded, B. "Israelite History". In *Israelite and Judaean History.* ed. John H. Hayes and J. Maxwell Miller, London: SCM Press, 1977: 469-488.

Oesterley, W.O.E. *The Book of Proverbs.* Westminster Commentaries. London: Methuen, 1929.

_____. *The Wisdom of Egypt and the Old Testament in the Light of the Newly Discovered 'Teaching of Amen-em-ope'.* London: Macmillan, 1927.

Oesterley, W.O.E., and G.H. Box. *The Religion and Worship of the Synagogue.* 2nd ed. London: Pitman & Sons, 1911.

Otzen, Benedikt. "Lov og Visdom". In *Lov og Visdom i Baruks Bog.* ed. E.K. Holt, J.L. Hans and K. Jeppesen, Frederiksberg: Anis, 1995: 36-48.

Parpola, S. ed. *Letters from Assyrian Scholars to the Kings Esarhaddon and Assurbanipal [LAS].* Neukirchen-Vluyn: Neukirchener Verlag, 1983.

Pautrel, R. "Ben Sira et le Stoïcisme". *Recherches de Science Religieuse* 51 (1963): 535-549.

Perdue, Leo G. "Liminality as a Social Setting for Wisdom Instruction". *Zeitschrift für die Alttestamentliche Wissenschaft* 93 (1981): 114-126.

Peters, Norbert. *Das Buch Jesus Sirach oder Ecclesiasticus.* EHAT 25. Münster: Aschendorffschen Verlagsbuchhandlung, 1913.

Pfeifer, Gerhard. *Ursprung und Wesen der Hypostasenvorstellungen im Judentum.* AT 1/31. Stuttgart: Calwer, 1967.

Pfeiffer, Robert H. *A History of New Testament Times with an Introduction to the Apocrypha.* New York: Harper & Bros, 1949.

_____. *Introduction to the Old Testament.* New York: Harper & Row, 1941.

Pie Y Ninot, S. *La Palabra de Dios en los Libros sapienciales.* CSP 17. Barcelona: Facultad de Teologia, 1972.

Plöger, Otto. *Sprüche Salomos (Proverbia).* BKAT 17. Neukirchen-Vluyn: Neukirchener Verlag, 1984.

Poland, Lynn M. *Literary Criticism and Biblical Hermeneutics: A Critique of Formalist Approaches.* AAR 48. Chico: Scholars Press, 1985.

Porten, B. "Elephantine Papyri". In *Anchor Bible Dictionary,* Vol. 2. ed. D.N. Freedman, G. Herion, D.F. Graf and J.D. Pleins, New York: Doubleday, 1992: 445-455.

Porten, B. and A. Yardeni. *Textbook of Aramaic Documents from Ancient Egypt: Letters.* Winona Lake: Eisenbrauns, 1993.

Preuss, Horst-Dietrich. *Einführung in die alttestamentliche Weisheitsliteratur.* Stuttgart: Kohlhammer, 1987.

_____. "Das Gottesbild der älteren Weisheit Israels". *Vetus Testamentum Supplements* 23 (1972): 117-145.

Priest, John F. "Where is Wisdom to be Placed?" In *Studies in Ancient Israelite Wisdom.* ed. James L. Crenshaw, New York: KTAV, 1976: 281-288.

_____. "Humanism, Skepticism, and Pessimism". *Journal of the American Academy of Religion* 36 (1968): 311-326.

Pritchard, James B., ed. *Ancient Near Eastern Texts Relating to the Old Testament.* Princeton: Princeton University Press, 1969.

Rahlfs, A. *Septuaginta.* Stuttgart: DBS, 1979.

Raitt, Thomas M. *A Theology of Exile: Judgement and Deliverance in Jeremiah and Ezekiel.* Philadelphia: Fortress, 1977.

Rankin, Oliver S. *Israel's Wisdom Literature: Its Bearings on Theology and the History of Religion.* Edinburgh: T. & T. Clark, 1936.

Ray, J. "Review of *Ben Sira and Demotic Wisdom* by J.T. Sanders". *Vetus Testamentum* 35 (1985): 383.

Reese, James M. *The Book of Wisdom, Song of Songs.* OTM 20. Wilmington: Glazier, 1983.

_____. *Hellenistic Influence on the Book of Wisdom and Its Consequences.* Analecta Biblica 41. Rome: PBI, 1970.

_____. "Plan and Structure in the Book of Wisdom". *Catholic Biblical Quarterly* 27 (1965): 391-399.

Reindel, J. "Weisheitliche Bearbeitung von Psalmen". *Vetus Testamentum, Supplements* 32 (1981): 340-341.

Reiner, E. "The Etiological Myth of the 'Seven Sages'". *Orientalia* 30 (1961): 1-11.

Reitzenstein, R. *Das iranische Erlösungsmysterium.* Bonn: Marcus & Weber, 1921.

_____. *Poimandres: Studien zur Griechisch-Ägyptischen und frühchristlichen Literatur.* Leipzig: Deichert, 1904.

_____. *Zwei religionsgeschichtliche Fragen nach ungedruckten Texten der Strassburger Bibliothek.* Strassburg: Strassburg Bibliotek, 1901.

Reusch, F.H. *Erkläung des Buches Baruch.* Freiburg: Universitätsverlag, 1853.

Rickenbacher, O. *Weisheitspericopen bei Ben Sira.* OBO 1. Göttingen: Vandenhoeck & Ruprecht, 1973.

Ricoeur, Paul. *Freud and Philosophy: An Essay on Interpretation.* New Haven: Yale University Press, 1970.

_____. "Towards a Hermeneutic of the Idea of Revelation". In *Essays on Biblical Interpretation.* ed. Paul Ricoeur and L.S. Mudge, Philadelphia: Fortress, 1980: 88-98.

Ringgren, Helmer. *Religions of the Ancient Near East.* Translated by John Sturdy. London: SPCK, 1973.

_____. "Israel's Place among the Religions of the Ancient Near East". *Vetus Testamentum Supplements* 23 (1970): 1-8.

_____. *Främre Orientens religioner i gammal tid.* Stockholm: Bonnier, 1967.

_____. *Sprüche/Predigers.* ATD 16/1. Göttingen: Vandenhoeck & Ruprecht, 1962.

_____. *Word and Wisdom: Studies in the Hypostatization of Divine Qualities and Functions in the Ancient Near East.* Lund: H. Ohlsson, 1947.

Robert, André. "Midrash Biblique". *Ephemerides Theologicae Lovanienses* 30 (1954): 283.

_____. "Les Attaches Littéraires Bibliques de Prov. I-IX. Parts 1 and 2". *Revue Biblique* 43 & 43 (1934-35): (1934): 42-68, 172-204; 374-384; 44 (1935): 344-365, 502 525.

_____. "Littéraires (genres)". In *Dictionnaire de la Bible,* Vol. 5. ed. L. Pirot, Paris: Letouzey et Ane, 1926: 410-411.

Roberts, J.M. "Of Signs, Prophets, and Time Limits: A Note on Ps 74:9". *Catholic Biblical Quarterly* 39 (1977): 474-481.

_____. "The Human Dilemma and the Literature of Dissent". In *Tradition and Theology in the Old Testament.* ed. D. A. Knight, Philadelphia: Fortress, 1974: 235-258.

Rüger, H.-P. "Amôn-Pflegekind: Zur Auslegungsgeschichte von Prv. 8:30a". In *Übersetzung und Deutung: A.R. Hulst gewidmet,* Nijkerk: F. Callenbach, 1977: 154-163.

_____. *Text und Textformen im hebräischen Sirach.* BZAW 12. Berlin: de Gruyter, 1970.

Rylaarsdam, J.C. *Revelation in Jewish Wisdom Literature.* Chicago: Chicago University, 1974.

Sanders, James A. *Ben Sira and Demotic Wisdom.* SBLMS 28. Chico: Scholars Press, 1983.

Savignac, J. de. "Interprétation de Proverbes 8:22-32". *Vetus Testamentum Supplements* 17 (1969): 196-203.

_____. "Note sur le sens du verset 8:22 des Proverbes". *Vetus Testamentum* 4 (1954): 429-432.

Scarpat, Giuseppe. "Un Hapax Assoluto: AIRETIS (Sap. 8:4)". In *Scritti classici e cristiani offerti a Francesco Corsaro,* Catania: Facolta di Lettere e Filosofia Universitá degli Studi di Catania, 1994: 643-647.

Schencke, Wilhelm. *Die Chokma (Sophia) in der jüdischen Hypostasenspekulation: Ein Beitrag zur Geschichte der religiösen Ideen im Zeitalter des Hellenismus.* Kristiana: Jacob Dybwad, 1913.

Schmid, Hans H. *Wesen und Geschichte der Weisheit.* BZAW 101. Berlin: Töpelmann, 1966.

Schmidt, J. *Studien zur Stilistik der alttestamentlichen Spruchliteratur.* Alttestamentliche Abhandlungen 13/1. Münster: Aschendorff, 1936.

Schmidt, Werner H. "ηνθ θνη ερωερβεν (Greek)". In *Theologisches Wörterbuch zum Alten Testament,* Vol. II. ed. G.J Botterweck and H. Ringgren, Munich: Kohlhammer, 1976: cols. 650-659.

Schmitt, A.K. "Struktur, Herkunft, und Bedeutung der Beispielreihe in Weisheit 10". *Biblische Zeitschrift* 21 (1977): 1-22.

Schrader, L. *Leiden und Gerechtigkeit: Studien zu Theologie und Textgeschichte des Sirachsbuches*. Beiträge zur biblischen Exegese und Theologie 27. Frankfurt: P. Lang, 1994.

Schröder, H.O. "Fatum (Heimarmene)". In *Reallexicon fur Antike und Christentum*, Vol. 7. ed. T. Klauser, Stuttgart: Anton Hiersemann, 1969: 524-636.

Schroer, Silvia. "Die göttliche Weisheit und der nachexilische Monotheismus". In *Der eine Gott und die Göttin: Gottesvorstellungen des biblischen Israel im Horizont feministischer Theologie*. ed. M.-T. Wacker and E. Zenger, Freiburg: Herder, 1994: 151-182.

_____. "Die personifizierte Sophia im Buch der Weisheit". In *Ein Gott allein? JHWH-Verehrung und biblischer Monotheismus im Kontext der israelitischen und altorientalischen Religionsgeschichte*. ed. W. Dietrich and M.A. Klopfenstein, Fribourg: Fribourg University, 1994: 543-558.

_____. "Weise Frauen und Ratgeberinnen in Israel". *Biblische Notizen* 51 (1990): 45.

Schuller, Eileen. *Post-Exilic Prophets*. MBS 4. Wilmington: Michael Glazier, 1988.

Schürer, Emil. *A History of the Jewish People in the Age of Jesus Christ*. Translated by G. Vermes, F. Millar and M. Black. Vol. 2. 5 vols. Edinburgh: T.&T. Clark, 1979.

Schüssler-Fiorenza, Elisabeth. "Wisdom Mythology and the Christological Hymns of the New Testament". In *Aspects of Wisdom in Judaism and Early Christianity*. ed. R. Wilken, Notre Dame: Notre Dame University, 1975: 17-41.

Scott, R.B.Y. "Wise and Foolish, Righteous and Wicked [Proverbs 10-29]". *Vetus Testamentum Supplements* 23 (1972): 146-165.

_____. *The Way of Wisdom in the Old Testament*. New York: Macmillan, 1971.

_____. *Proverbs, Ecclesiastes*. AB 18. Garden City, N.Y.: Doubleday, 1965.

_____. "Wisdom in Creation: The 'Amôn of Proverbs 8:30". *Vetus Testamentum* 10 (1960): 213-223.

_____. "Solomon and the Beginnings of Wisdom in Israel". *Vetus Testamentum Supplements* 3 (1955): 262-279.

Sellin, E. *Introduction to the Old Testament*. Translated by W. Montgomery. London, 1923.

Sheppard, Gerald T. *Wisdom as a Hermeneutical Construct: A Study in the Sapientializing of the Old Testament*. BZAW 151. Berlin: de Gruyter, 1980.

_____. "Wisdom and Torah: The Interpretation of Deuteronomy Underlying Sirach 24:23". In *Biblical and Near Eastern Studies: Essays in Honor of William Sanford LaSor*. ed. Gary A. Tuttle, Grand Rapids: Eerdmans, 1978: 166-176.

Simonetti, Manlio. *Biblical Interpretation in the Early Church: An Historical Introduction to Patristic Exegesis*. Edinburgh: T & T Clark, 1994.

Simpson, J.A. and E.S.C. Weiner. "Personification". In *The Oxford English Dictionary*, Vol. 11, 1989: 64 col 3.

Singer, Simon, and Marcus Adler. *The Authorised Daily Prayer Book [Siddur. Hebrew and English]*. London: Eyre & Spottiswode, 1962.

Skehan, Patrick W. "Structures in Poems on Wisdom: Proverbs 8 and Sirach 24". *Catholic Biblical Quarterly* 41 (1979): 365-379.

_____. *Studies in Israelite Poetry and Wisdom*. CBQM 1. Washington DC: CBA, 1971.

_____. "The Text and Structure of the Book of Wisdom". *Tradito* 3 (1945): 1-12.

Smend, R. *Die Weisheit des Jesus Sirach erklärt*. Berlin: Reimer, 1906.

Smith, Daniel L. *The Religion of the Landless: A Sociology of the Babylonian Exile*. Bloomington: Meyer Stone, 1989.

Smith, Duane E. "Wisdom Genres in RS 22.439". In *Ras Shamra Parallels: The Texts from Ugarit and the Hebrew Bible*, Vol. 2. ed. L.R. Fisher, Rome: PBI, 1975: 215-247.

Smith, Mark S. *The Early History of God*. San Francisco: Harper & Row, 1990.

Smith, Sidney. "An Inscription from the Temple of Sin at Huraidha in the Hadhramawt". *Bulletin of the School of Oriental and African Studies* 11, no. 3 (1945): 451-464.

Soden, W. von. "Die Unterweltsvision eines assyrischen Kronprinzen". *Zeitschrift für Assyriologie* 43 (1936): 1-31.

Soggin, J.A. "Amos and Wisdom". In *Wisdom in Ancient Israel*. ed. J. Day, R. Gordon and H. Williamson, Cambridge: Cambridge University, 1995: 119-123.

Soll, William M. "Babylonian and Biblical Acrostics". *Biblica* 69/3 (1988): 305-323.

Spicq, C. *L'Ecclésiastique*. La Sainte Bible 6. Paris: Letouzey et An, 1951.

Stamm, J.J. *Die akkadische Namengebung*. MVAG 44. Leipzig: J.C. Hinrich'sche, 1939.

Stecher, R. "Die persönliche Weisheit in den Proverbien Kap. 8". *Zeitschrift für Katholische Theologie* 75 (1953): 411-451.

Steck, Odil H. *Das apokryphe Baruchbuch: Studien zu Rezeption und Konzentration "Kanonischer" Überlieferung*. Göttingen: Vandenhoeck & Ruprecht, 1993.

Steiert, Franz-Josef. *Weisheit Israels: Ein Fremdkörper im Alten Testament? Eine Untersuchung zum Buch der Sprüche auf dem Hintergrund der ägyptischen Weisheitslehren*. FTS 143. Freiburg: Herder, 1990.

Stern, David. "Language". In *Contemporary Jewish Religious Thought*. ed. A.A. Cohen and P.R. Mendes-Flohr, New York: Free Press, 1988: 543-551.

_____. *Parables in Midrash: Narrative and Exegesis in Rabbinic Literature*. Cambridge, Mass: Harvard University, 1991.

Stone, Michael E. "Lists of Revealed Things in the Apocalyptic Literature". In *Magnalia Dei, the Mighty Acts of God : Essays on the Bible and Archaeology in Memory of G. E. Wright*. ed. F. Moore Cross, W.E. Lemke and P.D. Miller, New York: Doubleday, 1976: 436-437.

Story, C.I.K. "The Book of Proverbs and Northwest Semitic Literature". *Journal of Biblical Literature* 64 (1945): 319-337.

Strugnell, John. "Notes en marge du volume V. Text in J. M. Allegro, Discoveries in the Judaean Desert of Jordan [*DJDJ*] V, Oxford 1968, 11–15, plates 4–5, with the corrections by J. Strugnell,". *Revue de Qumran* 7 (1969-71): 183-186.

Suggs, M.J. "Wisdom of Solomon 2:10-5:1: A Homily Based on the Fourth Servant Song". *Journal of Biblical Literature* 76 (1957): 26-33.

Swete, H.B. *The Old Testament in Greek according to the Septuagint*. Cambridge: Cambridge University, 1912.

Tena, P. *La Palabra Ekklesia*. Barcelona: Facultad Teologia, 1958.

Terrien, Samuel. "Wisdom in the Psalter". In *In Search of Wisdom: Essays in Memory of John G. Gammie*. ed. L.G. Perdue, B.B. Scott and W.J. Wiseman, Louisville: Westminster John Knox, 1993: 51-72.

_____. "The Play of Wisdom: Turning Point in Wisdom Theology". *Horizons in Biblical Theology* 3 (1981): 125-153.

Tigay, J.H. *The Evolution of the Gilgamesh Epic*. Philadelphia: Fortress, 1982.

Tov, E. *The Book of Baruch*. Alpharetta: Scholars Press, 1975.

Toy, Crawford H. *A Critical and Exegetical Commentary of the Book of Proverbs*. ICC. Edinburgh: T. & T. Clark, 1899.

Trible, Phyllis. "Wisdom Builds a Poem. The Architecture of Proverbs 1:20-33". *Journal of Biblical Literature* 94 (1975): 509-518.

Turner, Victor W. *The Ritual Process: Structure and Anti-Structure*. Chicago: Aldine Publishing Company, 1969.

Urbach, Ephraim E. *The Sages: Their Concepts and Beliefs*. Translated by Israel Abrahams. 2nd ed. Jerusalem: Magnes, 1979.

Vaccari, A. "Quasi plantatio rosae in Iericho (Eccli 24:18)". *Verbum Domini* 3 (1923): 289-294.

Van Leeuwen, Raymond C. "Scribal Wisdom and Theodicy in the Book of the Twelve". In *In Search of Wisdom*. ed. J.G. Gammie, L.G. Perdue, B.B. Scott and W.J. Wiseman, Louisville: Westminster John Knox, 1993: 31-49.

_____. "The Sage in the Prophetic Literature". In *The Sage in Israel and the Ancient Near East*. ed. J.G. Gammie and L.G. Perdue, Winona Lake: Eisenbrauns, 1990: 295-306.

Vandebeek, G. *De Interpretatio Graeca van de Isisfiguur*. Studia Hellenistica 4. Louvain: University of Louvain, 1946.

Vogels, Walter. "The God Who Creates Is the God Who Saves: The Book of Wisdom's Reversal of the Biblical Pattern". *Eglise et Théologie* 22 (1991): 315-335.

Wasserman, Earl R. "The Inherent Values of Eighteenth-Century Personification". *PMLA* 65 (1950): 435-463.

Webster, T.B.L. "'Personification' as a Mode of Greek Thought". *The Journal of Warburg and Courtauld Institutes* 17 (1954): 10-21.

Weeks, Stuart. *Early Israelite Wisdom*. Oxford Theological Monographs. Oxford: Clarendon, 1994.

Weiden, W.A. van der. *Le Livre des Proverbes*. Rome: PBI, 1970.

Weinfeld, Moshe. *Deuteronomy and the Deuteronomic School*. Oxford: Clarendon, 1972.

Weiser, Artur. *The Old Testament: Its Formation and Development*. Translated by Dorothea M. Barton. New York: Associated Press, 1960.

Westermann, Claus. *Theologie des Alten Testaments in Grundügen*. Göttingen: Vandenhoeck & Ruprecht, 1978.

Whedbee, J. William. *Isaiah and Wisdom*. Nashville: Abingdon, 1971.

Whybray, R.N. *The Book of Proverbs: A Survey of Modern Study*. Leiden: Brill, 1995.

_____. *Proverbs*. NCBC. Grand Rapids: Eerdmans, 1994.

_____. "Prophecy and Wisdom". In *Israel's Prophetic Tradition. Essays in Honour of P.R. Ackroyd*. ed. R. Coggins, M. Knibb and A. Phillips, Cambridge: Cambridge University, 1982: 181-199.

_____. *The Intellectual Tradition in the Old Testament*. BZAW 115. Berlin: de Gruyter, 1974.

_____. *The Book of Proverbs*. CBC. Cambridge: Cambridge University, 1972.

_____. *The Heavenly Counsellor in Isaiah XI:13-14: A Study of the Sources of the Theology of Deutero-Isaiah*. Cambridge: Cambridge University, 1971.

_____. "Proverbs 8:22-31 and Its Supposed Prototypes". *Vetus Testamentum* 15 (1965): 504-514.

_____. *Wisdom in Proverbs: The Concept of Wisdom in Proverbs 1-9*. SBT 45. London: SCM Press, 1965.

Wilcken, Ulrich. *Archiv für Papyrusforschung und verwandte Gebiete 3*. Leipzig: Teubner, 1900.

Wildeboer, G. *Die Sprüche*. Freiburg: Mohr, 1897.

Wilder, Amos N. "Story and Story World". *Interpretation* 37 (1983): 353-364.

Williams, Daniel H. "Proverbs 8:22-31". *Interpretation* 48 (1994): 275-279.

Williams, James G. *Those who Ponder Proverbs: Aphoristic Thinking and Biblical Literature*. BL 2. Sheffield: Almond Press, 1981.

Williams, Ronald J. "The Sages of Ancient Egypt in Light of Recent Scholarship". *Journal of the American Oriental Society* 101 (1981): 1-19.

_____. "The Alleged Semitic Original of the Wisdom of Amenemope". *Journal of Egyptian Archaeology* 47 (1961): 100-106.

Williamson, H.G.M. *The Book Called Isaiah: Deutero-Isaiah's Role in Composition and Redaction*. Oxford: Clarendon, 1994.

_____. "The Concept of Israel in Transition". In *The World of Ancient Israel*. ed. R.E. Clements, Cambridge: Cambridge University, 1989: 141-162.

Winston, David. "Wisdom in the Wisdom of Solomon". In *In Search of Wisdom: Essays in Memory of John G. Gammie*. ed. L.G. Perdue, W.J. Wiseman and B.B. Scott, Louisville: Westminster John Knox, 1993: 149-164.

_____. "Wisdom of Solomon". In *Anchor Bible Dictionary*, Vol. 6. ed. D.N. Freedman, New York: Doubleday, 1988: 120-127.

Wischmeyer, O. *Die Kultur des Buches Jesus Sirach*. BZNW 77. Berlin: de Gruyter, 1995.

Wolff, Hans W. *Amos the Prophet: The man and his background*. Philadelphia: Fortress, 1973.

_____. *Joel und Amos*. BKAT 14/2. Neukirchen-Vluyn: Neukirchener Verlag, 1967.

_____. *Amos' geistige Heimat*. WMANT. Neukirchen-Vluyn: Neukirchener Verlag, 1964.

Wright, Addison G. "Wisdom". In *The New Jerome Biblical Commentary*. ed. R.E. Brown, J. Fitzmeyer and R.E. Murphy, New Jersey: Prentice Hall, 1990: 510-522.

_____. *The Literary Genre Midrash*. New York: Alba House, 1967.

_____. "Numerical Patterns in the Book of Wisdom". *Catholic Biblical Quarterly* 29 (1967): 391-399.

_____. "The Structure of the Book of Wisdom". *Biblica* 48 (1967): 165-184.

_____. "The Structure of Wisdom 11-19". *Catholic Biblical Quarterly* 27 (1965): 391-399.

Würthwein, E. "Der Sinn des Gesetzes im Alten Testament". *Zeitschrift für Theologie und Kirche* 55 (1958): 255-270.

Ziegler, J. ed. *Sapientia Salomonis*. Vol. XII/1. Septuaginta Vetus Testamentum Graecum. Göttingen: Vandenhoeck & Ruprecht, 1981.

_____. *Sapienta Iesu Filii Sirach*. Vol. XII/2. Septuaginta Vetus Testamentum Graecum. Göttingen: Vandenhoeck & Ruprecht, 1980.

_____. ed. *Ieremias, Baruch, Threni, Epistula Ieremiae*. Vol. XV. Septuaginta Vetus Testamentum Graecum. Göttingen: Vandenhoeck & Ruprecht, 1957.

Ziener, G. *Die Theologische Begriffssprache im Buche der Weisheit*. Bonner Biblische Beiträge 11. Bonn: Hanstein, 1956.

Zimmerli, Walther. "Ort und Grenze der Weisheit im Rahmen der alttestamentlichen Theologie". *[SPOA]* (1963): 121-138 (*SAIW* 314-326).

_____. "Zur Struktur der alttestamentlichen Weisheit". *Zeitschrift für die Alttestamentliche Wissenschaft* 51 (1933): 177-204.

Index